Global Economic Prospects

Global Economic Prospects

Technology Diffusion in the Developing World

2008

1818 H Street NW
Washington DC 20433
Telephone: 202-473-1000
Internet: www.worldbank.org
E-mail: feedback@worldbank.org

1 2 3 4 11 10 09 08

ISBN: 978-0-8213-7365-1
eISBN: 978-0-8213-7366-8
DOI: 10.1596/978-0-8213-7365-1

ISSN: 1014-8906

Cover photos: Irrigation by Chris Stowers/Panos; Man with Cell Phone by Jacob Silberberg/Panos; Train by Qilai Shen/Panos; Map Projection by Chris Stowers/Panos; and Researcher by Jenny Matthews/Panos.
Cover design: Critical Stages

The cutoff date for the data used in this report was December 12, 2007. Dollars are current U.S. dollars unless otherwise indicated.

Contents

Figures

Tables

Boxes

Foreword

EACH YEAR, *Global Economic Prospects* explores critical "here and now" economic developments that are relevant to low- and middle-income countries. Past editions have examined the economic implications of international and regional trade liberalization, and migration and remittances. Last year's report looked at the recent acceleration in growth among developing countries and its sustainability over the longer term.

This year we take a closer look at technology, a critical determinant of sustainable growth and poverty reduction. We do so by directly measuring the extent to which countries use technological inputs (including scientific technologies embodied in goods and services and business processes) and produce technological outputs. The report also examines trends in the major channels through which technology is transmitted internationally, and in the country-specific factors that determine how well it is absorbed domestically.

Encouragingly, this *Global Economic Prospects* finds that, since the early 1990s, technological progress in both low- and middle-income countries has increased more rapidly than in high-income countries. As a result, the level of technology used in developing countries is catching up with high-income countries. However, the technology gap between them remains wide. Globalization has underpinned much of the recent progress by exposing developing countries to foreign technology through imports of high-tech consumption, intermediate and capital goods. Countries have also benefited from rising levels of foreign direct investment that often brings with it knowledge of important process technologies and foreign markets. Finally, highly skilled international diasporas are exposing developing countries to technology, both through the trade and marketing contacts that they provide to their countrymen and through the return of former émigrés.

Unfortunately, progress in improving the capacity of developing countries to absorb and make use of those technologies throughout their economies has been much weaker. Whether technological progress in developing countries will continue to outpace high-income countries will depend on the improvements in this regard. The main impediments to further progress is not access to technologies, but the weakness of domestic skills and competencies, which prevents many developing countries from exploiting these technologies, and rigidities in the regulatory environment that prevent innovative firms from being created and expanding. The diffusion of technologies within countries is often slow, which means that although some firms may have technologically sophisticated operations, most do not. Moreover, most of the population and most firms operate in a low-tech environment. As a result, despite having technologically sophisticated cities and world-class firms, the economy-wide level of technological achievement in countries like China and India is not very different from that in other countries at similar levels of development.

This report suggests a number of policy directions to bolster technology diffusion and absorption within developing countries. *First*, developing countries should safeguard the principle of openness and actively strengthen skills in the domestic population to ensure that they are able to take advantage of future opportunities. *Second*, to assist diffusion throughout the economy, policy needs to reinforce technological absorptive capacity at the subnational and regional levels and to strengthen dissemination channels within countries, including the outreach, testing, marketing, and dissemination activities of applied R&D agencies. *Third*, authorities should ensure that publicly supplied technological services and technology-enabling infrastructure are widely available, whether they are delivered directly by the state or by private firms. *Fourth*, in low-income countries and in those middle-income countries with uneven access to quality secondary and tertiary schooling, efforts should concentrate on raising the quality and quantity of schooling.

Finally, governments may need to intervene directly to encourage the rapid diffusion of technology and a domestic culture of "new-to-the-market" innovation. However, caution is required. Although direct interventions have sometimes been associated with some important technology successes, in many instances they have not. Policies that have succeeded have tended to make subsidies conditional on performance and put in place high-quality and independent-of-industry oversight systems.

Alan Gelb
Acting Senior Vice President and
Chief Economist
The World Bank

Acknowledgments

THIS REPORT WAS produced by staff from the World Bank's Development Prospects Group. Andrew Burns was the lead author and manager of the report. The principal authors of chapter 1 were Hans Timmer and Elliot (Mick) Riordan. Chapter 2 was written by Andrew Burns and William Shaw, with written contributions from Antonio David, Yvan Decreux, and Annette De Kleine. Chapter 3 was written by Andrew Burns and William Shaw with written contributions from Dilek Aykut, Antonio David, Yvan Decreux, Annette De Kleine, Mariem Malouche, Sanket Mohapatra, and Olga Sulla. Both Chapters 2 and 3 benefitted from the expert research assistance of Taras Chernetsky, Shuo Tan, and Teng Jiang.

Several people contributed substantively to chapter 1. The Global Trends Team, under the leadership of Hans Timmer, was responsible for the projections, with written contributions from John Baffes, Paul Brenton, Maurizio Bussolo, Betty Dow, Teng Jiang, Annette De Kleine, Donald Mitchell, Denis Medvedev, Gauresh Rajadhyaksha, Elliot (Mick) Riordan, Cristina Savescu, Shane Streifel, and Dominique van der Mensbrugghe. The poverty numbers originated with Shaohua Chen from the Development Research Group.

The accompanying online publication, Prospects for the Global Economy (PGE), was produced by a team led by Cristina Savescu and including Sarah Crow, Teng Jiang, Shunalini Sarkar, and Jennifer Vito, with technical support from Gauresh Rajadhyaksha.

Martha Grotton edited the report, Nigar Farhad Aliyeva and Michael Paul managed the publication process, and Merrell Tuck managed the dissemination activities. Roula Yazigi provided invaluable assistance with the design of some figures. Book production was coordinated by Mary Fisk from the World Bank Office of the Publisher.

The report was produced under the guidance of Uri Dadush, François Bourguignon, and Alan Gelb. Several reviewers offered extensive advice and comments throughout the conceptualization and writing stages. These included Jean-François Arvis, Kevin Barnes, Vandana Chandra, Prof. Carl Dahlman, Mark Dutz, Alan Gelb, Mary Hallward-Dreimeier, Daniel Lederman, Jeffrey Lewis, William Maloney, Claudia Paz Sepulveda, and Alfred Watkins.

Abbreviations

BACI	Banque Analytique de Commerce International (International Trade Analytical Database)
CAGR	compound annual growth rate
CAT scan	computerized axial tomography scan
CEPII	Centre d'Etudes Prospectives et d'Informations Internationales (Institute for Research on the International Economy)
CIS	Commonwealth of Independent States
DAX	Deutsche Aktien Exchange
DJIA	Dow Jones Industrial Average
DPT	diphtheria, pertussis, and tetanus
DSL	digital subscriber ink
EAF	electric arc furnace
EAP	East Asia and the Pacific
ECA	Europe and Central Asia
EMBIG	Emerging Market Bond Index-G
EPO	European Patent Office
EU	European Union
FDI	foreign direct investment
GDP	gross domestic product
GNI	gross national income
HIV/AIDS	human immunodeficiency virus/acquired immune deficiency syndrome
ICB	International Crisis Behavior
IEA	International Energy Agency
IMF	International Monetary Fund
ISO	International Organization for Standardization
LAC	Latin America and the Caribbean
LME	London Mercantile Exchange
MENA	Middle East and North Africa

MSCI	Morgan-Stanley Composite Index
NASDAQ	National Association of Securities Dealers Automated Quotations
OECD	Organisation for Economic Co-operation and Development
OHF	open hearth furnace
OPEC	Organization of the Petroleum Exporting Countries
PC	personal computer
PPP	purchasing power parity
R&D	research and development
SAR	South Asia region
SMEs	small and medium enterprises
SSA	Sub-Saharan Africa
TFP	total factor productivity
TOPIX	Tokyo Stock Price Index
UN Comtrade	United Nations Comtrade database
UNCTAD	United Nations Conference on Trade and Development
UNDP	United Nations Development Programme
UNESCO	United Nations Educational, Scientific, and Cultural Organization
UNIDO	United Nations Industrial Development Organization
USPTO	U.S. Patent and Trademark Office
WTO	World Trade Organization

Overview

This edition of *Global Economic Prospects* is being released during a period of increased uncertainty following four years of record growth in developing countries. In addition to examining economic prospects over the near and longer term, it takes an in-depth look at the current level of and recent trends in technological achievement and the main factors that determine the extent to which developing countries succeed in implementing foreign technologies.

Notwithstanding the financial turmoil provoked by a reassessment of risks in the U.S. mortgage market, and despite large losses in some financial markets, exposure to asset-backed securities appears to be broadly based. Losses so far have been manageable, although credit conditions have tightened. For developing economies, sovereign risk premiums have increased but remain low by historical standards. Equity values, exchange rates, and commodity prices have become more volatile, and the vulnerability of countries with large current account deficits or pegged exchange rates has become more visible.

Against this background, global growth slowed modestly in 2007, coming in at 3.6 percent after a strong 3.9 percent in 2006. Most of the slowdown was attributable to weaker growth in high-income countries. Growth in developing economies was a robust 7.4 percent, broadly unchanged from 2006 (figure 1). This strong performance in the developing countries has offset somewhat the slowdown in U.S. domestic demand that started with the unwinding of the housing bubble early in 2006. During 2007, developing countries accounted for more than half the growth in world imports, contributing—along with the depreciation of the dollar—to strong net exports for the United States and furthering the reduction in global imbalances.

Global growth in 2008 should moderate to 3.3 percent, as the robust expansion in developing countries partly compensates for weaker results in high-income countries. World output should pick up in 2009, expanding by 3.6 percent, as the U.S. economy regains momentum.

Several serious downside risks cast a shadow over this soft landing for the global economy. External demand for the products of developing countries could weaken much more sharply and commodity prices could decline if the faltering U.S. housing market or further financial turmoil were to push the United States into a recession. Alternatively, monetary authorities might overreact to the current climate of uncertainty and overstimulate the economy. This would be particularly dangerous for developing countries if the bulk of the resulting liquidity were to move into rapidly growing developing regions, provoking the same kind of overinvestment conditions that arose in the U.S. housing market.

Prospects for the U.S. dollar represent an additional risk factor. A recession in the United States or an excessive easing of U.S. monetary policy could contribute to further sharp declines in the dollar. A weaker dollar would benefit developing countries with dollar debt, but impose losses on those that hold dollar-denominated assets. It would hurt the competitiveness of firms exporting to the United States

Figure 1 Robust growth among developing countries should cushion the developed country slowdown

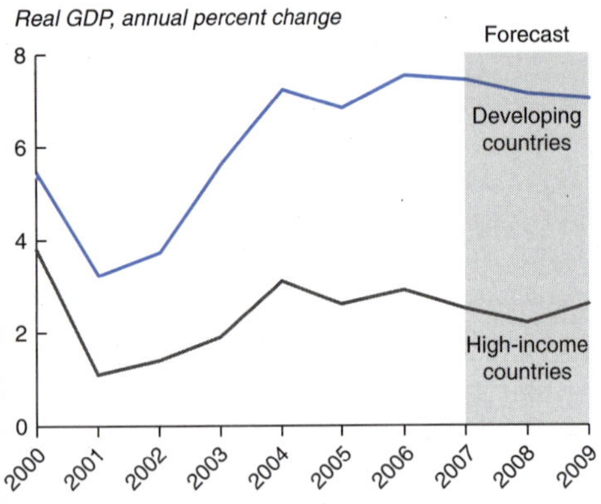

Source: World Bank.

(and those producing close substitutes for U.S. imports), while benefiting countries with currencies pegged to the dollar—at least temporarily. However, the main impact of a precipitous decline of the dollar would likely derive from the increased uncertainty and financial-market volatility it would provoke, which would increase trading costs, and spreads on developing-country debt—resulting in weaker export and investment growth throughout the global economy.

Even should such risks not materialize, several developing countries may be quite vulnerable to sudden adjustments in financial markets. Most exposed are those countries that combine large current account deficits with pegged exchange rates and with increasing domestic inflation. Also at risk are countries whose domestic banking sectors have balance sheets characterized by large currency mismatches.

Technological achievement and diffusion in developing countries

The special topic of this edition of *Global Economic Prospects* is technology and its diffusion within the developing world. Much of the economic and social progress of the past few centuries has been due to technology. Technology has been central to both economic growth and many elements of social welfare that are only partly captured by standard measures of gross domestic product (GDP), including health, education, and gender equality. As measured by total factor productivity, it explains much of the differences in both the level and rate of growth of incomes across countries (Easterly and Levine 2001; Hall and Jones 1999; King and Levine 1994). And, looking forward, it is expected to play a central role in meeting the environmental and climate-change challenges of the remainder of this century.

The private sector and the efficient functioning of markets are key to technological progress. At the same time, the efficient delivery of socially relevant technological goods and services depends on the direct contribution of nonmarket actors, including governments, nongovernmental organizations, and international organizations. Of course, policy also supports technological progress by facilitating the smooth operation of markets, by ensuring the acquisition of technological competencies by the general population, and by providing the physical infrastructure that is often a necessary complement to technologically sophisticated activities. Active measures to promote technology diffusion and strengthen the linkages between firms and research and development (R&D) agencies are also vital.

In exploring technological achievement and diffusion, this report adopts a broad definition of technology and technological progress, one that encompasses the techniques (including the way the production process is organized) by which goods and services are produced, marketed, and made available to the public. Understood in this way, technological progress at the national level can occur through scientific innovation and invention; through the adoption and adaptation of preexisting, but new-to-the-market, technologies; and through the spread of technologies across firms, individuals, and the public sector within the country.

Figure 2 Scientific innovation and invention is almost exclusively a high-income activity

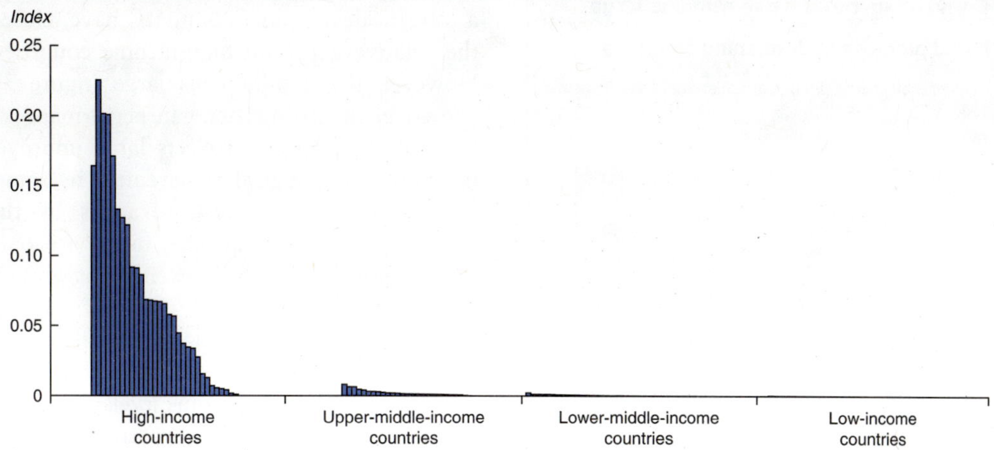

Source: World Bank.

The following discussion traces the structure of the overall report, which in chapter 2 explores the level of—and recent trends in—technological achievement, as well as the process by which technology diffuses between and within countries. Chapter 3 concentrates on the process by which countries absorb foreign technology, both the mechanisms through which they are exposed to foreign technologies and the domestic factors that dictate how successfully they absorb those technologies. Although the chapter identifies a number of important, policy-relevant trends, and it explores their policy implications, it leaves to future work a more normative analysis of the policies that developing countries should follow to maximize the development benefits of technological progress.

Policy needs to actively promote technological adoption and adaptation as well as nurturing domestic innovative capacity

A central finding of the report is that most developing countries lack the ability to generate innovations at the technological frontier. Although the number of patents and scientific journal articles is strongly correlated with GDP per capita for high-income countries, almost none of this activity is being performed in developing countries (figure 2). The lack of advanced technological competencies in these countries means that technological progress in developing countries occurs through the adoption and adaptation of pre-existing but new-to-the-market or new-to-the-firm technologies. Moreover, relatively thin domestic technology sectors and much better economic and scientific opportunities abroad mean that many nationals of developing countries perform cutting-edge research in high-income countries. For example, 2.5 million of the 21.6 million scientists and engineers working in the United States were born in developing countries (Kannankutty and Burelli 2007).

The level of technological achievement in developing countries has converged with that of high-income countries over the past 15 years

A sustained policy of increased openness to foreign trade and foreign direct investment (FDI), plus increased investments in human capital, have contributed to substantial improvements in technological achievement in developing countries over the past 15 years. And despite rapid progress at the technological frontier, technological achievement in both low- and

Figure 3 Technological achievement: Converging, but the gap remains large

Rapid progress in developing countries...

Percent change in technological achievement, 2000s versus 1990s

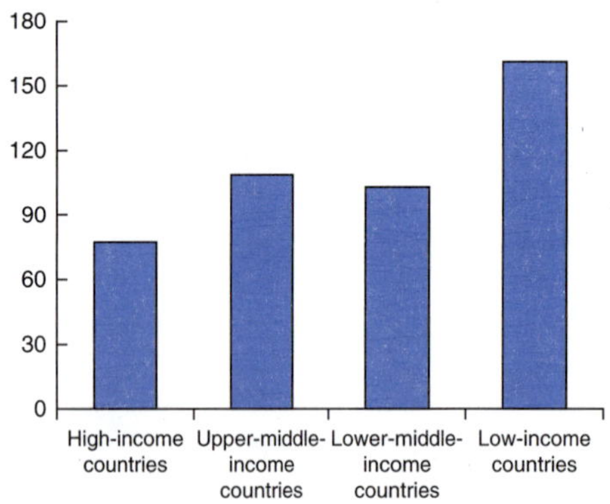

...fueled relative convergence...

Index, high-income countries = 100

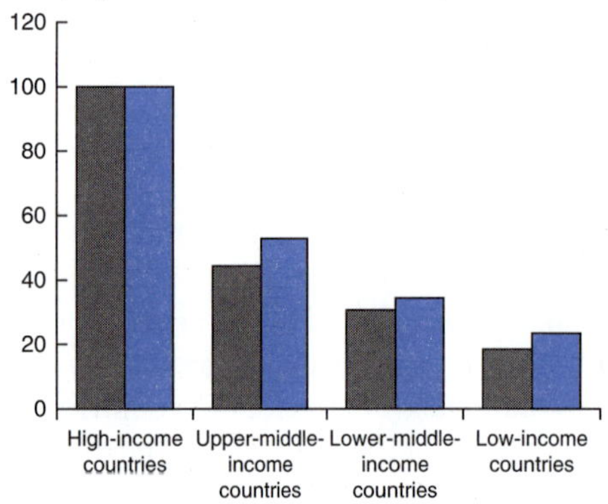

...but the gap remains large

Technological achievement index

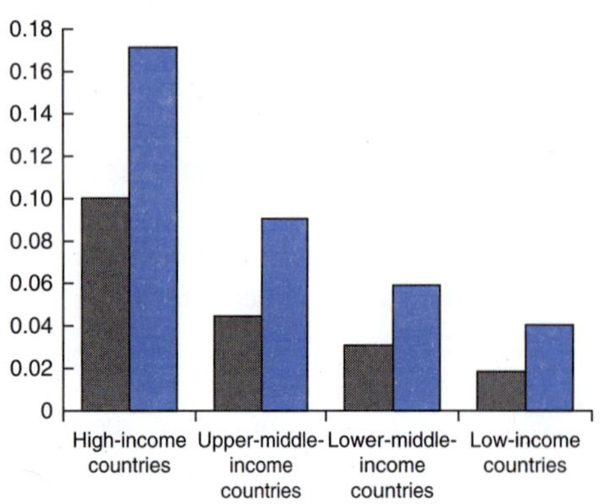

Source: World Bank.

middle-income countries has increased much more rapidly than in high-income countries. As a result, developing countries have closed the relative gap with high-income countries. However, the gap remains large (figure 3). Moreover, the strong aggregate performance of low-income countries reflects large improvements in technological achievement by some, but much more modest advances by the majority. As a consequence, many are only maintaining pace with, or even losing ground to, high-income countries.

In general, the level of technological achievement observed in a country is positively correlated with income levels. However, considerable variation is apparent within income groups. Among other things, this variation reflects the nature of the technology being observed, the impact of the overall policy framework on the ability of technologically sophisticated firms to grow, and the extent to which governments have given priority to and had success in delivering services with a strong technology component.

The penetration of older technologies, such as fixed-line telephones, electrical power, transportation, and health care services—many of which were originally provided by governments—is only weakly correlated with income. The low-income countries with the highest utilization rates of these older technologies tend to have rates as high as those of the average lower-middle-income country (figure 4). Similarly, the lower-middle-income and upper-middle-income countries with the highest utilization rates tend to have rates that match the average rate of the next highest income group.

In part, this reflects the nature of the technologies in question, such as electrical networks, road infrastructure, fixed-line telephony, and sanitation networks. Many of these technologies require an infrastructure that is relatively expensive to create and maintain, and which relies on large numbers of individuals with scarce technical skills. In addition, the observed diffusion of older technologies today depends on the intensity and efficiency with which government services have

Figure 4 The penetration of older and more recent technologies depends on more than income

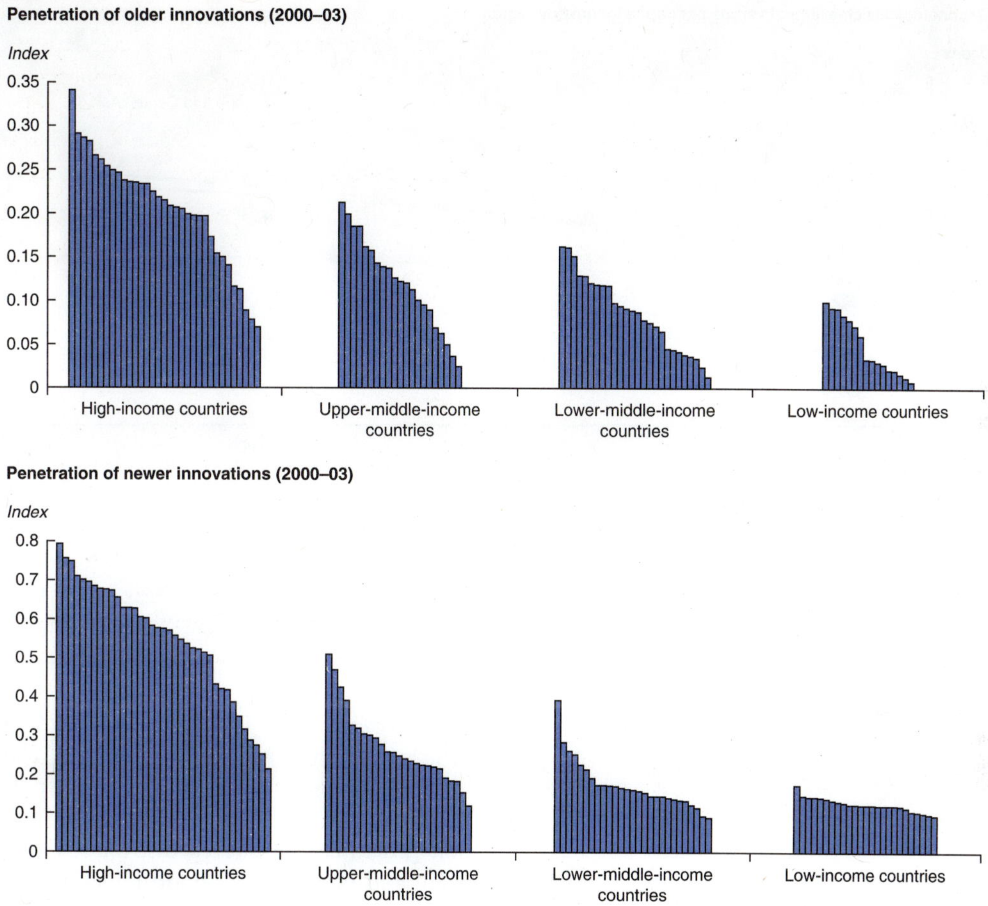

Source: World Bank.

been delivered in the past. Part of the strong technological showing of the countries in the former Soviet bloc is explained by the heavy emphasis that past governments placed on providing basic infrastructure and education to a wide range of the population. Similarly, past governance problems and civil strife help explain the relatively weak penetration of these technologies in many Sub-Saharan African countries, whereas macroeconomic turmoil and a relatively unequal distribution of incomes and skills in Latin America may have contributed to weak outcomes in that region.

The penetration rates of newer technologies have risen relatively rapidly and are more directly correlated with income than is the case for older technologies. The infrastructure for newer technologies such as mobile phones, computers, and the Internet is generally less expensive to create and requires fewer (though more skilled) workers to maintain. Moreover, in many countries, regulatory reform has meant that the private sector now offers these services in a competitive environment as compared with the state-owned, monopolistic environments of the past. As a result, supply of

Figure 5 Technological achievement tends to level off at different income levels in different regions

Technological achievement versus per capita income by region

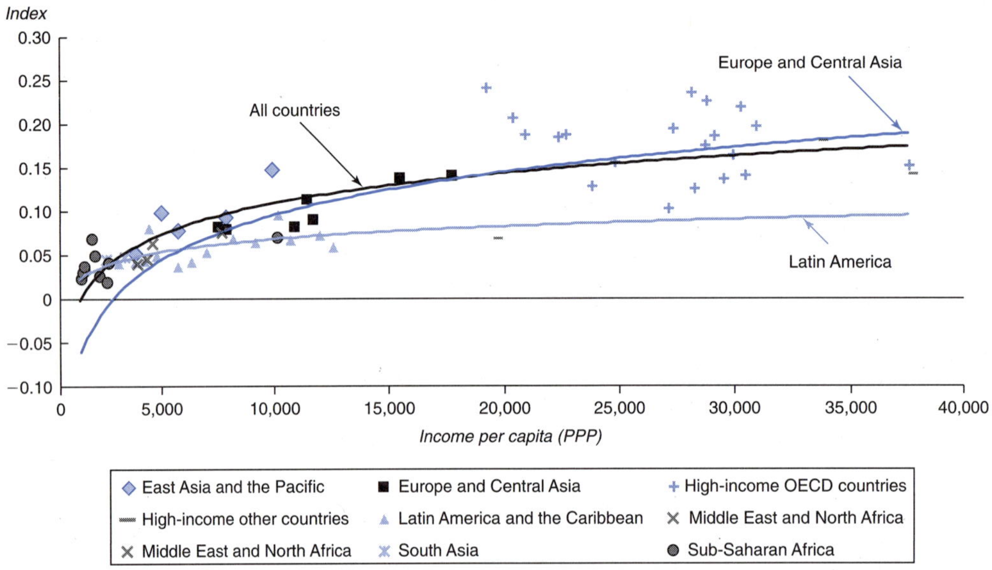

Source: World Bank.

these new technologies has been more responsive to market demand and less restrained by the budget constraints of governments or state-owned-enterprises. Furthermore, demand for these products has been boosted by low end-user costs as a result of competitive pricing strategies and because some of these newer technologies lend themselves more easily to sharing than do some older technologies.

Overall, although technological achievement tends to rise with incomes, this relationship is nonlinear and shows a tendency to level off. Moreover, it is not uniform across regions. Thus countries in Europe and Central Asia tend to have somewhat higher levels of achievement than would be expected on the basis of income alone, but the overall relationship between technological achievement and income in the region tracks relatively well that of all countries (figure 5). In contrast, technological achievement in Latin America tends to be lower than what would be expected given incomes, and the overall relationship suggests that other factors appear to be restraining achievement even as incomes progress. These results are consistent with the view that policy choices over the long term (such as those that generated the uneven distribution of income and educational opportunities in Latin America and the region's history of weak links between R&D communities and the business world) are important determinants of absorptive capacity and technological progress.

The level of technology in developing countries reflects the pace at which technology diffuses within countries

Although it can take time for a technology to gain a foothold in developing countries, the more serious impediment to technological achievement is the speed with which technologies spread within these countries. On average, the time it takes before official statistics in a developing country record significant exploitation of a new technology has declined from almost 100 years for innovations

Figure 6 Most technologies fail to penetrate deeply into developing economies

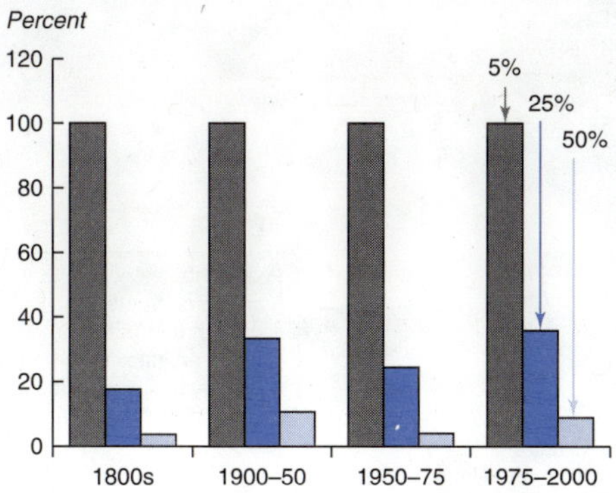

Source: World Bank calculations using data from Comin and Hobijn 2004.

Figure 7 The urban–rural gap in telephone access in India is huge

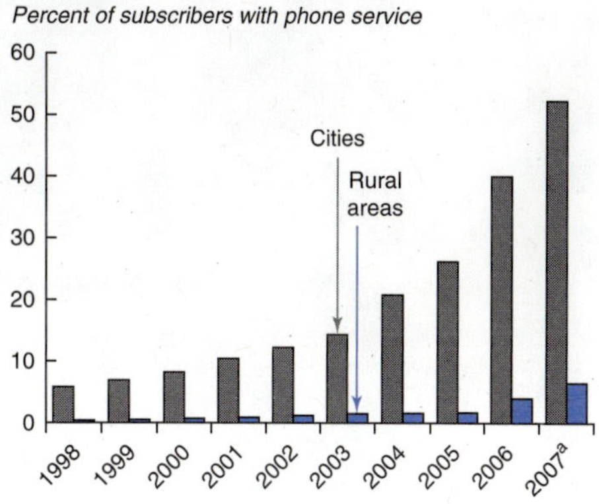

Source: Telecommunications Regulatory Authority of India.
a = estimated.

discovered in the 1800s to about 20 years today.[1] However, technological progress also depends on how rapidly the technology spreads within the country. Here the story is less encouraging. For technologies discovered during 1950–75, only a quarter of the developing countries that have achieved at least a 5 percent penetration level have gone on to reach the 25 percent threshold, and all of these are upper-middle-income countries (figure 6).

The story is somewhat better for newer technologies. Not only have these technologies spread more quickly between countries, but also the share of countries that have achieved the 25 percent threshold is higher, at 33 percent. Indeed, developing countries have now reached the same average level of penetration of mobile phones as was observed in high-income countries in 1995.

The unevenness of technological diffusion across countries is often mirrored within countries, especially large countries. Although technology spreads relatively rapidly among elites living in major cities, it takes much longer for it to find its way to the rest of the population or from top-performing companies to the average firm. Specific sectors in advanced urban centers in China and India, for example, use world-class levels of technology, but the incidence of these technologies elsewhere in the country, and in rural areas in particular, remains low (figure 7). Even within sectors, technology may diffuse only slowly. In Brazil and India, for example, the most sophisticated firms use technologies and achieve levels of productivity that rival world leaders, but the vast majority of firms operate at levels of productivity that are less than one-fifth those of the top performers.

A framework for understanding the diffusion of technology within developing countries

The bulk of technological progress in developing countries has been achieved through the absorption and adaptation of preexisting and new-to-the-market or new-to-the-firm technologies, rather than the invention of entirely new technologies. Given the still wide technology gap, this is likely to remain the case for the vast majority of developing countries.

A developing country's ability to absorb and adopt foreign technologies depends on two main factors: the extent to which it is exposed to foreign technologies (the pace at

Figure 8 Domestic absorptive capacity both conditions and attracts external flows

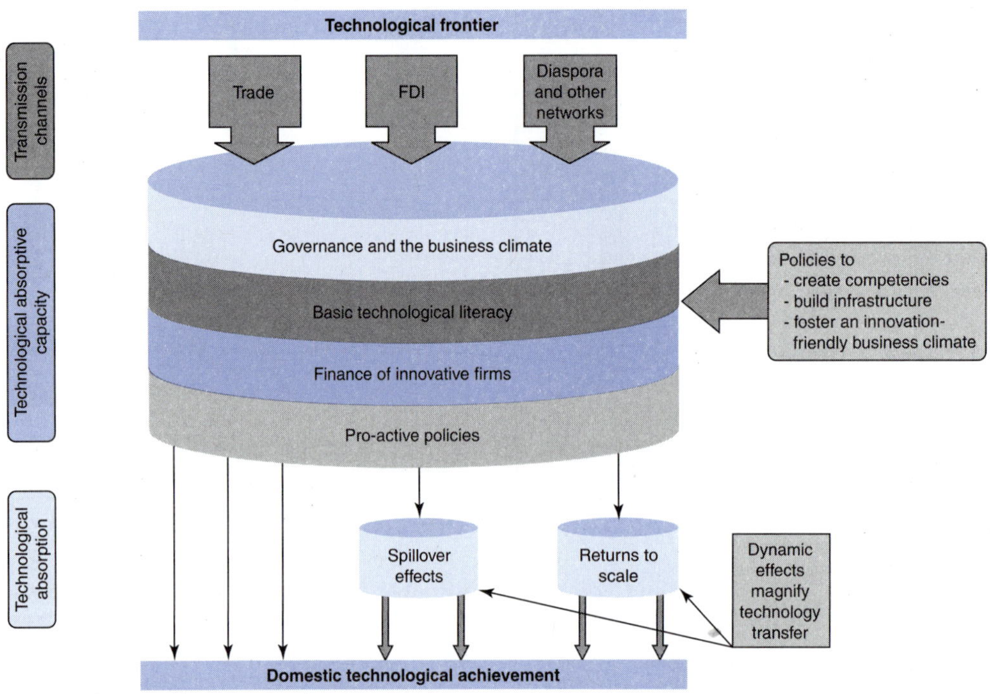

Source: World Bank.

which technologies diffuse across countries) and its ability to absorb and adapt those technologies to which it is exposed (the pace at which technology diffuses within the country). Figure 8 presents a stylized description of how a developing country absorbs technology. As a first step, an economy is exposed to higher-tech business processes, products, and services through foreign trade; foreign direct investment; and contacts with its diaspora and other communications channels, including academia and international organizations (the large arrows at the top of the figure). The larger these flows, the greater the exposure of the economy to the global technological frontier.

However, exposure to new ideas and techniques is not sufficient to ensure that the technology diffuses throughout the economy. Successful absorption of foreign technology depends on the technological absorptive capacity of the economy (represented by the multiple-ringed drum). Absorptive capacity depends on the overall macroeconomic and governance environment, which influences the willingness of entrepreneurs to take risks on new and new-to-the-market technologies; and the level of basic technological literacy and advanced skills in the population, which determines a country's capacity to undertake the research necessary to understand, implement, and adapt them. In addition, because firms are the basic mechanism by which technology spreads within an economy's private sector, the extent to which financing for innovative firms is available—through the banking system, remittances, or government support schemes—also influence the extent to and speed with which technologies are absorbed.

Government policy also has a crucial role to play. Governments are often the primary channel through which certain technologies, such as electricity, fixed-line telephones, transportation infrastructure, and medical and educational services, are delivered. Moreover, government policy is largely responsible for creating a business environment that facilitates easy firm entry and exit and that is not hostile to the profits to be made from exploiting new technologies. Too often, rules and/or specific features of the domestic market prevent firms from making money by exploiting a new technology, and, as a result, the technology does not spread within the country. Policy should also ensure that R&D and dissemination efforts give priority to creating and introducing products for which a market (domestic or foreign) exists and to helping firms exploit those opportunities.

The overall process is, of course, much more complicated and much less mechanistic than is depicted in Figure 8. Technological flows and technological absorptive capacity influence each other. How well technology diffuses depends on various market imperfections, including increasing returns to scale and technological spillovers (the smaller light blue rings toward the bottom of the figure). Here the existence of a financial sector that intermediates between savers and innovators may be necessary to overcome the initial cost of some new technologies. In particular, access to finance may be essential if innovative firms are to achieve the necessary scale to unleash a potential virtuous circle, so that the additional income garnered by the successful exploitation of one new technology permits the acquisition of another, thus resulting in further gains.

Increased openness to trade, FDI, and diaspora contacts have boosted technological diffusion

The dismantling of trade barriers in many developing countries over the past two decades has dramatically increased developing countries' exposure to foreign technologies. Their imports of capital and intermediate goods (which permit the production of technologically sophisticated goods and services) now represent between 6 and 14 percent of their GDP, an increase of more than 80 percent since 1994. The ratio of high-tech imports to GDP more than doubled during the same period. Partly as a result, developing-country exports of high-tech goods have also increased, rising from 11 percent of total exports in the mid-1990s to 19 percent in 2002–04 (figure 9). In the case of lower-middle-income countries, high-tech goods represent broadly the same 23 percent share in total exports as in high-income countries (15 percent if China is excluded).

The easing of restrictions on FDI also has contributed to technology diffusion within developing countries. FDI is a major source of process technology and learning by doing opportunities for individuals in developing countries. Over the past 15 years, FDI inflows to developing countries have almost doubled as a percentage of GDP. In addition, foreign firms are making important contributions to the technological capacity of host countries, performing more than 40 percent of the total R&D in some countries. At the same time, the competition, standards and knowledge of foreign markets that foreign firms bring to the domestic market can have important spillover effects. Finally, many firms in developing countries have increased their access to cutting-edge technology by purchasing technologically sophisticated firms domiciled in high-income countries.

In addition to dismantling barriers to foreign investment, some middle-income countries have encouraged greater FDI flows by implementing stronger regimes governing intellectual property rights (evidence suggests that stronger intellectual property rights are associated with a rise in knowledge flows to affiliates and in inward FDI flows toward middle-income and large developing countries, but not in poor countries). A few countries have encouraged joint ventures rather than FDI to maximize technology transfers to

Figure 9 Developing countries' trade in technology goods has risen

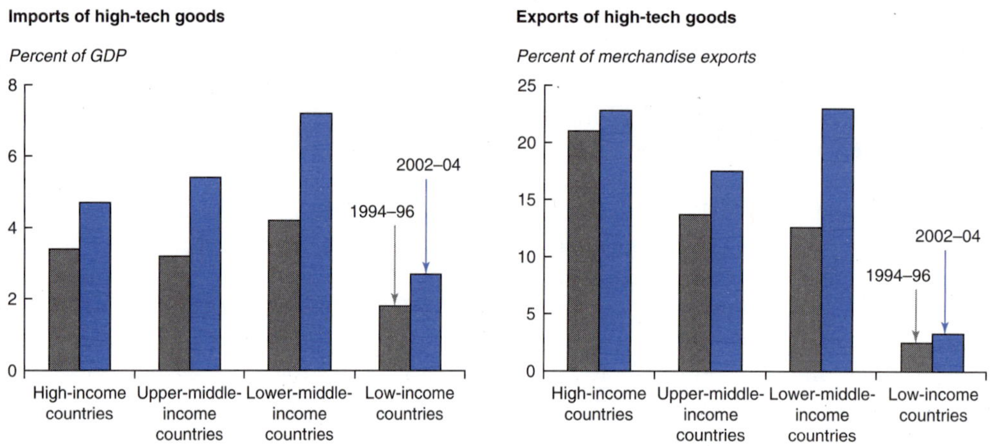

Source: World Bank.

local firms. However, this strategy seems to work only for countries with substantial market power. In particular, fear of losing control over cutting-edge technologies sometimes causes multinational firms forced into joint ventures to reserve their best technologies for the domestic market and transfer only older less efficient ones.

Substantial technology transfers are also associated with international migration and the diasporas of developing countries. Not all of these are positive. Even though 93 percent of university-educated individuals from developing countries return to or remain in their country of origin (Docquier and Marfouk 2004), the brain drain is a serious problem for a number of mostly small countries. However, the existence of a well-educated diaspora (more highly-skilled individuals migrate than lower-skilled individuals) constitutes an important technological resource for the home country—a brain bank, as it were. This is especially the case when weak employment prospects in the home country reduce the economic benefits initially forgone by the individual's departure.

For most countries, high-skilled out-migration remains at managable levels and these technologically savvy diasporas contribute to technological transfers by strengthening trade and investment linkages with more advanced economies through networks that provide access to technology and capital and through remittances. Remittances not only contribute to domestic entrepreneurship and investment, but also, along with the introduction of mobile phone services, have greatly expanded the provision of banking and other arm's-length financial services within developing countries—themselves a critical enabling process technology. Finally, returning migrants can provide important resources, such as entrepreneurship, technology, marketing knowledge, and investment capital. The effect of a single returning émigré armed with skills acquired in a developed economy can have (and has had) large economic and technological effects on the country of origin.

Better macroeconomic and educational policies have improved absorptive capacity in developing countries...

Although increases in the flows of the principal international transmitters of technology have been marked, improvement in the factors that determine the capacity of developing countries to absorb and effectively use that technology has been much more gradual. On the positive side, most developing countries

Figure 10 Macroeconomic stability has improved since the early 1990s

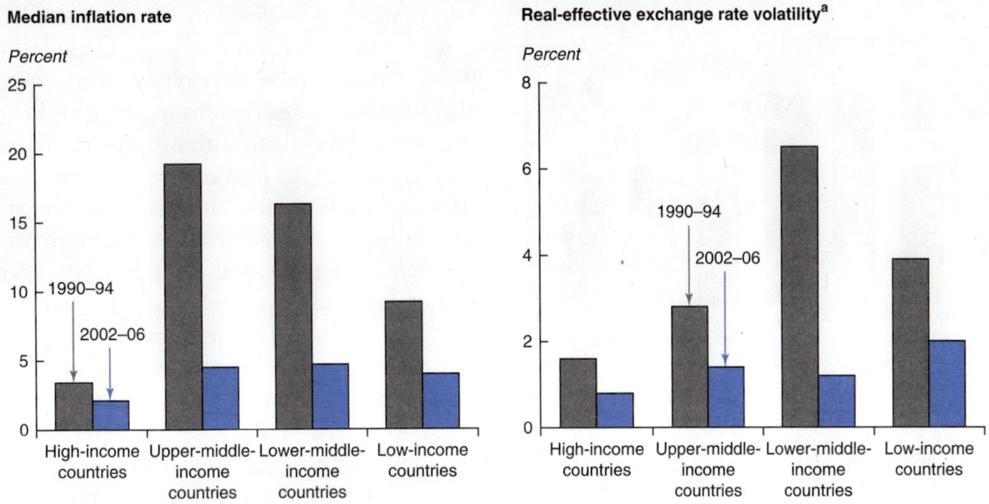

Source: World Bank.

a = average absolute value of the monthly change in the real-effective exchange rate.

have improved their investment climates. Their macroeconomic and political environments have become more stable over the past 15 years. The number of international conflicts has fallen by more than 50 percent since the 1990s, median inflation has dropped from about 20 percent in the early 1990s to less than 5 percent, and exchange rate volatility has fallen by more than 50 percent in every developing region (figure 10). All these changes reduce risk and increase the likelihood that entrepreneurs will take a chance and introduce a new technology within a country. These same changes have contributed to improved per capita GDP and a significant decline in the number of people living in absolute poverty, which has eased the constraints on the ability of poor countries to generate resources for investment, and has increased the willingness of firms and individuals to take risks.

Improvements in the quality of human capital in most developing countries have increased the countries' capacity to adopt and adapt technologies. Poor health is receding as a factor that impedes technological progress. Life expectancy in middle-income countries has reached 70 years and continues to rise. In low-income countries outside of Sub-Saharan Africa, life expectancy is up from 59 years in 1990 to 64 years in 2005 (in Sub-Saharan Africa, extremely low incomes and the HIV/AIDS epidemic have led to a drop in life expectancy since 1990). The labor force in most developing countries has also become better educated. Adult literacy rates have increased in every developing region over the past 15 years (figure 11). The share of children graduating from primary school has also increased in all regions except East Asia and the Pacific (where it stood at 98 percent in 2005). Meanwhile, secondary school and college enrollment rates are up across the board. Increased school enrollment has raised youth literacy rates to close to 100 percent in all the predominantly middle-income regions. According to official statistics, almost 75 percent of 15- to 24-year-olds in Sub-Saharan Africa can read and write. That rate compares favorably with an adult literacy rate of 60 percent and suggests that over time, the technological literacy of the population will rise. Although policies to promote literacy and extend school

Figure 11 Literacy rates have increased in all regions

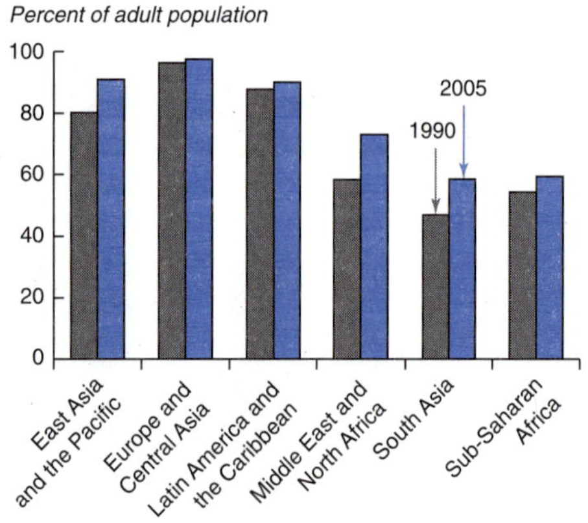

Source: World Bank.

attendance are critical, in too many cases, the quality of the education delivered in many developing countries remains low. Large proportions of students officially classified as literate fail to pass international standardized tests of literacy and numeracy.

Technological progress requires additional improvements in the quality of the labor force beyond strengthening educational systems. Training can make an important contribution to both the productivity of private firms and the efficiency of public services. For example, the dissemination of the simple skills required to build rainwater collection systems can improve access to clean drinking water and to reduce the incidence of disease. And investing in the domestic skills required to support high-skill and high-value-added industries can help maximize the technology spillovers from FDI.

...but improvements in the business climate and governance lags

In contrast to improvements in the quality of human capital, business climate and governance indicators have shown little improvement, on average, over the past decade. Governance in several countries has improved, notably in Central Europe and the Baltic countries, proving that motivated political leadership can make a difference. But, in many other countries, the quality of governance has declined or remained stable.

Progress in the dismantling of regulatory barriers that impede technology diffusion has also been slow. Restrictions on labor mobility that constrain firms' ability to reallocate workers within the firm can be important barriers to the adoption of new technologies, and restrictions on firm entry and exit tend to prop up inefficient firms and limit the expansion and creation of innovative ones. Overall, the time and cost involved in starting a business, the efficiency of contract enforcement, the time required to resolve insolvencies, the average amount recovered, and the degree of corruption in developing countries generates an overall investment climate that is much less conducive to innovation than that observed in the industrial countries (figure 12).

Along with eliminating unnecessary requirements, technological progress often requires the strengthening of regulatory initiatives. For example, improvements in the effectiveness of public-sector institutions have contributed to more efficient logistics services, a key determinant of trade competitiveness. Strengthening contract enforcement, the efficiency of court operations, the security of property rights (including the reliability and timely update of property registries), and the effective regulation of financial markets can be critical to ensuring an adequate return to investments in technology. Governments also can play a key role in boosting technological progress through the definition and promotion of product standards, and in helping firms comply with them.

Despite the limited amount of at-the-frontier scientific innovation performed in developing countries, technological progress depends on R&D and especially technology dissemination activities. In most developing countries and sectors, R&D should focus on the adoption and adaptation of preexisting technologies, not on efforts to expand the global technological frontier. For low-income countries, policy should focus on strengthening

Figure 12 Developing regions have much poorer governance than do OECD countries

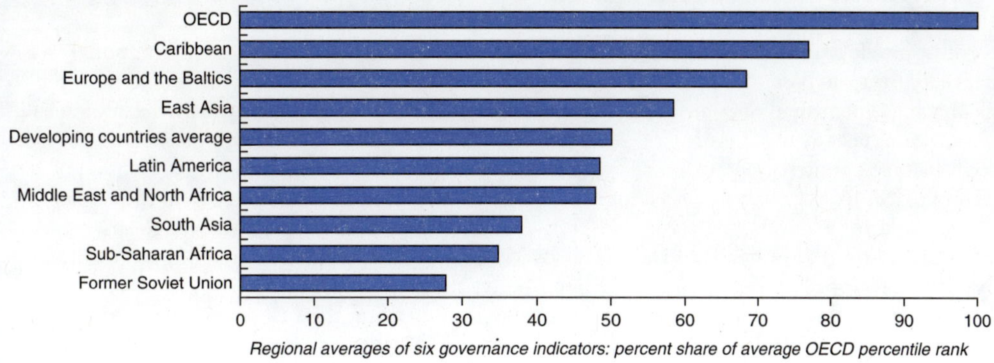

Source: Kaufman, Kraay, and Mastruzzi 2007.
Note: OECD = Organisation for Economic Co-operation and Development.

the infrastructure necessary for the successful diffusion and implementation of technologies, on facilitating the diffusion of already existing technologies, and on developing domestic competencies. More technologically advanced middle-income countries should emphasize the same points but should strengthen their R&D and technical competencies in order to increasingly compete at the global technological frontier. In both low- and middle-income countries, policy should place special emphasis on incentives and on maintaining strong ties to private-sector firms.

Some policy directions

This review of the level of and trends in technological achievement in developing countries, of the major transmitters of technological knowledge, and of the determinants of countries' ability to absorb them suggests a number of empirical conclusions (box 1). This report does not offer a comprehensive explanation of why technological progress occurs, nor does it include an in-depth analysis of the policies that governments can adopt to increase the rate of technological progress. Nevertheless, the preceding analysis makes clear that some combination of openness to foreign technology, strong domestic technological competencies, a motivated public sector, and a well-financed private sector are key ingredients for success. In addition, several general policy directions suggest themselves.

First, much of the technological progress in developing countries over the past 15 years has been associated with the increase in openness that occurred during the same period. This openness has increased developing countries' exposure to foreign technologies, but their capacity to absorb them has improved much less. To the extent that technological absorptive capacity limits the level of technological achievement that an economy can reach (as suggested by the tendency for technological achievement in Latin America to level off), the relatively weak improvement in absorptive capacity may result in a future slowing of the rate of technological progress in some countries unless they take significant steps to raise the quality of domestic human capital, improve the regulatory environment, and increase the efficiency with which they deliver government services. This risk may be most marked for those countries such as Indonesia and Mexico that have taken advantage of globalization in a relatively passive manner, exploiting their low-wage comparative advantage without taking strong steps to improve domestic competencies.

Box 1 Summary of empirical results

First, on most fronts, developing countries have progressed markedly over the past 15 years. As a result, technological achievement in all income groups and in every region has advanced more quickly than in high-income countries.

Second, the technological frontier has advanced as high-income countries (and some developing countries) continue to innovate at a rapid rate. Thus the technology gap between developed and developing countries remains large, particularly for low-income countries.

Third, to a large extent the convergence in technological achievement reflects a substantial increase in the openness of developing countries to foreign trade, foreign direct investment, and international migration, which has dramatically increased both the exposure of developing countries to new technologies and the opportunities to use foreign markets to exploit increasing returns to scale.

Fourth, progress has also been made in increasing countries' absorptive capacity through improved literacy, enhanced educational attainment, and better macroeconomic stability. However, progress in improving the business climate and governance indicators has been much more mixed. As a result, technological absorptive capacity has advanced much less quickly than technological achievement.

Second, because of the complementarity of technologies and infrastructure, countries where older technologies have yet to penetrate particularly deeply may also face limits to the extent to which other technologies are able to diffuse. Therefore, the authorities should focus on ensuring that publicly supplied technological services are available as widely, reliably, and economically as possible, whether they are delivered directly by the state or by private firms.

Third, a main remaining challenge is to ensure that technologies diffuse throughout the country, not just to major centers or top-performing firms. This does not mean trying to create research centers everywhere, but it does require reinforcing absorptive capacity at the subnational level. Moreover, it means paying attention to dissemination channels within countries, including domestic transportation infrastructure, and the essential role to be played by the outreach, testing, marketing, and dissemination activities of applied R&D agencies.

Fourth, notwithstanding the relatively strong improvement in technological achievement by some low-income countries, many others have improved only marginally or not at all. In particular, improvements in technological absorptive capacity have been limited. Efforts to concentrate on increasing the quality of human capital must continue, not only by ensuring that more students stay in school longer, but also by raising standards, which in too many cases are too low.

Fifth, given the importance of market failures (for example, increasing returns to scale, the potential for coordination failures, the difficulties in appropriating the full returns to innovation owing to imitators, and capital-market imperfections), governments may need to intervene directly to encourage the rapid diffusion of technology and the growth of a vibrant domestic culture of technology adaptation and new-to-the-market innovation. Policies that have been tried include, among others, support for industry-specific research, subsidies for specific products, barriers to trade that favor technology-intensive activities, and directed credit programs. Such policies have been associated with economic miracles, particularly in several East Asian countries. However, they have also been associated with significant failures, notably in some Latin American and Sub-Saharan African countries. In those cases where direct interventions have been successful, they have tended to make support conditional on performance and have maintained high-quality government monitoring programs that have avoided being "captured" by industrial interests.

Note

1. Significant is defined here to be a penetration rate that is at least 5 percent of the average level in countries with the highest rate of exploitation.

References

Comin, Diego, and Bart Hobijn. 2004. "Cross-Country Technology Adoption: Making the Theories Face the Facts." *Journal of Monetary Economics* 51(1): 39–83.

Docquier, Frederic, and Abdeslam Marfouk. 2004. "Measuring the International Mobility of Skilled Workers (1990–2000)." Policy Research Working Paper Series 3381. World Bank, Washington, DC.

Easterly, William, and Ross Levine. 2001. "It's Not Factor Accumulation: Stylized Facts and Growth Models." *The World Bank Economic Review* 15(2):177–219.

Hall, Robert E., and Charles I. Jones. 1999. "Why Do Some Countries Produce So Much More Output per Worker Than Others?" *The Quarterly Journal of Economics* 114(1):83–116.

Kannankutty, Nirmala, and Joan Burrelli. 2007. "Why Did They Come to the United States? A Profile of Immigrant Scientists and Engineers." *Info Brief.* National Science Foundation: Directorate for Social Behavioural and Economic Sciences. Arlington, VA. June.

Kaufmann, Daniel, Aart Kray, and Massimo Mastruzzi. 2007. "Governance Matters: Governance Indicators for 1996–2006." World Bank Policy Research Working Paper No. 4280, World Bank, Washington, DC.

King, Robert G., and Ross Levine. 1994. "Capital Fundamentalism, Economic Development, and Economic Growth." *Carnegie-Rochester Conference Series on Public Policy* 40:259–92.

1

Prospects for Developing Countries

Following the sudden and sharp drop in market valuations of U.S. mortgage-backed securities in mid-2007, global markets have entered a phase of heightened uncertainty. This has been reflected in increased volatility in equity markets, commodity prices, and exchange rates.

Notwithstanding the increased volatility, the impact on developing countries has been relatively minor to date. Risk premiums have escalated, but remain relatively low in a historic context, and capital inflows remain plentiful, although bank lending has dropped off. Aggregate growth in developing countries continues to be strong, reflecting improved fundamentals in many countries, sizable revenues from commodity exports, and continued access to international finance at moderately higher cost. Their strong gross domestic product (GDP) growth is partially offsetting weaker U.S. domestic demand, which is now expected to remain subdued well into 2008.

Despite the resilience demonstrated by the global economy, risks exist and increased volatility has made several developing countries more vulnerable to financial disturbance, especially those with large current account deficits, pegged exchange rates, or domestic banking sectors that have borrowed heavily in international markets.

Growth outlook

On average, developing countries have been affected only modestly by the slowdown in the United States during 2007, which is now anticipated to continue into 2008 before picking up in 2009. GDP growth among low- and middle-income economies eased just 0.1 percentage point in 2007 from the strong 7.5 percent recorded in 2006. Despite weaker U.S. import growth, continued robust spending by oil-exporting countries and vibrant expansions in China and India are projected to keep developing-country growth strong at 7 percent or more in 2008 and 2009.

Over the longer term, the resilience of developing countries' improved fundamentals will be tested. More prudent macroeconomic management and technological progress (see chapters 2 and 3) have contributed to an increase in total factor productivity (TFP) and real income growth over the past 15 years. Over the next 10 years, these same factors are expected to enable developing countries to achieve annual per capita income gains of 3.9 percent, and perhaps as much as 3.4 percent in the following decade. These projections imply per capita income growth that is more than twice as fast as that in high-income countries. Growth of such magnitude would reduce the number of people living on less than a dollar a day from 1.2 billion in 1990 and 970 million in 2004 to 624 million by 2015. Such aggregate outcomes are not guaranteed, however, and performance across individual countries is likely to be diverse.

Inflation has remained remarkably muted worldwide despite four years of strong growth. Many developing countries have contained domestic inflation following a tightening of monetary and fiscal policies. The sharp increases in commodity prices mainly had one-time direct impacts on inflation, with only limited second-round effects. Moreover, the increasing integration of developing countries into global markets and their rising shares in world trade have helped dampen inflation globally through heightened international competition. In some countries, however, inflation may become an increasing challenge. In several oil-exporting countries, spending of vast export revenues is heating up domestic markets. In China, efforts to slow growth may not succeed in quickly reversing a recent acceleration of inflation, and demand pressures remain pronounced in several countries in Europe and Central Asia and Latin America and the Caribbean. In Sub-Saharan Africa, the combination of strong domestic demand and rising international grain prices could push already mounting inflation still higher, particularly in import-dependent coastal states.

Continued high and increasing oil prices have stimulated the use of food crops for biofuels and raised fertilizer costs. Prices of maize and vegetable oils increased by 33 and 50 percent, respectively, during 2007. Wheat production fell short of consumption partly because it has been displaced by maize and partly because of adverse weather conditions. As a result, stocks have reached historic lows, and wheat prices have jumped 30 percent. From a macroeconomic perspective, these price increases have hit low-income countries the hardest, resulting in a terms-of-trade loss equal to 0.5 percent of their GDP, with the poorest urban and nonfarming rural segments of the population bearing the greatest burden. While experience shows that direct and targeted income support, rather than price controls, is the most effective way to help these vulnerable consumers, the institutional requirements for social safety nets can be daunting.

Risks

The financial turbulence that emerged in mid-2007 has demonstrated how sudden and pervasive adjustments in financial markets can be. Because the dynamics of financial behavior are inherently difficult to control, and because new securitized instruments have made identifying the location or magnitude of underlying risk difficult, the possibility of a breakdown in a key financial institution or system cannot be fully discounted. Moreover, the likelihood of financial problems would increase rapidly if home prices in the United States were to fall precipitously, an event that could push the U.S. economy into recession. Such circumstances, and the likely U.S. monetary policy reaction, would reinforce the dollar's slide, with a consequent destabilizing effect on global markets.

To date, strong fundamentals in developing countries have helped mitigate the slowdown in the United States, but in the case of a major disruption, adverse effects in emerging markets are unlikely to be avoided, which at some point would exacerbate the U.S. slowdown. Substantially tighter financial conditions could generate a credit crunch that would have consequences for investment and growth in middle-income countries. Low-income countries would also suffer substantial repercussions resulting from weaker global demand for commodities, price declines, and terms-of-trade losses. Even without further turmoil in international financial markets, several developing countries have become more vulnerable to financial pressure as a result of heightened anxiety and increased volatility in foreign exchange markets.

Another important risk is that the loosening of monetary policy in response to the U.S. subprime mortgage crisis could cause growth to overshoot. Commodity markets could tighten further, inflationary pressures would mount, and financial imbalances would increase rather than recede. Such a scenario could sow the seeds of a much sharper slowdown in the medium term and illustrates the current challenge facing monetary authorities in both high-income and developing countries.

Financial markets: Needed correction or major disruption?

The financial market turmoil of the second half of 2007 resulted from the interaction of several factors. An extended period of abundant liquidity and low interest rates worldwide sparked a search for yield that induced many investors to take on additional risk. This was supported by robust global growth and favorable financial conditions, fueling a four-year expansion in the global credit cycle. Rapid growth in the market for asset-backed securities and structured financial products (collateralized debt obligations in particular) throughout major financial centers facilitated both lending (by making the calibration and offloading of risk easier) and borrowing (by effectively increasing liquidity and the availability of credit). Emerging market bond spreads declined to record lows, and equity prices increased rapidly in many developing countries during the first half of 2007. However, the degree of risk was especially underestimated in the lower credit segments of the U.S. mortgage market (subprime and "alt-A" loans), and hence the value of many asset-backed securities was grossly overestimated.

Corrections to this overvaluation began suddenly in late July, and rising default rates in the U.S. subprime mortgage market spilled over into equity, currency, and bond markets worldwide. Credit conditions for corporate borrowers tightened significantly, while government bond yields declined sharply in what is known as a "flight to quality." Spreads on noninvestment grade U.S. corporate securities widened by 200 basis points in July and the first half of August, indicating that investors' appetite for risk had diminished considerably (figure 1.1). In mid-August, the U.S. Federal Reserve and the European Central Bank provided ample liquidity to the banking system to help stabilize financial conditions.

The sell-off in risky assets served to widen emerging market bond spreads by about 100 basis points by mid-August, raising the cost of capital for corporate borrowers in both mature and emerging markets. As financial conditions tightened once more near the end of the year, U.S. high-yield spreads jumped to 600 basis points by the end of November and emerging market spreads retreated, then increased to 270 basis points, with the overall widening attributable to the current episode moving to 170 points.

Figure 1.1 The perceived riskiness of high-yield corporate bonds increased more than that of emerging market bonds

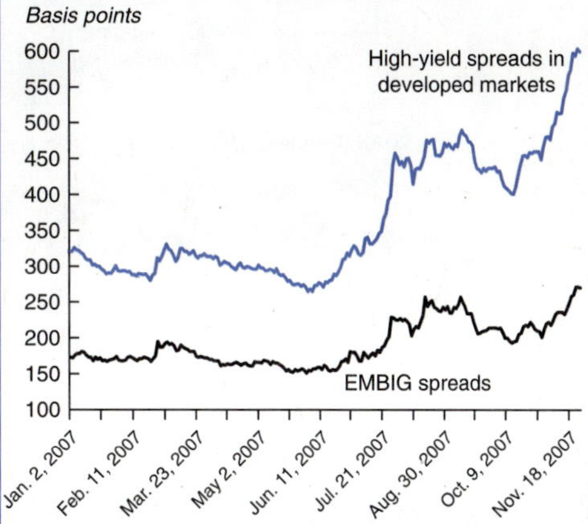

Sources: Bloomberg, JPMorgan-Chase, and World Bank.
Note: EMBIG = Emerging Market Bond Index-G.

Even though the turmoil has affected emerging markets, so far the financial fallout has been limited, though nevertheless more serious than other, fairly short-lived episodes of market turbulence and volatility that have occurred since 2005 (figure 1.2). Flight to

Figure 1.2 Emerging market asset sell-off more severe than during earlier periods of market turbulence

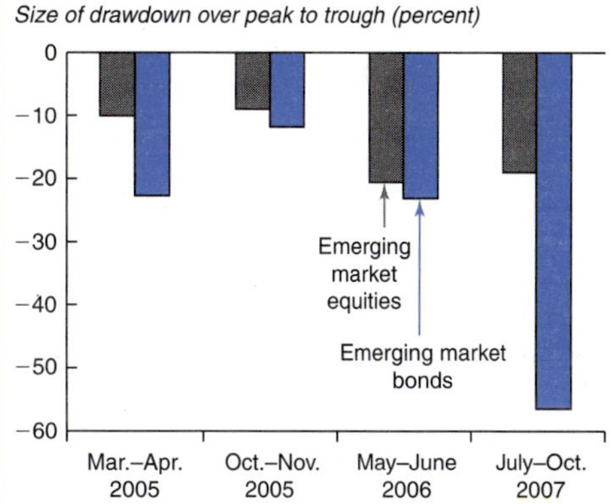

Sources: Bloomberg and World Bank.

Figure 1.3 Global equity markets fall, then recover led by emerging markets

Equity market index (January 1, 2007 = 100)

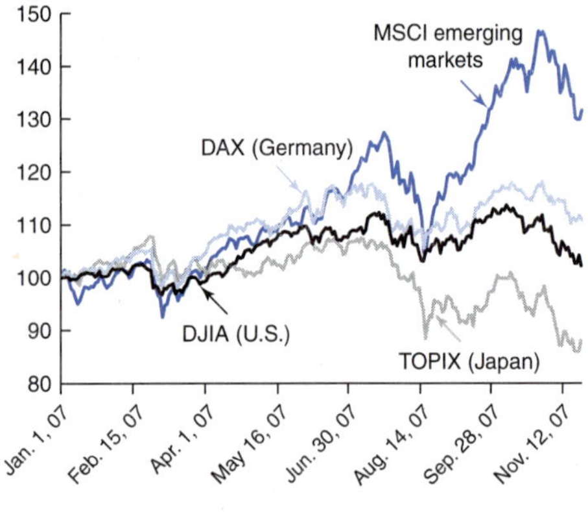

Source: Thomson/Datastream.

Note: DJIA = Dow Jones Industrial Average; MSCI = Morgan-Stanley Composite Index; TOPIX = Tokyo Stock Price Index; DAX = Deutsche Aktien Exchange.

quality and the need to cover losses in the subprime market provoked a sell-off across the entire spectrum of high-yield assets in mature and emerging markets. Equity price declines in emerging market economies initially exceeded those in mature markets, but emerging markets rebounded sharply, outpacing gains in mature markets (figure 1.3). The Morgan-Stanley composite index of emerging-market stocks picked up close to 50 percent from the beginning of the year, well above the developed markets, before both retreated in tandem by late November. The rebound in emerging market equities was underscored by a resumption of inflows to equity funds, which had experienced outflows of some $5 billion during late July and early August. Until recently, corrections were global in nature, and stock exchanges in East Asia and the Pacific and Latin America and the Caribbean were continuing to drive solid recovery in emerging market equities.

Gross capital flows to developing countries showed strong gains in 2007 before financial uncertainties arose. Bond issuance, bank loan commitments, and equity placements together averaged $53 billion a month from January through July, up from $41 billion during 2006, but a decline in August dropped flows to $42 billion (table 1.1). The surge in flows before August was concentrated in bond issuance and equity placements, and these categories initially experienced the steepest falloff after the turmoil. By October, bond and equity flows had recovered fully or almost fully, but a sharp falloff in bank lending emerged, with commitments dropping $25 billion during the month. Viewed on the basis of only moderate increases in sovereign spreads, the lack of bond issuance in August and September may have reflected decisions by governments in developing countries to postpone new issuance because of limited financing needs rather than an inability to access the market. However, for corporate borrowers in emerging economies, which accounted for 80 percent of bond issuance during 2007, financial conditions have deteriorated. The decline in banking flows is a concern, possibly reflecting a partial near-term withdrawal from

Table 1.1 Gross capital flows to developing countries, 2005–07

(monthly averages, $ billions)

			2007		
	2005	2006	January–July	August	October
Total	30	41	53	42	50
Bond issues	11	11	22	3	15
Bank loan commitments	15	20	18	35	10
Equity placements	5	9	13	4	25

Source: Dealogic Loanware and Bondware.

emerging markets, as banks tighten credit criteria and assume a more risk-averse posture as they replenish reserves after sharp losses in subprime securities.

Global growth

After four years of robust GDP and trade growth, steadily increasing commodity prices, low bond market spreads, gradually changing interest rates, and relatively stable exchange rates, volatility in international markets has increased. Conditions in global financial markets have turned from exceptionally favorable to less stable and less predictable.

More than in recent years, reserves and other buffers will be needed to absorb unexpected shocks. Policy makers must prepare both for the possibility that their economies may slow sharply and for the possibility that growth may continue to exceed potential. Similarly, they must prepare for the possibility of an abrupt depreciation of their currencies as well as the possibility that continued capital inflows could push them up. Commodity prices may spike, or they could give up part of the gains realized this decade.

Despite such a volatile climate, aggregate growth is likely to remain robust for the developing countries, mainly because of strong domestic momentum in most of them. Indeed, economic performance for many developing economies was exceptionally robust during the first half of 2007, much stronger than anticipated in *Global Development Finance* in early 2007 (World Bank 2007a).

Table 1.2 and figure 1.4 summarize recent developments and the base case outlook. World growth eased from 3.9 percent in 2006 to 3.6 percent in 2007, with the slowdown led by members of the Organisation for Economic Co-operation and Development (OECD). Their GDP dipped by 0.3 percentage points to 2.5 percent in the year. The downturn was more marked in the United States, with growth slowing from 2.9 percent in 2006 to 2.2 percent in 2007. Much of the decline reflected the direct fallout of the weakening housing market, with residential investment falling rapidly, and credit conditions for both firms and consumers tightening.

Among developing countries, growth remained firm at 7.4 percent in 2007, after an equally strong 7.5 percent in 2006, underpinned by continued strength in East and South Asia. If China and India are excluded, activity in low- and middle-income countries slipped by 0.2 percentage points to 5.7 percent in the year.

In 2008, global growth is expected to moderate further, as the effective cost of capital remains elevated for financial institutions, firms, and households. Weak domestic demand is expected to keep U.S. GDP growth below 2 percent in 2008, while growth in Europe and Japan should continue to ease under the additional weight of appreciating currencies. OECD import demand is projected to move from a solid 6.8 percent gain in 2007 to 5.4 percent during 2008, slowing export growth in developing countries by a point to 11 percent and dampening their output growth to 7.1 percent.

The OECD countries are anticipated to recover during the course of 2009, as returning stability in financial markets helps revive consumer and business confidence and residential

Figure 1.4 A step-down in growth in 2008

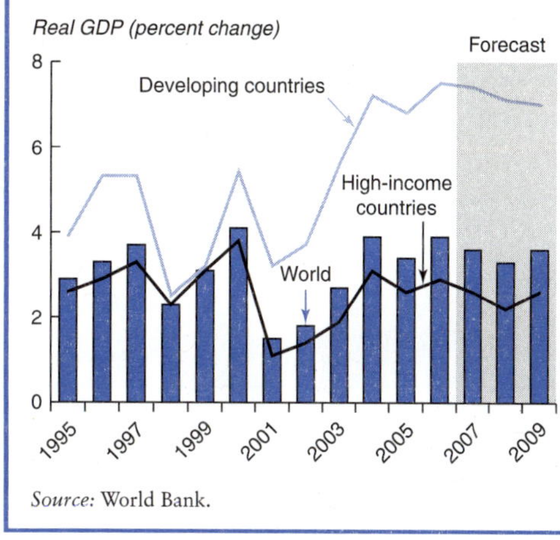

Source: World Bank.

Table 1.2 The global outlook in summary, 2005–09

(percent change per annum, except where otherwise indicated)

			Estimate	Forecast	
	2005	2006	2007	2008	2009
Global conditions					
World trade volume	7.8	10.1	9.2	7.6	9.2
Consumer prices					
Group of seven countries [a,b]	2.0	2.0	1.7	1.7	1.9
United States	3.4	3.2	1.9	1.5	1.9
Commodity prices (US$ terms)					
Non-oil commodities	13.4	24.5	15.3	−0.7	−4.6
Oil price					
US$ per barrel [c]	53.4	64.3	71.2	84.1	78.4
Percentage change	41.5	20.4	10.8	18.1	−6.8
Manufactures unit export value [d]	0.0	1.6	2.3	0.8	0.8
Interest rates					
$, 6-month (percent)	3.7	5.2	5.3	4.8	5.0
€, 6-month (percent)	2.2	3.2	4.3	4.0	4.3
Real GDP growth [e]					
World	**3.4**	**3.9**	**3.6**	**3.3**	**3.6**
World (PPP weights) [f]	4.8	5.3	5.2	4.9	5.1
High-income countries	**2.6**	**2.9**	**2.6**	**2.2**	**2.6**
OECD countries	2.4	2.8	2.5	2.1	2.4
Euro Area	1.5	2.8	2.7	2.1	2.4
Japan	1.9	2.2	2.0	1.8	2.1
United States	3.1	2.9	2.2	1.9	2.3
Non-OECD countries	5.8	5.6	5.1	4.8	5.0
Developing countries	**6.8**	**7.5**	**7.4**	**7.1**	**7.0**
East Asia and the Pacific	9.1	9.7	10.0	9.7	9.6
China	10.4	11.1	11.3	10.8	10.5
Indonesia	5.7	5.5	6.3	6.3	6.5
Thailand	4.5	5.0	4.3	4.6	5.2
Europe and Central Asia	6.1	6.9	6.7	6.1	5.7
Poland	3.6	6.1	6.5	5.7	5.1
Russian Federation	6.4	6.7	7.5	6.5	6.0
Turkey	7.4	6.1	5.1	5.4	5.7
Latin America and the Caribbean	4.6	5.6	5.1	4.5	4.3
Argentina	9.2	8.5	7.8	5.7	4.7
Brazil	2.9	3.7	4.8	4.5	4.5
Mexico	2.8	4.8	2.9	3.2	3.6
Middle East and North Africa	4.3	5.0	4.9	5.4	5.3
Algeria	5.1	1.8	3.4	4.0	3.8
Egypt, Arab Rep. of	4.4	6.8	7.1	7.0	6.8
Iran, Islamic Rep. of	4.3	4.6	5.0	5.0	4.7
South Asia	8.7	8.8	8.4	7.9	8.1
Bangladesh	6.0	6.6	6.5	5.5	6.5
India	9.2	9.4	9.0	8.4	8.5
Pakistan	7.7	6.9	6.4	6.5	6.7
Sub-Saharan Africa	5.8	5.7	6.1	6.4	5.8
Kenya	5.8	6.1	6.3	5.3	5.1
Nigeria	6.6	5.6	5.9	7.4	6.1
South Africa	5.0	5.4	5.0	5.1	5.3
Memo items					
Developing countries					
Excluding transition countries	6.9	7.5	7.5	7.2	7.1
Excluding China and India	5.2	5.9	5.7	5.3	5.2

Source: World Bank.
Note: OECD = Organisation for Economic Co-operation and Development; PPP = purchasing power parity.
a. Canada, France, Germany, Italy, Japan, the United Kingdom, and the United States.
b. In local currency, aggregated using 2000 GDP weights.
c. Simple average of Dubai, Brent, and West Texas Intermediate.
d. Unit value index of manufactured exports from major economies, expressed in U.S. dollars.
e. GDP in 2000 constant dollars; 2000 prices and market exchange rates.
f. GDP measured at 2000 PPP weights.

investment bottoms out. On aggregate, growth in developing countries is expected to be robust in both 2008 and 2009, remaining at or above 7 percent.

The high-income countries

Among OECD countries, the first quarters of 2007 appeared to be a prelude to more volatile growth (figure 1.5). U.S. GDP weakened sharply in the first quarter before rebounding to 3.8 and 4.9 percent in the second and third quarters on the strength of business investment in the second quarter, surprisingly strong consumer demand and stock-building in the third, and strong net exports in both. But high-frequency data point to weaker consumption growth in the fourth quarter, and for the year as a whole, 2.2 percent growth is expected, 0.7 percentage points below 2006 results (figure 1.6).

In contrast, Japan and the Euro Area maintained a favorable pace of growth in the first quarter, with business confidence breaching record highs, but developments in the second quarter were disappointing. In Europe, a retrenchment in business capital outlays more than halved GDP gains of the previous quarter, while in Japan, a slide in fixed investment turned growth into a decline. Third quarter results for Europe provided an upside surprise,

Figure 1.5 Volatile patterns of growth among OECD countries

Growth at seasonally adjusted annualized rates

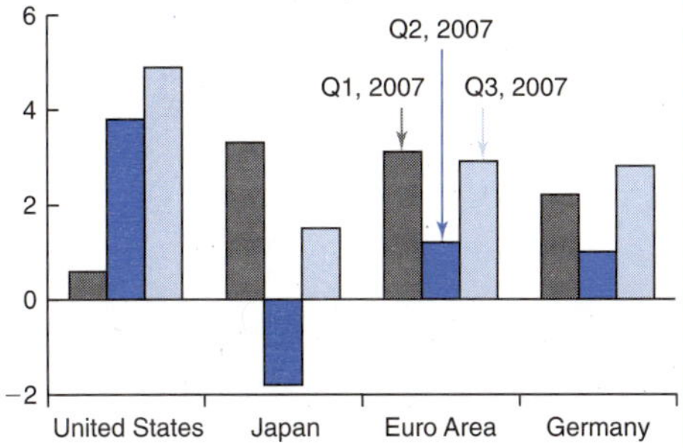

Source: National agencies and Eurostat.
Note: Q = quarter.

Figure 1.6 Tighter credit and weak housing yield slower U.S. growth

Real GDP growth at annual rates (percent)

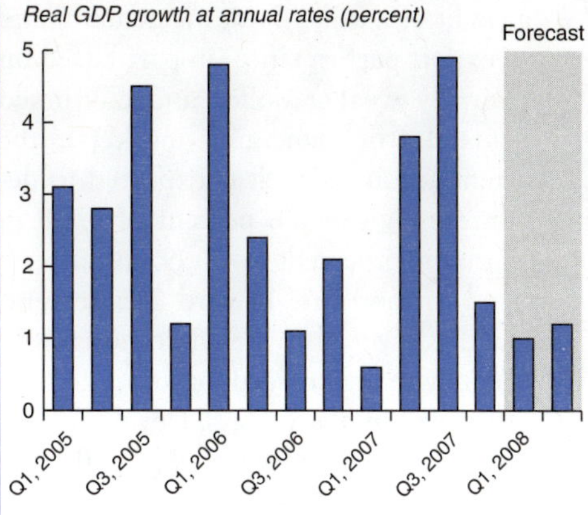

Source: World Bank.
Note: Q = quarter.

with growth returning to a favorable 2.9 percent. GDP gains were broadly based across countries, while business investment, stocks, and consumer spending in France and Germany revived to spur overall growth.

The Japanese economy rebounded modestly in the third quarter as well to register growth of 1.5 percent after a 1.8 percent decline in the previous quarter based on much improved net exports and a moderate boost to household spending. For 2007 as a whole, European growth is expected to register a strong 2.7 percent, eclipsing the United States for the first time in more than a decade, and growth in Japan should register 2 percent.

GDP growth in the United States is projected to weaken further in 2008, falling to 1.9 percent. During the year, continuing difficulties in the commercial paper market, the source of working capital for most U.S. business, implies a boost in the effective cost of short-term funds, despite a cumulative reduction of 100 basis points in Federal funds over September through December, which carried the rate to 4.25 percent. Recovery is anticipated for 2009, with growth registering

2.3 percent, grounded in a stabilization of financial markets and a revival of business and household spending.

As a result of weaker domestic demand and stronger export performance (in part based on a substantially weaker dollar and continued solid demand from emerging markets), the U.S. current account deficit is expected to decline from its high of 6.6 percent of GDP in 2006 to around 5 percent by 2009. Inflation is anticipated to moderate toward 2.5 percent, in step with slower growth, while household savings could move toward positive ground for the first time in many years. Developments in the United States are expected to influence conditions in Japan, both because of Japan's reliance on trade as a source of growth and because of the sensitivity of business investment to the costs of long-term capital. This is of particular note given Japan's experience with the yen carry trade.[1] Because such trade can potentially unwind rapidly, with local currency proceeds used to redeem yen, substantial appreciation of the currency could hamper exports, production, and incomes. Growth in Japan is expected to slow to 1.8 percent in 2008 before picking up to 2.1 percent by 2009.

Household spending in the Euro Area has not yet fully recovered from the increase in the German value added tax of January 2007, although unemployment in Europe eased to 7.3 percent in September 2007, the lowest level since figures began to be compiled in 1993. Business investment continues to move in close step with export performance, which deteriorated toward the end of the year, in part because of the appreciation of the euro and slowing U.S. demand. As exports soften and business investment declines, GDP growth is projected to slip to 2.1 percent in 2008 before reviving to 2.4 percent in 2009.

The developing countries

The first half of 2007 was marked by an acceleration in industrial production across developing regions, notably in East Asia (20 percent, year over year) (figure 1.7 and table 1.3).[2] A pickup in China's production, together with momentum gains in Indonesia (7.3 percent) and Thailand (6.0 percent), resulted partly from a bottoming out of the high-tech slump in the second quarter of the year. South Asia's continued buoyant production gains are linked to double-digit growth in India, which is tied in turn to strong domestic demand. Latin America and the Caribbean achieved a 6.4 percent increase in industrial production during the second quarter, at a seasonally adjusted annual rate, up from 2.4 percent during the first. Within the region, strong performance in Brazil (10 percent), Colombia (13 percent), and Mexico (5.5 percent) have offset weakening output

Figure 1.7 Robust growth in developing country industrial production

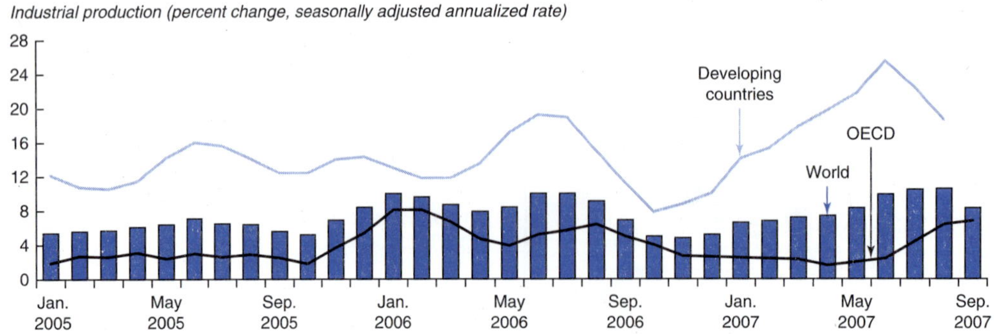

Source: World Bank.

Table 1.3 Recent economic indicators, developing regions, 2005–07

	Growth year-on-year		Seasonally adjusted annualized growth		Growth year-on-year	
Indicator and region	2005	2006	Q1, 2007	Q2, 2007	H1, 07	Latest
GDP growth (percent) [a]						
Developing countries	6.8	7.5	8.5	7.0	7.5	—
East Asia and the Pacific	9.1	9.7	10.3	10.5	9.8	10.2
Europe and Central Asia	6.1	6.9	3.8	4.3	6.3	—
Latin America and the Caribbean	4.6	5.6	7.5	5.0	5.9	5.7
Middle East and North Africa	4.3	5.0	4.8	4.5	4.7	—
South Asia	8.7	8.8	15.6	7.7	9.2	—
Sub-Saharan Africa	5.8	5.7	4.9	4.0	5.0	—
Industrial production growth (percent)						
Developing countries	9.3	10.1	14.6	18.5	14.0	11.4
East Asia and the Pacific	13.8	14.3	19.6	28.9	19.6	16.4
Europe and Central Asia	1.4	4.5	5.6	0.0	3.7	5.0
Latin America and the Caribbean	3.9	4.3	2.4	6.4	3.8	4.6
Middle East and North Africa	4.4	−0.3	−1.9	1.5	−0.5	−1.2
South Asia	9.1	11.0	15.6	11.3	13.0	8.0
Sub-Saharan Africa	5.0	5.3	—	—	—	—
Consumer prices (year over year growth rates in percent)						
Developing countries	6.4	6.2	5.7	6.1	5.9	6.1
East Asia and the Pacific	7.2	4.9	4.3	3.4	3.8	3.1
Europe and Central Asia	4.4	5.6	4.5	4.8	4.7	7.1
Latin America and the Caribbean	5.4	5.6	5.8	5.0	5.4	4.7
Middle East and North Africa	2.8	1.8	4.9	4.2	4.5	5.0
South Asia	7.0	7.6	7.1	6.4	6.7	6.9
Sub-Saharan Africa	3.4	4.6	6.3	7.1	6.7	7.1
Spreads on debt (basis points)						
Developing countries	306	198	176	162	169	243
East Asia and the Pacific	265	180	138	129	134	207
Europe and Central Asia	185	137	147	134	141	192
Latin America and the Caribbean	364	213	183	167	175	259
Middle East and North Africa	324	338	418	434	426	548
South Asia	199	199	166	171	169	482
Sub-Saharan Africa	277	266	283	270	277	321

Source: National statistical agencies through Thomson/Datastream; spreads: JPMorgan.
Note: Q = quarter.
Quarterly 2007 growth for developing regions based on data available for key economies.
EAP: China, Indonesia, Malaysia, Philippines, Thailand. SAR: India. ECA: Hungary, Poland, Russian Federation, Turkey.
LAC: Argentina, Brazil, Chile, Colombia, Mexico. MENA: Arab Rep. of Egypt. SSA: Nigeria, South Africa.
— = not available; H1 = 1st half.
a. Growth rates at annual or annualized rates unless otherwise indicated.

gains in Argentina and the República Boliviarana de Venezuela.

Robust production data are also reflected in GDP results. Led by the large economies, notably China, India, and the Russian Federation, output for the developing countries averaged 7.5 percent (year-on-year) in the first half of 2007, matching the record pace of 2006 (table 1.3 and figure 1.8). Because developing economies have been less affected by the fallout from the subprime crisis than high-income economies, the anticipated slowdown of growth in 2008 should be less pronounced. Gains among developing countries are projected to slow from 7.4 percent in 2007 to 7.1 percent in 2008, with easing across all regions except the Middle East and North Africa and Sub-Saharan Africa, in part because of higher oil revenues. For the remaining countries, slower export market growth, only gradual improvement in financing conditions, and declines in the terms of trade account for most of the slowdown. Though a further easing of growth to 7 percent is anticipated for 2009,

Figure 1.8 Developing growth retains strong momentum during the first half of 2007...

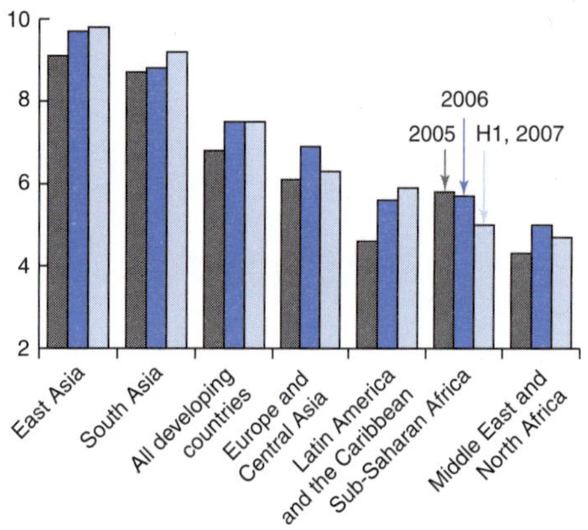

Sources: World Bank and National agencies.
Note: H1 = 1st half.

Figure 1.9 ...with growth moderating through 2009

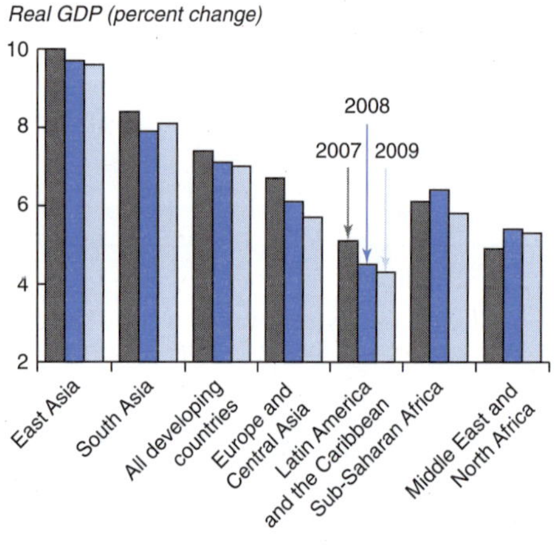

Source: World Bank.

global conditions should favor a smoother step-down in activity for those countries and regions more dependent on trade, notably East Asia and Latin America (figure 1.9).

Developing region perspectives

GDP in **East Asia and the Pacific** is expected to grow about 10 percent in 2007, the strongest performance since 1994. Growth in China is expected to exceed 11 percent (table 1.2). Elsewhere in the region, strong investment demand boosted growth in Indonesia by almost a percentage point, from 5.5 percent in 2006 to 6.3 percent in 2007. Tighter monetary policy and the economy's absorption of the direct effects of the removal of energy subsidies in 2006 have nearly halved inflation, from 13 percent in 2006 to 7 percent in 2007. Growth is expected to remain in the 6 percent range. Growth in Malaysia and the Philippines appears to have picked up as well, coming in at near 6 percent or better, reflecting a relaxation of monetary policies and improved external demand for electronics. Growth in Thailand has been more subdued during 2007, at a little over 4 percent, tied in part to political unrest, as well as a lagging response to the high-tech revival.

Assuming that China continues its double-digit growth and that the authorities succeed in dampening overheated sectors, GDP growth in East Asia should slow gradually to 9.7 percent in 2008 and to 9.6 percent by 2009. Many countries in the region could, however, experience a stalling of export growth and a loss of business and consumer confidence, leading to a moderate falloff in GDP gains in 2008.

The effects from the turmoil in the world's financial centers may be minimal for most economies in East Asia. Except for China, direct exposures of financial institutions in the region to mortgage-backed securities (or subprime risks) are limited.[3] Economies in East Asia and the Pacific are entering this more turbulent period from a position of relative strength: improved macroeconomic fundamentals, further movement into current account surplus, and rapidly increasing reserves. Yet several of these economies have been the object of international investor interest through carry trades.[3] Should conditions in the mature markets deteriorate so that assets are shifted out of classes perceived as risky to cover other losses, the threat of an unwinding of the yen carry trade, with attendant down-spikes in local equity markets and rapid currency depreciation, is a concern for policy makers.

Possible side effects related to financial market turbulence—notably a distinct softening of U.S. and European import demand—could affect all East Asian countries. The Euro Area and the United States together account for 43 percent of China's export market, while Japan accounts for 7.5 percent. With the development of China as a hub for the final assembly and shipment of goods to destination markets, with parts and materials supplied by other East Asian economies (figure 1.10), slower import demand from developed countries could adversely affect the entire region. Some East Asian economies could experience a double hit, sustaining a loss of both direct and indirect import demand.

In the **Europe and Central Asia** region, investment and external demand are both slowing, leading to a moderate easing of growth from 6.9 percent in 2006 to 6.7 percent in 2007. Private consumption, fed by robust credit creation, accounted for 4.6 percentage points of the advance in 2007. Investment, which accounted for 3.4 percentage points of growth in 2007, was driven by policy reforms, improved business confidence tied to European Union (EU) accession by several Central and Eastern European countries, and continuing high oil prices that have fueled a construction boom in several countries of the Commonwealth of Independent States (CIS).

The falloff in external demand took hold in the second half of 2007, slowing growth by 2 percentage points, as net exports continued to deteriorate. Inflation has risen in several countries, tied to sustained strong growth in domestic demand, rising fuel and food prices (the latter aggravated by drought in Bulgaria and Romania), and higher world grain prices. Rapid credit expansion in most of the region has contributed to a worsening of external balances while exerting upward pressure on asset, goods, and labor market prices (figure 1.11). Signs of overheating are evident in Bulgaria and the Baltic states, for example, where external positions have deteriorated from already high levels. Effects on the region stemming from the crisis in the U.S. subprime mortgage market have thus far been limited. Initial downward adjustments to asset prices

Figure 1.10 East Asia now accounts for one-quarter of China's imports

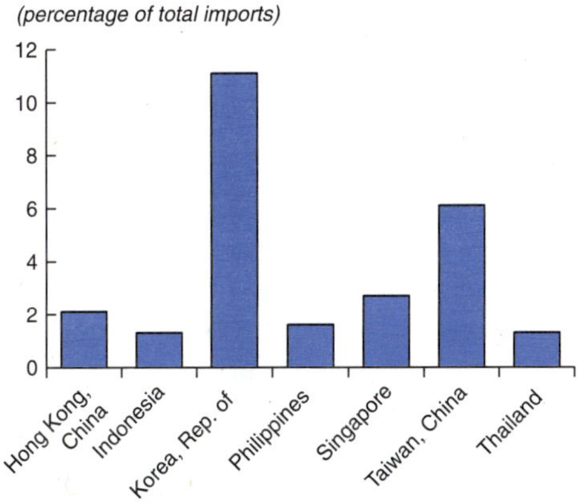

Source: National sources through Haver Analytics.

Figure 1.11 External positions vary widely across Europe and Central Asia

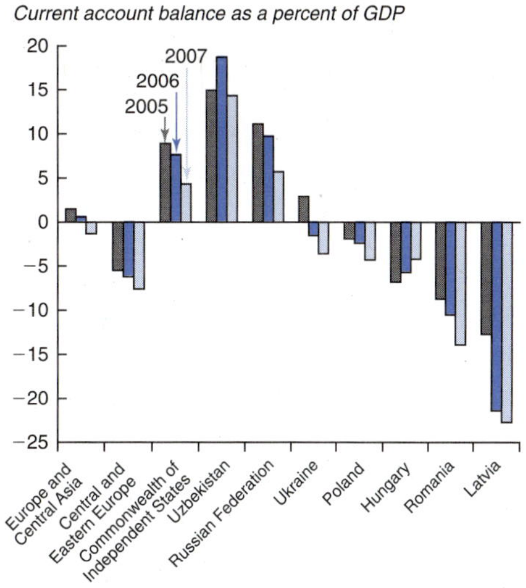

Source: World Bank.

and currencies have since been recouped and bond spreads increased, but to a lesser extent than in other markets.

Regional GDP growth is expected to slow to 6.1 percent in 2008 and 5.7 percent in 2009. Given tighter international credit conditions and weakening external demand, the growth falloff in 2008 is likely to affect almost the entire region. Domestic demand is also projected to soften slightly from its recent strong growth, with contributions to GDP of both private consumption and investment dropping by 0.2 percentage points during 2008.

Three exceptions to this growth forecast for 2008 are Albania, Hungary, and Turkey. In Albania, growth is likely to firm on continued strong domestic demand, including an increase in public investment. That investment is crucial to overcome substantial problems in infrastructure, as power shortages now form a significant bottleneck to growth. In Hungary and Turkey, further easing in monetary policy is expected to strengthen domestic demand, leading to a pickup in growth.

External demand is projected to revive by 2009 as GDP growth among the OECD countries picks up. After slowing GDP by 2.2 percentage points in 2008, net exports are projected to boost growth by 1.7 percentage points in 2009. This gain is expected to be offset by further slowing in domestic demand, particularly investment in the CIS countries, yielding GDP growth of 5.7 percent in 2009. The expected falloff in investment in the CIS is driven by the completion of hydrocarbon infrastructure projects that have supported production and export capacity in recent years.

In **Latin America and the Caribbean,** GDP advanced by 5.1 percent in 2007, the fourth consecutive year of sustained growth. The average rate of output gains over 2005–07 was 5.3 percent, twice the 2.7 percent registered during the previous 15 years. Recent growth has also been broadly based, with positive results shared across subregions: South America, Central America, and the Caribbean (figure 1.12). A favorable external environment, together with better macroeconomic management, helped improve fundamentals, reduce the volatility of economic indicators, and sustain growth. GDP in the region picked up to a 5.9 percent pace in the first half of 2007 on the back of continued strong activity in Argentina, Brazil, Chile, and the República Boliviarana de Venezuela. In addition, the mid-2007 credit market turmoil that hit the United States seems to have had limited effects on Latin America and the Caribbean to date. To a degree, the recent upturn in growth will serve as a buffer. Even though any stagnation in the United States will eventually affect regional prospects, countries seem better prepared for exogenous shocks than during prior episodes of financial market disturbance.

Figure 1.12 Growth eases in 2007 for the Latin America and Caribbean region

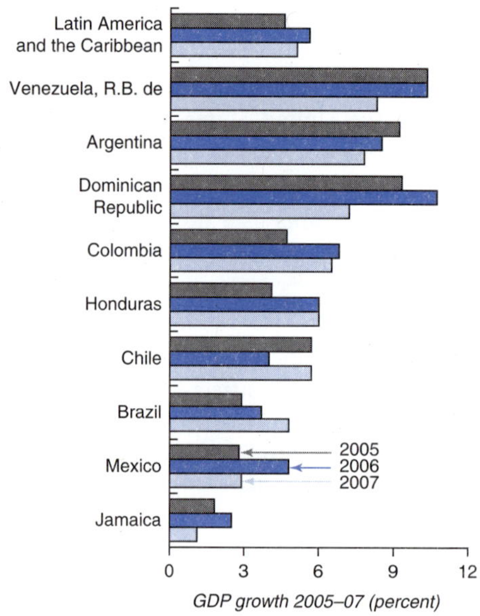

Sources: World Bank and national agencies.

In contrast with previous expansion phases—and indeed, with previous episodes of crisis—Latin America and the Caribbean is now recording a healthy current account surplus and accumulating large stocks of international reserves. The improvements of recent years might indeed be sufficient to ward off some of the adverse effects of developments in the United States. For example, at the time of the 1998 Russian crisis, the current account deficit for the region was close to $89 billion or 4.4 percent of GDP. In 2003, the deficit reversed to a surplus, and in 2006, the region had a surplus of more than $46 billion, equivalent to 1.6 percent of GDP. Trade liberalization and flexible exchange rates are among the frequently cited policies that facilitated these improvements in external balances.

On the heels of strong growth in 2007, regional GDP growth is expected to ease to 4.5 percent in 2008 and further to 4.3 percent by 2009. Such measured regional slowdown is underpinned by continued strong growth in Brazil and a rebound from a weak 2007 in Mexico, while growth in other countries—notably Argentina and the República Boliviarana de Venezuela—is likely to slow. Excluding the latter two countries, GDP moderated slightly from 4.7 percent in 2006 to 4.4 percent in 2007 and, following an anticipated dip to 4.2 percent in 2008 because of weak import demand in the United States, is expected to recoup to 4.3 percent by 2009. Should these outturns be realized, they would represent the longest positive growth spell for Latin America and the Caribbean since the 1960s. Despite a gradual worsening of current account positions because of stabilizing commodity prices and slower growth in global demand, strong growth is likely to persist, supported by continued expansion in consumption and investment, buoyed by an environment of low inflation (excluding Argentina and the República Boliviarana de Venezuela), improved fiscal policy (particularly in Mexico), and continued strong capital inflows (especially to Brazil).

High oil prices have continued to support growth for the oil-exporting countries in the **Middle East and North Africa,** coming on the heels of a 5 percent regional GDP advance in 2006, the fastest in a decade for the region's developing countries.[4] Oil prices, which spiked to almost $100 per barrel late in the year and averaged $71 per barrel for 2007, are further buttressing government revenues, some of which are dedicated to infrastructure spending in the developing oil exporters (principally Algeria and the Islamic Republic of Iran). At the same time, a solid pickup in European growth over the course of 2007 has favored economic activity among the diversified exporters in the Maghreb and Mashreq, which have especially close trade and services ties with the Euro Area. GDP in the Middle East and North Africa appears to have fared well over the first half of 2007, though easing from 2006 to a 4.7 percent pace during the period, with the slowing tied in part to a return to drought conditions that have affected several countries in the Maghreb, notably Morocco.

The run-up of surplus funds among oil exporters and the availability of new investment opportunities across the region boosted foreign direct investment (FDI) flows to new highs of more than $24 billion in 2006, or 3.4 percent of regional GDP. At the same time, recovery of local equity markets offers promise that after bouts of overheating during 2004–05 and stabilization following the recent tensions in global financial markets, a less volatile source of funds may play a larger role in the region's growth.

Developing country oil exporters in the Middle East and North Africa registered growth of 4.5 percent in 2007, half a percentage point up from 2006, as GDP in the Islamic Republic of Iran advanced to 5 percent, while output in Algeria almost doubled from the poor 1.8 percent showing of 2006. Hydrocarbon revenues (oil and natural gas) flowing to developing country exporters amounted to $167 billion in the year, representing an increase of 5.7 percent, or $9 billion, over 2006 results. In contrast, export revenues for the high-income country exporters grew by 6 percent to $360 billion, an increment of $20 billion, over 2006 levels (figure 1.13).[5]

For diversified exporters, trade responded well to increased European demand, and to a degree by a depreciation of local currencies in relation to the euro. Exports of goods and

Figure 1.13 Continued oil revenue gains support growth among Middle East and North Africa oil exporters

Crude oil and product revenues ($ billions) oil price, World Bank ($/barrel)

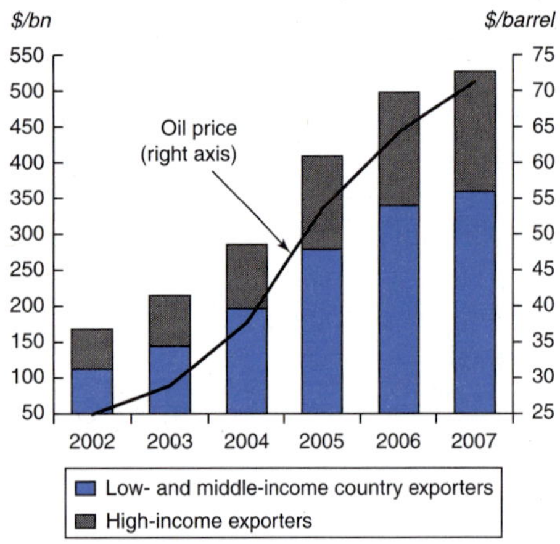

Sources: UN Comtrade database; International Monetary Fund; International Energy Agency; World Bank.

services for Jordan, Morocco, and Tunisia as a group jumped to 10.2 percent growth in the year, in step with a 2.5 percent increment in Euro Area demand, setting the stage for improved output growth. At the same time, a risk facing the region's textiles and clothing exporters, as well as many other low- and middle-income country exporters, is the coming removal of remaining barriers to Chinese exports of specific textiles and clothing products (box 1.1).

A number of factors are likely to shape the growth profile for the Middle East and North Africa region. A softening of OECD demand is anticipated for 2008, although it may be accompanied by additional firming of global oil prices tied to continued robust demand in emerging markets. This should benefit the oil exporters for a time, and should support regional growth of 5.4 percent. As the global environment improves by 2009, the Middle East and North Africa region should be able to maintain the broader pace of growth established in 2008 for several more years. Domestic conditions will vary decidedly across the disparate economies of the region, as will efforts at reform, which in most cases are aimed at spurring private sector or non-oil activity. Tensions related to continuing conflict in Iraq, unsettled conditions in the Levant, and international disputes with the Islamic Republic of Iran will tend to affect global and regional investors' confidence concerning the region, and any projections exercise about the region should take these into account as a risk.

In **South Asia,** regional GDP growth remained vibrant at 8.4 percent in 2007, though easing somewhat from the stellar 8.8 percent gains of 2006. Industrial production and GDP growth are being driven by strong domestic demand, with private consumption and investment each contributing about 4 points to GDP growth in the year. An expansion of credit, rising incomes, and strong worker remittance receipts are underpinning private consumption, while improvements in business sentiment—both foreign and domestic—along with rising corporate profits, are providing a further boost to investment. Despite more restrictive monetary policy and progress toward greater fiscal consolidation in a number of countries, domestic demand growth has picked up, building on the momentum of reforms undertaken in recent years. Moreover, because of tighter policy conditions, inflation pressures moderated during the first half of 2007 in the larger regional economies of India and Pakistan. The risks of revived inflation remain, in part because of the still incomplete pass-through of high energy prices and upward pressures on food prices.

Current account balances deteriorated in a number of countries in 2007, with deficits reaching close to 5 percent of GDP in Pakistan and Sri Lanka and about 2 percent in India. Pakistan's current account deficit is a concern, having deteriorated by the equivalent of more than 5 percentage points of GDP during the last four years. In India, monetary tightening and large capital inflows led to substantial appreciation of the rupee over the year, with the currency reaching a near decade high of Rs 39.30 against the dollar by late November

Box 1.1 Developing country exports in the wake of the removal of barriers to Chinese exports

The system of quantitative restrictions that managed rich countries' imports of textiles and clothing from developing countries for 30 years, especially those produced in China and India (the Multi-Fiber Arrangement), was finally dismantled at the end of 2004, although restrictions for a number of categories of Chinese textile and clothing exports to the EU and the United States remained because of measures that are due to expire in 2008.

China's exports of clothing soared 22 percent in 2005 and 32 percent in 2006, increasing its market share in those two years to 24 percent and 28 percent, respectively, but the impact on competitors has been less drastic than some had feared. The increase in the size of the world market for clothing has allowed exports from many other countries to grow, including the Arab Republic of Egypt, India, Peru, Sri Lanka, and Turkey. In Bangladesh, where 1 million jobs were predicted to be lost, exports to the EU and the United States gained continuously between 2004 and the first four months of 2007.

Nevertheless, some countries have seen declines in clothing exports that may entail substantial adjustment. For example, exports to the U.S. and EU markets from Brazil, the Dominican Republic, Swaziland, and Taiwan (China) declined substantially in 2005 and 2006. With the exception of Swaziland, clothing exports from these countries continued to decline into 2007. In addition, for Sub-Saharan Africa as a whole, where the end of the clothing sector had been foreseen, exports to the EU and the United States fell by 7 percent in 2004 and 17 percent in 2005 (on a trade weighted average). In 2006, Sub-Saharan African textile exports to the EU grew 3 percent, whereas exports to the United States declined by 6 percent. In 2007, to the extent that data are available, Sub-Saharan African textile exports to both the EU and the United States grew by 7 and 2 percent, respectively. A number of countries, including Madagascar, Mauritius, and Swaziland, managed to reverse an initial decline in clothing exports and return to growth in 2006 or early 2007.

How vulnerable are other countries when the final restrictions on Chinese textile and clothing exports to the EU and the United States expire? In 2006, 19 percent of Chinese exports to the EU and 20 percent of exports to the United States were subject to quota restrictions, and exports of these products will likely grow significantly after removal of the quotas. In the EU market, Colombia, the Dominican Republic, Mauritius, Peru, and Sri Lanka appear to be most at risk with more than 40 percent of their 2006 exports in product categories for which China is currently still subject to quotas. For other countries, the ratio is between 20 and 40 percent, and for Sub-Saharan Africa as a whole stands at 51 percent, mainly driven by the high exposure of Mauritius (74 percent). In the U.S. market, exposure is generally lower: only the Dominican Republic, India, and Sri Lanka export more than 20 percent of their textiles and clothing in categories where Chinese exports are currently subject to quotas. For most other countries, the ratio is between 5 and 20 percent. However, looking at the impact of the elimination of Multi-Fiber Arrangement quotas in 2004, many competitors managed to defend their market shares in recent years, and they might be able to do so in 2008 as well.

The clothing sector still provides an opportunity for export diversification and the expansion of manufactured exports for low-wage countries, even in the face of unfettered competition from China. The countries best able to expand their exports of clothing will be those that have a supportive business environment, low trade costs (efficient customs, ports, and transport infrastructure), and competitive firms that are flexible enough to meet the changing demands of the global buyers that now dominate the industry.

At the same time, significant adjustment pressures may arise as more efficient firms expand, while those unable to compete in the global market decline. In the absence of other employment opportunities, especially for women, workers made redundant from the textile and clothing sector may fall back into poverty. Minimizing the costs incurred by released workers and their families and facilitating their adjustment into alternative employment will be a major challenge for a number of developing countries.

Figure 1.14 South Asia growth is slowing as the Indian rupee appreciates

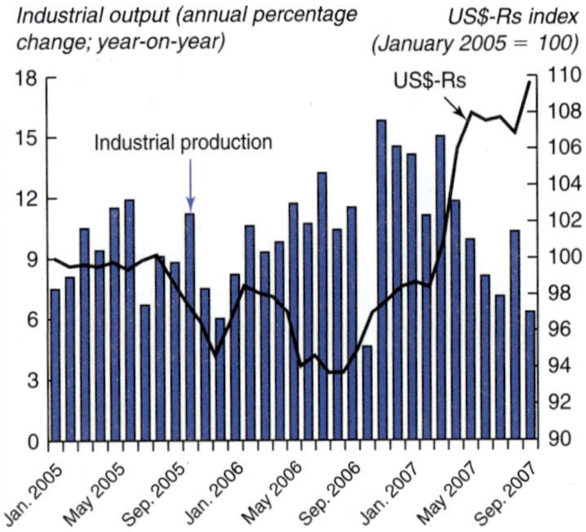

Source: World Bank.

(figure 1.14). The initial effects of increased volatility in international credit markets during the latter part of mid-2007 led to a fall-off in equity prices for both India and Pakistan, though both countries have recouped losses in the interim and returns remain well in the positive territory for the year. In local currency, equity markets are up 36 percent in India (50 percent in dollar terms) and 20 percent in Pakistan (19 percent in dollar terms) as of the end of November 2007.

Tighter credit conditions, greater market volatility, increased risk of recession in the United States, and easing growth in the EU will place downward pressures on regional exports before improvement sets in by 2009. At the same time, increased competition from China will be a factor in shaping the path of export growth over the next few years, and an additional 18 percent increase in crude oil prices in 2008 will contribute to a marked deterioration in external balances. On balance, these factors should lead to an easing of regional growth from 8.4 percent in 2007 to 7.9 percent in 2008. Growth is projected to pick up to 8.1 percent in 2009 as external demand revives and given easing pressures on the import bill as oil price gains diminish. Domestic demand is anticipated to revive into 2009, assuming inflation conditions permit some easing of monetary policy in the second half of 2008.

Growth in **Sub-Saharan Africa** looks poised to remain buoyant by historic standards, maintaining a growth pace near 6 percent from 2007 through 2009, notwithstanding slowing demand in the United States and the Euro Area. GDP continued to grow strongly in 2007, with output expanding 5 percent in the first half of the year, and is expected to amount to 6.1 percent for 2007 as a whole. This follows a solid 5.7 percent advance in 2006, grounded in sharp gains for regional oil exporters and South Africa (figure 1.15). Global commodity demand and prices were pushed higher in recent years, notably by continued brisk economic expansion in China. Sub-Saharan Africa is one of few regions that has witnessed a strong supply response to higher oil prices, with crude oil production up 14.3 percent in 2004, an additional 7.6 percent in 2005, and 8.1 percent in 2006 (when Nigeria, which suffered from a number of shutdowns of facilities, is excluded).

Figure 1.15 Oil exporters drive 2007 growth results for Sub-Saharan Africa

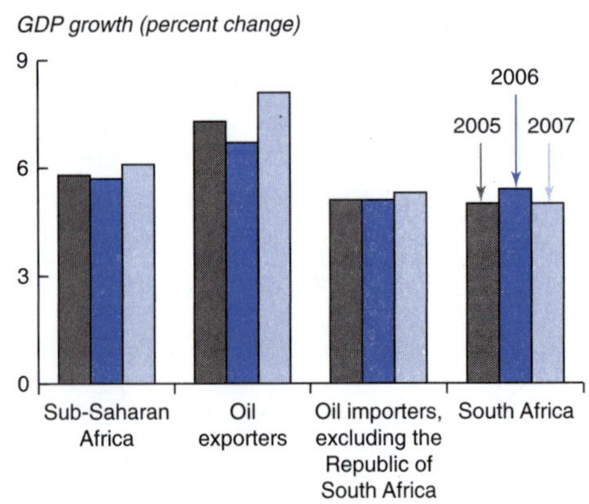

Sources: World Bank and national agencies.

Improved macroeconomic stability is also playing an important role in sustaining growth, as is a pickup in both domestic and foreign investment. Debt relief in recent years has freed budgetary resources for spending on infrastructure and social programs. A common trait across economies is a notable pickup in capital spending focused on the transport, telecommunications, and construction sectors. In addition, recovery from drought in many areas of the region is translating into improved performance in agriculture, adding impetus to growth, while the income effects stemming from several years of high non-oil commodity prices are stimulating private consumption.

Recent turbulence in international financial markets resulted in a moderate depreciation of the South African rand against the dollar, but this followed a period of appreciation of the rand because of anticipated capital inflows related to merger and acquisition activity. Due to weakness in the U.S. dollar, the nominal effective exchange rate of the rand has returned to levels prevailing in July, declining 11.2 percent during the first 10 months of the year. There are as yet no signs of a sharp sell-off of South African assets, and there appears to be little evidence of marked adverse effects on the domestic growth outlook.

Much of the impetus for regional growth over 2008–09 will come from strong domestic demand, notwithstanding softer private demand in South Africa, the region's powerhouse, where higher interest rates and an erosion of real incomes are curbing real outlays. A sharp decline in farmers' income in countries affected by recent floods will constitute a near-term drag on growth, and on private consumption in particular, although government and donor transfers and assistance may mitigate some of the effects. Investment is expected to remain strong, notwithstanding the tightening of international credit conditions and lower commodity prices, in part because of large strategic investments by rapidly growing developing economies such as China and India. A notable activity is the Moatize coal project in Mozambique, investment in which amounted to $1.44 billion in the first half of 2007. Madagascar is also experiencing huge investments in its economy. Against this background, Sub-Saharan African GDP is anticipated to be sustained at a pace above 6 percent through 2008, before slipping to 5.8 percent growth in 2009 as oil exporters respond to international conditions and restrain output moderately.

World trade

The globalization of markets for goods and services is continuing at an unabated pace. Over the past seven years, world trade volumes have increased at an average rate of 6.7 percent, virtually the same as during the 1990s (table 1.4). Trade volumes are expanding more than twice as fast as industrial production (global GDP has grown 3 percent a year since 2000, up from 2.8 percent a year during the 1990s). In current dollar terms, world trade doubled during the 1990s and has doubled again since 2000.

While world trade has grown steadily for the last 15 years, developing country trade has accelerated in recent years. During the 1990s, developing country export volumes increased at an annual pace of 6.8 percent, roughly the same as the 6.9 percent export gains of the high-income countries. Since 2000, however, developing countries' exports have been growing twice as fast as exports from high-income countries: 10.8 percent a year versus 5.1 percent a year.

On the import side, the acceleration is even more impressive. During the 1990s, developing countries' import growth of 5.7 percent a year lagged behind that in high-income countries (7.0 percent), but over the last seven years, those positions have reversed. In 2006, import growth in developing countries registered 14.3 percent, compared with 7.9 percent in the high-income countries. Imports across developing regions were growing at double-digit rates during 2006, as export revenues, which had been boosted by high-volume growth and sharp increases in commodity prices, were

Table 1.4 Developments and prospects for world trade and payments

Growth in percent	1991–2000	2000–05	2006	Estimate 2007	Forecast 2008	Forecast 2009
World trade volume[a] (growth in percent)	6.8	5.7	9.8	8.7	7.4	9.3
World exports (growth in percent)	**6.9**	**5.7**	**10.1**	**9.2**	**7.6**	**9.2**
High-income countries	6.9	4.3	9.2	8.2	6.3	7.6
OECD high-income	6.8	3.6	8.8	8.7	6.5	7.7
United States	7.1	1.9	8.4	7.8	8.5	9.0
Japan	4.4	5.9	9.6	6.5	4.0	4.3
Euro Area	6.9	3.6	9.0	11.9	7.2	8.6
Developing countries	**6.8**	**10.4**	**12.7**	**12.0**	**11.0**	**13.1**
East Asia and the Pacific	11.7	15.4	17.7	17.8	15.2	18.5
Europe and Central Asia	0.9	9.1	10.3	9.2	8.5	8.7
Latin America and the Caribbean	8.1	5.3	7.8	4.8	5.5	5.8
Middle East and North Africa	4.4	6.1	9.5	4.3	3.8	5.2
South Asia	9.0	11.2	9.0	8.5	8.4	10.5
Sub-Saharan Africa	4.7	5.4	4.4	5.7	7.3	6.6
World imports (growth in percent)	**6.7**	**5.8**	**9.5**	**8.3**	**7.2**	**9.5**
High-income countries	**7.0**	**4.5**	**7.9**	**6.8**	**5.4**	**7.9**
OECD high-income	6.8	4.1	7.4	6.8	5.0	7.8
United States	9.3	4.3	5.9	2.0	1.3	6.8
Japan	3.6	3.9	4.6	3.6	3.0	5.2
Euro Area	6.3	3.4	7.5	10.1	7.4	9.4
Developing countries	**5.7**	**10.1**	**14.3**	**12.5**	**11.9**	**13.3**
East Asia and the Pacific	11.3	13.7	14.8	14.9	14.3	19.2
Europe and Central Asia	−0.9	10.5	14.2	12.8	11.6	10.4
Latin America and the Caribbean	10.7	4.2	13.3	9.2	9.3	8.1
Middle East and North Africa	1.6	9.7	19.1	12.0	10.0	7.4
South Asia	7.9	12.9	12.1	12.1	10.5	11.9
Sub-Saharan Africa	4.4	8.5	12.4	8.2	8.7	8.8
Current account (percent of GDP)						
High-income countries	**−0.1**	**−0.8**	**−1.1**	**−0.7**	**−0.6**	**−0.5**
OECD high-income	−0.2	−1.1	−1.9	−1.5	−1.4	−1.2
United States	−1.8	−4.9	−6.6	−6.0	−5.4	−5.1
Japan	2.4	3.1	3.9	4.1	3.7	3.8
Euro Area	0.0	0.2	−0.2	0.4	−0.1	0.1
Developing countries	**−1.5**	**1.4**	**3.6**	**3.1**	**2.5**	**1.8**
East Asia and the Pacific	0.1	3.3	8.4	10.1	8.6	7.6
Europe and Central Asia	−1.0	1.4	0.6	−1.3	−1.9	−2.6
Latin America and the Caribbean	−2.6	−0.6	1.6	0.5	0.1	−0.2
Middle East and North Africa	−0.3	5.5	9.6	8.2	9.5	6.2
South Asia	−1.6	0.3	−1.3	−2.4	−3.0	−2.7
Sub-Saharan Africa	−1.9	−0.3	0.9	0.4	0.9	−0.2

Source: World Bank.
Note: a. Exports and imports of goods and non-factor services in 2000 US$.

being expended. The pickup of trade in developing countries also shows in their shares of world markets: in current dollars, developing countries' market share increased gradually in the 1990s from 20 to 25 percent, but since 2000, their share has jumped to 35 percent, supported in part by higher commodity prices.

The rapid growth of trade and production in developing countries, seemingly independent of growth in the high-income countries, is sometimes referred to as "delinking." At the same time, the rapid integration of developing countries into global markets, a key factor underlying high growth rates, could also be considered as an intensification of the linkage of developing countries to high-income countries, as they have become an integral part of the global business cycle. The combination of delinking in terms of growth rates and increased linkage in terms of cyclical changes in growth gives developing countries a prominent role in the current economic environment: they have become a driving force for global trade, and their strong trade links can help mitigate the slowdown in high-income countries. In 2007 and the years following, developing countries are expected to be the source of more than half of growth in global imports.

The shift of import demand away from the United States (and high-income countries generally) and toward developing countries is clearly visible in recent high-frequency data. The slowing of high-income countries' imports and of developing countries' exports reflects much weaker investment and consumption growth in the United States in line with the fallout in the housing market (figure 1.16).

At the global level, the slowing of U.S. imports has been offset in part by a strengthening of import demand across developing countries driven, among other factors, by robust domestic demand, especially in the large emerging market economies (figure 1.17). Looking forward, vibrant growth in developing countries should offer a cushion from recessionary conditions in the key OECD economies over the critical 2008 period.

Figure 1.16 Weak U.S. growth reduces demand for developing country exports

Growth of investment and imports, four quarter moving average, (percent)

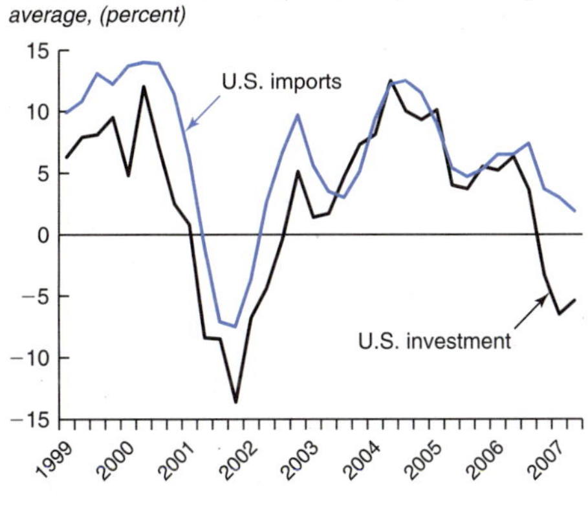

Source: World Bank.

Figure 1.17 Export opportunities for high-income countries

(Percent) nominal growth in US$, 12-month moving average

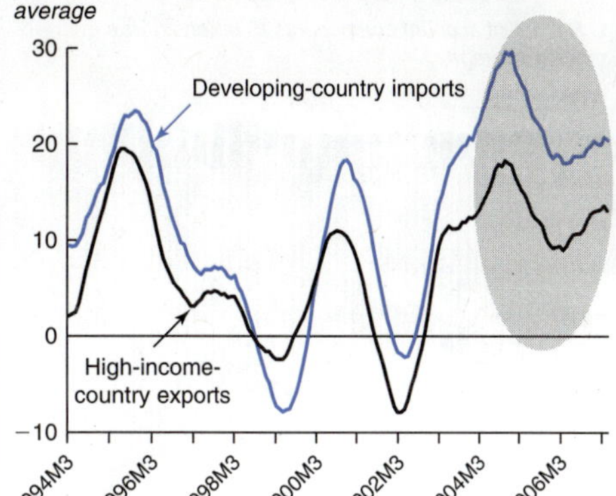

Source: World Bank.
Note: M3 = March.

Indeed, among recent regional developments, dollar-based import growth has been strong: Sub-Saharan African imports increased 23 percent over the year to May 2007; South Asian imports jumped 32 percent through August, driven by strong investment and import demand in India; and Latin America and East Asia were importing at rates of 15 and 14 percent, respectively, through September. However, the key contribution to the pickup in imports stems from Europe and Central Asia (an increase of 28 percent through September, up from 20 percent a year earlier), where in Central and Eastern Europe, EU accession countries are increasing their import potential in dollars with currencies effectively pegged to an appreciating euro, while in the CIS, exporters of oil and other hydrocarbons continue to spend portions of their accumulated revenues.

Such rotation of trade growth is contributing to an unwinding of global imbalances that

Figure 1.18 U.S. current account narrows over 2007 and is likely to continue doing so

U.S. current account components ($ billions, three quarter moving average)

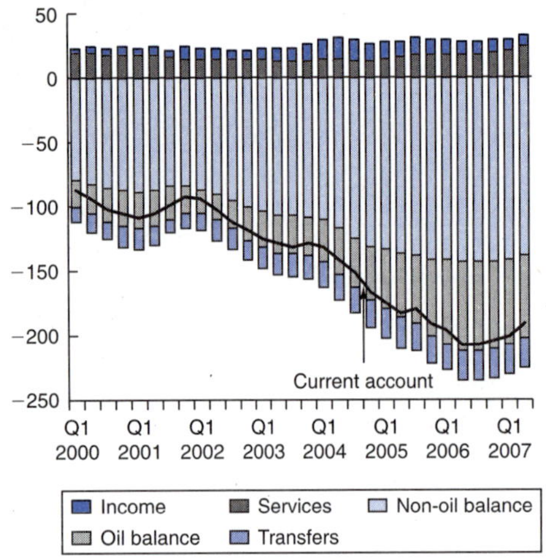

Source: U.S. Department of Commerce.

started in 2006. The U.S. current account deficit declined from a peak of 6.8 percent of GDP in the fourth quarter of 2005 to 5.5 percent by the second quarter of 2007. The shrinking deficit reflected weaker U.S. imports, caused in part by the housing slump, and stronger exports, supported by demand in developing countries and the falling dollar (figure 1.18). The mirror image of the narrowing U.S. current account may be found in developing countries, as well as selected OECD countries, where surpluses are broadly in decline. Based on the strong correlations shown in figure 1.16, export revenues in developing countries are likely beginning to slow in line with the softening of import demand in the high-income countries. At the same time, spending in developing countries remains strong. Such gradual unwinding of global imbalances is expected to continue, at least through 2009, as oil price levels decline, driven by the same elements that emerged in 2007.

Inflation and commodity markets

In high-income countries, inflationary pressures were sufficiently under control during 2007 to allow central banks to end a period of monetary tightening. In the United States, the Federal Reserve had become more concerned about a possible recession than about accelerating inflation and lowered Federal funds by 50 basis points to 4.75 percent on September 18—the first reduction in four years. A further 25 basis point cut was enacted on October 31 and a like reduction on December 11, carrying Federal funds to 4.25 percent. In Japan, inflation is not yet permanently in positive territory, making it unlikely that the Bank of Japan will follow its initial tightening steps with further increases in interest rates. In Europe, inflation is fluctuating around the European Central Bank's upper target, recently with more upward than downward momentum. Given expectations for softening growth in 2007, as well as an appreciating currency, the European Central Bank will probably hold its policy rate at 4 percent.

The inflation picture is more diverse across developing countries. In several rapidly growing economies, where inflation had picked up over the last two years, policy interest rates have been increased gradually. This occurred across South Asia (India, Pakistan, and Sri Lanka), where signs of overheating became evident, and also in several Latin American and Caribbean countries (Argentina, Chile, Colombia, and the República Bolivariana de Venezuela). China and the Czech Republic are examples of economies where monetary tightening continues. But in some countries (Belarus, Brazil, the Lao People's Democratic Republic, and the Philippines) inflation eased and monetary policy, which was tight, is now loosening moderately. In several countries monetary policy has reversed. In Hungary and Turkey, for example, policy rates were cut in 2007 after being on a long uptrend. This turnabout was a reaction to the recent slowdown in growth after a long period of strong gains in domestic demand that led to large current account deficits and inflation pressures.

Inflation has remained remarkably muted after four years of global growth that has been stronger than that experienced in the last 30 years. Average consumer price inflation in high-income countries registered 1.8 percent in 2007, slightly below that experienced during the downturn of 2001. Median inflation in developing countries registered a moderate (in a historic context) 5.9 percent, only 0.6 percentage points higher than at the beginning of the decade. Hyperinflation, once a trademark of several developing countries, has been eliminated, with Zimbabwe now being the notable exception. The number of developing countries with double-digit inflation has halved since the beginning of the decade.[6] Inflation was lower in the first half of 2007 than it was in the previous year in more than 60 percent of all countries, and among the 56 developing countries for which inflation data are available for the first half of 2007, more countries experienced an easing than a pickup of pressures. Moreover, average inflation is still on the rise in just two of six developing regions (figures 1.19 and 1.20). In Sub-Saharan Africa, inflation is volatile, but is trending higher, reflecting rising food prices, and the Middle East and North Africa region shows a clear uptick in inflation, likely triggered by the expenditure of burgeoning oil revenues in the region, notably in the Islamic Republic of Iran. In other regions, inflation is volatile, but broadly trending flat or slightly downward.

Figure 1.20 Inflation is broadly stable elsewhere, though at high levels

Consumer prices (percent change, year-on-year)

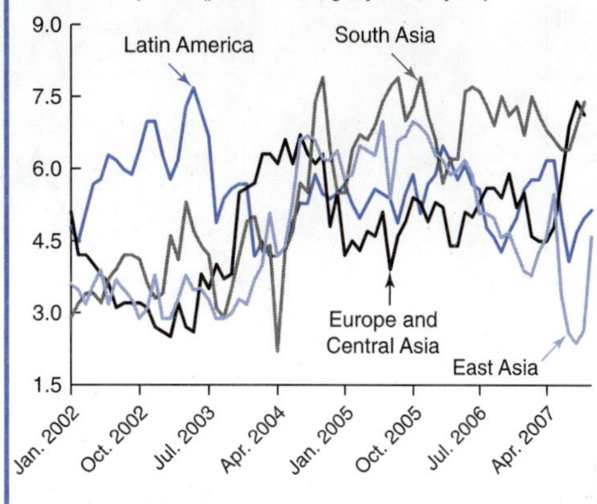

Source: World Bank.

Developing countries have played an important part in restraining inflation worldwide. Improved macroeconomic policies have tended to reduce domestic pressures on inflation across a wide range of countries. Independent monetary policy, more cautious fiscal stances, strong currencies, and rapid TFP growth have increasingly kept domestic inflation under control. In addition, greater engagement in international trade and competition has helped spread price restraint across trading partners. In many countries, passing cost pressures through to output and to consumer prices has become progressively more difficult.

The lack of pass-through, in particular, has enabled monetary policy in the high-income countries to remain fairly passive in the face of rising non-core prices. Partly as a consequence, global growth has been maintained at

Figure 1.19 Inflationary pressures are rising in the Middle East and North Africa and Sub-Saharan Africa

Consumer prices (percent change, year-on-year)

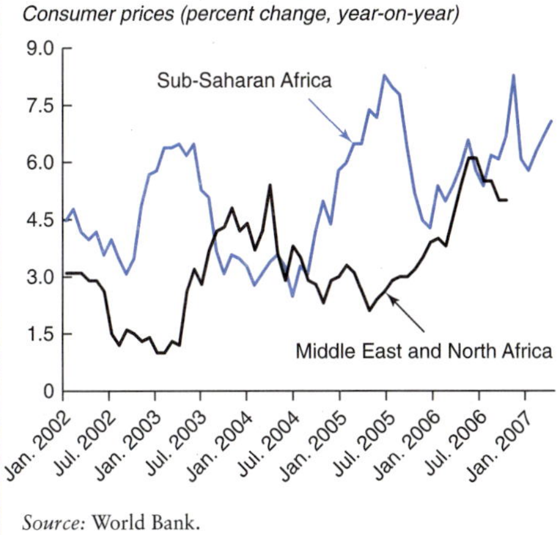

Source: World Bank.

Figure 1.21 Commodity prices continued gains through 2007 led by metals

Commodity price indexes (January 2003 = 100)

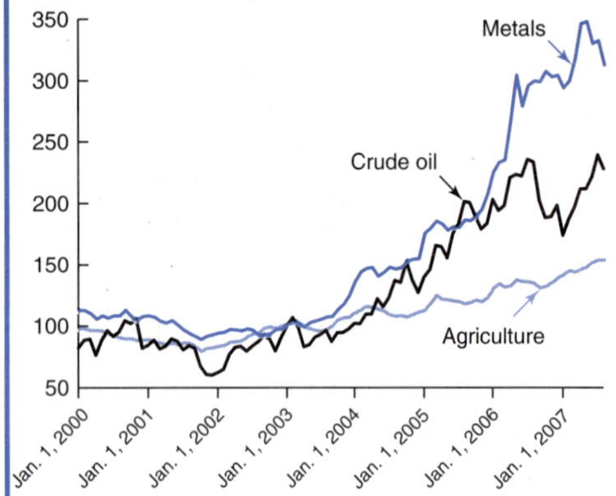

Source: World Bank.

Figure 1.22 Copper, zinc, and aluminum prices sharply affected by China

$/metric ton

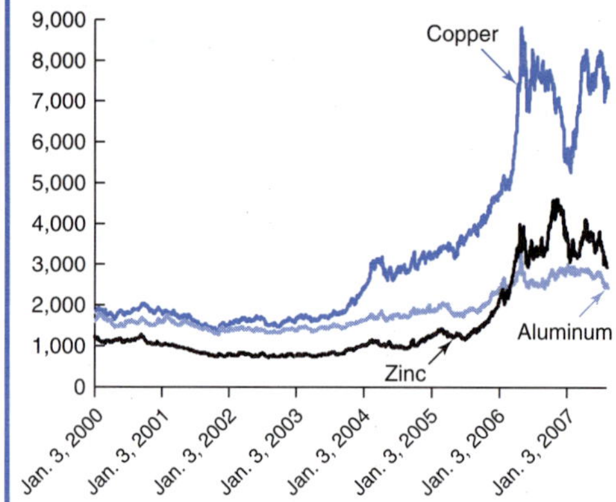

Sources: London Mercantile Exchange and World Bank.

a higher rate much longer than in the past, generating increasing capacity constraints in commodity markets. As a result, commodity prices continued to increase and remained elevated into the fourth quarter of 2007. Commodities have become more volatile, however, and the increase in several commodity prices is now moderating (figure 1.21).

The increased use of food crops for production of biofuels is an important factor that led to large increases in the prices of vegetable oils and grains in 2007, which in turn contributed to an overall 15 percent increase in the index of agricultural prices and a 20 percent rise in food prices. The latter is of special concern for poor consumers in developing countries.

The prices of metals have increased more than other commodity prices over the last four years, largely because of especially strong demand in China. Underinvestment during earlier periods of low prices and numerous supply problems and delays in bringing on new capacity have also played a part. Shortages of equipment and skilled workers have significantly increased development costs, and ore grades are deteriorating. The price of metals for which China is a net importer, especially copper, have experienced sharp gains, while those for which China is a net exporter—mainly aluminum and to some extent zinc—have increased much less (figure 1.22). Following the global credit squeeze in August and September, the prices of metals dropped more than 10 percent (metals tend to be particularly sensitive to slowing economic activity and may have been exposed to speculative pressures when investors closed their positions to finance other losses in their portfolios). The prices of metals are generally expected to peak in 2007, to decline by 5 percent in 2008, and to continue lower into 2009 as rising capacity tips markets into surplus.

Nominal oil prices, measured in dollars, broke historic records in November, reaching nearly $100 a barrel. Measured in euros, oil prices stood 4.5 percent above their 2006 peak, while in real terms (corrected for overall inflation) oil prices remain 4.2 percent below the peaks reached in November 1979.

Higher oil prices have reduced growth in global oil demand, particularly in high-income countries. Oil demand in the OECD declined for six consecutive quarters beginning in the fourth quarter of 2005, with an average drop of more than 0.4 million barrels a day (figure 1.23).

Figure 1.23 Growth in the world's demand for oil slows

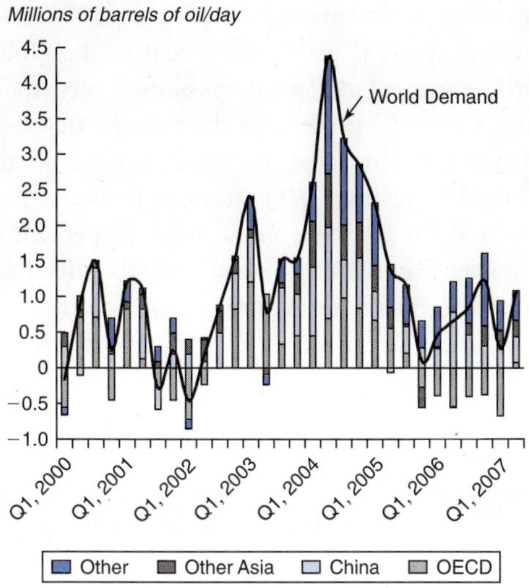

Sources: International Energy Agency and World Bank.

Figure 1.24 OPEC reduces output to support prices

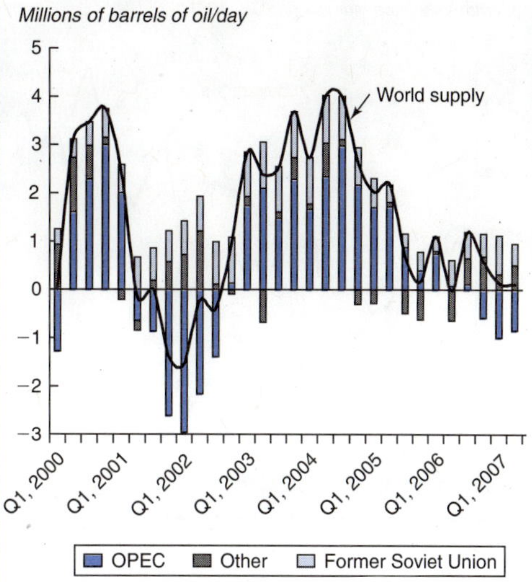

Sources: International Energy Agency and World Bank.

In non-OECD economies, the demand for oil has grown by just over 1 million barrels of oil a day since 2005, down sharply from the surge of 2004. Supply in several producers that are not members of the Organization of Petroleum Exporting Countries (OPEC), especially Russia and countries in western Africa, has increased in recent months, and among OECD countries, Canadian production continues to grow, predominantly from oil sands, while significant new output in the deep water U.S. part of the Gulf of Mexico is starting up. These increases have been partially offset by moderately falling production in the North Sea. As demand eased and non-OPEC supply increased, OPEC countries reduced their output to prevent further increases in stocks and a fall in prices (figure 1.24).

Because OPEC has limited spare capacity and is holding down production, oil prices will likely remain quite elevated and volatile; however, high prices and increasing environmental concerns should continue to moderate growth in demand. At the same time, rising upstream investment in oil-producing countries (both in OPEC and in non-OPEC countries) should result in new capacity that exceeds the growth in oil demand. Nevertheless, oil markets are expected to remain finely balanced over 2007–09, in part because of production discipline by exporters, and prices are expected to remain above $75 a barrel for the coming two years. In the longer term, the oil market balance is expected to loosen and prices are projected to fall toward $50 per barrel.

The rise in agricultural prices during 2007 was underpinned by strong demand for food imports, especially by oil-exporting countries, which contributed to a 20 percent increase in global food prices for the year. Higher cocoa and robusta coffee prices raised beverage prices by 13 percent, while raw materials prices were moderately higher (figure 1.25). The increase in food prices was led by fats and oils, up 50 percent for the year, and grains, up 22 percent (figure 1.26).[7] Among other commodities, sugar prices declined 32 percent, as

Figure 1.25 Agricultural prices surge over 2006–07

Commodity price indexes (2003 = 100)

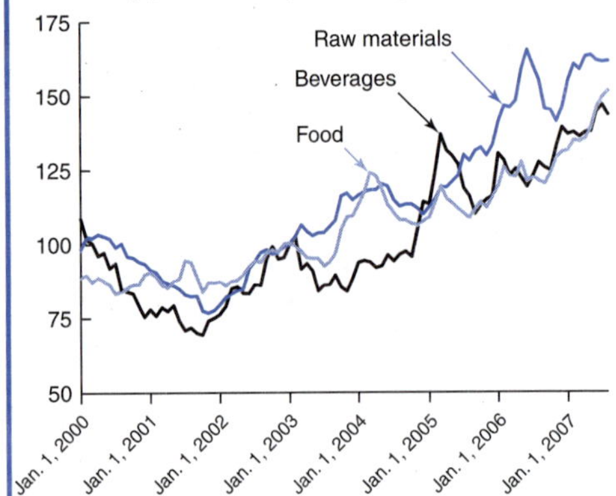

Source: World Bank.

Figure 1.26 A rise in food prices, led by a ramp-up of the prices of fats, oils, and grains

Commodity price indexes (1990 = 100)

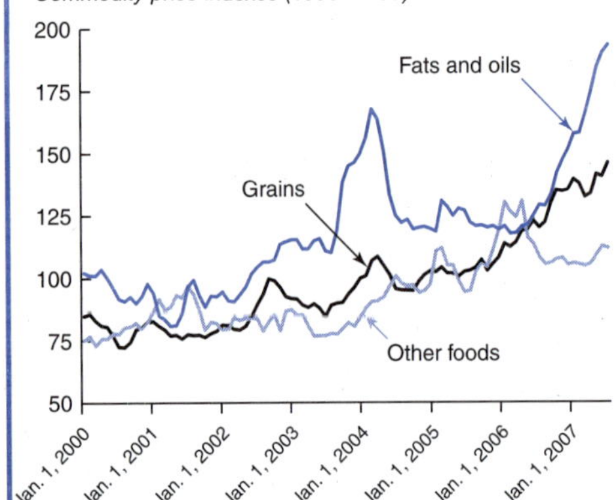

Source: World Bank.

growing conditions in India, Pakistan, and Thailand improved, and new plantings and favorable weather boosted Brazilian production.

Food prices have risen nearly 75 percent since their lows of 2000. The increases stem partly from the stepped-up use of food crops for biofuels and partly from other more fundamental factors, such as rapid income growth in developing countries, high fertilizer prices, low stocks, and droughts. Biofuels are playing an increasingly important role in agricultural commodity markets as their share of global production and trade increases. In 2006, biofuels accounted for 5–10 percent of the global production of the primary biofuel feedstocks and up to 77 percent of the volume of trade. Among the largest biofuel producers, the United States used 20 percent of its maize production for biofuels; Brazil used 50 percent of its sugarcane for biofuels; and the EU used 68 percent of its vegetable oil production, primarily rapeseed, and also imported additional vegetable oils. Such large usage reduces supplies of these crops for food and feed and has contributed to substantial price gains (box 1.2).

The anticipated spike in grains prices, identified as a concern in the World Bank's *Global Development Finance* report published in May 2007 (World Bank 2007a), has largely materialized. Monthly wheat prices have increased 90 percent since mid-2007. Wheat stocks are expected to fall to record lows relative to consumption, and prices may increase further in 2008 before production recoups enough to rebuild stocks. In the meantime, a large number of food-importing countries may suffer substantial terms-of-trade losses over the course of 2007 and into 2008 (box 1.3). Price increases for vegetable oils and grains primarily affect low-income countries, with the rise in prices since the end of 2004 leading to a terms-of-trade loss equivalent to 0.5 percent of GDP. This represents 1 percent of GDP in 29 countries, and nearly 5 percent of GDP for the most affected country, Eritrea. The impact on middle- and high-income countries is considerably less because imports of these commodities represent a smaller share of trade, and higher prices on other commodity exports tends to offset terms-of-trade losses resulting from higher food prices. Agricultural prices are expected to remain nearly flat at high levels in 2008, as biofuels production continues to ramp up in response to consumption mandates and production subsidies, drawing resources from other crops.

Box 1.2 Biofuels

Biofuels are not new: the first Ford automobile was originally intended to run on ethanol. However, the interest in biofuels has increased in recent years along with increases in energy prices and heightened concern about the environment. Countries want not only to achieve greater energy security, but also to reduce the use of fossil fuels to lower greenhouse gas emissions and improve air quality. The demand for biofuels also got a boost when methyl tertiary-butyl ether was banned as a fuel additive to meet clean air regulations in many U.S. states and localities and for fear it was contaminating groundwater. The political gain attached to supporting new demand for agricultural products, and thus enhanced crop prices, has added to interest on the part of politicians and encouraged generous support policies in many countries, including EU countries and the United States.

Biofuels can be produced from a variety of feedstocks. Current technology, often called first-generation technology, relies primarily on food crops such as sugarcane and maize to produce ethanol and on vegetable oils from rapeseed, soybeans, palms, and other crops to produce biodiesel fuel. So-called second-generation technology may be able to produce biofuels from an even wider range of feedstocks, such as switch grass, timber waste, and municipal garbage, but such technology is not yet commercially viable and many experts do not expect it to become so for at least a decade.

Global production of biofuels totaled about 45 billion liters in 2006, representing slightly more than 1 percent of global road transport fuels on an energy equivalent basis. Biofuels can be used to replace their fossil fuel counterparts or can be blended with fossil fuels to achieve certain benefits, such as reduced tailpipe emissions and increased octane levels to improve engine performance. One of their greatest advantages is that they can be used in conventional gasoline and diesel engines without modification of the engines and can be dispensed through existing distribution channels.

Nevertheless, their use has some limitations. Ethanol can be used in conventional gasoline engines only up to about a 10 percent blend with gasoline without engine or fuel system modifications. It also requires special handling in transport to prevent contamination. Specially designed flex-fuel engines can use a wider range of blends of ethanol and gasoline and are available in Brazil and the United States. Biodiesel fuel can be used in any blend with fossil fuel diesel in standard diesel engines, but its use is limited in colder climates. The energy content of ethanol is lower than that of gasoline, providing about 20–30 percent fewer miles per gallon than gasoline, while biodiesel provides 5–10 percent lower mileage than diesel.

While biofuels have thus far had little impact on crude oil prices, they have already had large effects on prices of commodities used as feedstocks for biofuels, as well as for competing crops. For example, maize prices rose by about 60 percent from mid-2005 to mid-2006, largely because of the increased use of maize for ethanol production in the United States. This prompted a huge shift of land from wheat into maize in the following season, which contributed to a sharp increase in wheat prices. Vegetable oil prices have also increased because of their stepped-up use for biodiesel production in Europe and the United States, with palm oil prices up 48 percent in the last year and soybean oil prices up 25 percent. These price shifts have set off a food versus fuel debate that is causing some to question the contribution of biofuels.

Risks and uncertainties: Danger of a banking crisis and a U.S. recession

The baseline projections assume, on the real side of the economy, that the U.S. housing recession does not spill over in a large-scale way to the rest of domestic demand, as the downward spiral in housing is mitigated by strong export growth. On the financial side of the economy, the projections assume that losses on holdings of asset-backed securities are widely distributed and that interventions by the Federal Reserve, the European Central Bank, and other institutions restore calm to financial markets. However, the effective cost

Box 1.3 Policy responses to rising food prices

Higher prices of imported staples, strong growth of domestic and regional demand that pushes up prices of domestically produced goods, and increased prices of production inputs such as fertilizers and energy are causing rapid rises in food prices in many countries. The price increases will hurt the poor, who spend a large share of their income on food, but will also help the rural poor who produce a marketable surplus. Governments are under pressure to take action to blunt the impact of higher food prices, but many countries have liberalized or partially liberalized their domestic food markets and imports (Bangladesh, Brazil, Egypt, India, Mali, Morocco, Russia, Ukraine, and the Republic of Yemen, to name a few) and no longer have policy instruments to control food prices. Those countries that have targeted safety net programs can rely on those channels to provide assistance to the poorest people, but countries without safety net programs will feel pressure to impose price controls or to reintroduce government controls. This would undo successful policy reforms and send a negative message to the private sector.

Bangladesh offers an example of the success of open market food policies. It has transformed its agricultural sector into one of the most productive in South Asia. The country is largely self-sufficient in rice, a basic staple, and is an emerging exporter of high-value agricultural products. One of the keys to this success was the government's decision to liberalize food imports in the early 1990s. Private traders imported food grains during times of domestic shortfall, providing needed supplies and price stabilization, as well as removing a financial burden from the government. By 2000, the private sector was importing 100 percent of imported food, and the government reoriented its large public food distribution system away from mass distribution in favor of a targeted safety net program for the poor. Such a response would be effective in the current situation of high food prices, but a complicating factor is that part of the current price increases might be more persistent than in the past.

Past periods of food price increases were temporary and lasted only two or three years, such as the increases during the 1970s or the more recent increases in 1995–96; however, the current increases have a structural component that may persist because it is closely tied to the rise in global energy prices. If energy prices remain high, food crop prices are unlikely to decline significantly. Over the longer term, supplies of food are expected to increase and prices to fall, but the current price increases are expected to continue for several years, and thus most countries will not be able to shelter their consumers from them. Current food price increases also have a temporary component caused by low stocks and production shortfalls stemming from drought. These can be expected to dissipate as supplies respond to high prices. Countries should aim to protect consumers from temporary price increases caused by shortages, but few countries can afford to protect consumers against structural changes in food prices.

Consumers in food-exporting countries are also seeing their food prices increase as supplies are exported at high international prices, and several countries have imposed export bans to contain domestic food price inflation. Such bans unfairly penalize the producers of these crops and may encourage smuggling and corruption. A more appropriate policy response is to provide a targeted safety net program for the poor while allowing exports to continue unfettered.

of capital is likely to increase further, reflected in tightened credit criteria for firms as well as households in the United States. Elsewhere, however, tightening is expected to be more moderate. Under such conditions, weakness in U.S. housing would continue, but the contraction in residential investment will have bottomed out by mid-2008.

Should unexpected and large-scale new losses occur in financial markets—concentrated among commercial and investment banks or among major investors—credit conditions globally could tighten much more. Such a scenario would tend to increase losses on asset-backed securities, potentially carrying financial markets and the real economy into a downward spiral and requiring an aggressive loosening of monetary policy.

Under such circumstances, contraction in quarterly GDP in the United States would become more likely, pushing growth in 2008 to 1 percent, or almost half of baseline growth. Equity markets in high-income countries would likely decline substantially, and the effective cost of capital could increase by some 200 basis points in 2008, compared with the baseline. Such a pronounced credit crunch would be reflected in a sharp decline in U.S. business investment, declining employment, weaker consumer outlays, and a prolonged period of depressed consumer prices.

Adverse developments in the United States would spill over to the rest of the world through weaker U.S. imports and a substantial further decline in the dollar, spurred by an aggressive loosening of monetary policy. The spillover could be exacerbated by a reversal of the yen carry trade and a reduced appetite for U.S. assets among international investors as growth slows and assets of financial institutions become more risky. Largely because of reduced exports and investment growth, GDP growth in Europe and Japan could fall to 1.5 and 1.3 percent, respectively, about half a percentage point below the baseline.

For a number of middle-income countries, the most important transmission channel of effects stemming from the OECD countries would be a tightening in international credit conditions, which would cut into investment and reduce growth. Middle-income economies with large current account deficits and countries whose currencies are pegged to the euro would likely feel the greatest effects. Growth in middle-income countries would fall a percentage point below the baseline; however, the impact would be quite diversified, in part depending on how economies are linked financially to the U.S. dollar. Central European economies that accumulated euro-denominated debt will be more vulnerable than countries that hold dollar debt.

The repercussions for low-income countries could also be sizable, as weaker global demand for commodities (metals, agricultural products, and fuels) could worsen their terms of trade by 2 percent of GDP, and the pace of expansion could decline by 0.6 points in 2008. Overall, given such a scenario, global growth might decline by three-quarters of a percentage point in 2008 compared with the baseline.

The loosening of monetary policy in response to the subprime crisis might also cause growth to overshoot. As a result, commodity markets could tighten further; inflationary pressures would mount, especially in developing countries; and financial imbalances would increase rather than recede. Such a scenario could sow the seeds of a much sharper growth slowdown in the medium term and illustrates the challenge facing monetary authorities in both high-income and developing countries.

Long-term prospects and poverty forecasts

A potential for catching up

Beginning in the mid-1990s, per capita income growth in developing countries has accelerated, with growth being particularly vibrant since 2000. Several factors suggest that this high growth will be sustained over the longer term. First, economic policies are on a more solid footing than in earlier periods, with both inflation and fiscal deficits broadly under control, and structural policies more conducive to taking advantage of more open global markets, and a business climate more favorable for investment. Second, many countries have entered, or are entering, a period of demographic transition that combines rapid labor force growth with declining dependency ratios. This shift provides a window of opportunity for rapid economic gains. Third, the income disparity between developing and developed countries is still large, but with broader access to information and technology-laden capital and imports, developing countries have the ability—and the incentive—to narrow this gap.

The long-term forecast for 2010–30 projects sustained growth across developing countries, albeit with a moderating trend (figure 1.27). For developing countries as a whole, per capita growth is expected to ease from an average of 3.9 percent in the first decade of the 2000s to 4.5 and 3.4 percent in the second and third decades, mainly reflecting slowing growth in the East Asia and the Pacific region. Sub-Saharan Africa could see a slight acceleration, with average per capita income growth of 3.0 percent in the current decade, increasing to a more sustainable 3.2 to 3.4 percent in subsequent decades. This is a substantial improvement over the 1980s and 1990s, when per capita incomes in Sub-Saharan Africa declined.

Years of sustained increases in per capita incomes should see average real incomes (stated in 2001 prices) more than double by 2020, rising from $1,300 in 2001 to $2,800 by 2020. By 2030, they are projected to reach nearly $4,000. However, significant variation will occur around these numbers, and despite a relatively optimistic growth scenario, the gap between rich and poor countries will remain extremely wide. The average citizen in a developing country is projected to earn only 7.8 percent as much as a citizen of a high-income country, a ratio that should rise to about 10.0 percent by 2030.

This year's long-term scenario represents a significant upward revision from last year's long-term forecast. The revision reflects a confluence of factors, including the simple recognition that developing country growth has accelerated over the last decade and has been broadly based and sustained. Among the factors that likely contributed to sustaining this high level of growth is the relatively rapid convergence in technological achievement between high-income countries and developing countries (see chapter 2). This progress is projected to continue over the next 20 years, and the returns to knowledge and capital will remain more or less constant. These sustained returns combined with rising incomes will translate into increased investment in education and research and development, helping to

Figure 1.27 Long-term growth, 1980–2030

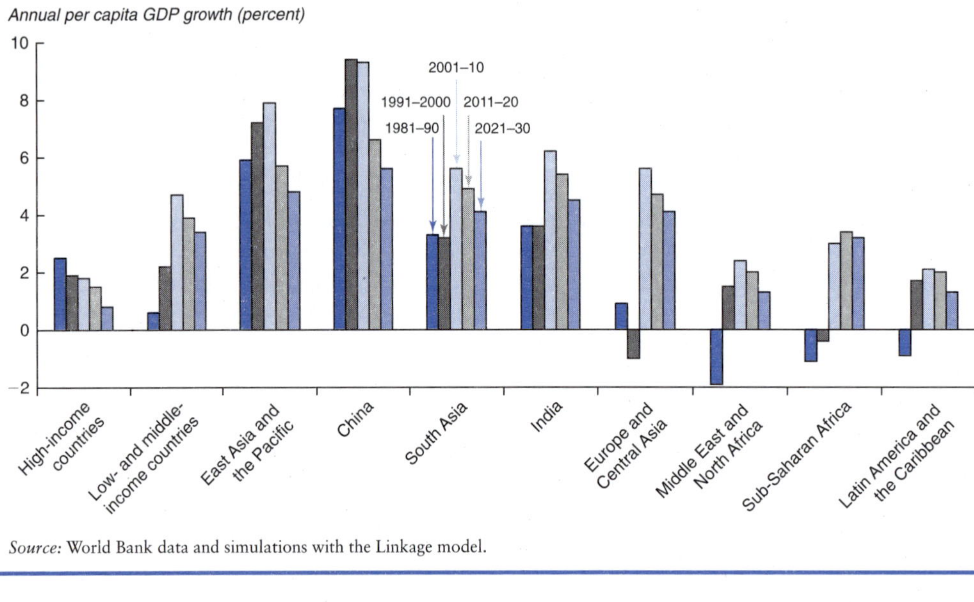

Source: World Bank data and simulations with the Linkage model.

Figure 1.28 Declining capital-led growth for developed countries, 2002–30

Growth decomposition (percentage contribution per year)

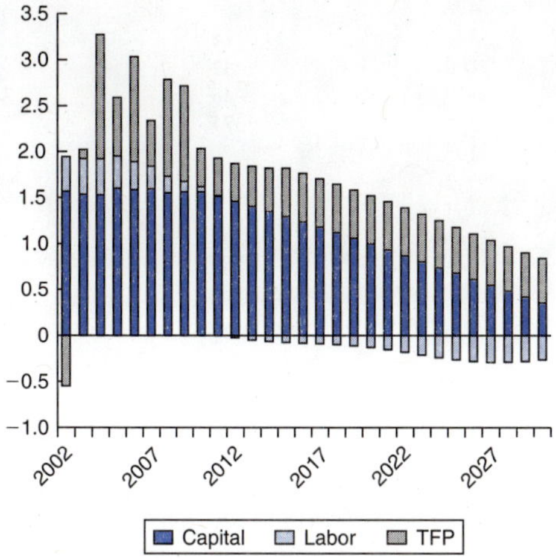

Source: Simulation results from the Linkage model.
Note: TFP = total factor productivity.

Figure 1.29 Sustained high productivity growth for developing countries

Growth decomposition (percentage contribution per year)

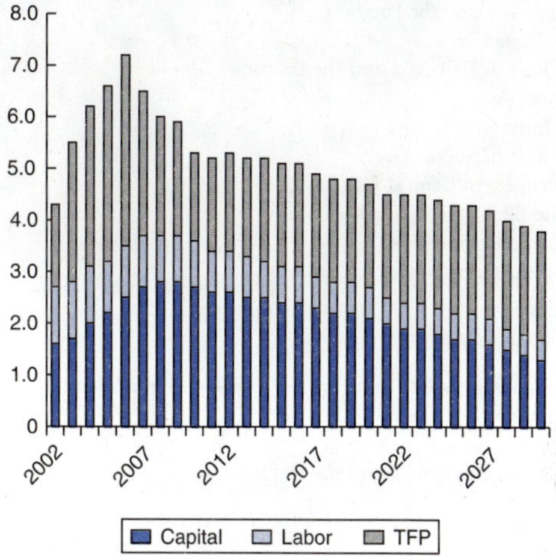

Source: Simulation results from the Linkage model.
Note: TFP = total factor productivity.

establish a virtuous cycle of further technological progress and increased incomes. Those countries where technological progress has stagnated are expected to benefit from a supportive global environment characterized by accelerating exports and continued strong income gains from commodities, partly explained by the growing importance of developing countries in global growth.

Part of the strong projected performance for developing countries derives from stronger labor force growth, but much can be attributed to technological progress, measured in figures 1.28 and 1.29 by TFP growth. The strong TFP growth in developing countries of the last several years is consistent with the findings in chapter 2 of this report, which suggest that (based on a different measure of technology) the technology gap between middle- and high-income countries has narrowed over the last 10 years. Over the forecast horizon, the relative strength of TFP growth in developing countries is expected to persist, which is also consistent with the finding in chapter 3 that the drivers of technological diffusion and absorption in developing countries have strengthened. However, as stressed there, the realization of this potential during the coming decades will depend on the extent to which countries, especially low-income countries, can strengthen their technological absorptive capacity and remain open to new technology flows.

Poverty declines significantly in the baseline, though not uniformly

The upward revisions to the long-term forecast generate a more positive poverty forecast for 2015, albeit a modest improvement compared to the forecast presented in the *Global Monitoring Report* for 2007 (World Bank 2007b). The percentage of the population in developing countries living on less than $1 a day in 2015 under the current long-term forecast is 10.2 percent, down from 11.8 percent in the *Global Monitoring Report* (table 1.5). The rapid improvements in reducing poverty in Asia since 1990 imply that the target of halving the percentage of the poor living on

Table 1.5 Poverty in developing countries by region, selected years

Region or country	1990	2004	2015
Number of people living on less than $1/day (millions)			
East Asia and the Pacific	476	169	40
China	374	128	29
Rest of East Asia and the Pacific	102	41	11
South Asia	479	446	256
India	376	371	217
Rest of South Asia	103	76	39
Europe and Central Asia	2	4	2
Middle East and North Africa	5	4	2
Sub-Saharan Africa	240	298	290
Latin America and the Caribbean	45	47	34
Total	1,247	970	624
Excluding China	873	841	595
Number of people living on less than $2/day (millions)			
East Asia and the Pacific	1,113	684	296
China	819	452	186
Rest of East Asia and the Pacific	294	232	110
South Asia	954	1,116	997
India	734	868	772
Rest of South Asia	220	248	226
Europe and Central Asia	20	46	16
Middle East and North Africa	49	59	38
Sub-Saharan Africa	396	522	567
Latin America and the Caribbean	115	121	102
Total	2,647	2,548	2,017
Excluding China	1,828	2,096	1,831
Percentage of the population living on less than $1/day			
East Asia and the Pacific	29.8	9.1	2.0
China	33.0	9.9	2.1
Rest of East Asia and the Pacific	22.1	7.1	1.6
South Asia	43.0	30.8	15.1
India	44.3	34.3	17.6
Rest of South Asia	38.9	20.6	8.5
Europe and Central Asia	0.5	0.9	0.3
Middle East and North Africa	2.3	1.5	0.7
Sub-Saharan Africa	46.7	41.1	31.4
Latin America and the Caribbean	10.2	8.6	5.5
Total	28.7	18.1	10.2
Excluding China	27.1	20.7	12.6
Percentage of the population living on less than $2/day			
East Asia and the Pacific	69.7	36.6	14.5
China	72.2	34.9	13.4
Rest of East Asia and the Pacific	63.7	40.4	16.9
South Asia	85.7	77.1	59.0
India	86.4	80.4	62.7
Rest of South Asia	83.4	67.6	49.2
Europe and Central Asia	4.3	9.8	3.4
Middle East and North Africa	21.7	19.7	10.3
Sub-Saharan Africa	77.1	72.0	61.5
Latin America and the Caribbean	26.3	22.2	16.3
Total	60.8	47.6	32.9
Excluding China	56.8	51.6	38.7

Source: World Bank.

$1 a day or less between 1990 and 2015 will be achieved at the global level, though not necessarily at the country or regional level. The new forecast leads to some improvement in the outlook for Sub-Saharan Africa, but the region is still significantly off target.[8,9]

Agricultural productivity has important poverty implications for low-income countries

Agricultural technology is a particularly important determinant of overall technology and poverty reduction in low-income countries (World Bank 2007c), mainly because in most economies the majority of workers remain in agriculture, and the poor are concentrated in rural areas. Moreover, productivity growth in agriculture is one of the main drivers of rising incomes in agricultural economies. Increased agricultural productivity frees up workers to take on more lucrative manufacturing jobs and reduces food costs relative to wages. Moreover, by increasing yields, high agricultural productivity generates a marketable surplus that can be used to purchase higher-quality inputs for production and consumer goods, which in turns leads to a virtuous cycle between the agricultural and nonagricultural sectors of the economy. The marketable surplus can also be used to increase exports or to reduce food imports.

In the baseline scenario, agricultural productivity is projected to increase by a uniform 2.5 percent a year (Martin and Mitra 1999). Historically, however, not all countries have achieved this average increase. For example, the green revolution that lifted agricultural productivity in South Asia over the last 40 years largely bypassed Sub-Saharan Africa, where yields have largely stagnated. Looking ahead, agriculture in Sub-Saharan Africa is faced with some of the same challenges as in the past, for example, lack of access to credit and poorly integrated markets. Both South Asia and Sub-Saharan Africa could be facing additional challenges that will threaten future gains in agricultural productivity, for instance, environmental degradation caused by global climate change or insufficient investment in new and locale-specific varieties of crops.

To illustrate the sensitivity of future outcomes to the possibility of weaker agricultural productivity performance, an alternative scenario looks at the impact on global growth, incomes, and poverty from assuming zero agricultural productivity growth over the period 2008–15 in the two largely low-income regions of South Asia and Sub-Saharan Africa.[10] One key result would be higher prices for agricultural produce compared with the baseline. Agricultural producer prices in Sub-Saharan Africa would increase around 6 percent, with a more modest increase of 2 percent for processed food. The increase in prices is more acute in South Asia: around 11 percent for primary agriculture, with a 4 percent increase in processed foods. These increases lead to a loss of competitiveness in both domestic and export markets.

In the case of Sub-Saharan Africa, imports of crops and livestock products rise by some 40 percent in 2015 relative to the baseline and exports drop by 30 percent. Overall output declines by some 12 percent. Agricultural labor demand barely changes, as the decline in output is offset by a decline in productivity, leaving overall labor demand more or less unchanged, albeit with depressed wages. In South Asia, labor demand actually increases. The output impact is a more modest drop of 9 percent, and the loss of productivity is reflected in an overall increase in labor demand of 1 percent, and thus less rural-to-urban migration occurs. The difference between the two regional impacts is linked to the degree of autonomy of their respective agricultural and food markets. A greater share of Sub-Saharan Africa's agricultural output is exported and a greater share of its demand is imported. The increase in domestic producer prices will therefore be dampened by external markets in Sub-Saharan Africa, compared with the more self-sufficient markets in South Asia.[11] South Asia therefore witnesses more price adjustment and less volume adjustment relative to Sub-Saharan Africa.

Lower agricultural productivity, higher prices, and lower wages for unskilled workers increase poverty in both South Asia and Sub-Saharan Africa. In Sub-Saharan Africa, overall consumer prices rise by 1.4 percent and food prices by 4 percent. In South Asia, the increases are even more marked: 10 and 3 percent, respectively. Combined with a significant fall in wages for the unskilled, which creates a sharp drop in food wages (the quantity of food that can be purchased with the average wage) that affects the poorest the most, the poverty headcount index in Sub-Saharan Africa would increase by some 5 percentage points in 2015 relative to the baseline, even though the average income loss would be a more moderate 3 percent, suggesting that the loss in agricultural productivity harms the poor, on average, more than others.[12]

Notes

1. Carry trade is an approach undertaken to leverage investments in higher-yielding securities intermediated through a low-interest cost center. For example, a purchase of emerging market equities or fixed income securities through borrowing in yen at low Japanese interest rates and converting yen to local currencies to complete the transaction would be classified as a carry trade. Even though estimates of funds intermediated through the yen carry trade are highly uncertain, an indicator of their potential size can be discerned from the substantial weakness of the yen-dollar exchange rate during 2006–7, when it fell some 5.8 percent.

2. A full analysis of recent developments and the outlook for each region is available on the World Bank's Web site at http://www.worldbank.org/prospects.

3. China is the largest overseas holder of U.S. mortgage-backed securities, around $260 billion, largely through China's official reserve holdings and holdings of Chinese commercial banks. However, almost all of these instruments enjoy the backing of U.S. government-sponsored enterprises Fannie Mae and Freddie Mac, and the risks associated with these holdings appear to be minimal.

4. Developing countries of the Middle East and North Africa region, which account for regional aggregate figures in this chapter, are Algeria, the Arab Republic of Egypt, the Islamic Republic of Iran, Jordan, Lebanon, Morocco, Oman, the Syrian Arab Republic, Tunisia, and the Republic of Yemen. Low- and middle-income economies with insufficient data for coverage are Iraq, Libya, and the West Bank and Gaza. High-income countries of the region, which are excluded from aggregates in the chapter, are Bahrain, Kuwait, Qatar, Saudi Arabia, and the United Arab Emirates.

5. Changes in the volume of oil and gas production have been modest in recent years, ranging from 0.5 to 1.0 percent annual gains in Algeria to a decline in the Islamic Republic of Iran and the Republic of Yemen. Hence the buildup in export revenues is largely due to the large-scale increases in global oil prices during 2005 through 2007.

6. Inflation now exceeds 10 percent in Angola, Argentina, Botswana, Costa Rica, Ghana, Haiti, Indonesia, the Islamic Republic of Iran, Kenya, Madagascar, Malawi, Mozambique, Sri Lanka, República Boliviarana de Venezuela, and Zimbabwe.

7. Among individual vegetable oils, palm oil was up 48 percent, coconut oil was up 41 percent, and soybean oil was up 25 percent. Among individual grains, maize prices rose 33 percent and wheat prices increased 30 percent.

8. Even though the revisions to the long-term forecast imply roughly a doubling of per capita growth for Sub-Saharan Africa, that growth will have more impact after 2015 than before, as recent poverty forecasts have already incorporated the strong upward trend in per capita growth rates since the end of the 1990s.

9. The poverty numbers presented here do not yet take into account the results of the recent International Comparison Project, which will provide an updated set of price levels across countries. New purchasing power parity exchange rates could—although not necessarily will—lead to a new set of poverty estimates.

10. These projections involved six modeled countries or regions—Bangladesh, India, Pakistan, the rest of South Asia, Nigeria, and the rest of Sub-Saharan Africa excluding South Africa.

11. One plausible explanation for South Asia's greater self-sufficiency has been its higher agricultural productivity over time because of the green revolution.

12. The poverty impact is generated by the World Bank's Development Economics Prospects Group's global income distribution dynamics poverty tool, and was performed only for Sub-Saharan Africa because of its high projected level of poverty in 2015. The global income distribution dynamics tool probably underestimates the true poverty impact, because information on consumption in most surveys is insufficient to factor in

price changes fully. To the extent that the poor spend a larger share of their meager budget on food, one would anticipate an even greater negative impact for the poor.

References

Martin, Will, and Devashish Mitra. 1999. "Productivity Growth and Convergence in Agriculture and manufacturing." Policy Research Working Paper Series 2171. World Bank, Washington, DC.

World Bank. 2007a. *Global Development Finance 2007*. Washington, DC: World Bank.

_____. 2007b. *Global Monitoring Report 2007*. Washington, DC: World Bank.

_____. 2007c. *World Development Report 2008: Agriculture for Development*. Washington, DC: World Bank.

2

Technology and Technological Diffusion in Developing Countries

Technological progress—improvements in the techniques (including firm organization) by which goods and services are produced, marketed, and brought to market—is at the heart of human progress and development. At the national level, technological progress can occur through invention and innovation; through the adoption and adaptation of preexisting but new-to-the-market technologies; and through the spread of technologies across firms, individuals, and the public sector within a country.

For developing countries, the bulk of technological progress occurs through the latter two channels. Much of this chapter is concerned with measuring the extent to which this process has occurred in countries in different regions and at different income levels. Although the current state of technological achievement is itself illuminating, the pace at which it is changing is equally important, and this is estimated by comparing the level of technological achievement in the early 1990s with its current level and inferring the pace of change for different countries. The chapter concludes by looking at the speed with which specific technologies spread both across countries and within them. Armed with this broad view of technological progress within developing countries, chapter 3 explores in more detail the main factors that influence technological progress in individual developing countries. That chapter places equal emphasis on the international connections and networks that expose firms and individuals in developing countries to cutting-edge technologies and on the domestic factors that determine how successfully countries are able to absorb and apply those technologies. To establish a baseline for future work, both chapters adopt a positive (empirical) rather than a normative or prescriptive approach. Nevertheless, some clear conclusions with policy implications do emerge from the analysis.

This chapter begins its empirical examination by reviewing existing estimates of the contribution of technological progress to economic growth as measured by gross domestic product (GDP) and of income levels in developing countries. It reviews the mechanisms by which technology contributes to GDP and incomes, but also stresses the contributions of technology to other important development goals that are not well captured by GDP alone, such as health, education, and the environment. In addition, it discusses some of the principal limitations of this kind of empirical analysis and accompanying caveats. The chapter then discusses a wide range of previously published indicators of the extent to which various technologies have penetrated the economies of developing countries. For ease of exposition, these indicators are arranged in three groups: those showing the extent of scientific innovation and invention; those measuring the penetration of older technologies, such as railroads and telephones; and those measuring the penetration of newer technologies, such as personal computers and mobile phones. The chapter then develops an aggregate measure of technological achievement using a statistical technique (principal components analysis) that combines some 20 separate indicators of technological achievement along these three dimensions, plus an additional dimension, the extent to which countries are exposed to external technologies (explored in more detail in chapter 3). The distribution of overall technological achievement across countries and changes over the past decade are examined to evaluate both the speed with which technological achievement in countries is advancing and the dimensions along which change is occurring most quickly. The chapter concludes by examining a new longitudinal data set (Comin and Hobijn 2004) that tracks both the speed with which individual technologies are transmitted across countries and the pace with which they diffuse within countries.

Eight main results emerge from this chapter:

1. *While technological achievement is related to income levels across countries, the nature of this relationship differs depending upon the dimension of technology being examined.*

- While a strong correlation exists between scientific innovation and invention and income in high-income countries, almost none of this kind of activity is being performed in developing countries. As a result, virtually all technological progress in developing countries comes from the adoption and adaptation of preexisting technologies.
- At an aggregate level, the use of older technologies is positively related to income in developing countries. However, the extent to which they are employed varies substantially within income groups, suggesting that developing countries' history, geography, and past government success in delivering infrastructural technologies are equally important determinants of the extent to which older technologies are used.
- Penetration rates of more recent technologies vary more regularly with income. In part this reflects their relatively lower start-up and infrastructure costs than those of older technologies and their more flexible delivery structure.

2. *While technological achievement tends to rise with income, it tends to level off.* The level of technological achievement at which this leveling off occurs differs across countries according to their geography, history, and level of technological absorptive capacity (discussed in more detail in chapter 3). Thus, reflecting an emphasis on equal access to education and state-provided technological services, countries within the Europe and Central Asia region have significantly higher levels of technological achievement than other countries at similar income levels. By the same token, countries in Latin America and the Caribbean are somewhat less advanced than might be expected, as earlier inward-looking policies and weak basic technological literacy in the overall population have limited the extent to which technologies have permeated economic activity.

3. *Technological achievement within countries can vary widely.* Despite a level of technological achievement in major cities that can rival that in high-income countries, low levels of technological advancement in rural areas mean that, viewed as a whole, countries such as China and India are not particularly technologically advanced. Moreover, because technology spreads slowly across firms, there are wide differences in the technological sophistication of production, even within the same sector in the same country.

4. *Overall, the technology gap between middle-income and high-income countries has narrowed over the past 10 years.* Evidence of catch-up is particularly strong in Chile, Hungary, and Poland, where the overall level of

technological achievement increased by more than 125 percent during the 1990s.

5. *On average, technology is advancing more rapidly among low-income countries.* Among those low-income countries for which sufficient data are available, the penetration of technology is progressing more rapidly than in either middle- or high-income countries. However, this reflects very strong catch-up in some countries and more modest improvements, or even relative declines, in the majority. Moreover, technology in high-income countries is also advancing, and the absolute increase in these countries is larger than in developing countries.

6. *The pace at which technology spreads between countries is accelerating.* Whereas a new technology in the 1800s could take as long as 100 years to reach 80 percent of the world's countries, for a new technology to reach 80 percent of the world's countries now takes less than 20 years.

7. *Ultimately, however, what matters most for technological achievement is the speed with which technology spreads within a country.* Here too the evidence suggests a pickup in the pace of internal diffusion, but there is also widespread divergence across countries, even across those at similar income levels.

8. *Changes in the regulatory environment and in the nature of technologies partly explain the acceleration in the rate at which they penetrate into developing countries.* Many old infrastructure technologies, such as roads, railroads, sanitation, and fixed-line telephone systems, are often provided by the government and are thus subject to public sector budget constraints and the risk of government failure. By contrast, the most common new technologies, such as the Internet, mobile phones, and computers, are being delivered in a regulatory environment that encourages competition and that harnesses private capital (domestic and foreign) to provide basic infrastructure. Moreover, the past 10 years have been more stable politically than the 1980s and 1990s, which has likely given a boost to the diffusion of newer technologies.

The role of technology in development

Technological progress is at the heart of human progress and development. As the 1998 *World Development Report* on the knowledge economy (World Bank 1998) emphasized, the understanding of how things are created and the communication of that knowledge are critical drivers of economic progress. Central to understanding the role of technology is the recognition that technology and technological progress are relevant to a wide range of economic activities, not just manufacturing and computers. For example, some estimates suggest that technological progress has boosted productivity in agriculture four times as quickly as in manufacturing (Martin and Mitra 2001). Indeed, seemingly low-tech products such as corn or flowers can be the result of relatively high-tech production processes, while in some countries the production of ostensibly high-tech products such as computers is an outcome of relatively low-tech assembly activities. Finally, in many cases technology is embodied in production and management systems rather than in physical goods or software algorithms. A computer loaded with the latest software that sits unused on a desk for most of the day is a very different manifestation of technology than the same computer that is running a production process or managing an accounts payable system.

This report defines technology and technological progress in this wider sense, although data limitations may give some of the measures developed the flavor of a more narrow, physical, and manufacturing-oriented definition.

Technology is both a critical determinant and an outcome of rising incomes

Traditionally, economists view the process by which goods and services are produced as one that combines capital, labor, and other factors of production (land and natural resources) using a particular technology. The relative efficiency with which a given economy produces

Table 2.1 Disparity among TFP levels remains wide

	TFP relative to that of the United States, 2005	Annual TFP growth, 1990–2005
Regions	*(index, U.S. = 100)*	*(annual percentage change)*
East Asia and the Pacific	8.4	5.1
Europe and Central Asia	21.7	2.2
Latin America and the Caribbean	19.3	0.2
Middle East and North Africa	13.3	0.5
South Asia	5.8	2.3
Sub-Saharan Africa	5.6	0.2
Income groups		
High-income OECD countries	77.1	1.3
High-income non-OECD countries	53.1	0.7
Upper-middle-income countries	23.7	1.2
Lower-middle-income countries	9.6	3.2
Low-income countries	5.2	1.7

Source: Poncet 2006.
Note: OECD = Organisation for Economic Co-operation and Development; TFP = total factor productivity.

goods and services given a certain quantity of labor and capital is called total factor productivity (TFP). TFP is commonly interpreted as a measure of the technology of production and its rate of growth as a measure of technical progress.[1]

International comparisons of TFP suggest that enormous gaps exist between high-income and low- and middle-income countries in the efficiency with which they produce goods and services (table 2.1). In 2005, the average level of TFP in low-income countries was only slightly more than 5 percent of U.S. levels. The technology lower-middle-income countries employed was roughly twice as efficient and that of upper-middle-income countries was approximately four times as efficient. While these gaps have been narrowing for low-income and lower-middle-income countries, upper-middle-income countries have only managed to maintain their relative position in relation to high-income countries. At the regional level, these gaps have widened or remained stagnant in three of six developing regions, with TFP growing faster in high-income countries than in Latin America and the Caribbean, the Middle East, and Sub-Saharan Africa.

The relationships between income growth, technological progress, capital accumulation, and welfare are, of course, much more complex than can be summarized in a simple measure of TFP, partly because each factor of production and the technology with which factors are combined are dependent on one another. As discussed in chapter 3, capital goods often embody significant technological progress and there is no simple way to distinguish between the contribution that each makes to growth. Similarly, technology in the form of knowledge of business processes and of science and general experience is embodied in labor. Moreover, the contribution of technology to welfare is only imperfectly measured by its impact on GDP (box 2.1).

Technological progress can lower costs, improve quality, create new products, and help reach new markets

Even though measures of TFP and its progress give us a sense of the relative dispersion of technological progress, they tell us little about the mechanisms by which technology influences development. Technological progress involves much more than doing the same things better or with fewer resources. It is more dynamic, involving both the creation of new and new-to-the-market products and production techniques, but also the spread of these techniques across firms and throughout the economy. While the mechanisms by which technological progress contributes to development are in some sense obvious, the following deserve special mention:

- *Technological progress can spur development by lowering the costs of production and enabling the exploitation of increasing returns to scale.* By improving the efficiency with which existing

Box 2.1 Technology can contribute to welfare without affecting measures of short-term output

While the relative level of TFP provides a sense of the efficiency with which factors are combined, it ignores the welfare contributions of technology that do not have an immediate impact on GDP. For instance, in national accounts, the purchase of machinery that reduces air and water pollution, such as scrubbers for smokestacks, may not increase GDP. While the purchase of machinery will be recorded as income accruing to the producing firm, this may be offset by reduced profits and other factor payments of the purchasing firm. Thus, even though over the longer term the machinery may contribute to a reduction in days of work lost because of respiratory illnesses, and therefore to an increase in national income, over the medium term the machinery would have little measurable effect on GDP or TFP despite the improvement in air quality, which would provide a general, if not monetized, benefit. Similarly, technological advances that reduce the cost of public services may have little impact on recorded income, but may have important implications for the quality of life.

In developing countries, the diffusion of such technology as water and sanitation systems, oral rehydration techniques to treat diarrhea, immunization, malaria prevention, and contraceptives have been tremendously important for improving household well-being, but such innovations will affect output only over time as improved child health eventually pays off in terms of greater adult productivity (Alderman, Hoddinott, and Kinsey 2006; Behrman and Rosenzweig 2004; Glewwe, Jacoby, and King 2001). These technologies may also have important noneconomic societal benefits, such as improved gender equality, which are not recorded in GDP because women are more likely to engage in nonmarket production, or may appear only with a lag as improved health technologies facilitate women's entry into the labor force over time (Bailey 2006; Miller 2005; Schultz 2007).

products are produced, new technologies can open up the possibility of increasing output and, assuming that markets are available, taking advantage of previously unexploited increasing returns to scale.

- *Technological progress in one sector can create new economic opportunities in other sectors.* Lower production costs can create whole new products, or even sectors. A new-to-the-market innovation in one sector can result in a flowering of activity in other sectors by creating a demand for and supply of goods and services that did not exist previously (box 2.2).
- *The benefits of a new technology can extend well beyond the immediate sector or good in which the technology exists.* This is the case if the initial product is an important intermediate good in the production of other goods, for example, telecommunications or reliable electrical service.
- *Technology can yield quality improvements.* Such improvements can enable a developing country to penetrate more demanding consumer and intermediate markets. This can be as simple as employing machinery and equipment that produce goods and services that correspond to the more exacting expectations and standards of consumers and business clients in high-income countries. Technology in this sense extends beyond engineering technology to include management techniques. For example, one of the big challenges facing Ugandan fisheries was creating systems of quality assurance that allowed them to meet phytosanitary standards in the European Union on a sustained basis (Chandra and Kolavalli 2006).

Box 2.2 Technological innovation may spur further innovation in upstream and downstream activities

In Chile, the creation of a viable international salmon farming industry involved the simultaneous development of a number of related new-to-the-market products, including the domestic production of fish tanks, fish eggs, salmon food, and vaccines, and eventually the introduction of additional varieties of farmed fish. New process technology was also introduced, including systems for feeding, processing, and stocking fish that met global quality and phytosanitary standards.

The introduction of a cut flower industry in Kenya to serve the European market represents the indirect effect of the successful introduction of the industry in Colombia to serve the U.S. market. The new activity generated a wide range of additional new-to-the-market innovations in the form of greenhouses and postharvest care facilities to preserve the freshness of blossoms. Process technology involved learning how to use chemicals and mastering the logistical challenge of delivering this fragile product to the local airport on time and with sufficient regularity to meet customers' just-in-time requirements.

Success in one activity may well lead to further innovation and technological deepening. The move from producing carnations to more fragile and expensive roses is an example. Another example is the shift to higher-quality products such as chilled rather than frozen fish fillets. Yet another example of deepening is palm oil production in Indonesia, where new processes include the production of new varieties of palms; the introduction of new crude and processed palm oil refining technologies; and, notably, the introduction of oleo chemical technologies.

Source: Chandra 2006.

Even relatively simple technologies can have far-reaching development impacts

Technological advances do not need to be extraordinarily complex or reliant on the most sophisticated technology to have important development impacts. In many low-income countries, fairly commonplace technologies are often in short supply because of weak capacities to implement them (box 2.3), and relatively simple innovations can have profound effects. The green revolution is a dramatic example of the effectiveness that even modest technological advances can have in boosting incomes among the poor. In addition, greater access to the technologies required to store and process food can increase food security, particularly in communities without access to reliable electricity or means of refrigeration. The use of sawmill waste (sawdust, planer shavings, and chipper dust) to produce carbonized briquettes for use in household cooking can increase access by the poor to fuel for cooking while reducing deforestation pressures.[2] Dissemination of the simple skills required to build rainwater collection systems can greatly improve access to clean drinking water and reduce the incidence of diarrhea, a major cause of infant mortality. Insecticide-treated mosquito nets are a well-known, cost-effective strategy for preventing the spread of malaria, but the main challenge in many countries remains developing and implementing a mechanism for distributing them to those most in need and ensuring that they are used.

Despite these advantages, technological change can also be disruptive

While technological progress generates substantial benefits, it can also be disruptive, because its benefits are not necessarily evenly distributed. In particular, while the introduction of an advanced technology may mean new opportunities for the innovator and reduced costs for consumers, it can result in significant short-term losses in incomes for competitors using older technologies. For

Box 2.3 Promoting appropriate technologies in Rwanda

A recent study of Rwanda identified simple technologies whose greater use could have a substantial impact on development. For example, the study identified a lack of qualified plumbers and water sanitation technicians as a major factor holding back the implementation of simple rainwater collection strategies that have helped improve the quality of drinking water supplies in neighboring countries. Similarly, a lack of basic skills, including those necessary to manufacture stainless steel products, prevents the implementation of simple food processing techniques, such as passion fruit pasteurization and pulping, that could reduce the share of crops lost to spoilage, which sometimes results in the loss of as much as 30 percent of a crop. Public sector dissemination of best practices is hindered by poor skills and inappropriate incentives, which result in research centers producing local products that take insufficient account of users' needs and requirements. The table provides a snapshot of the status of efforts to promote the diffusion of simple technologies in Rwanda.

Diffusion of selected "appropriate" technologies in Rwanda

Rural energy	• Biogas for institutions: installations ongoing and spreading • Biogas for households: pilot program of 163 units to start 2007 • Micro hydropower: 6 projects in preparation, more in future? • Biofuel: no national program or policy as yet • Wind: no program or policy as yet • Peat: large stocks but limited exploitation • Efficient stoves for urban areas: national program ongoing • Efficient stoves for rural areas: some programs ongoing • Rice and coffee husks for briquette production: limited programs • PV systems: technology available but slow market • Solar water heating: technology available but slow market
Water and sanitation	• Roof water harvesting: only on limited scale for households • Boreholes: few and expensive • Hand pumps: imported from region or India • VIP and Ecosan latrines technology: available, limited uptake
Agricultural technologies and transport	• Irrigation through treadle and motorized pumps: limited uptake • Drip irrigation: starting • Animal traction for tillage and transport: promoted in certain areas • Small tractors for rice puddling and transport: few units imported • Rice threshing and winnowing: few machines available and locally produced • Rice hulling: opportunities for small-scale processing • Maize milling: machines imported and locally made • Oil presses for sunflower, soya, essential oils: starting • Livestock spraying: locally made machine now available
Low-cost building	• Rice and coffee husks and peat for brick burning: some use • Hand brick press machines: locally made and imported • Engine brick press machines: imported

Source: Watkins and Verma 2007.

example, improved production and processing of sugarcane in Brazil has allowed production, incomes, and employment in that country to increase significantly, but it has done so at the expense of sugar producers in other countries, who have been unable to compete. While the associated income losses may be painful, the global impact tends to be positive, because the income losses promote the reallocation of resources and activity to more effective uses.

Technological progress may also benefit certain classes of workers over others. Technological change that uses high-level skills more intensively may hurt less skilled workers in high-income countries by increasing the demand for skilled workers and simplifying tasks or allowing the outsourcing of tasks that previously were accomplished by relatively well-paid semiskilled workers. Many economists cite the recent tendency for technological progress to benefit more skilled workers as a major source of the rise in earnings inequality in most advanced countries.[3] Note, however, that technical change does not always raise the demand for skilled workers relative to unskilled workers, nor does the disruption necessarily occur to the detriment of low-skill workers. Thus the weaving and spinning machines that benefited lower-skilled workers by enabling them to produce textiles formerly produced by skilled artisans were destroyed in the Luddite and Captain Swing riots of the 19th century (Acemoglu 2002).

Moreover, if changes in earnings in developing countries are taken into account, it is no longer clear that technical change has been biased toward skilled workers. By some measures, global inequality has not increased over the past two decades.[4] Global income distribution has benefited from the rapid growth in China and India, which has enabled hundreds of millions of people to escape poverty. Technical change interacting with increased globalization may have increased inequality within some countries by increasing the demand for skilled workers. By opening up opportunities for technical progress through the production of export goods that require relatively high-level skills, greater participation in international trade has led to increasing demand for skilled workers, and thus to greater income inequality in some countries (Arbache, Dickerson, and Green 2004; Zhu and Trefler 2005). At the same time, technical progress can be strongly pro-poor, for example, the discovery of simple technologies to store and process food in areas with insufficient access to electricity or to enable low-cost approaches to combating disease.

The disruptive nature of technological progress can generate important benefits to society by spurring competition. For example, the introduction of mobile phone technology in several developing countries has introduced an important element of competition not only in the telecommunications sector, but also in banking and other information-sensitive sectors. Partly as a result, many of the informational asymmetries generated by a lack of effective communications that various middlemen used to exploit have been eliminated, raising producer prices and lowering consumer prices.[5] These benefits are often accompanied by shifts in the distribution of income whereby some groups can lose either relative to others or in absolute terms. These losses can be difficult for the poor to absorb, underlining the importance of safety nets to minimize social conflict and to ensure that overall progress does not come at too high a cost for some individuals.

Measuring technology in developing countries

The remainder of this chapter is concerned with measuring the level of technological achievement in developing countries and recent progress in this regard. This first section goes beyond indirect measures of technology like TFP, and seeks a more direct measure of technological achievement by exploring the extent to which specific technologies have permeated economic activity in developing countries and the intensity of scientific innovation and invention.

Measuring technology directly is difficult, mainly because, unlike pencils or automobiles, technology has no easily counted physical presence. Nor does it have a well-defined price that would allow it to be measured and aggregated in the same way that services are. Rather, technology is embodied in products, intermediate inputs, and processes. As a result, most efforts to measure it have been forced to use indirect techniques (see Archibugi and Coco 2005 for a review). Some indexes emphasize inputs into technological advancement, such as education levels, numbers of scientists and engineers, and expenditures on research and development (R&D) or R&D personnel, for example, the index of innovation capability put out by the United Nations Conference on Trade and Development (UNCTAD 2005). Other indexes also incorporate information on the diffusion of technologies and on indicators of innovation, such as the number of patents granted. The technology achievement index, published by the United Nations Development Programme is an example. Still other indexes focus on outputs, such as the share of high-tech activities in manufacturing value added and exports, for instance, the index of competitive industrial performance published by the United Nations Industrial Development Organization (UNIDO 2002). Some indexes focus more on the mechanisms by which technological progress is achieved (Sagasti 2003) or by which technological learning occurs (Soubattina 2006). For example, the national innovative capacity index reflects government and firm-level policies associated with successful innovation (Porter and Stern 2003).

Each of these approaches has its strengths, but none of them is entirely satisfactory, both because the indicators used fail to do justice to the broad definition of technology adopted here (box 2.4), and because the methods by which these indexes are constructed are sometimes arbitrary (Archibugi and Coco 2005). To overcome these deficiencies, the indexes developed in the remainder of this chapter include a number of indicators not previously included in technology indexes. Summary indexes are derived from these along three dimensions of technological achievement: the extent of scientific innovation and invention, the diffusion of older technologies, and the diffusion of newer technologies. We begin by reviewing current levels of technology and their dispersion and recent trends in a number of indicators that the literature pertaining to these three dimensions of achievement has used.

In a subsequent section, summary indicators of achievement along each of these dimensions are derived using principal components analysis. Their current levels and recent trends are discussed, an overall index of technological achievement is generated from these summary indicators, and a fourth indicator (developed in chapter 3) summarizes the extent to which external technology is used in the production process.

Scientific innovation and invention

Most technological improvements in developing countries are at least partially dependent on the diffusion of technology from more advanced countries. Nevertheless, scientific innovation is important in some developing countries, and advanced technologies often need to be adapted to local conditions, which may require further innovation.

The intensity of innovation is closely related to per capita income . . .

The degree of scientific innovation in developing countries, as measured by the number of journal articles and patents granted (scaled by population), varies sharply with per capita income (table 2.2).[6] Authors from high-income countries report 7 times as many published articles than those from upper-middle-income countries and 88 times as many as authors from low-income countries. Variations for measures of patents granted and license fees earned are even larger. This result is generally reflected in regional data, with countries in regions with higher incomes such as Latin America and the Caribbean reporting higher levels of patents and journal articles than regions such as South

Box 2.4 Shortcomings of available measures of technological achievement

Available indicators provide only a partial view of the level of technological achievement in developing countries and of the gap with high-income countries. Most available indicators reflect the quantity of technology used, whereas the quality of delivery is often what is critical. For example, the value of electricity in production is a function of both the amount consumed and its reliability. In general, global indicators of technology levels do not take differences in quality sufficiently into account. To the extent that quality of delivery varies systematically with income levels, the indicators likely understate the differences between rich and poor countries. For example, Kaufmann, Leautier, and Mastruzzi (2005) find that access to infrastructure services (similar to what we measure here) and the quality of infrastructure services in urban areas are both closely related to the strength of governance, which is itself highly correlated with income levels.

Nor do the available indicators reflect the disparity of achievement within countries. National indicators of technological achievement are based on country averages, but large gaps exist in the extent to which technologies are used within regions, income groups, and countries. For example, the relatively low performance of South Asia reflects the slowness of technology diffusion from the relatively advanced major cities to rural areas, as well as from the rich to the poor within urban areas. Indeed, the degree of technological diversity across Chinese regions or Indian states mirrors the extent of diversity across developing countries, with regions containing large technologically sophisticated cities, such as Mumbai or Delhi, being well ahead of areas that lag behind in economic development.

Finally, most indicators tend to be biased toward goods (as opposed to services), and among these, toward electronic and other high-tech goods. Most measures also focus on product technology (goods and services that themselves are highly technical) rather than final (or intermediate) goods and services that may be technologically unremarkable, but which are the result of a technologically sophisticated production process, for example, maize that is produced using sophisticated crop rotation methods, enhanced irrigation and fertilization strategies based on satellite imaging, and bioengineered seeds.

Asia or Sub-Saharan Africa, which are dominated by lower-income countries. The ratio of patents granted to residents to the total number of patents a country grants (an indicator of the extent to which innovations are generated domestically) is only weakly correlated with income. Equally important influences include the domestic economic structure, the country's openness to foreign direct investment (FDI) (see chapter 3), the domestic costs of making a patent application, local intellectual property rights, and the legal environment—all factors that dictate the potential benefits from holding a patent.

Patent activity in middle-income countries has increased over the past 20 years (figure 2.1), primarily because of a sharp jump in patenting (relative to population) among upper-middle-income countries in the early 1990s following the integration of the transition economies of the former Soviet Union into the world economy. The continuous increase in patent activity among lower-middle-income countries mainly reflects activity in China, whose share in world patent applications rose from about 1.5 percent in the late 1980s to a peak of nearly 10 percent in 2004. Excluding China, additional patenting activity in lower-middle-income countries has been relatively modest. While patent activity has also risen in low-income countries, it remains far below that in middle-income countries both in the absolute numbers of patents issued and relative to the population.

Table 2.2 Scientific and innovative outputs

Regions and income groups	Scientific and technical journal articles, 2003	USPTO patents, 2006	EPO patents, 2005	Total patents, 2003	Number of patents to nonresidents 2003	Royalty and license fee receipts 2004
Regions	*(Number per million people)*				*(percent of total)*	*(percent of GDP)*
East Asia and the Pacific	17	0.7	0.01	37	77	0.02
Europe and Central Asia	90	0.9	0.40	95	28	0.06
Latin America and the Caribbean	35	0.7	0.21	46	98	0.03
Middle East and North Africa	18	0.1	0.03	—	—	0.02
South Asia	9	0.5	0.07	1.4	60	0.00
Sub-Saharan Africa	5	1.4	1.16	157	100	0.06
Income groups						
World	*111*	*38.6*	*11.4*	*127*	*41*	*0.27*
High-income countries	584	135.1	42.6	331	38	0.33
Upper-middle-income countries	85	1.4	0.40	91	42	0.04
Lower-middle-income countries	21	0.6	0.01	46	64	0.03
Low-income countries	7	0.4	0.07	3.5	56	0.00

Source: World Development Indicators, USPTO, EPO, and World Intellectual Property Office data.
Notes: EPO = European Patent Office, USPTO = U.S. Patent and Trademark Office. To reduce home bias, the total patents granted by the USPTO to high-income countries exclude those granted to the United States, and the total patents granted by the EPO exclude those granted to high-income European Union countries.
— = not available.

. . . although the Europe and Central Asia region is an outlier

Reflecting a history of advanced scientific and engineering work in a number of former Soviet bloc countries, the Europe and Central Asia region has relatively high levels of scientific innovation and invention (table 2.2).

Figure 2.1 Patent activity is rising in middle-income countries

Total patent applications per 10,000 people

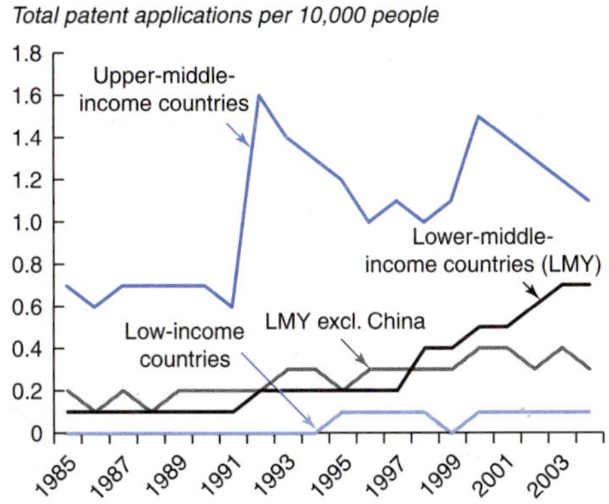

Source: World Development Indicators.

Publication rates there are equal to those in many high-income countries, and patent activity is more than twice the level in any other developing region. The region is also the most self-reliant of developing regions in terms of patent activity, with only 28 percent of patents being filed by nonresidents, a figure that is even lower than the high-income country average of 38 percent. The East Asia and Pacific region also scores high in terms of patents, although its publication record is more in keeping with that of other developing regions. In some countries, such as China and India, conscious efforts to raise R&D spending have led to higher levels of scientific innovation than might be expected based on income (Lederman and Saenz 2005), while low levels of innovation in Latin America and the Caribbean reflect an academic research tradition with few links to industry (Maloney 2006).

Penetration of older technologies

The clear dominance of high-income countries in the number of scientific and technical journal articles published, the number of patents

Box 2.5 Deepwater petroleum technology in Brazil

Experience in the extractive sectors can help generate new technologies that in turn can be used as a source of global comparative advantage. The experience of Brazil's Petrobras, a majority state-owned company, in exploiting that country's considerable deepwater oil and natural gas resources provides an interesting example.

To exploit the Campos Basin, which lies in the Atlantic at a depth of more than 100 meters and now accounts for nearly 84 percent of Brazil's oil production, Petrobras created the anticipated production system on a floating platform. This advanced system, developed with the help of foreign experts, cut the delay between discovery and early production of deepwater fields from as long as six years to a mere four months and has since become a model for the industry worldwide.

Petrobras has successfully leveraged this experience, developing many patents both on its own and in conjunction with the rest of the industry, universities, and research institutes. It has invested heavily in research and education, creating its own R&D center, to which it allocates 1 percent of its gross income. The center, whose staff is increasingly made up of Brazilian experts, has contributed significantly to Petrobras's many patents and continues to help develop cutting-edge technology for the company.

Petrobras is now recognized as a world leader in all phases of deepwater technology—from drilling; to underwater completion, pumping, and production using floating structures; to mooring and processing—with its particular expertise is in the areas of unmanned subsea installations, marine engineering, and floating production systems. About two-thirds of its production is at a depth of more than 300 meters, and at various times Petrobras has set a number of records, including oil production at a water depth of 1,853 meters and the then-deepest exploration well (2,853 meters) in the giant Roncador field.

Petrobras has used its advanced technology to perform exploration and production work in Angola, Argentina, Bolivia, Colombia, Nigeria, Trinidad and Tobago, and the United States and has acquired offshore exploration blocks and interests in Equatorial Guinea, Libya, Senegal, and Turkey (Black Sea). It has also recently signed various agreements in China, India, Mexico, Mozambique, and Tanzania.

Source: World Bank.

granted, and the extent of licensing and royalty fees realized points to the relatively minor role that at-the-frontier innovation plays in determining technological progress in developing countries and the relative importance that adoption and adaptation of existing technologies must play. We look first at the diffusion of older technologies.

The major technological innovations of the past two centuries—such as steam power, electricity, the internal combustion engine, the telephone, radio, and television—exist to some degree in virtually every country in the world. However, the extent to which they are available within countries varies enormously, depending both on the technical adaptive capacity of the country (chapter 3) and on the affordability of the technology.

Many of the most prominent technologies are in the manufacturing sector. However, the efficient extraction of natural resources often requires advanced technology and can encourage technological progress. Indeed, the failure to absorb new technologies is an important reason for the slow growth of many natural resource-based economies in Latin America (box 2.5).

Affordability limits the penetration of electrical networks in some countries . . .

Affordability, exacerbated by fiscally constrained governments, helps explain the modest diffusion of many technologies critical to development. This appears to be the case for a number of infrastructure technologies such as electricity (figure 2.2), rail and road transportation, and fixed-line telephony. In each of these cases, a reliance on governments to provide these services, coupled with weak institutions and a lack of domestic capacity to

Figure 2.2 Electrical consumption varies markedly even at similar income levels (2004)

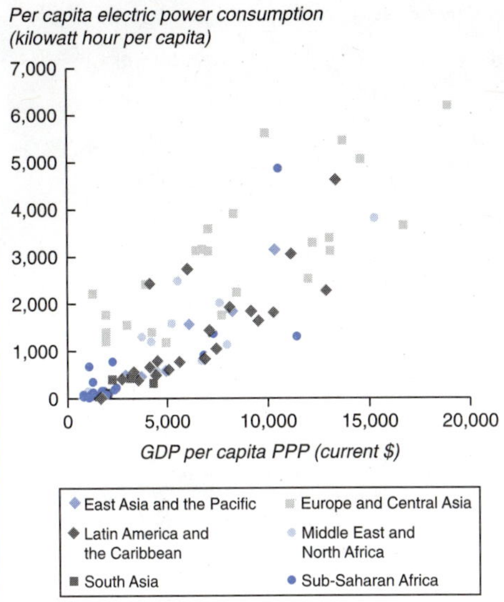

Sources: World Bank; World Development Indicators.

maintain systems, has limited their diffusion in a number of low- and middle-income countries.

Other factors, such as industrial structure, climate, tax policies, and preferences, are also at play. In the case of electricity, the way a country organizes its power sector (the process technology employed) can also have a strong bearing on the diffusion of the specific technology within the economy. For example, many countries in the former Soviet bloc enjoy near-universal access to electrical power and per capita consumption rates that are more than double those in any other developing region (table 2.3). This reflects a much earlier decision to emphasize electrification and the provision of subsidies under communist rule. Access to power in other regions is more spotty, with most of the population in most large cities having access (or at least the possibility of access) to the electrical power grid, but with a large share of the rural population, particularly in the poorest countries, having no or only limited service. In India for example, only 85 percent of rural villages have access to the power grid. In Sub-Saharan Africa, only 8 percent of the rural population has access to electricity, compared with 51 percent of the urban population. In South Asia, only 30 percent of the rural population has access to electricity, compared with 68 percent of the urban population (Besant-Jones 2006).

Moreover, the reliability of the grids varies enormously, partly because of the amount of electricity lost through pilferage or in transmission. Because of electricity's importance as an intermediate input, the reliability of the electrical supply may be even more important to the diffusion of other technologies than its availability. Many machines are sensitive to the quality of electrical power and many processes are intolerant of interruptions. As a result, unreliable power can be an important factor in preventing the implementation of these technologies in some countries. For the world as a whole, electricity losses amount to an average of 9 percent of the power produced. Countries in East Asia and the Pacific and Sub-Saharan Africa and members of the Organisation for Economic Co-operation and Development (OECD) do better than this average, while losses in South Asia approach 30 percent. Furthermore, the impact of power reliability differs across countries. In Bangladesh, for example, where transmission and distribution losses represent only 9 percent of produced power, some 70 percent of managers indicate that unreliable power is a serious constraint to business. In contrast, in Cameroon and Moldova, where transmission losses are much greater than in Bangladesh, the share of managers making this complaint is much lower—13 percent in Cameroon and less than 4 percent in Moldova (World Bank 2007e).

. . . and restricts access to efficient transportation . . .

Like the electrical network, transportation systems are old technologies that enable other technologies, and their dissemination within countries has been closely affected by

Table 2.3 Indicators of the diffusion of older technologies

	Electric power consumption 2004	Electric power transmission and distribution losses 2004	Telephone mainlines 2004
Regions	*(kilowatt-hours/capita)*	*(percentage of output)*	*(per 100 people)*
East Asia and the Pacific	1,343	7	19
Europe and Central Asia	3,637	12	26
Latin America and the Caribbean	1,674	17	18
Middle East and North Africa	1,289	16	13
South Asia	414	26	4
Sub-Saharan Africa	550	9	2
Imcome groups			
World	*2,606*	*9*	*19*
High-income countries	9,609	6	54
Upper-middle-income countries	3,454	12	23
Lower-middle-income countries	1,448	10	19
Low-income countries	375	23	3

	Price basket for residential fixed telephone line 2004	Road density 1999	Rail density 2005
Regions	*(percentage of gross national income/capital/month)*	*(kilometers of road/100 square kilometers of land area)*	*(kilometers of rail/100 square kilometers of land area)*
East Asia and the Pacific	—	14.2	0.42
Europe and Central Asia	3.5	11.8	0.81
Latin America and the Caribbean	3.2	16.1	0.31
Middle East and North Africa	4.4	6.8	0.27
South Asia	10.6	80.6	1.55
Sub-Saharan Africa	29.3	6.4	0.18
Income groups			
World	*2.2*	*22.1*	*0.66*
High-income countries	1.0	41.2	1.17
Upper-middle-income countries	3.9	11.9	0.70
Lower-middle-income countries	6.0	14.5	0.39
Low-income countries	20.7	19.0	0.36

	Agricultural machinery and tractors 2003	Irrigated land 2003	Air transport 2004
Regions	*(per 100 square kilometers of arable land)*	*(as a percentage of cropland)*	*(number of registered carrier departures/1,000 people)*
East Asia and the Pacific	93	—	1.1
Europe and Central Asia	184	11	2.1
Latin America and the Caribbean	123	11	2.8
Middle East and North Africa	141	32	1.2
South Asia	143	39	0.3
Sub-Saharan Africa	13	4	0.5
Income groups			
World	*202*	*18*	*3.7*
High-income countries	433	12	18.0
Upper-middle-income countries	173	10	3.2
Lower-middle-income countries	113	24	1.3
Low-income countries	90	24	0.3

Sources: World Bank; World Development Indicators.
Note: — = not available.

government regulation and affordability. Many process technologies (for example, the assembly, sorting, refrigeration, and delivery of fresh fruit) depend on an effective transportation network. The diffusion of railroads among developing countries varies widely, with the countries of the former Soviet bloc having a much more extensive rail transport system than other developing countries at similar income levels. This variance is explained in part by differences in population density (figure 2.3). The cost per passenger mile of a rail system tends to fall with population density, which helps explain the particularly low density of railroads observed in Sub-Saharan Africa (Stelling and Jensen 2001). Interestingly, with the exception of Europe and Central Asia, per capita income does not appear to be an important factor in explaining the diffusion of either rail or road networks. Moreover, the observed distribution of road networks is only weakly correlated with population density. Relative to other regions, Latin America and the Caribbean has significantly more roads

Figure 2.3 Rail and road densities rise with income and population density (2004)

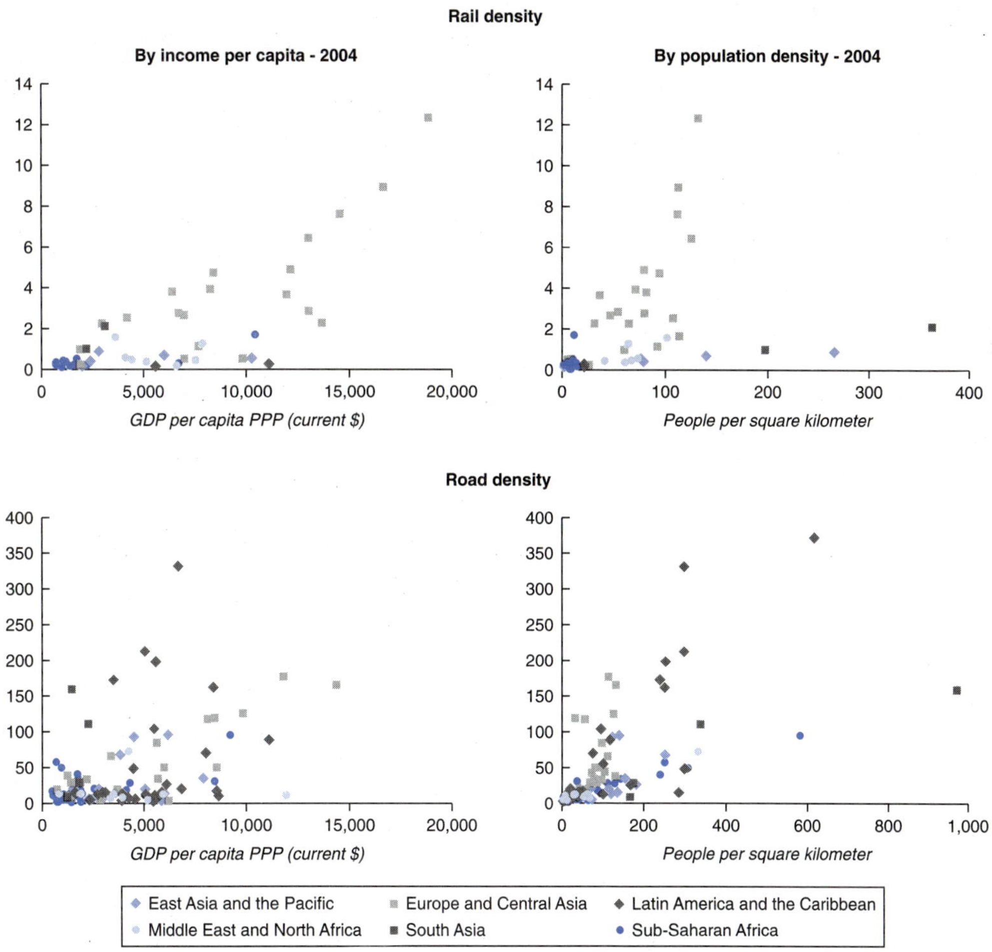

Sources: World Bank; World Development Indicators.

than would be expected on the basis of population and income, while the high average road density in South Asia mainly reflects high densities in Bangladesh and India and low densities elsewhere in the region.

Considerable disparities in access to road and rail transport services are found within many developing countries. Rural areas in particular suffer from poor access to transport services. During 1994–2001, only an estimated 61 percent of the rural population in low-income countries lived within two kilometers of an all-season road (Briceno-Garmendia, Estache, and Shafik 2004). Poor access to transport facilities can cause the neglect of potentially productive land, limit yields of used lands to levels below their potential, and reduce profits from the sale of produce, all of which weakens incentives for farmers to maximize production, thereby limiting the prospects for alleviating poverty (World Bank 2006). Improving road access can thus have a dramatic impact on growth in remote areas.

. . . and air transport and telephones

A well-developed air transport network is also essential for some technologies and may be a particularly important enabling technology for landlocked economies with poor access to ports in neighboring countries. Air transport is a newer technology, and its distribution across countries tends to follow income at the most aggregated level. Thus high-income countries registered 18 carrier departures per 1,000 people in 2004, compared with 0.3 departures for low-income countries. Although middle-income countries have a higher number of carrier departures relative to population than do low-income countries, the cross-country correlation between income and air transport intensity is relatively low for all developing countries (figure 2.4). This suggests that factors such as the importance of tourism to the economy and access to alternative forms of transport—especially relevant for island nations—are among the most important determinants of the intensity of air transport use.

The delivery of fixed-line telephone services follows a similar pattern. On average, the incidence of this mature technology among upper-middle-income countries is less than half that in high-income countries, and in low-income countries falls to almost 5 percent of developed country levels. Across regions, the

Figure 2.4 Telephone densities are highly correlated with income, but air transport is not

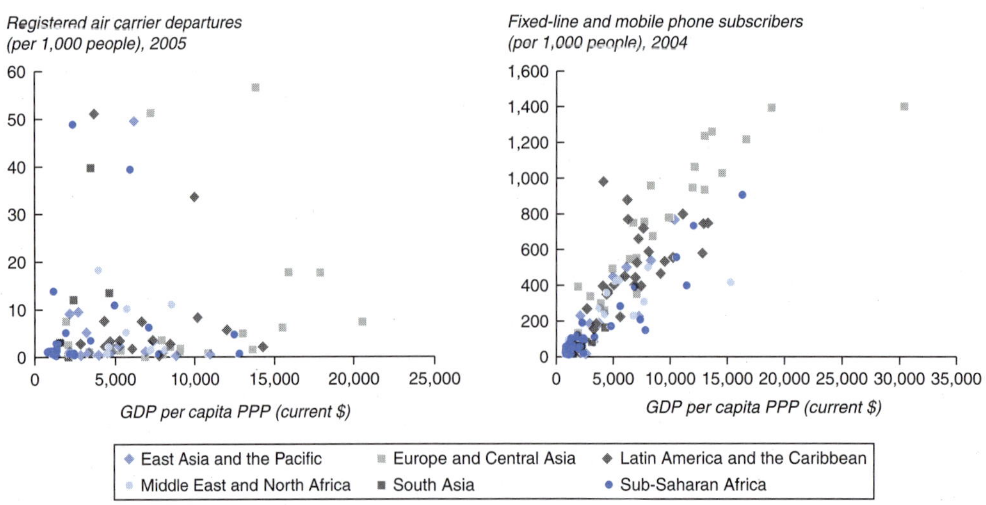

Sources: World Bank; World Development Indicators.

Table 2.4 Affordability of fixed-line phones falls rapidly with lower incomes

(cost of fixed-line phone service as a percentage of monthly income in dollars and PPP)

	Per capita income			Price as a % of monthly income	
	GNI	PPP	Monthly price fixed-line phone	GNI	PPP
Regions					
East Asia and the Pacific	1,630	5,194	5.9	4.3	1.4
Europe and Central Asia	4,143	9,152	9.5	2.8	1.2
Latin America and the Caribbean	4,045	8,116	10.0	3.0	1.5
Middle East and North Africa	2,198	6,084	7.3	4.0	1.4
South Asia	692	3,142	5.1	8.8	1.9
Sub-Saharan Africa	746	2,004	14.0	22.5	8.4
Income groups					
World	*7,011*	*9,424*	*11.7*	*2.0*	*1.5*
High-income countries	35,264	32,550	27.6	0.9	1.0

Sources: World Bank; World Development Indicators.
Note: GNI = gross national income; PPP = purchasing power parity.

incidence is once again much higher in Europe and Central Asia, reflecting the heritage of the communist era. Elsewhere, East Asia and Latin America have fewer than 20 phone lines per 100 people and South Asia and Sub-Saharan Africa have fewer than 5 lines per 100 people.

In contrast to air transport, the cross-country correlation between the availability of telephones and income levels is strong (figure 2.4). The cost of residential service is significantly higher in the low-income regions of South Asia and especially Sub-Saharan Africa (8.4 percent) than in the predominantly middle-income regions (table 2.4).

The adoption and adaptation of old technologies varies by sector

The diffusion of old technologies has contributed to rapid growth in the agriculture sector in many developing countries. During 1967–92, TFP (often used as a proxy for increases in technology) is estimated to have increased four times as quickly in agriculture as in the manufacturing sector in both high-income and developing countries (Martin and Mitra 2001). In part this growth represents the exit of underemployed farm workers to better paying jobs in other sectors, but it also represents significant improvements in seeds; more capital intensive forms of embodied technology such as tractors, fertilizer, and irrigation systems; and better process technology, such as crop rotation and management techniques for disease-resistant crops (box 2.6).

At the same time, the diffusion of medical technologies within low-income countries has been slow. Some of the most important technological developments of the past 100 years have been medical, including the discovery and widespread distribution of antibiotics and the eradication and effective treatment of a wide range of previously deadly or debilitating viruses, including retroviruses such as those that cause HIV/AIDS.

The diffusion of knowledge about treatments is generally relatively speedy and efficient within the medical community, but their diffusion and application within the population of the developing world is much slower. In Europe and Central Asia, Latin America and the Caribbean, and the Middle East and North Africa, the average share of children immunized for measles, diphtheria, pertussis (whooping cough), and tetanus is 89 percent or better, bringing them close to the immunization rates in high-income countries. East Asia and the Pacific also posts immunization rates above 80 percent. However, immunization

Box 2.6 The green revolution

The green revolution is an example of the dramatic effects that modest technological advances can have in boosting the incomes of the poor. The green revolution was a decades-long effort, guided primarily by public sector and nonprofit institutions, to create and disseminate agricultural technologies to developing countries. The principal technologies involved were pesticides, irrigation, and synthetic nitrogen fertilizer, which had long been available in industrial countries, along with the development of high-yielding varieties of maize, wheat, and rice. Asia's green revolution doubled cereal production between 1970 and 1995 while increasing the land area devoted to cereals by only 4 percent (World Bank 2007b). Even though the impact of the green revolution on the poor was initially a source of controversy, by the late 1990s it was clear that poor people had reaped substantial benefits from higher incomes, less expensive food, and increased demand for their labor. The public sector was critical to this effort, because the development of new seed technologies has some aspects of a public good: developers cannot capture the full benefits, because once the seed is widely available, it can be easily reproduced. The green revolution also demonstrates some of unintended effects that can accompany the adoption of new technologies: the excessive use of agrochemicals has polluted waterways, wasteful irrigation has contributed to water scarcity, and high livestock concentrations near urban areas have contributed to the spread of disease.

Source: World Bank 1998, 2007b.

rates in South Asia and Sub-Saharan Africa average 59 to 63 percent (table 2.5). In part, this reflects particularly low immunization rates in some of the larger countries in these regions, notably India (less than 60 percent) and Nigeria (less than 35 percent), which outweigh the better performance of some of the smaller countries, for example, in Sri Lanka, 99 percent of children aged 12 to 23 months are immunized. The disappointing failure to deliver this basic technological service arises despite the intense involvement of the international community in assisting, and in some instances taking full responsibility for, this process. Moreover, the pace at which these rates are rising is disappointingly low as countries continue to struggle to implement effective delivery systems. Partly as a result,

Table 2.5 Immunization rates lag significantly in South Asia and Sub-Saharan Africa
(children aged 12–23 months immunized)

	DPT		Measles		DPT	Measles
	1993	2003	1993	2003	2003	2003
Regions	*(percent immunized)*		*(percent immunized)*		*(ratio to high-income countries)*	*(ratio to high-income countries)*
East Asia and the Pacific	83	83	79	83	0.87	0.90
Europe and Central Asia	80	89	84	91	0.94	0.99
Latin America and the Caribbean	78	90	82	93	0.95	1.01
Middle East and North Africa	85	91	84	92	0.96	1.00
South Asia	59	63	59	61	0.66	0.66
Sub-Saharan Africa	49	59	51	61	0.62	0.66
High-income countries	88	95	83	92	1.00	1.00
World	*71*	*76*	*71*	*75*	*0.80*	*0.82*

Sources: World Bank; World Development Indicators.
Note: DPT = diphtheria, pertussis, and tetanus.

Table 2.6 Diffusion of both water and sanitation technology is low in rural areas

	Improved water sources					
	Total population		Rural population		Urban population	
	1990	2004	1990	2004	1990	2004
Regions			*(percent of population with access)*			
East Asia and the Pacific	71.8	78.5	61.4	69.8	97.3	91.9
Europe and Central Asia	91.7	91.7	83.4	79.8	97.0	98.7
Latin America and the Caribbean	82.8	91.0	60.0	73.0	92.6	96.0
Middle East and North Africa	87.5	89.5	78.9	80.8	96.1	96.3
South Asia	70.6	84.4	64.9	81.3	88.6	93.6
Sub-Saharan Africa	48.9	56.2	36.1	42.4	81.9	80.1
Income groups						
World	*76.4*	*82.7*	*63.2*	*72.2*	*95.2*	*94.5*
High-income countries	99.8	99.5	99.1	98.5	99.8	99.8
Upper-middle-income countries	88.1	92.7	73.5	77.8	94.8	97.7
Lower-middle-income countries	74.2	80.8	62.9	70.9	96.4	93.1
Low-income countries	64.3	75.0	56.7	69.4	87.0	88.1
	Improved sanitation facilities					
	Total population		Rural population		Urban population	
	1990	2004	1990	2004	1990	2004
Regions			*(percent of population with access)*			
East Asia and the Pacific	29.7	50.6	15.3	36.1	65.5	72.4
Europe and Central Asia	86.1	85.0	72.0	70.3	93.7	93.0
Latin America and the Caribbean	67.4	77.1	35.4	48.7	80.7	85.7
Middle East and North Africa	69.9	76.2	52.0	57.9	87.1	92.3
South Asia	17.4	37.2	6.3	26.6	50.3	62.7
Sub-Saharan Africa	31.5	37.2	23.8	28.2	52.4	53.3
Income groups						
World	*44.4*	*57.0*	*22.8*	*37.7*	*77.2*	*79.4*
High-income countries	100.0	100.0	100.0	100.0	100.0	100.0
Upper-middle-income countries	76.7	81.4	52.6	59.9	87.1	88.6
Lower-middle-income countries	37.3	55.4	19.7	38.8	72.9	76.2
Low-income countries	21.3	38.3	11.6	28.5	49.6	60.5

Sources: World Bank; World Development Indicators.

child mortality rates remain elevated in these regions.

The health benefits of clean drinking water and sanitation facilities have been understood for centuries. Nevertheless, one in five people living in developing countries lack access to improved water sources and only half have access to improved sanitation facilities (table 2.6). In South Asia and Sub-Saharan Africa, only some 37 percent of the population has access to improved sanitation services, while only slightly more than half of the Sub-Saharan African population has access to improved drinking water (this share rises to 65 percent if Nigeria, where only 35 percent of the population has access to improved water, is excluded). The rest of the developing world does much better on these measures. For example, close to 90 percent of the population in Europe and Central Asia has access to improved water (91.7 percent) and sanitation sources (85 percent). Nevertheless, the diffusion of these basics technologies is weak in rural parts of all developing areas, reflecting more intense affordability issues and the relative scarcity of basic technological literacy and the competencies necessary to install and maintain such systems (see the discussion on basic technological literacy in chapter 3). For example, in China and India, only 44 and 33 percent, respectively, of the rural population have access to improved sanitation.

Older technologies have become widely diffused in many countries, but large disparities remain

Older technologies have penetrated less completely into developing countries than into developed countries, but the gap is much less pronounced than the gap for indicators of scientific innovation and invention. Moreover, the relationship between income levels and the diffusion of older technologies within the developing world is relatively weak, suggesting that the efficiency of the regulatory environment and the diffusion of basic skills within countries are more important than incomes in determining the actual level of diffusion of these technologies. Countries with the highest achievement in each income group find themselves at about the median level of achievement of the next highest income group. Once again, the level of diffusion of the older technologies tends to be higher for countries of the former Soviet bloc than for other countries at the same income level, while both the upper-middle-income and lower-middle-income countries of Latin America and the Caribbean tend to report lower levels of diffusion than other countries at similar income levels.

The striking differences between Europe and Central Asia on the one hand and Latin America and the Caribbean on the other hand in the diffusion of older technologies may reflect differences in income distribution and in the nature of R&D activities (box 2.7). Europe and Central Asia had more equal access to education combined with greater government investment in infrastructure, which facilitated more rapid diffusion of technologies than in Latin America and the Caribbean. In addition, whereas R&D activity was clearly linked to the industrial strategy of Soviet-era firms in Europe and Central Asia, R&D in Latin America was concentrated in universities, was oriented toward research at the global frontier (but generally not of cutting-edge quality), and had few links to firms (Maloney 2006).

Penetration of recent technologies

The relatively slow diffusion of many old technologies in developing countries contrasts sharply with the relatively rapid penetration of newer technologies (table 2.7). Macroeconomic turmoil, civil strife, and fiscal constraints limited the within-country diffusion of many older technologies, but more hospitable circumstances—including low inflation, low government deficits, and a technical and regulatory environment that has better harnessed private sector financing of new technologies—have contributed to the spread of more recent technologies. In a few cases, newer technologies have leapfrogged over older ones, for example, mobile phones now have higher penetration rates in some countries than fixed-line telephones.

Distinguishing between old and recent technologies is necessarily arbitrary. To a certain extent, road infrastructure is an ancient technology, and yet the technology embodied in producing a kilometer of German autobahn is completely different from that required to construct a kilometer of dirt track in Somalia. Similarly, exports that are currently classified as high-tech are in some cases evolutionary developments from relatively old technology (mobile phones, for example, evolved from radios and fixed-line telephones).[7] Nonetheless, the distinction is useful, because in many cases the factors that have impeded the diffusion of old technologies within developing countries are qualitatively different from those that impede the distribution of more recent technologies. For instance, the diffusion of many of the older technologies depended upon the creation and maintenance of expensive government infrastructure at a time when many governments were grappling with severe budget constraints and weak technical and governance capacity. Not only are today's technologies being exploited in a more

Box 2.7 Technology and growth in Latin America's natural resource-based economies

While much of the value added from extractive industries, such as crude oil production and mining, is a return to land, the technology employed in these activities is often very sophisticated. Some economies, such as Australia, Canada, and Sweden, achieved rapid rates of growth over the 20th century through the efficient exploitation of natural resources. By contrast, Latin America's natural resource-based economies achieved relatively limited growth; until recently, substantial mineral deposits have gone unexploited. Two central reasons explain the failure to capitalize on Latin America's natural resource opportunities.

First, the region had low levels of human capital and weak institutions that slowed the adoption and creation of new technologies. Latin American countries invested much less than other regions in promoting education systems, with the result that by 1870, the literacy rate was only one-third to one-fourth as high as in Canada and the United States. Early industrialization reflected the cumulative impact of numerous small advances made by many individuals, but in Latin America, the lack of access to education translated into limited innovation and slower technological progress, because colonial institutions deemphasized technical education and universities failed to produce sufficient engineers and scientists through the 19th century.

Second, innovation was discouraged and firm entry was inhibited by anticompetitive guilds, labor markets that were excessively protective of insiders' rights, concentrated credit markets that only lent to insiders, explicit trade barriers that impeded knowledge spillovers from trade interactions, and barriers to FDI. The concentration of wealth also discouraged innovations by newcomers. Rights to organize corporations and financial institutions were rationed to protect the value of rights held by powerful interests and the costs associated with filing patents were exorbitant. After the Great Depression, attempts to force rapid industrialization through import substitution policies led to sectors that were out of line with comparative advantage, that were walled off from competition and sources of innovation, and that required substantial subsidies to survive. Natural resource sectors, the likely source of Latin America's comparative advantage, were starved of capital and workers who were drawn to the heavily subsidized and inefficient manufacturing enterprises.

The combination of inefficient industrialization with the stifling of natural export sectors left many countries in the region vulnerable to balance of payments crises and severely constrained growth.

Source: Lederman and Maloney 2007.

relaxed and stable regulatory environment, but also many of them are being financed and built by private sector investors with access to ample funds and outside expertise.

Exports of high-tech goods are only loosely related to incomes

One frequently used indicator of the diffusion of recent technology is the share of high-tech goods in total merchandise exports. To be sure, the informational content of this measure has decreased with the proliferation of relatively low-tech assembly operations of high-tech goods, which in turn has reduced the level of technological competence associated with a given level of export of high-tech goods. Nevertheless, the share of high-tech exports is generally positively correlated with other indicators of technological achievement.[8]

Middle-income countries as a group have a much higher share of high-tech exports than low-income countries. Within the middle-income group, however, the lower-middle-income countries average a higher share of high-tech exports than the upper-middle-income countries (table 2.8). The East Asian countries have much higher shares of high-tech exports than the other regions, and the Middle East and North Africa region has much lower shares than the

Table 2.7 Diffusion of recent technologies

	Internet users		Internet bandwidth		Broadband subscribers	
	2005	Percentage change 1999–2005	2004	Percentage change 1999–2004	2005	Percentage change 2001–05
Regions	*(per 1,000 people)*		*(megabytes/second)*		*(per 1,000 people)*	
East Asia and the Pacific	89	48	8,735	149	26	236
Europe and Central Asia	190	48	6,670	132	21	208
Latin America and the Caribbean	156	41	4,513	121	16	89
Middle East and North Africa	89	64	899	91	—	—
South Asia	49	66	2,249	114	1	131
Sub-Saharan Africa	29	42	114	62	—	—
Income groups						
World	*137*	*20*	*43,856*	*108*	*42*	*59*
High-income countries	527	14	121,433	107	163	45
Upper-middle-income countries	196	36	5,611	126	21	147
Lower-middle-income countries	95	50	5,533	134	23	187
Low-income countries	44	72	708	120	1	143

	Personal computers		Cellular subscribers		Digital cellular subscribers	
	2004	Percentage change 1997–2004	2004	Percentage change 1995–2004	2004	Percentage change 1999–2004
Regions	*(per 1,000 people)*		*(per 100 people)*		*(per 1,000 people)*	
East Asia and the Pacific	38	26	24	58	257	54
Europe and Central Asia	98	20	44	79	512	43
Latin America and the Caribbean	88	17	32	51	337	42
Middle East and North Africa	48	17	13	73	142	70
South Asia	12	29	4	87	40	88
Sub-Saharan Africa	15	11	8	61	83	47
Income groups						
World	*130*	*14*	*28*	*37*	*284*	*29*
High-income countries	579	12	77	28	768	19
Upper-middle-income countries	113	18	48	58	521	37
Lower-middle-income countries	45	23	24	61	255	54
Low-income countries	11	25	4	92	43	88

Sources: World Bank; World Development Indicators.
Note: Period growth rates are compound annual growth rates.
— = not available.

other predominantly middle-income regions. In part these differences reflect the impact of long-standing policies in several East Asian countries that emphasized exports of increasingly sophisticated products and these countries' proximity to transport corridors that facilitated their participation in international production networks.

Although well below half the level of East Asia and the Pacific, Latin America and the Caribbean's share of high-tech exports relative to the total of manufactured exports of 13 percent in 2004 was larger than that of the other regions (table 2.8). This mainly reflects a high share of high-tech exports in Mexico (20 percent). The average share for individual countries in Latin America and the Caribbean is 8.6 percent, with high-tech exports representing 7 percent or less of the total merchandise exports of Argentina, Colombia, Honduras, Nicaragua, and Paraguay.

Personal computers have diffused relatively slowly . . .

Personal computers (PCs) are among the recent technologies for which data exist for a wide number of countries. PCs are a relatively new technology that, despite their present-day ubiquity in high-income countries, have

Table 2.8 Share of high-tech products in total exports

(high-tech exports as a percent of manufactured exports)

	2004	1999–2004
		Percentage point change
Regions		
East Asia and the Pacific	33.4	2.7
Europe and Central Asia	8.7	−0.7
Latin America and the Caribbean	13.1	−1.4
Middle East and North Africa	3.2	−0.4
South Asia	4.1	0.5
Sub-Saharan Africa	—	—
Income groups		
World	*21.3*	*−0.4*
High-income countries	22.3	−0.4
Upper-middle-income countries	16.2	−3.1
Lower-middle-income countries	22.2	4.0
Low-income countries	—	—

Sources: Centre d'Etudes Prospectives et d'Informations Internationales; World Bank.
Note: — = not available.

actually diffused relatively slowly throughout the world since their introduction in the 1980s, at least compared with the speed at which the use of mobile phones and the Internet has spread. Thus in 1995, France had just under 145 computers per 1,000 inhabitants, fewer than half as many as in the United States at the time (325) and roughly the same as in Hungary today. France now has 575 computers per 1,000 inhabitants, compared with 762 in the United States, and many developing countries in Europe and Central Asia and Latin America have PC ownership rates similar to Hungary's. Indeed, the regional average for Europe and Central Asia is brought down by low penetration rates in Turkey and Ukraine (the second and third most populous countries in the region, respectively), which have only 52 and 28 computers per 1,000 individuals, respectively. If we use the simple average of the penetration rate in individual countries in the region, there are about 150 computers per 1,000 people, with many countries posting penetration levels close to the unweighted average for high-income countries (460 PCs per 1,000).[9]

Nevertheless, three-quarters of low-income countries have 15 or fewer PCs per 1,000 people and one-quarter have fewer than 5 per 1,000 people. Yet, several low-income countries have substantially more. Mongolia, for example, reports having 133 PCs per 1,000 people, illustrating that even though the density of PC ownership is correlated with income, substantial variations exist across countries at similar income levels.

. . . while diffusion of the Internet and mobile phones has been extremely rapid

The penetration of Internet use, a more recent technology,[10] offers an interesting comparison (figure 2.5). Internet bandwidth consumption and the number of broadband subscribers more than doubled from 1999 to 2004 in both middle- and low-income countries. High-income countries have almost as many PCs per capita as there are Internet users in developing countries, which have twice as many Internet users as PCs. The ratio rises as per capita incomes decline, with four times as many Internet users as PCs in the Middle East

Figure 2.5 The incidence of Internet use varies widely across countries

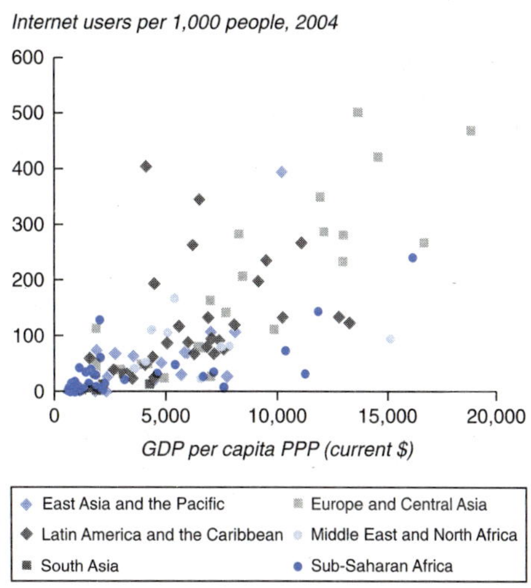

Sources: World Bank; World Development Indicators.

and North Africa and South Asia. The capacity to share an Internet connection, either formally through a commercial venture such as an Internet café or informally, makes Internet use much more affordable than owning a PC and lies at the root of this difference.

A lack of infrastructure helps explain weak penetration rates in some low-income countries. For example, even though Internet penetration rates rose by 41 percent in Sub-Saharan Africa from 1999 to 2005, Internet penetration in the region remains the lowest among developing regions, in part because no high-speed, low-cost backbone exists to connect eastern and central Africa to the rest of the world. As a result, Internet transactions must be made via satellite, which provides lower bandwidth at higher cost than fiber optics (Kenyan call center operators pay $7,000 per megabyte of bandwidth compared with around $500 for operators connected by fiber optic cable in India). As a result, prospects for Sub-Saharan Africa are expected to improve following the recent installation of a fiber optic backbone along the western coast of the continent and the expected completion of a similar backbone along the eastern coast in 2008.

Technology is also providing solutions for overcoming infrastructure costs. In a number of countries, wireless broadband connections are outpacing digital subscriber line (DSL) and cable as a mechanism for distributing Internet access to customers. So-called 3G mobile phones already provide reasonable bandwidth in many countries, while more advanced standards offer hope for even faster implementation and diffusion. Some 23 developing countries are planning to, or already have begun to, deploy WiMax systems, a wireless, broadband Internet standard touted as the successor to today's WiFi and 3G systems. Those with existing WiMax implementations include the Dominican Republic, Pakistan, South Africa, and Uganda.

The ability to share the fixed costs of a mobile phone and its monthly subscription costs, along with its portability, have facilitated the diffusion of this technology in developing countries. Although lack of competition and difficulties innovative entrepreneurs encountered in getting licenses slowed the initial diffusion of mobile phone technology, much has changed in recent years (Sullivan 2007). Mobile phone ownership rates in developing countries—even in the poorest countries—are rising rapidly, having almost doubled in low-income countries between 2000 and 2004. Indeed, new subscribers are signing up at such a fast pace that the data in table 2.7 are already broadly out of date.

Because the market is evolving so rapidly, with new applications for mobile phone technology being developed on a regular basis, evaluating its overall impact is difficult. Penetration rates in Europe and Central Asia and Latin America and the Caribbean are already high, rivaling those observed in high-income countries less than 10 years ago. Penetration rates in East Asia and the Pacific are somewhat lower on average; however, looking at only the middle-income countries in the region and excluding small island economies, the average penetration rate in East Asia and the Pacific is higher than in Latin America and the Caribbean. Penetration rates in low-income countries are much lower, on average, although some countries have reached levels comparable to those in middle-income countries. As of 2005, six Sub-Saharan African countries (Botswana, Gabon, Mauritius, the Seychelles, Sierra Leone, and South Africa) had mobile phone penetration rates above 30 percent. Although penetration rates in South Asia are also low, the large populations of these countries and the pace at which firms are adding customers means that globally, a substantial proportion of new mobile phone subscribers comes from developing countries.[11]

The rapid penetration of mobile phone technology reflects in part the process by which it has been financed. Unlike most fixed-wire telephone systems, railroads, and electrical grids, mobile phone technology has been introduced into most developing countries by well-funded private operators working within a relatively competitive environment. As a result, the creation of the necessary infrastructure for these systems has not been held back by the government financing and bureaucratic constraints that slowed the diffusion of older technologies. Moreover, microfinance techniques have facilitated expansion of the demand side of the business (Sullivan 2007).

The technological and economic implications of the rising penetration of mobile phones are only now being assessed. In poor, rural areas, where the transportation of goods and people is heavily constrained by poor infrastructure, the introduction of cheap, personal communications may be of great value both as a substitute for moving people and to assure that the movement of people or goods is worthwhile. In particular, the availability of relatively cheap and efficient communications has reduced informational asymmetries in a number of sectors, increasing producers' revenues and lowering consumers' costs (albeit at the expense of middlemen). In addition, this technology is increasingly being used to enable a degree of arm's-length financial intermediation that many argue is critical to development, but that has largely been unavailable in the past because of a lack of infrastructure (box 2.8).

The diffusion of new technologies has encouraged rapid growth in business services

The Internet, greater availability of computers, and faster communications have combined to greatly expand the potential for developing countries to supply services from a distance in a process called offshoring. Initially offshoring services were concentrated on lower-end software services and business

Box 2.8 Innovative use of communications technology is improving financial access for the poor

The poor confront considerable challenges in gaining access to well-functioning savings and payments services. Financial institutions do not exist in many rural areas, and those that do often impose high minimum balance requirements (reflecting high unit transaction costs for small accounts) that are well beyond the reach of poorer households. However, the adaptation of technology has allowed some innovative financial institutions in Sub-Saharan Africa to extend financial outreach to the poor.

For example, the Equity Bank in Kenya has outfitted a series of vans with laptops and telecommunications facilities to act as mobile banking units. It has also designed flexible savings mechanisms with emergency loan facilities. Teba Bank of South Africa has developed a smart card that uses existing mobile phone technology to provide low-cost, electronic banking services (savings and payments) for low-income customers. The program was originally developed to handle wage payments for migrant workers. The value of the cards can be topped up or the cards can be used to make purchases at any of the simple wireless terminals that have been placed in shops frequented by low-income clients. Remote Transaction Systems in Uganda is introducing a similar, but more sophisticated scheme. A system developed by Celpay allows clients in the Democratic Republic of Congo and Zambia to use their mobile phones to pay bills. The client establishes an account with Celpay and can then make purchases by texting a request to Celpay, which will transfer money to the merchant's account. Security is provided by the use of a personal identification number, which is needed to complete the transaction.

In a series of surveys of banking services in three middle-income and four low-income countries, Bankable Frontier Associates (2007) found that even though only 1.5 percent of the adult population in South Africa was using mobile phone banking, the potential for the service was large. Between 7 and 41 percent of the unbanked population of the countries surveyed (Botswana, Kenya, Namibia, South Africa, Tanzania, Uganda, and Zambia) has access (including shared access) to a mobile phone, and these penetration rates are rising.

Source: Bankable Frontier Associates 2007; World Bank 2007c.

processes as well as call centers. More recently, offshoring has moved into such areas as investment and financial services, human resources, health services, retail functions, logistics, and customer support functions (World Bank 2005). In addition to increasing demand for labor and boosting export revenues, offshoring of services to developing countries can improve their incentives to provide education and training, help improve the quality of services provided domestically, encourage technology and knowledge transfers, and minimize (compared with manufacturing) the environmental consequences of economic growth. By one account, the most attractive locations for offshoring global services (based on costs, the availability of workers with appropriate skills, and the overall business environment) include Brazil, Chile, China, the Czech Republic, India, Malaysia, the Philippines, and Thailand (A. T. Kearney 2007). As the complexity of services offshored increases, geographic proximity to major markets has become more important and has provided greater opportunities, for example, for the Czech Republic to supply Western Europe and for Mexico to supply Canada and the United States. The advantages of fluency in English and French, along with shared time zones, have increased the potential for African countries to supply services to the European market.[12]

While India has dominated the outsourcing market, rapid expansion of the business may be running into capacity constraints as the pool of unemployed and underemployed skilled workers dries up and wages are bid up.[13] Eventually, rising labor costs may partly erode the advantage of the current major offshore centers, providing greater room for competition from poorer countries. A recent survey found that the relative cost advantage of the leading offshore destinations fell in 2006 (A. T. Kearney 2007). However, partly because of learning by doing, these countries' scores along other dimensions, including people skills and the business environment, have increased. As a result, they have been able to move up the value added ladder by increasing the sophistication of the services they deliver even as their costs rise. This development underlines a major message for policy makers and businesses in developing countries: improving the skills of the labor force by devoting more resources to education and training, along with improving the overall climate for investment, is essential for competing in technologically sophisticated markets.

Logistics represent an important process technology

As noted earlier, the spread of modern communications technology and the diffusion of computers, coupled with quality improvements in transportation services, have combined to greatly improve the rapid and efficient delivery of goods and services, enabling just-in-time inventory processing and more efficient supply chain management (this subsection is based on Arvis and others 2007). The World Bank's logistics performance index provides an overall evaluation of the perceived sophistication with which countries are able to deliver goods and services (figure 2.6). It contains several subindexes that measure services critical to logistics, including customs, infrastructure, ability to track shipments, and business processes (competence) along with the timeliness and cost of deliveries of domestic logistics companies (table 2.9).

The overall quality of logistics services is clearly correlated with income. The top performers are high-income countries (Singapore, with an index of 4.19, ranks number 1), while the worst performers are the poorest countries that are landlocked or that suffer from severe governance problems or conflict (Afghanistan, with an index of 1.21, ranks last). On average, low-income countries score significantly lower than middle-income countries.

Nevertheless, index levels show considerable dispersion among countries with similar income levels. Countries where trade has played a significant role in promoting growth (for example, Chile, China, India, Malaysia, South Africa, Thailand, and Vietnam) tend to score high relative to their income level.

Figure 2.6 Logistics performance in the world (score on logistics performance index, 2005)

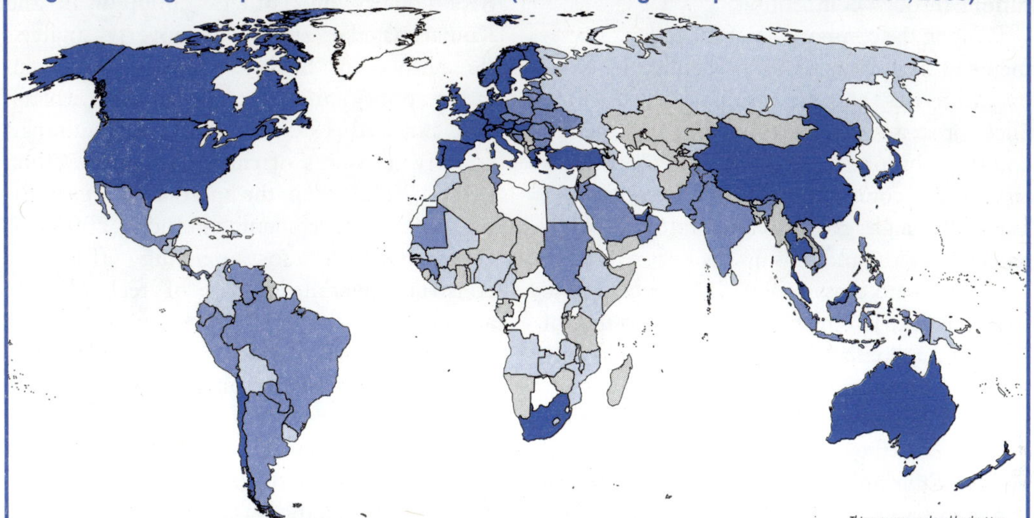

Source: Arvis and others 2007.

Note: The maximum score attainable is 5; the minimum is 1.

Vietnam, a low-income country, ranks 53rd among 150 countries, or slightly above the average for upper-middle-income countries. In contrast, countries where growth has been generated by oil and mineral assets, for example, Algeria, Bahrain, and Saudi Arabia, score low relative to income. The absence of a strong manufacturing sector in these latter countries tends to reduce the political impetus for the reforms that would improve logistics. Ultimately, countries that achieve high scores on the logistics performance index are those that have vigorously pursued reforms to improve the effectiveness of public sector institutions and to

Table 2.9 The quality of logistics services in 2005 varies by income

(score on logistics performance index)

	Overall	Customs	Infrastructure	International shipments	Logistics competence	Tracking and tracing	Domestic logistics costs	Timeliness
Regions					*(Index)*			
East Asia and the Pacific	2.58	2.41	2.37	2.64	2.54	2.53	3.04	3.01
Europe and Central Asia	2.59	2.39	2.39	2.61	2.53	2.55	2.97	3.04
Latin America and the Caribbean	2.57	2.38	2.38	2.55	2.52	2.58	2.97	3.02
Middle East and North Africa	2.42	2.24	2.27	2.44	2.33	2.35	2.95	2.88
Sub-Saharan Africa	2.35	2.21	2.11	2.36	2.33	2.31	2.98	2.77
South Asia	2.30	2.06	2.07	2.28	2.32	2.32	3.12	2.73
Income groups								
High-income countries	3.67	3.45	3.66	3.52	3.64	3.71	2.58	4.05
Upper-middle-income countries	2.85	2.64	2.70	2.84	2.80	2.83	2.94	3.31
Lower-middle-income countries	2.47	2.31	2.27	2.48	2.40	2.45	3.01	2.93
Low-income countries	2.29	2.12	2.06	2.32	2.29	2.25	2.99	2.71

Source: Arvis and others 2007.

Note: The maximum score attainable is 5; the minimum is 1.

encourage the efficiency of private sector institutions through competition.[14]

Among the components of the index, assessments of the quality of infrastructure, the quality of services, and the ease of customs clearance processes are highly correlated across countries. In contrast, the cost of services varies less across countries (with the exception of markedly high road freight rates in Sub-Saharan Africa) and thus makes a more limited contribution to cross-country differences in the overall index. This highlights the importance of the speed and reliability of shipping in globally integrated production networks. Interestingly, the gap between the best and worst performers in relation to the overall assessment of the reliability of the supply chain is twice the average gap across various dimensions of supply chain performance. The reliability of the supply chain tends to be determined by its weakest link.

Evaluating overall technological progress

The preceding sections of this chapter have discussed technological achievement in developing countries along three dimensions: scientific innovation and invention, the diffusion of old technologies, and the diffusion of new technologies. In this section we calculate summary indexes of technological achievement along each of these dimensions, as well as an overall index that combines these subindexes with additional information about the extent to which countries are exposed to technology through trade and FDI, issues that are discussed in more detail in chapter 3.

Summary indicators for scientific innovation and technology penetration

A statistical approach to summarizing technological progress

In creating the summary indexes, a statistical technique, principal components analysis, is used to combine subindicators in a flexible manner.[15] This approach has been widely used in health economics (Gwatkin and others 2000a, 2000b, 2000c; McKenzie 2003; Montgomery and others 2000; Vyas and Kumaranayake 2006), in poverty analysis (Sricharoen and Buchenrieder 2005), in regulatory policy analysis (Nicoletti, Scarpetta, and Boylaud 1999), in constructing cross-country measures of capital controls (Chinn and Ito 2006) and in the analysis of e-readiness in India (Government of India 2006). It contrasts with most existing efforts to construct overall indexes of technological achievement, which tend to aggregate subindexes using arbitrary weights with a weak theoretical or empirical basis, by using the statistical properties of the underlying data to determine the weights used in calculating the summary and overall indexes. Principal components analysis is used to generate aggregate indexes at two points in time, the early 1990s and the early 2000s,[16] for scientific innovation and invention, the penetration of older technologies, and the penetration of newer technologies. These summary indexes are then combined with an index of the extent to which countries are exposed to foreign technologies (through trade and FDI), which is developed in chapter 3, to generate an aggregate index of technological achievement. Table 2.10 lists the indicators that are summarized in both the overall index and each of the summary subindexes. The technical annex to this chapter explains the steps taken to calculate these weights in more detail.

The relationship between technological achievement and income varies depending on the dimension observed

Figure 2.7 reports the distribution of the summary subindex for each of the three dimensions of technological achievement discussed in this chapter (the summary index of the extent of exposure to foreign technologies is presented in chapter 3). A quick glance reinforces the earlier conclusion that, by and large, developing countries are not participating in scientific innovation at the technological frontier. Indeed, only a handful of countries, eight of which are former

Table 2.10 Indicators included in summary indexes of technological achievement

Indicator	Measure	Source
Scientific innovation and invention		
Scientific and technical journal articles	population	World Development Indicators
Patents granted by the U.S. Patent and Trademark Office	population	Lederman and Saenz 2005
Patents granted by the European Patent Office	population	Lederman and Saenz 2005
Penetration of older technologies		
Group A		
Electrical power consumption	kilowatt-hours/capita	World Development Indicators
International outgoing telephone traffic	minutes	World Development Indicators
Air transport, registered carrier departures worldwide	% of GDP	World Development Indicators
Agricultural machinery: tractors	per 100 hectares of arable land	World Development Indicators
Group B		
Main lines	per 100 inhabitants	World Development Indicators
Exports of manufactures	% of merchandise exports	World Development Indicators
Medium-tech exports	% of merchandise exports	CEPII BACI database
Penetration of recent technologies		
Internet users	per 1,000 people	World Development Indicators
Personal computers	per 1,000 people	World Development Indicators
Cellular subscribers	per 100 inhabitants	World Development Indicators
Percentage of digital mainlines		World Development Indicators
High-tech exports	% of total exports	CEPII BACI database
Exposure to external technology		
FDI net inflows	% of GDP	World Development Indicators
Royalties and license fee payments	% of GDP	World Development Indicators
Imports of high-tech goods	% of GDP	CEPII BACI database
Imports of capital goods	% of GDP	CEPII BACI database
Imports of intermediary goods	% of GDP	CEPII BACI database

Source: World Bank.
Note: BACI = Banque analytique de commerce internationale, CEPII = Centre d'Etudes Prospectives et d'Informations Internationales, EPO = European Patent Office, FDI = foreign direct investment, GDP = gross domestic product, USPTO = United States Patent and Trademark Office.

Soviet bloc countries, have anything like the same level of at-the-frontier scientific activity as the high-income countries. While this may reflect an innate bias in the indicators used (number of journal citations and patent applications), the results are consistent with the view that most technical progress in developing countries occurs through the adaptation and adoption of new-to-the-market or new-to-the-firm technologies rather than through the creation of new-to-the-world technologies. Moreover, notwithstanding that some firms—and even some cities—in developing countries do participate actively at the technological frontier, when viewed from the national level, not even the most advanced developing countries participate at levels comparable to those prevalent in high-income countries.

The distribution of technological achievement across the other indicators (diffusion of old innovations and of new innovations) is also skewed toward high-income countries, but much less so. Thus the intensity with which upper-middle-income countries exploit both older and newer technologies is between 50 and 60 percent of the level in high-income countries. This ratio is between 30 and 40 percent for lower-middle-income countries and is about 23 percent for low-income countries (table 2.11). However, the dispersion of the summary indicator of the penetration of older technologies within income groups is very wide. Many low-income countries report higher utilization rates for older technologies than do many upper-middle income countries. This report suggests that other factors—such as

Figure 2.7 Distribution of technological achievement by dimension

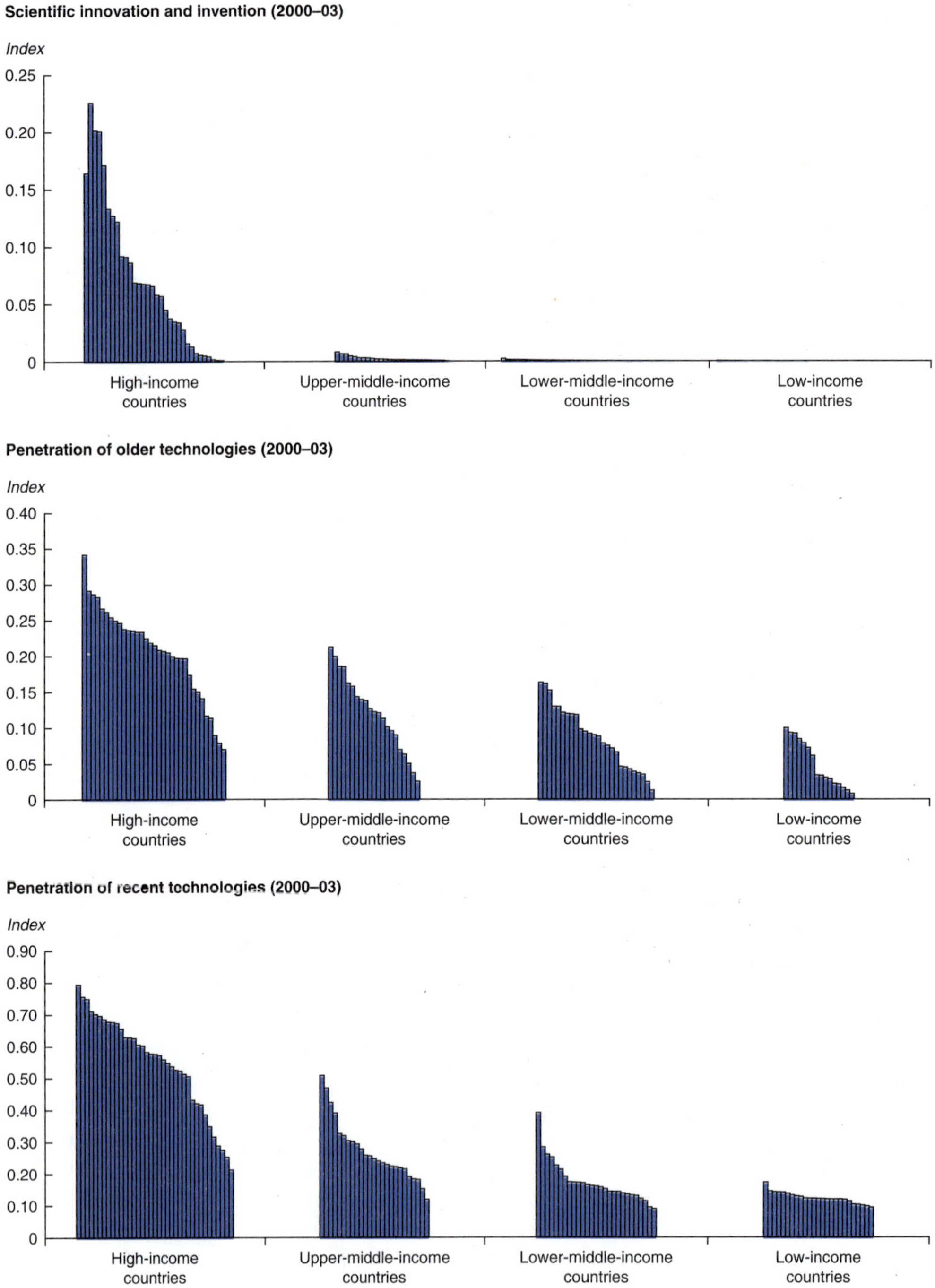

Source: World Bank.

Table 2.11 Technological achievement in developing countries relative to that in high-income countries

(percent of level in high-income countries)

	Scientific innovation and invention	Penetration of older technologies	Penetration of recent technologies
High-income countries	100.0	100.0	100.0
Upper-middle-income countries	3.3	58.4	49.6
Lower-middle-income countries	0.6	41.6	31.8
Low-income countries	0.1	23.7	22.7

Source: World Bank.

Table 2.12 Increase in technological achievement in developing countries relative to that in high-income countries

(index, percent increase in high-income countries = 100)

	Scientific innovation and invention	Penetration of older technologies	Penetration of recent technologies
High-income countries	100.0	100.0	100.0
Upper-middle-income countries	191.6	220.8	162.3
Lower-middle-income countries	157.1	251.8	145.8
Low-income countries	63.7	480.4	411.3

Source: World Bank.

history, effectiveness with which governments have delivered some public sector technological services, and past turmoil—may have had a greater influence than income in explaining the integration of these technologies into their economies.[17] In contrast, the diffusion of recent technologies is more correlated with income and shows both much less variation and less overlap across income groups. These results are consistent with the view that nonfinancial impediments to technological diffusion have constrained the diffusion of more recent technologies by less than they have for older ones.

In terms of scientific innovation and invention, middle-income countries have been catching up, at least in relative terms, but as already noted, the gap between them and high-income countries remains large. In addition, the gap between most low-income countries and the technological frontier has widened further both in relative and in absolute terms.

The story on the diffusion of technology is more encouraging. On average, in middle-income countries older technologies are diffusing at 2.5 times the rate as in high-income countries and more than four times as fast as in low-income countries (table 2.12). While this result appears to be robust for middle-income countries (figure 2.8), the variance is much higher among low-income countries. Several low-income countries have recorded substantial increases in technological progress, for example Benin, Ghana, and Togo record more than 100 percent improvements. In many others, however, progress has been slower than in high- and middle-income countries, implying that the technology gap for these countries is either stable or widening.

Not surprisingly, the most rapid increases in technological achievement recorded over the past decade or so are for more recent technologies, whose starting points are relatively low even in high-income countries (figure 2.8). Clear indications of catch-up are evident for newer technologies, with the penetration rates in upper-middle-income countries increasing 1.5 times as quickly as in high-income countries. The pace of increase among low-income countries was more than four times as rapid, but this reflects, to a significant degree, very large percentage improvements in a few countries that started off with very low levels. Notwithstanding these caveats, most developing countries are maintaining pace with high-income countries and many, especially among the upper-middle-income countries, are gaining ground.

New technologies are not as diffused as old technologies, but the gap between income groups is smaller

Overall, the penetration of recent technologies in the economic life of developing countries is less extensive than for older technologies, which is entirely understandable given the length of time that has passed since the older technologies were introduced. Nevertheless, the gap between countries at different income levels is not as striking as one might expect. Many upper-middle-income countries have achieved levels of technological achievement

Figure 2.8 Increase in summary technological achievement subindexes, 1990s–2000s

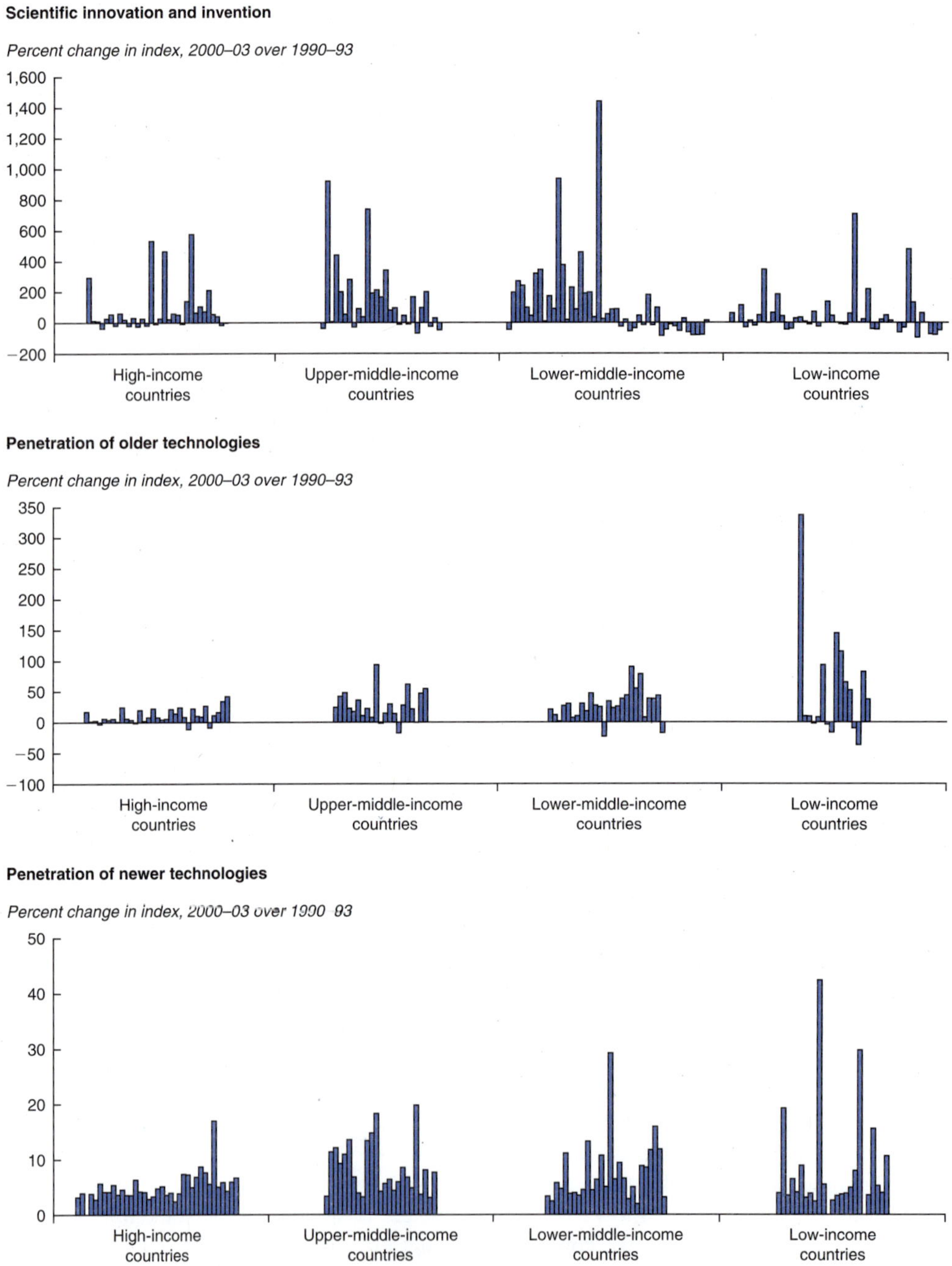

Source: World Bank.

Note: Countries are ranked according to the level of technological achievement in 2000.

similar to those in high-income countries, and substantial overlap is apparent between upper- and lower-middle-income countries and between lower-middle-income and low-income countries. Interestingly, the clear advantage countries in Europe and Central Asia enjoy along other dimensions of technological achievement is less marked here, with East Asian countries performing better than might be expected.

Overall technological achievement

To understand overall technological achievement, two alternative summary indexes were generated. The first combines the three summary subindicators of achievement discussed earlier, while the second includes an additional summary indicator that measures the extent to which economies are using imported technology in their production processes. The underlying components and their recent evolution are discussed in more detail in chapter 3 in the context of the channels by which external technology is transmitted to developing countries. These overall summary indexes are calculated using the same basic technique used to calculate the subindicators (see the technical annex to this chapter for details), with one difference: rather than using the raw data as inputs, the previously calculated summary indicators are used.

Figure 2.9 reports levels of technological achievement in 2000 according to these two summary indicators. The country coverage differs somewhat between the two indexes. To

Figure 2.9 Alternative summary indexes of technological achievement (2000s)

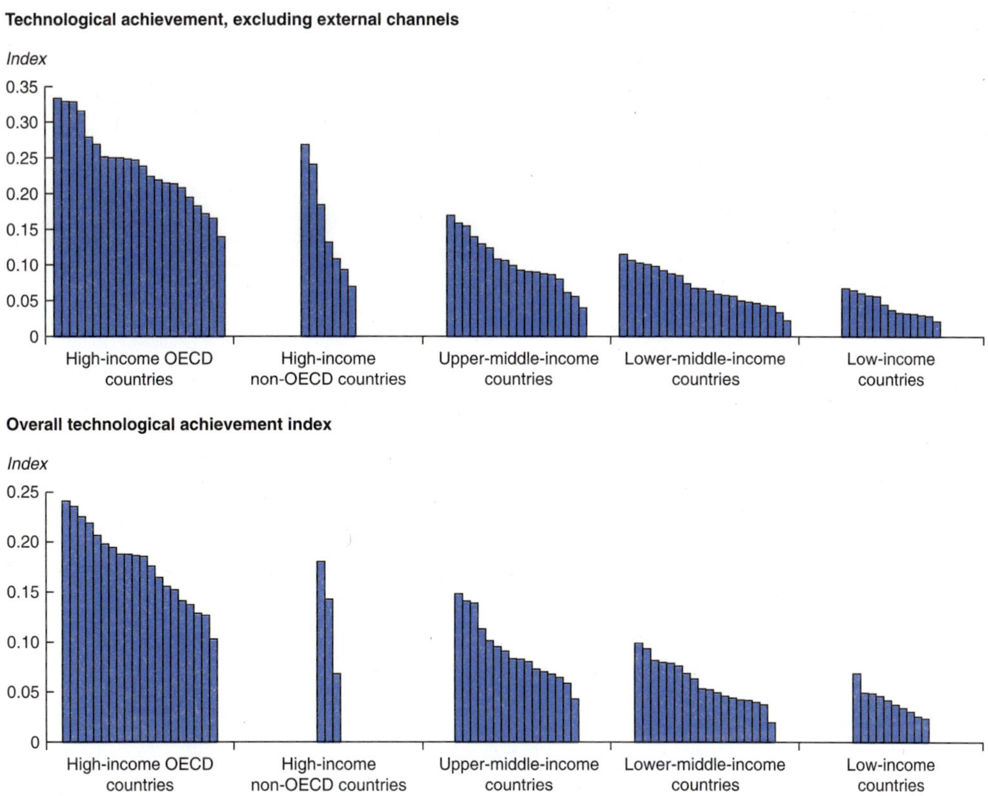

Source: World Bank.

be included, each country must have data for all variables, and as additional variables are added, some countries are lost from the sample. Reflecting this requirement, only 20 low-income countries are included in the first index and 16 in the second, down from 46 in the case of the subindicator with the best coverage.[18] Although these are relatively diverse groups of countries, they cannot be considered representative of all developing countries. Particular care should be taken in extrapolating results derived from these countries to all low-income countries.

Countries with similar income levels can have very different levels of technological achievement

While the influence of income on technological achievement is well established, considerable variation occurs within income groups (figure 2.10). The top performers within developing country income groups achieve a technology rating about equal to that of the median country in the next highest income group, and scores for countries at roughly the same income level show substantial dispersion. Overall, the relationship between technological achievement and income per capita is nonlinear, with the rise in technological achievement tending to flatten out for countries with per capita incomes between $10,000 and $25,000, a group that includes upper-middle-income countries and some of the less wealthy high-income countries such as Greece and Portugal. Countries in Latin America have weak technology scores given their income levels. Despite the perceived technological prowess of countries in East Asia, except for Malaysia, the highest-scoring country in the region, the developing countries in the region do not particularly distinguish themselves, in part because technological diffusion in these countries remains concentrated in a few urban centers and has not diffused widely elsewhere.

Focusing only on developing countries in the second panel of figure 2.10, the correlation with income remains, but the same

Figure 2.10 Technological achievement rises with income levels

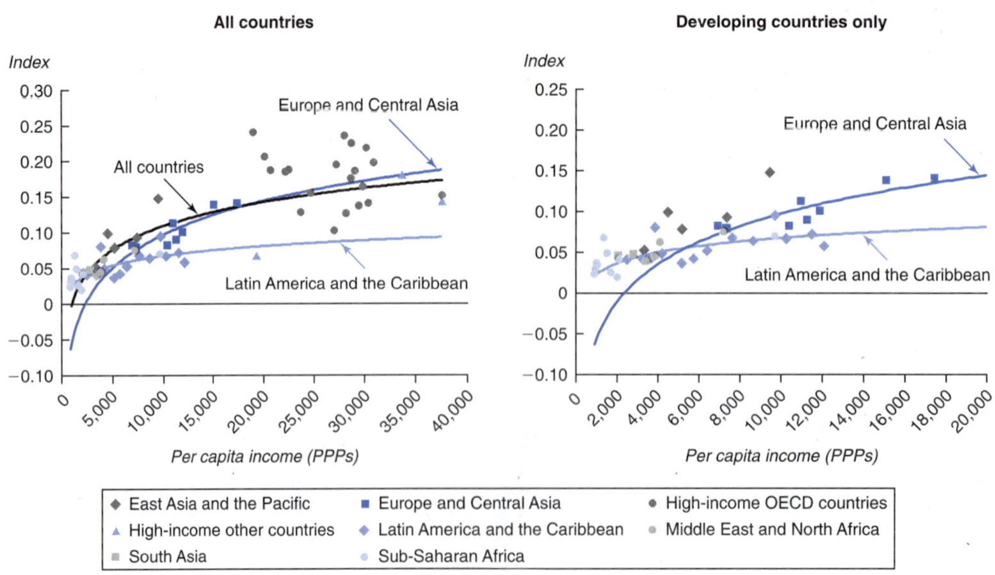

Source: World Bank.

tendency for a flattening in the relationship is still observable. For countries in Latin America and the Caribbean, the relationship between technological achievement and income per capita flattens out at even lower income levels, while for countries in Europe and Central Asia, the pattern follows more closely that of the overall sample, which includes high-income countries. Among developing countries (excluding those in the Europe and Central Asia region), technological achievement flattens out at an index level of around 0.15 for countries with per capita incomes around $5,500. While not conclusive, these results are consistent with a view that other factors, such as technological absorptive capacity (see chapter 3) limit the level of technological achievement that some developing countries can attain even as incomes continue to rise.

Technological convergence appears to be constrained by weak absorptive capacity in some regions

Figure 2.11 reports values for the two overall summary indexes at two points in time,

Figure 2.11 Comparison of levels of technological achievement, early 1990s and early 2000s

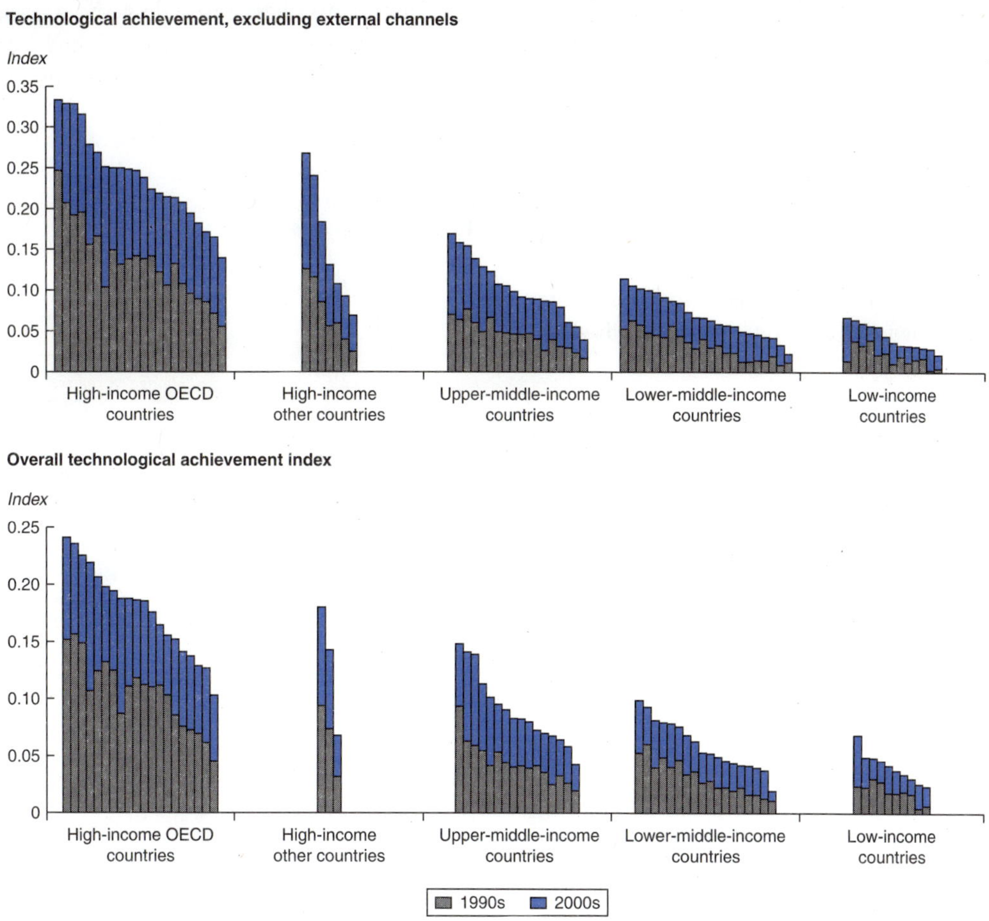

Source: World Bank.

roughly the early 1990s and the early 2000s. Both indexes offer a broadly consistent view of technological achievement. They both confirm that the absolute size of the increases in technological progress over the decade is larger among higher-income countries than lower-income countries, but that the relative improvement in developing countries has outpaced that in high-income countries, implying that catch-up is occurring.

The extent of apparent catch-up is strongest when considering the narrower definition of technological achievement that includes only scientific inputs and the penetration of old and new technologies. According to this measure, low-income countries for which data are available have shown the largest percentage improvement. If changes in the extent to which countries are making use of external technologies through imports and FDI are included, the extent of convergence declines for all developing country groups except the upper-middle-income countries. This finding reflects that high-income countries have also increased their imports of high-tech goods and have also benefited technologically from the operation of technologically sophisticated foreign-owned firms on their soil. However, trade may contribute more to technological improvement in the South than in the North (Lumenga-Neso, Olarreaga, and Schiff 2005).

Among upper-middle-income countries, catch-up is particularly strong in Chile, Hungary, and Poland, where the level of technological achievement rose by more than 125 percent during the 1990s. For most countries the pace of convergence was much slower. As indicated earlier, relatively weak data coverage across low-income countries makes generalizing about their progress difficult. Only 16 low-income countries (10 in the case of the summary index that includes imports of technology and FDI) have sufficient data for both the early 1990s and the early 2000s to permit an estimate of their rate of technological progress. Although generalizations to all low-income countries are not possible, some commonalities do emerge from this subsample, namely:

- The absolute increase in the overall index of technological achievement for low-income countries is about the same as for lower-middle-income countries (and thus the percentage increase in low-income countries is much greater), strongly suggesting a catch-up effect relative to the lower-middle-income countries (table 2.13).
- The percentage increase in achievement along the scientific innovation and invention dimension for all eight Sub-Saharan African countries for which data are available, along with Bangladesh and India, lies well below the average for middle-income countries. Only Vietnam approaches the performance of middle-income countries.
- The picture for the diffusion of old innovations is decidedly more mixed, with 5 of

Table 2.13 Overall technological progress in absolute and relative terms

	Technological achievement excluding external channels	Overall technological achievement
	(Percent change in the index)	
High-income	94	77
Upper-middle-income	127	109
Lower-middle-income	137	103
Low-income	227	161
Low-income (excluding Sudan)	160	124
	(Percent change relative to high-income countries)	
High-income	100	100
Upper-middle-income	135	141
Lower-middle-income	146	133
Low-income	241	208
Low-income (excluding Sudan)	170	160
	(Absolute change in the index)	
High-income	0.096	0.068
Upper-middle-income	0.057	0.046
Lower-middle-income	0.036	0.028
Low-income	0.024	0.022
Low-income (excluding Sudan)	0.024	0.022

Source: World Bank.

16 low-income countries showing stagnation or declines in the index between the early 1990s and early 2000s, while 6 recorded large percentage increases, comparable to those displayed by the more successful middle-income countries.

- Even for the diffusion of recent innovations, where successful examples of mobile phone and Internet diffusion have been much publicized, only 5 of 25 low-income countries (Guinea, Mongolia, Pakistan, Sudan, and Zimbabwe) achieved increases in the index that exceeded the middle-income average. However, low-income countries did increase penetration rates for recent innovations more quickly than high-income countries.[19] Given that new technologies sometimes substitute for older technologies, such as mobile phones for fixed-line telephones, transmission of information over the Internet for transmission involving travel and telephones, the previous finding suggests that the overall pace of convergence in low-income countries may be accelerating, particularly as data for 2005 and 2006 suggest continued high growth in the diffusion of mobile telecommunications and Internet technologies.[20]

Econometric evidence supports the view that the relationship between income and technological diffusion follows an S-curve: technological diffusion is slow at very low incomes, in part because of difficulties in affording new technologies, in part because low levels of human capital severely constrain technological progress. As incomes rise, technological diffusion increases rapidly, particularly in percentage terms, because of the low base level. At some level of income, however, the pace of technological diffusion slows. One explanation for this slowdown at higher income levels is the slow pace of improvement in an economy's ability to absorb new technologies (its technological adaptive capacity), as determined by the level of human capital, the governance structure, and the infrastructure (Howitt and Mayer-Foulkes 2005; Klenow and Rodriques-Clare 2004; Lederman and Saenz 2005). According to this view, technology in a country tends to converge toward a level consistent with the country's technological adaptive capacity. As a result, countries may experience relatively rapid technological progress for a period, but may subsequently stagnate at a given level unless they take steps to further raise their technological adaptive capacity. Chapter 3 develops the components of technological adaptive capacity and describes trends in developing countries.

Technological diffusion over the long term

So far, we have emphasized the technological performance of countries at different income levels over the recent past. Thanks to a new data set developed by Comin and Hobijn (2004), we can now analyze the process of technological diffusion over the longer term. This data set traces the extent of diffusion of some 100 technologies in 157 countries during the period 1750–2003.[21] For each technology, only countries for which published data exist are included, implicitly restricting the sample to countries (and technologies) where a significant degree of diffusion has occurred. The data analyzed here are further restricted to include only those country-technology pairs (a data set with one country and data for 7 technologies would have 7 country-technology pairs) where the intensity of use has reached at least 5 percent of the average level of the 10 countries with the highest recorded level of diffusion. Under this restriction, there are 1,181 country-technology pairs, 699 of which correspond to developing countries, heavily weighted to technologies discovered in the late 19th or early 20th centuries.[22]

Two important points emerge from this analysis. First, the diffusion of technology across the globe has accelerated over time.

Table 2.14 Successful diffusion has accelerated

	Period technology was initially discovered				
Technology	1750–1900	1900–50	1950–75	1975–2000	Number of countries
	(years following discovery until technology reached 80 percent of reporting countries)				
Transportation					
Shipping (steam)	83				21
Shipping (steam motor)	180				57
Rail (passenger)	126				93
Rail (freight)	124				99
Vehicles (private)	96				153
Vehicles (commercial)	63				123
Aviation (passenger)		60			109
Aviation (freight)		60			103
Communications					
Telegram	91				77
Telephone	99				156
Radio		69			154
Television		59			156
Cable television		50			98
PC			24		134
Internet use			23		151
Mobile phone				16	150
Manufacturing					
Spindle (ring)	111				50
Steel (open hearth furnace)	125				50
Electrification	78				155
Steel (electric arc furnace)		92			91
Synthetic textiles		36			75
Medical (OECD only)					
Cataract surgery	251				19
X-ray		93			27
Dialysis		33			29
Mammography			33		18
Liver transplant			28		29
Heart transplant			28		27
Computerized axial tomography (CAT) scan			18		29
Lithotriptor				15	26
Average (excluding medical)	106.9	60.9	23.5	16.0	
Average (including medical)	118.9	61.3	25.7	15.5	

Source: Calculations from CHAT database (Comin and Hobijn 2004).

Table 2.14 reports, for several old and new technologies, the number of years that elapsed between the discovery of the technology and the time it reached 80 percent of the countries currently reporting data for that technology.[23] The acceleration in the pace at which technologies spread across countries is particularly striking in the communications field, for which data are relatively good and country coverage is extensive. Thus telephone and telegram services were invented in the middle of the 19th century, and more than 90 years passed before those services reached 80 percent of the countries that currently report data

Table 2.15 The pace at which technology diffuses has picked up among successful adaptors

	1800–99		1900–50		1950–75		1975–2000	
	Threshold		Threshold		Threshold		Threshold	
	5%	25%	5%	25%	5%	25%	5%	25%
	(years from discovery until threshold reached)							
Regions								
East Asia and the Pacific			60	69	23	28	18	21
Europe and Central Asia	91	117	47	57	25	30	18	21
Latin America and the Caribbean	71	105	54	72	30	35	18	21
Middle East and North Africa	97	118	58	67	25	29	18	21
South Asia			52	62	—	—	—	—
Sub-Saharan Africa	85	109	56	69	—	—	18	21
Income groups								
High-income OECD countries	63	91	46	60	20	24	13	17
Other high-income countries	95	112	57	65	20	25	15	18
Upper-middle income countries	83	110	51	64	26	31	18	21
Lower-middle-income countries	86	114	57	69	—	—	20	22
Low-income countries			56	68	—	—		
World	76	102	52	65	22	26	16	19
Developing countries	84	111	54	67	26	31	18	21

Source: World Bank calculations using the CHAT database (Comin and Hobijn 2004).
Note: The sample is restricted to only those 567 country-technology pairings where the 25 percent threshold was reached and that were below 10 percent when they appeared in the database; — = no data.

for them. In contrast, mobile phones, computers, and cable television reached 80 percent of the countries that currently report data in less than 25 years. The same sort of acceleration can be observed for the dissemination of transportation, manufacturing, and medical technology.

Second, and consistent with the first point, technological diffusion appears to accelerate above a certain threshold. Table 2.15 considers only those country-technology pairs that have reached a level of penetration equal to 25 percent of the average level observed in the 10 countries where the technology is employed most intensively. Looking at the results for the world as a whole, the amount of time required to go from the 5 percent level to the 25 percent level (averaged across country-technology pairs) is much smaller than the time required to reach the 5 percent level. For example, in the first half of the 20th century, for a technology to reach the 5 percent threshold took, on average, 52 years, but only an additional 13 years to reach 25 percent. Moreover, the pace of acceleration has increased over time. For technologies introduced since 1975, a group dominated by electronics and information technologies, on average, it took 16 years from its invention for a technology to reach the 5 percent threshold in a given country, but only another 3 years to reach the 25 percent threshold. Although the pace of diffusion was somewhat slower in developing countries than in high-income countries, it too follows the same pattern. Because table 2.15 excludes country-technology pairs where the 5 percent threshold has been reached, but not the 25 percent threshold, the recorded diffusion times are probably lower-bound estimates.[24] This pattern is consistent with the existence of significant economies of scale and barriers to entry among these technologies, such that once the barriers are overcome and the technology is in place, scaling up occurs relatively quickly.

While diffusion has occurred relatively rapidly among successful diffusers, successful

Table 2.16 Slow diffusion means that many developing countries never reach the 25 or 50 percent threshold

	1800s			1900–50			1950–75			1975–2000		
	Threshold			Threshold			Threshold			Threshold		
	5%	25%	50%	5%	25%	50%	5%	25%	50%	5%	25%	50%
	(number of country-technology pairs that have reached threshold)											
Regions												
East Asia and the Pacific	18	0	0	38	9	3	7	2	1	6	2	0
Europe and Central Asia	56	19	6	47	23	6	40	18	3	23	13	6
Latin America and the Caribbean	80	11	1	95	34	8	31	3	0	19	4	0
Middle East and North Africa	28	4	1	44	16	6	9	1	0	6	2	0
South Asia	7	0	0	11	3	3	0	0	0	1	0	0
Sub-Saharan Africa	27	4	0	83	21	8	11	0	0	12	3	0
Income groups												
High-income OECD countries	150	114	75	134	93	55	96	87	75	28	26	23
Other high-income countries	25	16	7	28	23	14	14	10	8	7	6	6
Upper-middle-income countries	90	30	6	112	53	16	61	24	4	29	19	6
Lower-middle-income countries	109	8	2	130	38	12	33	0	0	33	5	0
Low-income countries	17	0	0	76	15	6	4	0	0	5	0	0
Total number of country-technology pairs												
World	391	168	90	480	222	103	208	121	87	102	56	35
Developing countries	216	38	8	318	106	34	98	24	4	67	24	6

Source: World Bank calculations using the CHAT database (Comin and Hobijn 2004).
Note: Sample restricted to only those 1951 country-technology pairings that were below 10 percent when they appeared in the database.

diffusion is the exception rather than the rule. For example, of 102 country-technology pairings first recorded in 1975–2000, only 56 (55 percent) have reached the 25 percent threshold and only about 35 (34 percent) have reached the 50 percent threshold (table 2.16). For developing countries, the pace (and extent) of diffusion is significantly slower (lower) than in high-income countries, with only 24 (36 percent) developing countries having reached the 25 percent threshold and only 6 (9 percent) having reached the 50 percent threshold. This slower diffusion is true even for extremely old technologies, a result consistent with the idea that affordability and competency issues are binding constraints on the further diffusion of technologies in these countries. This result is broadly consistent with the observation that for some groups of countries, overall technological achievement appears to stop increasing after a given level is reached, and many developing countries may thus face severe barriers to achieving accelerated technological progress.

Slow diffusion within countries reflects a nonlinear process

As noted earlier, the surprisingly low level of overall technological achievement in countries such as China and India contrasts with popular perceptions, which are based on the relative technological sophistication of some of the two countries' major cities and trading centers. However, the same kind of technological diversity observed across countries is visible within countries as well (see box 2.9 for the case of India). For example, although one might have expected India to have scored substantially better than many Sub-Saharan African countries in overall technological diffusion, in fact, it does not. Several technologically advanced cities in India notwithstanding, technologies have not penetrated deeply in many parts of the Indian countryside. Here the challenge is to put in place a basic infrastructure in the countryside that can support the kind of sophisticated technologies that the elites in the country are capable of supporting. As one observer put it, an energy technology revolution must precede

Box 2.9 The technological divide within India

Large segments of the Indian economy are technology sophisticated. Its high-tech industries are important global players, its premier education and R&D institutions are recognized internationally. Along with China, it has the largest pool of skilled manpower, including those with degrees in engineering and other technical disciplines. Moreover, India has become one of the world's largest markets for telecommunications technology, is a leader among developing countries in exports of software and information technology-enabled services, and has demonstrated its potential to be a major player in biotechnology-pharmaceuticals and the automobile and engineering sectors, with Bangalore having emerged as a major international center for technological production and innovation.

Nevertheless, on a per capita basis, India continues to lag behind middle-income countries in the rate of technological diffusion, R&D expenditures, attainment levels of basic and higher education, availability and quality of logistics services, and size of revenues and employment in software and other high-tech industries. In addition, India does not score substantially better than many Sub-Saharan African countries in terms of the overall penetration of technologies.

The juxtaposition of India's increasing technological prowess and relatively poor access to technology in per capita terms largely reflects the limited penetration of technology in rural areas, which account for more than 70 percent of the population, but less than 30 percent of GDP. For example, in June 2007 tele-density—the number of subscribers (wired and wireless combined) per 100 individuals—was 52.3 percent for urban dwellers compared with 6.5 for rural inhabitants (see the box figure). Although the gap remains large (especially in terms of quality and reliability), and indeed, has widened, a surge in rural mobile phone access means that by mid-2007, tele-density in rural India was equal to the level recorded for urban areas in 1998. Older technologies, such as radio, television, bicycles, and motorized two-wheelers, tend to be more evenly diffused than newer ones, such as mobile phones, computers, and the Internet, given the longer time since the former were introduced.

The digital divide between rural and urban areas promises to narrow over the long term, particularly in high-income states and near major cities. However, in some states, in the more remote rural areas, and among tribal and other linguistic groups that lag behind in economic development, the gap may well increase over time.

Source: Mitra 2007.

Urban and rural teledensity (fixed and mobile), India, 1998–2007

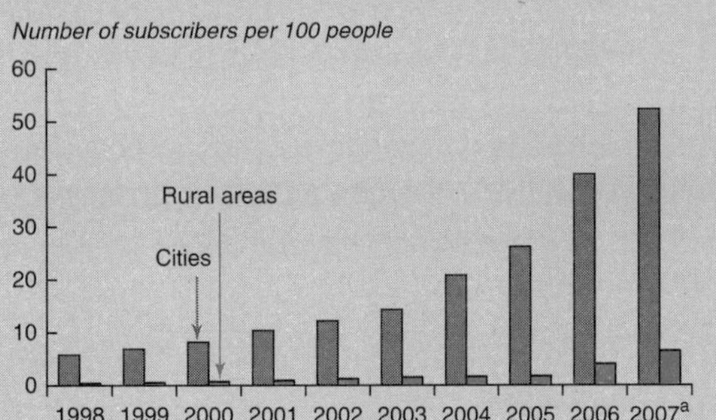

Source: Telecommunications and Regulatory Authority of India.
a. Estimated.

any information technology revolution (Friedman 2007). The rise in China's index of diffusion of new technologies is almost double that of India, in part because the more technologically backward regions in China have made progress in closing the gap with the more technologically advanced regions on the coast (Jefferson, Rawski, and Zhang 2007).

The technology employed by firms within sectors in individual countries also exhibits tremendous variation. In India, most firms, especially small ones, tend to use low levels of technology, and only a few operate near the national technological frontier. In most sectors, productivity at the national technological frontier is about five times the mean level for all firms (Dutz 2007). For small formal enterprises, average productivity is even lower: about one-sixth of the level at the technological frontier for each sector and only one-eighth that of top local performers. Smaller informal enterprises are likely to be even less productive.

The skewed distribution of enterprise productivity implies potentially huge productivity and output increases are possible, if already existing within-country knowledge were to diffuse from top performers to the rest of the economy. Assuming that domestic competencies were available (or created) to efficiently use the technologies employed by enterprises at the national frontier, Indian GDP could be 4.8 times higher if those technologies were successfully applied by their less productive rivals. Similarly, in Brazil, the productivity of innovative firms with more than 10 employees, which account for 26 percent of total sales, is, on average, 6.5 times higher than that of similarly sized firms classified as weakly innovative (which account for 11 percent of sales, but 38 per percent of employment).

Conclusion

All told, the evidence reviewed in this chapter suggests that for most developing countries technological progress is mainly a process of adaptation and adoption of technologies from abroad rather than the creation of new-to-the-world technologies. The pace of technology dissemination across countries has picked up considerably over the past 100 years, and most technologies are available at some level in most countries, but the extent to which technologies are available differs enormously. Many developing countries made progress in closing the technology gap with advanced countries during the 1990s. However, despite more rapid improvement in technological achievement among the poorest countries, enormous gaps in technological achievement remain. Even upper-middle-income countries have less than one-third of the level of TFP of high-income OECD countries, and low-income countries have only 7 percent. The gap in TFP levels between high-income countries and Latin America and the Caribbean, the Middle East and North Africa, and Sub-Saharan Africa has widened since 1990. Moreover, the gap between major centers and lesser cities and rural economies remains large even in the most successful countries.

At the same time, income is not the only determinant of technological progress. Although innovation at the technological frontier (as measured by patents and scientific journal articles) drops off quite sharply as income levels decline across countries, considerable overlap among income groups exists in the extent of diffusion of old technologies. Thus the most advanced middle-income countries demonstrate greater technological achievement in old technologies than the least sophisticated high-income countries, while the more advanced low-income countries rate higher than the lowest-ranking middle-income countries.

The technological gap between high-income and developing countries is more pronounced for new technologies; however, many developing countries are acquiring new technologies at a more rapid pace than older technologies. Given that some new technologies, such as mobile phones and to some extent computers, are substitutes for old technologies, the rapid diffusion of new technologies holds promise for a substantial, widespread advance in technological achievement. This progress likely reflects several factors: the reduction of regulatory constraints on economic activity that has occurred over the past 15 years in many developing countries; the enabling of private sector investors, who are free of local government budget constraints), to take the lead in implanting many of these technologies; the growing incomes in developing countries that have improved the affordability of new technologies; and the improvements in the technological absorptive capacity of developing countries and the increased exposure to international technology through trade flows, FDI, and a growing international diaspora. This last issue is the subject of chapter 3.

Technical Annex: Construction of the summary indexes

The summary indexes, the overall index of technological achievement, and the technological adaptive capacity index reported in chapter 3 were calculated by aggregating some

34 separate variables, with the weights used in the aggregation calculated by principal components analysis (see below). This approach distinguishes these indexes from most of those reported in the literature, which even though they are based on similar underlying base data, use arbitrary weighting schemes with limited theoretical or empirical bases (see Archibugi and Coco 2005 for a review).

A number of existing measures of technological achievement or technological progress emphasize inputs into technological advancement (numbers of scientists and engineers, R&D expenditure, or levels of R&D personnel), including, in some cases, even more indirect inputs, such as the general level of education of the population and governance factors that facilitate the absorption of technology (see, for instance, UNCTAD 2005). Other measures focus on outputs, that is, on indicators of technological performance, such as the shares of high-tech industries in exports and in manufacturing value added (UNIDO 2002). Still others focus more on the mechanisms by which technological progress is achieved (Sagasti 2003) or technological learning occurs (Soubattina 2006). A noncomprehensive list of prominent technology indicators includes the following:

- The index of innovation capability is published by the United Nations Conference on Trade and Development (UNCTAD 2005) and consists of an unweighted average of an index of human capital (calculated as a weighted average of tertiary and secondary school enrollment rates and the literacy rate) and a technological activity index (calculated as an unweighted average of three indicators: R&D personnel, U.S. patents granted, and scientific publications, all per million population).
- The index of competitive industrial performance is published by the United Nations Industrial Development Organization (UNIDO 2002) and is calculated as a simple average of four basic indicators: manufacturing value added per capita, manufactured exports per capita, share of medium- and high-tech activities in manufacturing value added, and share of medium- and high-tech products in manufactured exports;
- The technology achievement index is published by the United Nations Development Programme (UNDP 2001) and combines (a) the indicators of human skills (mean years of schooling in the population age 15 and older and enrollment ratio for tertiary-level science programs); (b) the diffusion of old innovations (electricity consumption per capita and telephones per capita) and of recent innovations (Internet hosts per capita and high- and medium-tech exports as a share of all exports); and (c) the creation of technology (patents granted to residents per capita and receipts of royalties and license fees from abroad). The index is constructed as simple averages of these indicators within subgroups and then across groups.
- The national innovative capacity index (Porter and Stern 2003) focuses on government- and firm-level policies associated with successful innovation. It is composed of four subindexes: proportion of scientists and engineers in the population, innovation policy, innovation linkages and what they call the cluster innovation environment. The overall index is calculated as an unweighted sum of the four subindexes, but the weights assigned to each indicator in the subindexes are determined by the coefficients obtained from a regression of the number of U.S. Patent and Trademark Office patents on the relevant indicators controlling for total population, the proportion of scientists and engineers employed, and the stock of international patents generated by the country between 1985 and 1994.

Estimating weights for variables using principal components

All the measures discussed above assign essentially arbitrary weights to the different indicators included in the indexes, or in the case of regression analysis, use weights derived from specific assumptions about functional forms and the data generating process. This report has followed a statistical approach, principal components analysis, to weighting variables. This approach is widely used in health economics (Gwatkin and others 2000a, 2000b, 2000c; McKenzie 2003; Montgomery and others 2000; Yvas and Kumaranayake 2006) and in poverty analysis (Sricharoen and Buchenrieder 2005). It has also been used in regulatory policy analysis (Nicoletti, Scarpetta, and Boylaud 1999) and in construction of cross country measures of capital controls (Chinn and Ito 2006). Most recently in the technology field, it has been used in a government of India study of e-readiness (Government of India 2006). Principal components analysis permits the calculation of weights for each indicator included in the overall index in an objective manner, with the weights being determined by the data—not by subjective judgment.

Principal components analysis is a statistical technique for reducing the dimensionality of data, thereby summarizing the informational content in a large set of data by calculating orthogonal linear combinations of the original data series. Essentially, it is a procedure that helps to reduce the number of variables in the analysis by calculating combinations of the underlying series that contain most of the information in the larger data set. It involves an examination of the correlation matrix for the variables and the extraction of the principal components of the data obtained from the eigenvectors of the correlation matrix whose eigenvalues are largest.

Intuitively, the procedure followed here is akin to an unobserved variable problem. It is assumed that there is some unobserved variable called *T* (technology), and that this variable is correlated with a number of other variables (***X***), such as R&D expenditures, share of high-tech goods in total manufacturing, and so on. These correlated variables are grouped together into a single data set and the eigenvalues of its correlation matrix are examined to identify a limited number of linear combinations (principal components) of the originating data that explain most of the variance in the original data set (at the limit, if all the eigenvalues were used, all the variance would be explained).

The first principal component is the linear combination of the underlying data that accounts for the largest amount of variability in the sample, the second principal component is the one that accounts for the next largest amount of variance, and so on successively until all the variance is explained. All components are orthogonal to (uncorrelated with) each other; therefore each can be interpreted as an underlying force (visible in varying degrees in each original variable). By selecting the n eigenvectors that explain a large share of the total variance, the overall dimensionality of the data set can be reduced to n.

It is assumed that the main correlate in the underlying data reflects some form of technology and therefore that the principal components can be used as an index of technology. This is essentially the same process as taking a simple average of several indicators, but with the attached weights being determined by the data rather than being imposed by the researcher.

As a large set of indicators are used that reflects a wide array of country characteristics, more than one principal component is required to adequately capture the information in the overall data set. One approach would be to calculate each of these purely data-driven, but necessarily arbitrary, components and use them to calculate the overall index. An alternative approach that uses a multistage procedure and subdivides the data into groups that are economically or statistically highly correlated or both was adopted. A principal components analysis on these subgroups can be used to create a subindex for those variables, which can then be used in a second stage to calculate an overall summary index.

Two methodologies for determining the subgroups were employed. The first was based on an ex ante grouping of the indicators following an economic rationale, and the second consisted of an ex post grouping of indicators based on an analysis of the correlation matrix and a graphical analysis of component loadings to identify groups of indicators that are highly correlated with each other. Because the overall technological achievement indexes obtained by these two methodologies are very similar, with correlation coefficients of 0.99, the remainder of the discussion is limited to the results obtained from the ex ante grouping given its more straightforward economic interpretation.

Data preparation

To maximize the economic comparability of the underlying cross-county data, all data were scaled, that is, expressed as a percentage of population, a percentage of GDP, a percentage of exports or imports, or a percentage of arable land, as relevant. So researchers could minimize the influence of outliers and one-off events, the scaled data were averaged over two time periods for each country: 1990–93 and 2000–03.[25] All data were converted into an index bound between 0 and 1 by subtracting from each variable the minimum observed value in the sample (across countries and time periods) and dividing by the difference between the maximum value in the sample and the minimum value.[26] Hence the value for indicator j for country i and time t is given by

$$x_{ijt} = (X_{ijt} - Min\ X_j)\ (Max\ X_j - Min\ X_j)$$

Applying principal components analysis to technology

For the purposes of this study, 34 variables were identified that bore an ex ante relationship with technology and for which adequate country coverage existed over the 1990–2006 period to support the calculation of two indexes, one for the early 1990s and the second for the early 2000s. The variables related to technological achievement and their sources are reported in table A2.1 and those related to technological absorptive capacity are reported in table A2.2.

Table A2.1 Indicators used to calculate the summary indexes and overall index related to technological achievement

Indicator	Source
Scientific innovation and invention	
Scientific and technical journal articles by population	World Development Indicators
Patents granted by the United States Patent and Trademark Office by population	Lederman and Saenz 2005
Patents granted by the European Patent Office by population	Lederman and Saenz 2005
Penetration of older technologies	
Electrical Power Consumption kilowatt-hours/capita	World Development Indicators
International outgoing telephone traffic percent of GDP per 1,000 people	World Development Indicators
Main lines per 100 inhabitants	World Development Indicators
Air transport, registered carrier departures worldwide percent of GDP per 1,000 people	World Development Indicators
Agricultural machinery: tractors per 100 hectares of arable land	World Development Indicators
Exports of manufactures percent of merchandise exports	World Development Indicators
Medium-tech exports percent of total exports	CEPII BACI database
Penetration of recent technologies	
Internet users per 1,000 people	World Development Indicators
Personal computers per 1,000 people	World Development Indicators
Cellular subscribers per 100 inhabitants	World Development Indicators
Percentage of digital mainlines	World Development Indicators
High-tech exports percent of total exports	CEPII BACI database
Exposure to external technology	
FDI net inflows percentage of GDP	World Development Indicators
Royalties and license fee payments percent of GDP	World Development Indicators
Imports of high-tech goods percent of GDP	CEPII BACI database
Imports of capital goods percent of GDP	CEPII BACI database
Imports of intermediary goods percent of GDP	CEPII BACI database

Source: World Bank.
Note: BACI = Banque analytique de commerce internationale, CEPII = Centre d'Etudes Prospectives et d'Informations Internationales, EPO = European Patent Office, FDI = foreign direct investment, GDP = gross domestic product, USPTO = United States Patent and Trademark Office.

Table A2.2 Indicators used to calculate the summary indexes and overall index of technological absorptive capacity

Macroeconomic environment	
General government balance as percentage of GDP	IMF/WEO and World Bank
Annual CPI inflation rate	Thomson Datastream and World Bank
Real exchange rate volatilty	J.P. Morgan, IMF and World Bank
Financial structure and intermediation	
Liquid liabilities percent of GDP	Beck, Demirgüç-Kunt, and Levine 2000
Private credit percent of GDP	Beck, Demirgüç-Kunt, and Levine 2000
Financial system deposits percent of GDP	Beck, Demirgüç-Kunt, and Levine 2000
Human capital	
Primary educational attainment percent of population aged 15 and over	Barro and Lee 2000
Secondary educational attainment percent of population aged 15 and over	Barro and Lee 2000
Tertiary educational attainment percent of population aged 15 and over	Barro and Lee 2000
Governance	
Voice and accountability	Kaufmann, Kraay, and Mastruzzi 2007
Political stability	Kaufmann, Kraay, and Mastruzzi 2007
Government effectiveness	Kaufmann, Kraay, and Mastruzzi 2007
Regulatory quality	Kaufmann, Kraay, and Mastruzzi 2007
Rule of law	Kaufmann, Kraay, and Mastruzzi 2007
Control of corruption	Kaufmann, Kraay, and Mastruzzi 2007

Source: World Bank.

An initial analysis of the two data sets revealed the existence of two principal components that explained 10 percent or more of the overall variance and three eigenvalues that exceeded 1—a widely used rule of thumb for determining the underlying dimensionality of a data set—in each of the data sets being used (tables A2.3 and A2.4). Bartlett's test for sphericity confirms that the basic indicators are correlated for both indexes, which confirms the meaningfulness of applying principal components analysis to this data. The Chi-square statistics are 1,520.88 (p-value of 0.00) and 1,572.10 (p-value of 0.00), respectively. Those statistics indicate a strong rejection of the null hypothesis that variables are not correlated.

Subsequently, as outlined earlier, principal components analysis was performed on ex ante economically motivated subgroups of the data for each summary index. In most cases, the first principal component from these subgroupings explained more than 60 percent of the total

Table A2.3 Share of total variance explained by principal components, technological achievement index

Technological achievement index (2000–03)

Component	Eigenvalues	Share of variance explained	Cumulative share of variance explained
1	9.91	0.52	0.52
2	3.59	0.19	0.71
3	1.49	0.08	0.79
4	0.92	0.05	0.84
5	0.85	0.04	0.88
⋮	⋮	⋮	⋮
19	0.00	0.00	1.00
Bartlett's test: Chi-sq (171)		1520.88 (p-value 0.00)	

Source: World Bank.

Table A2.4 Share of total variance explained by principal components, technological absorptive capacity index

Technological absorptive capacity index (2000–03)

Component	Eigenvalues	Share of variance explained	Cumulative share of variance explained
1	8.76	0.58	0.58
2	1.95	0.13	0.71
3	1.27	0.09	0.80
4	0.89	0.06	0.86
5	0.66	0.04	0.90
⋮	⋮	⋮	⋮
15	0.01	0.00	1.00
Bartlett's test: Chi-sq (105)		1572.09 (p-value 0.00)	

Source: World Bank.

variance for the subgroup,[27] suggesting that it adequately summarized the information in the overall grouping (table A2.5). Bartlett's test for sphericity rejects the null hypothesis of no correlation between variables in all cases at the 1 percent level.

Indicators of the penetration of old technologies constitute a notable exception. When all seven indicators were included, two eigenvalues exceeded unity. In addition, while the first principal component explained 55 percent of the variance, the second component

Table A2.5 Share of total variance explained by principal components for each sub-group of indicators

Technological achievement index (2000–03)

Component	Eigenvalues	Share of variance explained	Cumulative share of variance explained
Scientific invention and innovation			
1	1.49	0.75	0.75
2	0.51	0.25	1.00
Bartlett's test:	Chi-sq (1)	126.58 (p-value 0.00)	
Penetration of recent innovations			
1	3.28	0.66	0.66
2	0.92	0.18	0.84
3	0.57	0.11	0.95
4	0.19	0.04	0.99
5	0.05	0.01	1.00
Bartlett's test:	Chi-sq (10)	605.16 (p-value 0.00)	

Component	Eigenvalues	Share of variance explained	Cumulative share of variance explained
Penetration of old innovations			
1	1.46	0.73	0.73
2	0.54	0.27	1.00
Bartlett's test:	Chi-sq (1)	26.32 (p-value 0.00)	
Exposure to external technology			
1	3.43	0.69	0.69
2	0.80	0.16	0.85
3	0.54	0.11	0.96
4	0.22	0.04	1.00
5	0.01	0.00	1.00
Bartlett's test:	Chi-sq (10)	250.32 (p-value 0.00)	

Technological absorptive capacity index (2000–03)

Component	Eigenvalues	Share of variance explained	Cumulative share of variance explained
Human capital			
1	1.87	0.62	0.62
2	0.77	0.26	0.88
3	0.37	0.12	1.00
Bartlett's test:	Chi-sq (3)	47.16 (p-value 0.00)	
Governance			
1	5.30	0.88	0.88
2	0.33	0.05	0.93
3	0.23	0.04	0.97
4	0.09	0.02	0.99
5	0.03	0.01	1.00
6	0.02	0.00	1.00
Bartlett's test:	Chi-sq (15)	2077.61 (p-value 0.00)	

Component	Eigenvalues	Share of variance explained	Cumulative share of variance explained
Macroeconomic environment			
1	2.36	0.79	0.79
2	0.55	0.18	0.97
3	0.09	0.03	1.00
Bartlett's test:	Chi-sq (3)	25.53 (p-value 0.00)	
Financial structure and intermediation			
1	2.69	0.90	0.90
2	0.30	0.09	0.99
3	0.02	0.01	1.00
Bartlett's test:	Chi-sq (3)	633.96 (p-value 0.00)	

Source: World Bank.

accounted for a non-negligible 22 percent of the variance. The group was therefore further divided into two subgroups: industrialization and penetration of other old innovations. For each subgroup only the first principal component presented an eigenvalue greater than 1 and accounted for more than 70 percent of the variance in both instances. Subsequently, another stage of principal component analysis was performed to calculate an aggregate subindex for the penetration of old innovations, and the results are presented in the table A2.9 on the following page.[28] The overall conclusions obtained do not change substantially when the two groups are entered separately into the overall technological achievement index (rather than combined into one subindex).[29]

As expected, the principal components analysis assigned each subindex unequal weights in the overall index. Table A2.6 summarizes the weights assigned to each indicator series in the summary subindex of technological achievement for each of the economic variables. Table A2.7 reports the same data for the components used to calculate the overall index of technological absorptive capacity.

In a second stage, we conducted a principal components analysis on the subindexes. In the case of the technological achievement and the technological absorptive capacity indexes, the first principal component explained 79 percent and 65 percent, respectively, of the overall variance (table A2.8), suggesting that the first eigenvector of the correlation matrix provided a satisfactory summary of the information included in each of the subindexes.

Table A2.6 Factor loadings and variable weights for technological achievement subgroups (2000–03)

	Factor loadings	Variable weights (%)
Scientific innovation and development		
Patents	0.7071	68.42
Scientific and technical articles	0.7071	31.58
Penetration of old innovations		
Industrialization	0.7071	67.43
Main telephone lines per 100 inhabitants	0.5815	30.82
Exports of manufactures	0.5597	42.67
Exports of medium-tech goods	0.5904	26.51
Other old innovations	0.7071	32.57
Electric power	0.4067	32.66
International telephone traffic	0.5137	21.00
Air transport	0.5396	20.06
Agricultural machinery	0.5288	26.28
Penetration of recent innovations		
Internet users	0.5282	25.45
Personal computers	0.5214	24.52
Cellular subscribers	0.5060	28.25
Percentage of digital mainlines	0.1846	6.39
Exports of high-tech goods	0.3987	15.40
Exposure to external technology		
Net FDI inflows	0.4969	28.55
Royalties and license fee payments	0.4384	16.35
Imports of high-tech goods	0.4624	17.59
Imports of capital goods	0.4914	28.20
Imports of intermediary goods	0.3248	9.30

Source: World Bank.
Note: FDI = foreign direct investment.

Table A2.7 Factor loadings and variable weights for technological absorptive capacity subgroups (2000–03)

	Factor loadings	Variable weights (%)
Human capital		
Primary educational attainment	0.4648	24.92
Secondary educational attainment	0.6153	39.27
Tertiary educational attainment	0.6367	35.82
Governance		
Voice and accountability	0.3918	19.14
Political stability	0.3760	15.42
Government effectiveness	0.4224	17.98
Regulatory quality	0.4140	11.85
Rule of law	0.4250	18.39
Control of corruption	0.4179	17.22
Macroeconomic stability		
General government balance	0.4990	28.95
Annual consumer price index inflation rate	0.6100	34.40
Real exchange rate volatility	0.6156	36.66
Financial structure and intermediation		
Liquid liabilities	0.5910	30.79
Private credit	0.5424	38.58
Financial system deposits	0.5971	30.63

Source: World Bank.

Table A2.8 Share of total variance explained by main principal components of technological achievement and technological absorptive capacity using the sub-indexes (2000–03)

Component	Eigenvalues	Share of variance explained	Cumulative share of variance explained
Technological achievement			
1	3.17	0.79	0.79
2	0.60	0.15	0.94
3	0.14	0.04	0.98
4	0.09	0.02	1.00
Bartlett's test: Chi-sq (6)	332.49 (*p*-value 0.00)		
Technological absorptive capacity			
1	2.61	0.65	0.65
2	0.80	0.20	0.85
3	0.32	0.08	0.93
4	0.27	0.07	1.00
Bartlett's test: Chi-sq (6)	138.31 (*p*-value 0.00)		

Source: World Bank.

Table A2.9 reports the implicit weights attached to each subindex in the two summary indexes.

A similar process was undertaken, with similar results, for the data from the 1990s. In calculating the percentage changes in each subindex and in the overall index, the factor loadings from the 2000s estimation procedure were used to ensure comparability of the data sets.

Table A2.9 Factor loadings and variable weights obtained from second-stage principal components analysis (2000–03)

	Scientific innovation and invention	Penetration of old innovations	Penetration of recent innovations	Exposure to external technology
Technological achievement				
Factor loadings	0.5272	0.5404	0.4409	0.4855
Subindex weights (%)	21.74	23.99	34.79	19.48
	Human capital	Governance	Macroeconomic environment	Financial structure and intermediation
Technological absorptive capacity				
Factor loadings	0.5392	0.5579	0.3493	0.5254
Subindex weights (%)	25.29	36.98	10.66	27.06

Source: World Bank.

Notes

1. TFP simply measures all influences on GDP growth other than increases in capital and labor. Thus changes in TFP could reflect changes in the composition of output (for example, a shift from agriculture to manufacturing), changes in the quality of labor or capital not reflected in the data (for example, education levels), or any other variable that is an important determinant of growth but whose influence is not explicitly accounted for in growth equations.

2. See http://www.itto.or.jp/live/PageDisplayHandler?pageId=217&id=280.

3. See, for example, Haskel and Slaughter (2002) and Krugman (2000). The rise in the global supply of goods produced by unskilled and semiskilled labor, and the influx of low-skilled immigrants, are also cited as contributing to earnings inequality in high-income countries.

4. This is an important conclusion of *Global Economic Prospects 2007*. Although intercountry inequality (where each country is accorded equal weight) has worsened, weighting country observations by population shows an improvement in income distribution. Taking into account within-country inequality, global inequality has remained roughly constant since the late 1980s.

5. Anecdotal evidence indicates that access to mobile phones improved returns to producers at the

expense of middlemen for fishermen in Porto da Manga, Brazil, and Moree, Ghana, and for farmers in a wholesale market in Sri Lanka (de Silva and Zainudeen 2007). The advent of the Internet and automated teller machines had a similar effect in the United States, overcoming the anticompetitive effects of state banking regulation and strong lobbying in state legislatures.

6. The focus on patents and scientific publications reflects academic research on technology. Patents have the advantage of being more clearly associated with processes rather than products (by definition, a patent is not granted on a product, but rather on the method by which it is produced). The disadvantage is that patents exclude a number of important forms of innovation, notably software (until recently) and processes for managing multinational production and distribution networks.

7. The definition of a high-tech export used here includes products with high R&D intensity, such as aerospace-related items, computers, pharmaceuticals, scientific instruments, and electrical machinery. As such, it excludes a number of services such as software engineering that may, by their nature, be even more technologically intensive.

8. For example, the correlation coefficient of the share of high-tech exports in total foreign sales with adult literacy was 43 percent in 2005 and with expected years of schooling was 22 percent.

9. Regional and income group data in table 2.7 are weighted averages of individual countries, with the weights given by their populations. The simple averages cited in the text give equal weight to every country independent of the size of its population.

10. The core technology for the Internet can trace its history back to the early 1960s and a network developed by the U.S. Defense Department's Advanced Research Projects Agency. However, the Internet as it is understood by most people today—the World Wide Web and HTML web pages—was first introduced in the early 1990s, with the first web browser, Mosaic, being released in 1993.

11. According to the Cellular Operators Association of India, the country had more than 121 million subscribers in March 2007.

12. For example, South Africa is beginning to attract companies for business process outsourcing. One British executive (Ranger 2006) noted that his U.K. customers were more comfortable with the South African accent than with the Indian accent and cited the advantages of working at similar times as the parent company.

13. A 2005 report from Gartner Inc. stated that India had captured 80 to 90 percent of total offshore outsourcing revenue (Tucci 2005).

14. The scores in large countries may be biased, better reflecting the scores in coastal trading cities and less the score in the interior. Thus the Russian Federation's weak overall score in comparison with China's may be explained by the relative absence of large port cities close to major Russian manufacturing centers, whereas in China, port cities and manufacturing centers tend to be in close proximity.

15. Principal components analysis involves examining the eigenvectors of the correlation matrix of a set of related data and extracting from it a weighting scheme that describes as much of the information contained within the data set as possible using a minimum number of orthogonal linear combinations of the original data. By construction, a data set that consists of 100 series will have 100 of these eigenvectors that fully describe all the information in the data set. However, the first five of these eigenvectors (five different linear combinations of the initial 100 series) may describe 90 percent of the total variance. In such a case, principal components analysis would involve calculating an overall index based on these five subindexes. In a two- or three-stage procedure such as the one used here, the data are divided into subgroups either based on the ex ante characteristics of the subindexes or on the basis of statistical correlations. Then a separate principal components analysis is done on each of these subindexes, which are subsequently combined in a second or third round to determine the overall index.

16. To minimize the influences of outliers, the component indicators of the subindexes for each time period are calculated as the four-year average of values for the period 1990–93 and 2000–03. To maximize country coverage, missing data are gap-filled by using more recent or older data generally from within the analytical period. For the transition economies of the former Soviet bloc, data as recent as 1995 are used for the early 1990s data point in cases where data do not exist or are unreliable.

17. The relationship between income and technological achievement is complex. The level of income affects the ability to gain access to technology, while the level of technology helps to determine income levels (see the earlier section on "The role of technology in development").

18. Low-income countries included in the first index are Bangladesh, Benin, Côte d'Ivoire, Ethiopia, Ghana, India, Kenya, the Kyrgyz Republic, Mozambique, Nepal, Nigeria, Pakistan, Senegal, Sudan, Tanzania, Togo, Vietnam, the Republic of Yemen, Zambia, and Zimbabwe. The second index includes all of these except Nepal, Vietnam, the Republic of Yemen, and Zimbabwe.

19. The penetration of new technologies during 1990–2000 increased by 102 percent in high-income OECD countries, 256 percent in upper-middle-income

countries, 219 percent in lower-middle-income countries, and 123 percent in low-income countries.

20. For low-income countries, the number of Internet users per 1,000 people rose by 172 percent between 1999 and 2005, the number of secure Internet servers per 1 million people increased by almost 30 percent a year between 2004 to 2006, and the number of mobile phone subscribers per 1,000 people rose by 92 percent between 1995 and 2005 (World Bank 2007d).

21. Measurements of the extent of diffusion differ by technology, but generally involve available statistics on technology flows per country scaled by income or population, whichever is more appropriate. For example, the diffusion of electricity is measured by kilowatt hours consumed per person and the diffusion of railroads is measured by tonnage moved divided by gross national product.

22. Of the 699 country-technology pairs related to developing countries, 216 refer to a technology that was first recorded in the 19th century, 318 date from the first half of the 20th century, 98 come from the third quarter of the 20th century, and 67 from the final quarter of the 20th century.

23. The data set includes an estimate of the date of discovery for each technology.

24. That is, there are country-technology pairs, not considered in this analysis, that have reached the 5 percent level but are taking a long time to reach the 25 percent level.

25. When missing data issues occurred over this time period, the earliest available observation for a given indicator in the period from 1988–96 and 1998–2006 was used so as to expand country coverage. The budget balance indicators and the real exchange rate volatility indicators were averaged over the periods 1990–96 and 2000–06 to purge out cyclical effects. The real exchange rate volatility series is the yearly average of the absolute value of monthly change in the real effective exchange rate.

26. For this operation the authors used a combined data set including observations from both the 1990s and 2000s to ensure that data for each period had the same underlying scaling.

27. Frequently more than 70 percent of the variance was explained by the first principal component.

28. A data-driven grouping of indicators was also conducted and used to generate a two-step index similar to the one reported in the main text. As the indexes derived from this procedure did not differ materially from the one reported here, they are not reported.

29. Furthermore, results for the overall technological achievement index remain unchanged when the entire old innovations indicator group is included, that is, when no division into subgroups is made and the second principal component is ignored.

References

Acemoglu, Daron. 2002. "Technical Change, Inequality, and the Labor Market." *Journal of Economic Literature* 40: 7–72.

Alderman, Harold, John Hoddinott, and Bill H. Kinsey. 2006. "Long Term Consequences of Early Childhood Malnutrition." *Oxford Economic Papers* 58 (3): 450–74.

Arbache, Jorge Saba, Andy Dickerson, and Francis Green. 2004. "Trade Liberalization and Wages in Developing Countries." *Economic Journal* 114: F73–F96.

Archibugi, Daniele, and Alberto Coco. 2005. "Measuring Technological Capabilities at the Country Level: A Survey and a Menu for Choice." *Research Policy* 34: 175–94.

Arvis, Jean-François, Monica Alina Mustra, John Panzer, Lauri Ojala, and Tapia Naula. 2007. *Connecting to Compete: Trade Logistics in the Global Economy.* Washington, DC: World Bank.

Bailey, Martha J. 2006. "More Power to the Pill: The Impact of Contraceptive Freedom on Women's Labor Supply." *Quarterly Journal of Economics* 121 (1): 289–320.

Bankable Frontier Associates. 2007. "Financial Service Access and Usage in Southern and East Africa: What Do FINSCOPE™ Surveys Tell Us?" Bankable Frontier Associates. http://www.bankablefrontier.com. Accessed October 2007.

Behrman, Jere, and Mark Rosenzweig. 2004. "Returns to Birthweight." *Review of Economics and Statistics* 86 (2): 586–601.

Besant-Jones, John. 2006. "Reforming Power Markets in Developing Countries: What Have We Learned?" Energy and Mining Sector Board Discussion Paper 19. World Bank, Washington, DC.

Briceno-Garmendia, Cecilia, Antonio Estache, and Nemat Shafik. 2004. "Infrastructure Services in Developing Countries: Access, Quality, Costs and Policy Reform." Staff Working Paper 3468. World Bank, Washington, DC.

Chandra, Vandana. ed. 2006. *Technology, Adaptation and Exports: How Some Developing Countries Got It Right.* Washington, DC: World Bank.

Chandra, Vandana, and Shashi Kolavalli. 2006. "Technology, Adaptation and Exports: How Some Developing Countries Got It Right." In *Technology, Adaptation and Exports: How Some Developing Countries Got It Right*, ed. Vandana Chandra, 1–48. Washington, DC: World Bank.

Chinn, Menzie D., and Hiro Ito. 2006. "What Matters for Financial Development? Capital Controls, Institutions and Interactions." *Journal of Development Economics* 81 (1): 163–92.

Comin, Diego, and Bart Hobijn. 2004. "Cross-Country Technology Adoption: Making the Theories Face the Facts." *Journal of Monetary Economics* 51 (1): 39–83.

de Silva, Harsha, and Ayesha Zainudeen. 2007. "Teleuse on a Shoestring: Poverty Reduction through Telecom Cccess at the 'Bottom of the Pyramid'." Paper prepared for the Centre for Poverty Analysis Annual Symposium on Poverty Research in Sri Lanka, Colombo, December 6–7. http://www.lirneasia.net.

Dutz, Mark A., ed. 2007. *Unleashing India's Innovation: Toward Sustainable and Inclusive Growth.* Washington, DC.

Friedman, Thomas. 2007. "If IT Merged with ET." *International Herald Tribune*, October 31.

Glewwe, Paul, Hanan G. Jacoby, and Elizabeth M. King. 2001. "Early Childhood Nutrition and Academic Achievement: A Longitudinal Analysis." *Journal of Public Economics* 81 (3:) 345–68.

Government of India. 2006. *E-Readiness Assessment Report of States/Union Territories 2005.* New Delhi: Ministry of Communication and Information Technology.

Gwatkin, Davidson R., Shea Rustein, Kiersten Johnson, Eldaw Suliman, Adam Wagstaff, and Agbessi Amouzou. 2000a. *Socio-economic Differences in Brazil.* Washington, DC: World Bank. http://www.worldbank.org/poverty/health/data/index.htm#lcr.

______. 2000b. *Socio-economic Differences in Ethiopia. Health, Nutrition, and Population in Ethiopia.* Washington, DC: World Bank.http://worldbank.org/poverty/health/data/index.htm#lcr.

______. 2000c. *Socio-economic differences in Nigeria. Health, Nutrition, and Population in Nigeria.* Washington, DC: World Bank. http://worldbank.org/poverty/health/data/index.htm#lcr.

Hanushek, Eric A., and Ludger Woessmann. 2007. "The Role of Education Quality in Economic Growth." Working Paper 4122. World Bank, Washington, DC.

Haskel, Jonathan E., and Matthew J. Slaughter. 2002. "Does the Sector Bias of Skill-Biased Technical Change Explain Changing Skill Premia?" *European Economic Review* 46: 1757–83.

Howitt, Peter, and David Mayer-Foulkes. 2005. "R&D, Implementation, and Stagnation: A Schumpeterian Theory of Convergence Clubs." *Journal of Money, Credit, and Banking* 37 (1).

Jefferson, Gary H., Thomas G. Rawski, and Yifan Zhang. 2007. "Productivity Growth and Convergence Across China's Industrial Economy." Draft. Brandeis University, Waltham, Mass.

Kaufmann, Daniel, Frannie Leautier, and Massimo Mastruzzi. 2005. "Governance and the City: An Empirical Exploration into Global Determinants of Urban Performance." Policy Research Working Paper 3712. World Bank, Washington, DC.

Kearney, A. T. 2007. "Labor Cost Advantages of 'Offshore' Locations Decline in 2006." A. T. Kearney. http://www.atkearney.com. Accessed March 2007.

Klenow, Peter J., and Andrés Rodriguez-Clare. 2004. "Externalities and Growth." Working Papers Series 11009. National Bureau of Economic Research, Cambridge, MA. http://www.nber.org/papers/w11009.

Krugman, Paul. 2000. "Technology, Trade and Factor Prices." *Journal of International Economics* 50: 51–71.

Lederman, Daniel, and William F. Maloney, eds. 2007. *Natural Resources, Neither Curse nor Destiny.* Palo Alto, CA: Stanford University Press.

Lederman, Daniel, and Laura Saenz. 2005. "Innovation and Development Around the World, 1960–2000." Policy Research Working Paper 3774. World Bank, Washington, DC.

Lumenga-Neso, A., M. Olarreaga, and M. Schiff. 2005. "On 'Indirect' Trade-Related R&D Spillovers and Growth." *European Economic Review* 49 (7): 1785–98.

Maloney, William. 2006. "Missed Opportunities: Innovation and Resource-Based Growth in Latin America." Unpublished report. World Bank, Washington, DC.

Martin, W., and D. Mitra. 2001. "Productivity Growth and Convergence in Agriculture and Manufacturing." *Economic Development and Cultural Change* 49 (2): 403–23.

McKenzie, D. J. 2003 "Measure Inequality with Asset Indicators." Working Paper 042. Cambridge, MA: Harvard University, Center for International Development, Bureau for Research and Economic Analysis of Development.

Miller, Grant. 2005. "Contraception as Development? New Evidence from Family Planning in Colombia." Working Paper 11704. National Bureau of Economic Research, Cambridge, MA.

Mitra, Raja M. 2007. "India's Emergence as a Global R&D Center." Working Paper R2007:012, Swedish Institute for Growth Policy Studies, Stockholm.

Montgomery, M. R., K. Gragnolati, A. Burke, and E. Paredes. 2000. "Measuring Living Standards with Proxy Variables." *Demography* 37: 155–74.

Nicoletti, Giuseppe, Stefano Scarpetta, and Olivier Boylaud. 1999. "Summary Indicators of Product Market Regulation with an Extension to Employment Protection Legislation." Economics Department Working Papers 226. Organisation for Economic Co-operation and Development, Paris.

Poncet, Sandra. 2006. "The Long Term Growth Prospects of the World Economy: Horizon 2050." Working Paper 2006–16. Centre d'Etudes Prospectives et d'Informations Internationales.

Porter, M., and S. Stern. 2003. "Ranking National Innovative Capacity: Findings from the National Innovative Capacity Index." In *Global Competitiveness Report,* World Economic Forum, Geneva.

Ranger, Steve. 2006. "South Africa Touts Its Offshore Charms." http://www.silicon.com. Accessed December 12, 2006.

Sagasti, Francisco. 2003. *Knowledge and Innovation for Development: The Sisyphus Challenge for the 21st Century*. Cheltenham, U.K.: Edward Elgar.

Schultz, T. Paul. 2007. "Population Policies, Fertility, Women's Human Capital, and Child Quality." Discussion Paper 954. Yale Economic Growth Center, New Haven, CT.

Soubattina, Tatanya. 2006. "Generic Models of Technological Learning by Developing Countries." Draft. World Bank, Washington, DC.

Sricharoen, Thitiwan, and Gertrud Buchenrieder. 2005. *Principal Component Analysis of Poverty in Northern Thailand.* Paper presented at the Conference on International Agricultural Research for Development, Stuttgart-Hohenheim, Germany, October 11–13.

Stelling, Petra, and Arne Jensen. 2001. "Train Operators' Economies of Scale and Business Strategies." Working paper. Handelshogskolan, Gotteborg, Sweden.

Sullivan, Nicholas P. 2007. *You Can Hear Me Now: How Microloans and Cell Phones Are Connecting the World's Poor to the Global Economy.* San Francisco: Jossey-Bass.

Tucci, Linda. 2005. "Offshore Comparison Shopping: Best Buys Abroad." http://www.searchcio.com. Accessed September 28. 2005.

UNIDO (United Nations Industrial Development Organization). 2002. *Industrial Development Report 2002/2003: Competing through Innovation and Learning*. Vienna: UNIDO.

______. 2005. *Industrial Development Report 2005—Capability Building for Catching-Up: Historical, Empirical and Policy Dimensions.* Vienna: UNIDO.

UNCTAD (United Nations Conference on Trade and Development). 2005 *World Investment Report: Transnational Corporations and the Industrialization of R&D*. New York and Geneva: UNCTAD.

______. 2007. *The Least Developed Countries Report 2007: Knowledge, Technological Learning and Innovation for Development.* New York and Geneva, UNCTAD.

UNDP (United Nations Development Programme). 2001. *Human Development Report 2001: Making New Technologies Work for Human Development.* New York: Oxford University Press.

Vyas, Seema, and Lilani Kumaranayake. 2006. "Constructing Socio-economic Status Indices: How to Use Principal Components Analysis." *Health Policy and Planning* 21 (6): 459–68.

Watkins, Alfred and Anubha Verma. 2007. "Government of Rwanda-World Bank, Science, Technology and Innovation Capacity Building Assistance Program: Developing Practical Solutions to Practical Problems." Internal report. World Bank, Washington, DC.

World Bank. 1998. *World Development Report: Knowledge for Development.* New York: Oxford University Press.

______. 2005. *Sri Lanka—Offshoring Professional Services: A Development Opportunity.* Washington, DC: World Bank.

______. 2006. *Transport for Development.* Washington, DC: World Bank.

______. 2007a. *World Development Indicators 2007.* Washington, DC: World Bank.

______. 2007b. *World Development Report 2008: Agriculture for Development.* New York: Oxford University Press.

______. 2007c. *Making Finance Work for Africa.* Washington, DC: World Bank.

Zhu, Susan Chun, and Daniel Trefler. 2005. "Trade and Inequality in Developing Countries: A General Equilibrium Analysis." *Journal of International Economics.* 65: 21–48.

3

Determinants of Technological Progress: Recent Trends and Prospects

As discussed in the previous chapter, the pace at which technologies spread between and within countries has picked up. As a result, most developing countries are narrowing the technological divide that separates them from high-income countries. Nevertheless, the technology gap remains large; for many, including several low-income countries, it is widening rather than closing, in part because of the slowness with which technologies spread within countries. For virtually all developing countries, the domestic pace of technological progress is determined mainly by the speed with which already existing technologies are adopted, adapted, and successfully applied domestically, and done so throughout the economy, not just in the main cities.

This chapter explores some of the major determinants of this kind of within-country diffusion of technology. It adopts an analytical framework that distinguishes between the factors that dictate the extent to which an economy is exposed to external technologies on the one hand and the efficiency with which it absorbs them on the other hand. Among the most important channels through which low- and middle-income countries are exposed to foreign technologies are trade; foreign direct investment (FDI); and contacts with highly skilled diaspora members (nationals working abroad) and with other information networks, including those of academia and the media. Maintaining an open environment to such flows is critical for accessing technology at least cost. However, no matter how compellingly useful a technology may be, the process by which it spreads within a country can be lengthy.

The speed with which a country absorbs and adopts technology depends on many factors, including the extent to which a country has a technologically literate workforce and a highly skilled elite; promotes an investment climate that encourages investment and permits the creation and expansion of firms using higher-technology processes; permits access to capital; and has adequate public sector institutions to promote the diffusion of critical technologies where private demand or market forces are inadequate.

The process of technology absorption is also subject to virtuous circles. Scale economies in technologically sophisticated sectors and in learning by doing tend to make the acquisition of technology a nonlinear process, characterized initially by slow penetration until some threshold is reached, followed by a period of rapid acceleration, and finally by a period of slower diffusion as saturation is achieved. As a consequence, while gaps in technological achievement create opportunities for accelerated growth and convergence in lagging economies, they can also lead to divergence if the conditions for technology adoption in lagging countries are insufficient. Many technologies operate synergistically to reinforce the demand for each other and the effectiveness and capacity of supply.

Although the process of technological diffusion has a clear logic, the process is by no means mechanical. It occurs through interactions among individuals, entrepreneurs, firms, and governments. The role of government is both direct, as a supplier of many technological services, and indirect. In particular, the efficiency with which firms can diffuse technology within the domestic economy depends on the overall political and economic context, the level and distribution of human capital, the quality of the macroeconomic environment, and the rules and regulations governing the conduct of business, all of which are heavily influenced by governments.

This chapter discusses the principal channels through which developing countries are exposed to advanced technology, analyzes the main determinants of domestic absorptive capacity, and indicates likely future trends in technological diffusion. The following six main messages emerge from this analysis.

> *The principal channels by which developing countries are exposed to external technology—which include trade, FDI, and a highly skilled diaspora—have increased substantially over the past several decades.* The share of imported high-tech products in gross domestic product (GDP) has risen by more than half in both low- and middle-income regions since the mid-1990s, that of imports of capital goods by 37 percent, that of imports of intermediate goods by 26 percent, and that of FDI inflows by sixfold since the 1980s. Finally, the size and sophistication of global diasporas has increased markedly, along with substantial improvements in the technology by which migrants can transmit their know-how and interact with their home economies.
>
> *The ability to absorb foreign technology, which depends on domestic policies and institutions, has also improved in many developing countries.* Reflecting rising school enrollment, literacy rates in low-income countries have increased from less than 50 percent in 1990 to more than 62 percent, and among youth they now exceed 74 percent. In addition, the macroeconomic, governance, and investment climate that innovative firms and entrepreneurs need to operate is improving. More countries are operating in a context of close to stable prices (median inflation in low-income countries declined from 9.2 to 4.2 percent between 1990 and 2006) and flexible exchange rate regimes, while government finances are better balanced.
>
> *Technological diffusion among middle-income countries has benefited from the reorientation of global production processes.* Advances in communications and transport technology have given rise to the growth of global production networks, facilitating increased trade and technological advances in many developing countries, particularly middle-income developing countries. Until recently, low wages and a solid, if low, level of basic technological literacy have been sufficient to capture a significant role in global networks in many countries. As wages rise, however, these countries will need to make substantial additional investments in human capital to maintain their share of global production and continue the technological convergence of the past few years. They will also need to adopt a more proactive approach to developing local competencies and to using research and development (R&D) and outreach programs to bolster the diffusion process.
>
> *For low-income countries, poor technological adaptive capacity and limited dissemination of often simple technologies to the countryside are severely constraining technological progress.* Despite progress in basic technological literacy, extremely low levels of income, weak governance structures, and, in some cases, ongoing conflict continue to stymie the ability of low-income, and

especially Sub-Saharan African, countries to obtain and absorb new technologies. Nevertheless, the potential for technological progress through the greater dissemination of relatively simple technologies is huge.

The absence or low quality of some basic technologies that governments historically provide hinders technological diffusion by the private sector. These basic technologies often represent essential complementary technologies whose absence can prevent the successful adoption of a new-to-the-market technology.

The relatively rapid dissemination of new communications technologies throughout the developing world, including in low-income countries, offers a ray of hope. These potentially transformational technologies are enabling, often for the first time, the kinds of arm's-length transactions that may be critical to firm development and the spread of technology in these countries. New technologies are frequently introduced and promoted by members of national diasporas, both directly through networks and indirectly through investments financed from remittances.

The rest of this chapter is devoted to exploring how developing countries absorb external technology. The next section presents an analytical framework for technological progress. This is followed by a discussion of how trade, FDI, and migration expose countries to new technologies and can promote internal diffusion of those technologies. The section also discusses trends in these flows and the potential magnitude of associated technological progress and how this may have changed over time. The chapter then turns to an analysis of the domestic factors that facilitate the absorption of new technologies. This section first examines how government policies, and the business environment in general, facilitate the creation and expansion of innovative firms. It then looks at how levels of human capital—from literacy rates to R&D capacity—affect countries' ability to absorb technology from abroad. The chapter concludes with a speculative view of the prospects for technological progress and some policy messages.

Drivers of technological progress: A framework

The process by which countries adopt, adapt, and absorb external technologies is complicated. The overall framework followed in this chapter (depicted in figure 3.1) draws on previous work done at the World Bank, in particular, the 1998 *World Development Report* on the knowledge economy (World Bank 1998) and several regional and country-specific policy analyses of technology and technological competencies. In addition, it relies upon the academic literature on technology diffusion, including an excellent review article by Keller (2004); several articles by Coe and Helpman concerning the role of FDI; case studies of the process of technology diffusion by Chandra and Kolavalli (2006); empirical work on the technological influence of imports by Lumenga-Neso, Olarreaga, and Schiff (2005); and the discussion by Rodrik (2004) on the impact of market failures on innovation incentives.

Exposure to external flows interacts with domestic capacity to diffuse technology

For the purposes of analytical simplicity, the framework presents technological progress in developing countries as a process whereby an economy is exposed to higher-technology business processes, products, and services through foreign trade; FDI; and contacts with its diaspora and other communication channels, including academic and international organizations (the large arrows at the top of the figure). Exposure to new ideas and techniques is, however, not sufficient to ensure technological progress on the ground. The extent to which these flows are translated into technological progress depends on the technical absorptive capacity of the economy (represented by the ringed drum). This in turn depends on

Figure 3.1 Domestic absorptive capacity both conditions and attracts external flows

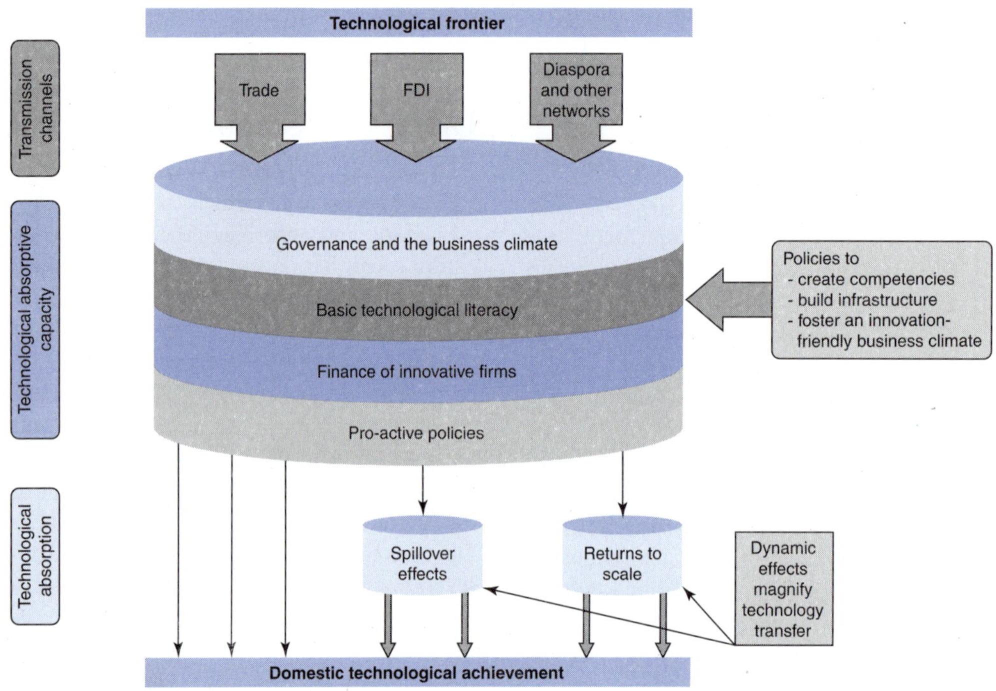

Source: World Bank.

the extent to which the business and macroeconomic climate fosters an environment in which firms—the main mechanism for technological diffusion within a country—are able to form, grow, and expand. Absorptive capacity also depends on the levels of basic technological literacy and advanced skills found in the country, which together dictate the country's capacity to implement technologies on the one hand and to do the research necessary to understand, implement, and adjust imported technologies on the other hand. Also important are government actions designed to help overcome market failures that might limit the financing of innovative activity, plus actions that focus technology policy on adapting and adopting those existing technologies for which there is a market and for which adequate domestic competencies exist. Critical here are outreach and dissemination policies, which need to serve as a two-way conduit, both informing the population about technological solutions and providing feedback to providers concerning the usability of and demand for proposed solutions. Taken together, these factors act as filters (the rings in the drum) that dictate how much of the potential technological flow is actually absorbed domestically.

The overall process is, of course, more complicated, with both technological flows and technological adaptive capacity influencing each other. For example, international trade is perhaps the most important vector for the transmission of technology, but the extent of a country's openness to trade depends significantly on the amount of FDI that has occurred, the existence of a vibrant and technologically literate diaspora, and the domestic business climate. Similarly, the quantity of FDI and its overall effectiveness depends on the quality and technological literacy of the labor force.

Increasing returns and spillover effects can magnify these effects...

Both domestic and external determinants of technological transfer are affected to varying degrees by increasing returns to scale and spillover effects that can magnify the absorptive impact of these flows. Access to foreign markets may allow domestic firms to grow and exploit economies of scale associated with some technologies, raising the overall wealth and technological sophistication of an economy. Meanwhile, the technological spillovers that can be expected from FDI, including demonstration effects and the transfer of business process and human capital to domestic firms through employee turnover, are likely to be greater the more qualified is the labor force. Both FDI and trade can contribute to cluster effects and networking externalities that increase the potential for spillovers and to technological diffusion from individual sectors and firms to the rest of the economy. Alternatively, economies of scale and agglomeration effects may prevent entry by new firms in some markets, cutting off otherwise promising opportunities for technological learning. In addition, imitators may limit entrepreneurs' ability to capture the returns to new-to-the-market innovations, thereby reducing incentives for technological progress.

... but a lack of financing can stymie innovation

Affordability issues can influence both the size of initial inflows and a country's technological absorptive capacity. Even if profitable investments in technology are available and the domestic environment encourages the absorption of new technologies, low incomes may make new technologies unaffordable to individuals and firms in developing countries. At the extreme, individuals near subsistence levels may be unwilling to risk adopting a new-to-the-market technique, may be unable to generate adequate savings to invest in a new technology, or may lack the collateral required to borrow. Thus poverty is a major cause, as well as a result, of low levels of technology.

Affordability is also an issue at the macro level. Low incomes constrain government finance, limiting the government's capacity to put into place both the level of physical infrastructure and the investments necessary to develop a level of domestic human capital capable of supporting and exploiting even simple technologies.

Policy should not impede innovative firms

Finally, firms, entrepreneurship, and government action that actively supports the diffusion of economically relevant and profitable technologies are the grassroots mechanisms by which technologies diffuse within countries. Firms must be able, and entrepreneurs permitted, to profit from the exploitation of new-to-the-market-technologies if those technologies and products are to diffuse. This means that policy must be welcoming of such profits and that both R&D and dissemination efforts not only need to focus on creating or adapting products and ideas (domestic or foreign) to the local market, but also must give priority to assisting firms to exploit them.

External transmission channels

This section presents data and describes recent trends concerning the external channels through which developing countries are exposed to foreign technologies. Where relevant, it also draws on the literature to comment on how specific elements in a country's technological absorptive capacity (discussed in more detail later in this chapter) interact with these external flows to determine the extent to which these channels translate into technological achievement.

Trade

Trade is one of the most important mechanisms by which embodied technological knowledge (in the form of both capital and intermediate goods and services) is transferred across countries. Imports of technologically sophisticated goods help developing countries raise the quality of their own products and the efficiency with which they are produced. Countries can also absorb new technology by exporting to customers who implicitly or explicitly provide guidance in meeting the specifications required for access to global markets. For developing countries with low R&D intensity, trade openness and exposure to foreign competition provide powerful inducements to adopt more advanced technology in both exporting and import-competing firms and are likely to produce large technology spillovers and productivity gains (Schiff and Wang 2006a).

However, the extent to which exposure to foreign technologies is reflected in the export and import patterns of individual countries depends on, among other things, the absorptive capacity of individual countries. As Soubbotina (2006) discusses, countries with relatively weak domestic scientific capacities tend to follow a more passive approach to technology absorption that is characterized by limited efforts to leverage the technology imported by foreign firms operating on their soil. For these countries, most technology transfers take place either through imports of high-tech goods, or perhaps through an apparently high-tech export sector that is, in reality, dominated by assembly operations associated with elevated imports of high-tech goods. Where sophisticated domestic capacities coexist with a significant degree of basic technological literacy in the population, technology diffusion is enhanced and, in general, the technological content of exports is higher.

Following Soubbotina (2006) classifications, "traditionalist slow learners," such as Bangladesh and Burkina Faso, which have low levels of technological competency and technological literacy, tend to rely to a large extent on imports of machinery and equipment. Other countries, such as Malaysia, Mexico, and the Philippines, appear to follow a "passive FDI-dependent" learning style. For these countries, the share of high- and medium-tech goods in their manufactured exports is higher than these goods' share in manufacturing value added, reflecting the dependence of their high-tech exports on imports of technologically sophisticated components and the relatively low technological complexity of domestic manufacturing operations. By contrast, "active FDI-dependent" countries, such as Chile and Hungary, strike a better balance between the share of high-tech goods and services in overall exports and domestic value added, reflecting greater domestic technological competencies. For the Russian Federation and some of the other countries that belonged to the former Soviet Union, a strong technological base and relatively low import shares of high-tech goods reflect their more advanced learning style, which places greater emphasis on domestically developed technologies. Nevertheless, these technologies mainly feed into products that serve the local market, because both high costs and quality concerns keep these sectors from being internationally competitive.

The potential for technology transfer through imports has risen

Imports improve domestic technology because embodied technology both allows firms to employ more efficient production processes and affords the possibility that firms can copy more advanced products and processes. At the same time, competition from technologically superior imports may boost domestic productivity.[1] Developing countries that have a large share of imports from high-income countries with large R&D expenditures have significantly higher productivity than developing countries that import from advanced countries with lower R&D expenditures (Coe, Helpman, and Hoffmaister 1997).[2] There also is evidence for a positive relationship between access to imported intermediate goods and performance (Handoussa, Nishimizu, and Page 1986). More recent literature highlights the indirect benefits for developing countries from North–North trade in R&D. The exchange of high-tech goods and services among high-income economies contributes to an increase in the global stock of knowledge and eventually becomes available to developing countries through North–South trade. Finally, technology diffusion, like trade, tends to be regional, with the largest transfers coming from natural trading partners, for example, Jordan benefits more from the European Union and Mexico benefits from Canada and the United States (Schiff and Wang 2006b).

However, the extent to which imported technology boosts the sophistication of domestic technological activity either directly or indirectly through spillovers depends on the quality of a country's technological absorptive capacity. Thus while using an imported capital good can lift the technological content of activity in a country, to the extent that importers pay competitive prices for the technology, there may be no net gain to the country (Eaton and Kortum 2001). Moreover, the business climate may be too weak or the technological literacy of the local labor force may be too low to successfully adapt the machinery to local conditions (Dahlman, Ross-Larson, and Westphal 1987; Rosenberg 1976). As a result, the country may not realize the potential productivity improvements available from imported technology (Pack 2006).

Developing countries' high-tech imports have increased

To the extent that a developing country can make use of or imitate sophisticated goods, its level of technological achievement should increase in line with the quality and technological sophistication of imported goods. Since the mid-1990s, the share of imported high-tech products in GDP has increased by more than 50 percent in low-income countries and by 70 percent in middle-income countries (table 3.1).[3] Among developing regions, East Asia and the Pacific has the highest share of high-tech imports in GDP (8.4 percent), with the highest share being for Malaysia (37 percent) and the Philippines (18 percent), but Europe and Central Asia has experienced the largest increase, reflecting the transition of many of the region's countries to market economies and their improved access to high-tech products following the relaxation of Cold War export restrictions. Among regions dominated by middle-income countries, high-tech imports represent 3.8 percent of GDP in Latin America and the Caribbean and 3.6 percent of GDP in the Middle East and North Africa, less than in Sub-Saharan Africa (4.5 percent).

Low-income countries have also improved their exposure to high-technology embedded in foreign products. After hovering around

Table 3.1 Trade in technology goods has increased in developing countries

	Imports of high-tech goods			Imports of capital goods			Share of high-tech exports in world high-tech exports		
	1994–96	2002–04	% change	1994–96	2002–04	% change	1994–96	2002–04	% change
	(% of GDP)			*(% of GDP)*			*(% of GDP)*		
Regions									
East Asia and the Pacific	5.9	8.4	42	11.6	12.8	10	9.9	19.0	93
Europe and Central Asia	3.2	7.2	125	7.1	14.7	107	1.0	2.7	163
Latin America and the Caribbean	2.4	3.8	61	5.4	7.2	32	2.1	3.4	61
Middle East and North Africa	2.5	3.6	44	6.3	8.9	42	0.1	0.2	29
South Asia	1.4	2.1	53	3.1	3.8	22	0.2	0.3	58
Sub-Saharan Africa	3.2	4.5	39	9.3	10.5	14	0.1	0.1	4
Income groups									
High-income countries	3.4	4.7	38	5.5	7.0	27	86.5	74.3	−14
Upper-middle-income countries	4.2	7.2	71	8.7	13.1	51	6.6	9.6	47
Lower-middle-income countries	3.2	5.4	70	6.9	9.2	33	6.7	15.7	137
Low-income countries	1.8	2.7	53	4.9	5.7	17	0.3	0.4	53

Source: World Bank calculations using Centre d'Etudes Prospectives et d'Informations Internationales' database, Banque Analytique de Commerce International.

Figure 3.2 Rising share of high-tech imports

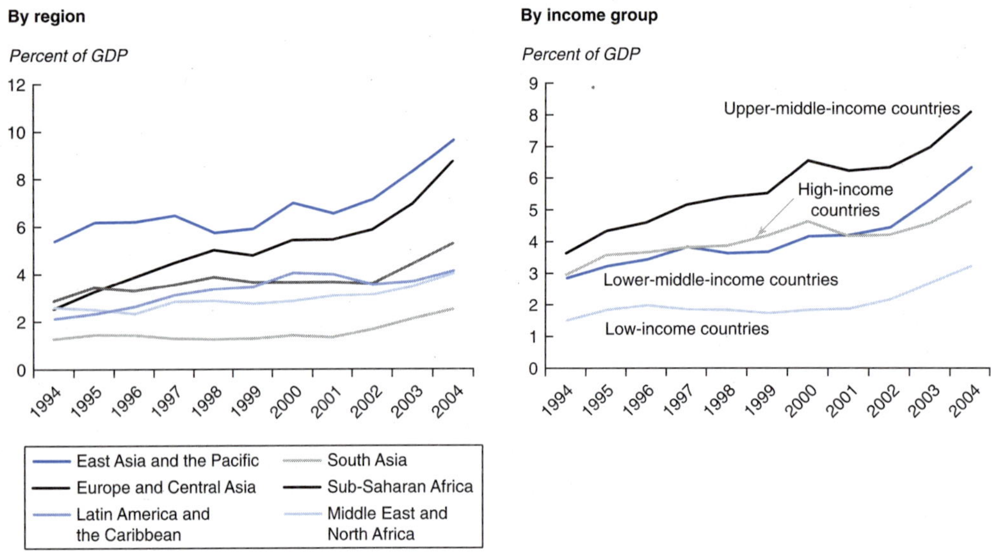

Source: World Bank calculations using Centre d'Etudes Prospectives et d'Informations Internationales database, Banque Analytique de Commerce International.

1.8 percent between 1994 and 2001, the average share of high-tech imports in low-income countries' GDP began to rise in 2002, reaching 3.2 percent in 2004 (figure 3.2). Both South Asia and Sub-Saharan Africa have enjoyed significant increases, although the ratio of high-tech imports to GDP remains extremely low in South Asia, less than 3 percent of GDP. In most countries in Sub-Saharan Africa, the share of imported high-tech goods fluctuates between 2 and 5 percent of GDP from year to year. Mauritius and South Africa import the most high-tech goods relative to the size of their economies, between 6 and 8 percent of GDP in any given year, while Somalia imports the least, less than 1 percent of GDP.

Despite developing countries' increased exposure to foreign technology through trade, its distribution across regions within countries tends to be extremely uneven, with foreign trade concentrated in a few major cities or regions. For example, 70 percent of high-tech trade (both imports and exports) in China originates in four regions and is highly correlated with R&D intensity and foreign firms (OECD 2007). As a result, the benefits of exposure to trade also tend to be unevenly distributed.

Capital goods imports have also increased

Although imports of high-tech goods provide an indication of an economy's exposure to technology, this indicator does not distinguish between imports of technology for consumption and imports for production, nor does it indicate the extent to which these imports improve the technological content of a country's economic activities. Technological content depends importantly on the structure of the economy and the nature (assembly or high valued added transformation) of the work done with the imports (box 3.1).

Imports of capital goods, such as machinery and equipment, which enable the production of higher quality and more technologically sophisticated goods, have a less ambiguous impact on a country's technological capacity. For countries operating within the technological frontier, a higher share of imported capital goods in GDP can reflect the presence of strong investment activity; a process of technological

Box 3.1 Technology imports: Different paths for different countries

Based on a breakdown of trade flows by technology level and by production stage, Lemoine and Ünal-Kesenci (2003) highlight the following divergent integration paths adopted by China, India, and Turkey, which all started from a relatively similar degree of industrial specialization about 10 years ago:

- *China* has become an assembly country, strongly integrated into the international segmentation-of-production processes in Asia. Most of China's imports of high-tech products are parts and components. These high-tech imports are predominantly incorporated into the production of exports and are not used to modernize domestic production capacities. Given its level of development, China's exports display an outstandingly strong high-tech content.
- *India* is characterized by limited participation in international division-of-production processes and by a low level of imports in high-tech products. These high-tech imports are evenly distributed among the different stages of production and the different sectors, while high-tech exports are concentrated in chemical industries.
- *Turkey's* high-tech imports consist mainly of capital goods and correspond to a classical form of technology transfer aimed at upgrading indigenous industrial capacities. Turkey's foreign trade is strongly structured by its traditional complementaries with Europe.

upgrading; and, over the longer term, a relatively sophisticated structure of production.[4] As a result, relatively technologically sophisticated middle-income countries import more capital goods (as a share of GDP) than less sophisticated low-income countries (table 3.1).

Overall, the share of capital goods in the GDP of developing countries has risen substantially over the past decade. Upper-middle-income countries saw a 51 percent increase in the share of these goods in GDP, while lower-middle-income countries have boosted their reliance on such goods by 33 percent. The former group of countries continues to have the largest share of capital goods in GDP, about 13 percent, more than double the share of low-income countries. As a consequence, the gap between low-income countries (especially the Least Developed Countries [UNCTAD 2007]) and other developing countries has widened. Europe and Central Asia saw the biggest regional increase in imports of capital goods, reflecting the substantial economic recovery in these countries following the recession that accompanied the transition to market economies. As was the case for high-tech imports, South Asia has the lowest level of imports of capital goods and has shown little improvement, presumably reflecting the relatively autarchic policies that governments in the region have followed until recently. By contrast, Sub-Saharan Africa imports substantially more capital goods, although the ratio of capital goods imports to GDP has increased less than in other developing regions since the mid-1990s, with the exception of East Asia and the Pacific. The story is particularly varied in Latin America, where some countries, such as Costa Rica and Mexico, increased their imports of capital goods following liberalization policies in the early 1990s, while others did not. The increase in the share of capital goods in GDP was particularly notable in Costa Rica, where it rose from about 7 percent in the mid-1990s to about 18 percent in 2002–04.

Exports of technological goods have also expanded

Participation in high-tech export markets has also been identified as a channel through which technology is diffused within developing countries. Many case studies suggest that exporting firms in developing countries benefit from implicit and explicit technological transfers that occur as a result of their interactions with foreign buyers. Benefits accrue because foreign buyers may have higher quality standards than domestic buyers. Foreign buyers may also assist with process improvements and provide information about and experience with foreign markets. Moreover, the additional demand that foreign markets provide may allow for the exploitation of economies of scale that justify more capital-intensive production (see, for example, Hobday 1995 and Rhee, Ross-Larson, and Pursell 1984 on the effects of learning by exporting in East Asia). Technology transfers through exports may be most important in production networks with clearly articulated supply chains (Gereffi 1999; Hobday 1995).[5] Spillovers may also be common in labor-intensive sectors where production processes are relatively simple and the relevant knowledge is widely available in industrial countries (Enos and Park 1987; Hou and Gee 1993).

Unfortunately, these efficiency benefits from exporting are not confirmed by econometric studies (Keller 2004), which generally find that the positive relationship between exporting and productivity results largely from the self-selection of firms into the export market.[6]

Whatever the magnitude of spillovers from exports and of concerns surrounding the re-export nature of some high-tech exports, the export of technology products is nevertheless an important indicator of technological achievement. High-tech exports offer better prospects for future growth than lower-tech goods because their market has been expanding more rapidly and because they offer superior spillover potential by transmitting skills and generic knowledge that can be used in other activities (Guerrieri and Milana 1998). High-tech exports are also less vulnerable to easy entry by lower-wage competitors, substitution by technical change, and market shifts (Lall 2001).

Although high-income countries continue to dominate the world market for high-tech goods,[7] middle-income countries have substantially increased their market share since the mid-1990s. Lower-middle-income countries more than doubled their global share of high-tech exports, increasing them from 6.6 percent in the mid-1990s to 15.7 percent in 2002–04 (3.4 to 5.0 percent if China is excluded). Moreover, the share of higher-technology goods in the total merchandise exports of these countries has also been increasing (figure 3.3). Much of this increase reflected the transfer of manufacturing processes from high-income countries to developing countries, notably those in East Asia and the Pacific. China was a major beneficiary of this process, increasing its global market share of high-tech exports from about 3 percent to 11 percent, but so too were other countries. The Philippines, for example, increased its market share from 0.9 percent to about 2.0 percent. Upper-middle-income countries made less spectacular progress, increasing their global market share from 6.5 percent to 10.5 percent, although some countries, such as Costa Rica, the Czech Republic, and Hungary, were able to increase their high-tech markets significantly.[8] In Sub-Saharan Africa, South Africa is the largest exporter of high-tech products, but its share has remained small and stable at about 0.08 percent.

The relative performance of different middle-income regions reflects different levels

Figure 3.3 Exports of low-, medium-, and high-technology goods

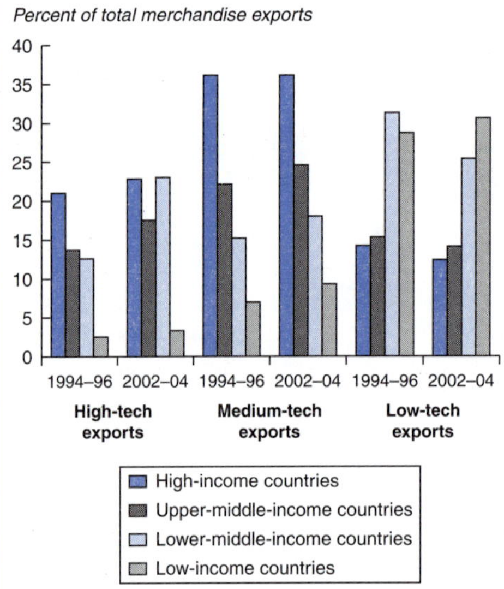

Source: World Bank calculations using Centre d'Etudes Prospectives et d'Informations Internationales database, Banque Analytique de Commerce International.

of technological capabilities and learning styles. Since the early 1990s, Latin America has almost doubled its share of high-tech products in world markets and now has the second largest market share after East Asia and the Pacific. However, in contrast with Europe and Central Asia and the Middle East and North Africa, it has done so with relatively little input from imported technology (imports of high-tech and capital goods as a share of GDP in Latin America and the Caribbean are half the rate of Europe and Central Asia). Partly as a consequence, Europe and Central Asia has gained market share in high-tech goods much more quickly than Latin America, and based on recent performance, is poised to overtake that region soon.

Low-income countries remain marginal players in the world market for high-tech goods, and even though their global share of exports of medium-tech goods has doubled, between the mid-1990s and 2002–04, it remains low at 0.8 percent. The share of low-income countries in world exports of low-tech goods is more substantial and has increased from 3.5 percent to 5.2 percent. Among these countries, Vietnam has improved its global market share of low-tech products from 0.2 to 0.8 percent, a 250 percent increase. India remains the most important exporter of low-tech products in this income group with 2 percent of the world market, second after China among developing countries, which accounts for about 17 percent of the world's low-tech exports.

Overall exposure to foreign technologies has increased

Overall, the increased participation of developing countries in global trade has substantially increased their exposure to foreign technologies. For middle-income countries, this exposure and the attendant expansion of high-tech exports have likely yielded important side benefits that are reflected in the sustained acceleration in developing country growth rates over the past 15 years. While the increase in trade openness has been generalized, the extent to which countries have been able to translate that into improved export performance and an increase in the technological sophistication of their own exports has varied, with countries like those in Europe and Central Asia that have relatively well-educated populations and a strong institutional structure having extracted the greatest benefits. Among other countries, notably low-income countries, weak absorptive capacity may be restricting the extent to which their economies have benefited from the increased exposure.

Foreign direct investment

Like trade, FDI can be a powerful channel for the transmission of technology to developing countries by financing new investment, by communicating information about technology to domestic affiliates of foreign firms, and by facilitating the diffusion of technology to local firms.

Foreign investors bring both equipment and know-how

Measuring the technological contribution of FDI is particularly difficult, in part because the standard measure from the balance of payments includes both physical (brownfield and greenfield) investments and financial investments (mergers and acquisitions). This said, FDI inflows to developing countries rose from \$10 billion in 1980 to an estimated \$390 billion in 2007, or from 0.4 to 2.9 percent of GDP, with the bulk of the increase occurring during the late 1990s in response to the liberalization of FDI policies.[9] Assuming that foreign firms employ a higher level of technology than the average domestic firm, then this rising trend will have increased the average level of technology in these countries, as well as their exposure to higher technologies.

FDI as a share of GDP has risen in all developing regions and income groups since the 1980s, but the increase has been concentrated in middle-income countries, where FDI rose to almost 3 percent of GDP (table 3.2). East Asia and the Pacific had the highest ratio during the 1990s, but it has since declined, in part because of a collapse in FDI inflows to a few

Table 3.2 Foreign direct investment as a percent of GDP

	1970–79	1980–89	1990–99	2000–06
All developing countries	0.5	0.4	1.5	2.7
By region				
East Asia and the Pacific	0.5	0.5	2.8	2.3
Europe and Central Asia	0.3	0.1	0.9	2.2
Latin America and the Caribbean	0.6	0.7	1.5	3.5
Middle East and North Africa	0.5	0.5	0.6	1.1
South Asia	0.0	0.1	0.4	0.7
Sub-Saharan Africa	0.7	0.4	1	2.5
By income groups				
Low-income countries	0.3	0.2	0.8	1.1
excluding India	0.6	0.4	1.4	1.8
India	0.0	0.0	0.3	0.7
Middle-income countries	0.5	0.4	1.6	2.9

Source: World Bank 2007a.

countries affected by the East Asian financial crisis in the late 1990s (particularly Indonesia), and in part because FDI inflows to China, although still high, have failed to keep pace with the rapid growth of output. Meanwhile in Latin America and the Caribbean, efforts to increase trade openness resulted in a boom of FDI inflows, which reached an average of 3.5 percent of GDP in 2000–06. In Europe and Central Asia, FDI rose from next to nothing before the breakup of the Soviet bloc to 2.2 percent of GDP in 2000–06. In the Middle East and North Africa and South Asia, FDI remains low at around or less than 1 percent of GDP. Most recently, FDI inflows to Sub-Saharan Africa have surged, reflecting substantial investment in oil and mineral production and a more generalized interest in the region stemming from increased political stability, liberalization of FDI policies over the past 15 years, and improved growth performance.

One way that FDI boosts technology transfer is by financing new machinery and equipment purchases. The share of FDI in developing countries' fixed capital formation increased from 2.9 percent in the 1970s to 10.7 percent in this decade (table 3.3), with the increase in middle-income countries being more pronounced than in low-income countries. However, FDI includes mergers and acquisitions that may involve no additional physical investment, and the share of mergers and acquisitions, including privatization transactions, in total FDI has been rising. Nevertheless, the foreign component of aggregate investment in developing countries has likely been rising along with the extent of technological transfer through this channel. Moreover, the transfers in know-how, business process technology, and market knowledge associated with mergers and acquisitions can occur whether or not any associated physical investment is involved, and may even be more important.

Foreign firms may also improve the technological capacity of developing countries by

Table 3.3 Foreign direct investment as a percent of fixed capital formation

	1970s	1980s	1990s	2000s
Regions				
East Asia and the Pacific	1.9	3.0	12.2	8.4
Europe and Central Asia	2.8	—	8.1	15.5
Latin America and the Caribbean	3.3	0.1	11.3	13.1
Middle East and North Africa	2.8	2.1	3.7	6.5
South Asia	0.3	0.4	2.5	4.1
Sub-Saharan Africa	3.6	2.2	9.3	18.6
Income groups				
Low-income countries	2.2	1.3	5.6	6.7
Middle-income countries	2.9	1.9	11.0	11.3
All developing countries	2.9	1.8	10.4	10.7
OECD countries	13.5	11.3	3.5	11.5

Source: World Bank 2007a.
Note: — = not available; OECD = Organisation for Economic Co-operation and Development.

Figure 3.4 Share of foreign affiliates in business R&D expenditure

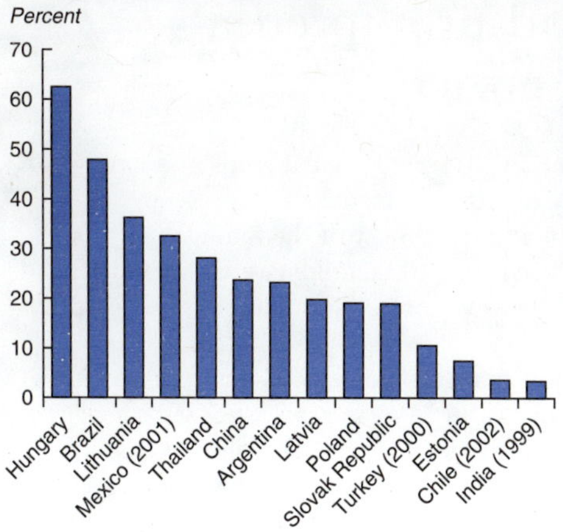

Sources: OECD; Activity of Foreign Affiliates database. http://www.sourceoecd.org; UNCTAD 2005; Eurostat; R&D statistics.

Note: The year is 2003 unless otherwise indicated.

financing R&D. Multinational corporations undertake most of their R&D activities in their home country or in other high-income countries.[10] Nevertheless, the role of developing countries appears to be rising. R&D spending in developing countries by majority-owned foreign affiliates of U.S. parent companies increased from $0.9 billion in 1999 to $1.6 billion in 2003 (Bureau of Economic Analysis 2007). The contribution of multinationals' R&D to total measured R&D activity in developing countries varies from more than 60 percent in Hungary to less than 5 percent in India (figure 3.4).

FDI may generate technology spillovers

In addition to its technological impact on the firm directly touched by the investment, FDI may also affect the level of technology in domestic firms.[11] Spillovers can arise when workers receive training or accumulate experience working for multinationals and then move to domestic firms or set up their own enterprise (Fosfuri, Motta, and Ronde 2001; Glass and Saggi 2002). For example, within six years of the beginning of FDI-led export growth in Mauritius, 50 percent of all firms operating in export-processing zones were locally owned, founded, managed, and staffed—in many cases by employees who had received on-the-job training in foreign enterprises and had left to set up their own companies (Rhee, Katterback, and White 1990).

Already existing local firms may also observe the actions of foreign firms and learn about new products, equipment, marketing techniques, and management practices. For example, 25 percent of the managers of Czech firms and 15 percent of the managers of Latvian firms report that they learned about new technologies by observing foreign firms as they entered their industry (Javorcik and Spatareanu 2005). In Morocco and Tunisia, domestically owned international call centers have risen in imitation of foreign firms (box 3.2).

If multinational entry leads to an increase in demand for intermediates, it may result in the expansion of upstream domestic industries (see the experience with Zambian supermarkets in box 3.3). Downstream industries may also benefit from the increased competition and added variety of inputs created by the foreign investment. In addition, foreign investors may provide advice, designs, direct production assistance, or marketing contacts to suppliers, which the latter can then deploy more broadly than simply providing cheaper or more reliable inputs to the foreigners.[12]

The entry of multinationals is likely to increase competition for the domestic firms within the industry, potentially forcing them to improve their efficiency and introduce new technologies or business strategies (Blomstrom, Kokko, and Zejan 2000), as in Wal-Mart's joint venture in Mexico (box 3.4). Such competition can make surviving domestic competitors stronger, but other domestic firms may be driven out of business, lose market share, and experience a loss of high-skilled workers and higher costs for intermediate goods resulting from increasing demand from the foreign-owned firms.[13] These effects may vary by industry depending on factors such as the market structure before the entry of

Box 3.2 European call centers in the Maghreb have inspired local entrepreneurs and prompted a specialization in high-value-added services

Leading call center companies from France and Spain have paved the way for domestically owned and export-oriented call centers in Morocco and Tunisia. Although call centers existed in Morocco and Tunisia before the first European call centers outsourced operations to the region in the early 2000s, domestically owned firms served the local market and provided only basic telecommunications services. Only after Atento (a Spanish-owned subsidiary) set up a call center in Morocco and Teleperformance (a French-owned firm) settled in Tunisia to serve clients in Europe did local entrepreneurs jump into the European market.

This transition was not without problems. Locally owned call centers lack the international name recognition of large foreign-owned firms and have had difficulty obtaining contracts from foreign companies. In addition, most of them are small, with a maximum of 100 to 200 employees, compared with more than 2,000 positions at some foreign-owned call centers.

Interestingly, many domestically owned firms, such as Outsourcia in Morocco, have chosen to differentiate themselves by targeting higher value added services. High turnover rates have also helped domestically owned firms to hire experienced agents who were trained in the foreign call centers.

Source: World Bank forthcoming.

Box 3.3 South African investment in Zambia's retail sector has improved the quality of local produce and farmers' earnings

The liberalization of the Zambian distribution sector allowed the inflow of foreign retail companies, which replaced some of the traditional retail sector with modern supermarkets and added both upstream and downstream benefits to the domestic economy. Consumers benefited from lower costs, while local suppliers learned new production and marketing techniques that enabled them to improve the quality, efficiency, and revenues of their operations.

When Shoprite of South Africa first opened supermarkets in Zambia, it found that the quality and quantities provided by individual local smallholder farmers were too low and too unreliable, and therefore imported 90 percent of its fresh produce from South Africa. Farmers' cooperatives that benefited from donor-funded technical assistance have since managed to improve the quality of their products and services, and Shoprite is now sourcing 90 to 95 percent of its fresh produce from Zambian farmers. In the case of one cooperative, farmers' cash income has increased from \$2 to \$3 a month to \$50 to \$70 a month, and local access to health care and education services has improved. The supermarkets themselves are providing local farmers with technical assistance. Agricultural experts from the retailer's subsidiary visit farms, give advice on crop sequencing, and provide inputs.

Source: Mattoo and Payton 2007.

Box 3.4 Wal-Mart's entry in Mexico boosted the Mexican soaps, detergents, and surfactants industry

The Aurerra–Wal-Mart joint venture, which created Walmex, followed Mexico's reduction in tariffs and liberalization of FDI in the late 1980s. By exercising its bargaining power, Walmex squeezed profit margins among the major soaps, detergent, and surfactants suppliers, offering them higher volumes in return.

Local firms that were not efficient enough to meet Walmex's terms lost market share, and many failed. Those that survived grew and became more efficient and innovative. The quality and efficiency of their overall operations benefited from their interactions with both their client (Wal-Mart) and with foreign-owned suppliers, with many firms adopting techniques and products first introduced into the market by their multinational competitors.

As a result of these spillovers and labor shedding, the surfactants sector rapidly improved its value added per worker. The newly found competitiveness and exposure to the requirements of Walmex and other foreign retailers on the domestic market has allowed the Mexican surfactants sector to expand its exports and market share in the United States, targeting the Latino community in which their brands are known.

Source: Javorcik, Keller, and Tybout 2006.

foreign multinationals, the R&D intensity of the products, and the links between foreign firms and domestic firms in upstream and downstream sectors.[14]

Outsourcing decisions, domestic policies, and absorptive capacity all affect spillovers

Evidence indicates that spillovers to local suppliers are not uniform across countries or across industries within a country.[15] Multinationals may choose not to source inputs locally because of concerns about the quality of local inputs or the time required to develop relationships with local suppliers or because of centralized sourcing arrangements that may provide volume discounts or access to customized inputs (UNCTAD 2001). In host countries with underdeveloped upstream sectors or in cases of FDI with very specialized input needs, the scope for spillovers to upstream sectors may be limited. Policies may also reduce the potential for spillovers. For example, in a highly protected market, foreign plants may operate at an inefficiently small scale (Moran 2007). Requirements that foreign firms enter into joint ventures with local companies may discourage use of the most advanced technology to avoid leakage to potential competitors (Beamish 1988).

The level of spillovers also depends on the domestic absorptive capacity. For example, other advanced countries tend to gain from technology spillovers from the activities of subsidiaries of U.S. multinationals, while poor countries do not (Xu 2000). Firms using advanced technology in low-income countries fail to achieve the same level of productivity as firms in industrial countries (Acemoglu and Zilibotti 2001) or the same kinds of spillovers as in middle-income countries, in part because the gap between the quality and human capital of the domestic workforce and that for which the equipment was originally designed is too large (Borensztein, de Gregorio, and Lee 1998). In general, spillovers may be more common when the difference in technological levels between the foreign multinational and the domestic economy is not too large.

As discussed earlier, the extent to which a country benefits from spillovers to the rest of the economy also depends on the country's policy stance on basic technological literacy and more advanced skills and on promotion of the adoption and diffusion of technologies within the economy. For example, some countries such as Mexico and the Philippines have benefited relatively little from FDI spillovers because FDI inflows, although abundant, have been oriented toward exploiting low wages and have not built many links to the domestic economy. In contrast, countries like Singapore have actively sought to maximize the technology spillovers from FDI by investing in the domestic skills and competencies necessary to support high-skill and high value added industries and by welcoming and promoting FDI in such sectors (Lall 2003).

Spillovers might be highly concentrated in certain regions within a country

Geographic proximity also determines the extent of technological spillovers observed. The closer a local firm is to a foreign-owned firm, the more frequently will the firms' employees interact with each other, increasing the likelihood that employees (and their acquired knowledge) will move between the two firms. The spatial aspect is also important for vertical spillovers between foreign-owned firms and their local suppliers, which are often located close to each other (Jaffe 1989).

The existence of such cluster effects may explain why FDI tends to be geographically concentrated within a country mainly around large cities or coastal states. In Russia, for example, more than two-thirds of the FDI stock in 2000 was in Moscow and three surrounding regions (Broadman and Recanatini 2005). Similarly, almost half of FDI flows in India go to the Mumbai and Delhi areas (Reserve Bank of India 2007), while in China, almost 90 percent of FDI flows go to the western coastal region (Kui-Yin and Lin 2007). This said, because of data limitations and conceptual problems, econometric support for the notion that such clusters generate important technology spillovers is limited (Lipsey and Sjohom 2005), with some studies supporting their existence (see Girma and Wakelin 2001 for the electronics sector in the United Kingdom) and others not (see Aitken and Harrison 1999 for Venezuela and Sjoholm 1998 for Indonesia).

Developing countries also purchase foreign high-tech firms

Outward FDI, that is, the purchase of foreign firms by domestically owned ones, and the licensing of technologies are two other, more direct mechanisms by which developing countries acquire foreign technologies and research expertise.

Over the past 20 years, firms domiciled in developing countries have increasingly turned to foreign acquisitions as a means of expanding their market share and gaining control over technology. Cross-border mergers and acquisitions by multinational corporations located in developing countries increased from $400 million in 1987 (less than 1 percent of global merger and acquisition transactions) to almost $100 billion in 2006 (almost 9 percent of global merger and acquisition transactions) (World Bank 2007a). Although technology may not be the primary motivator in many of these purchases, technology transfer is associated with nearly all of them in the form of control over patents and knowledge of manufacturing processes, marketing, and business process expertise. Table 3.4 summarizes some of the more technologically important recent acquisitions of high-tech firms by developing country firms.

Developing country firms may seek to acquire a brand or a marketing or distribution network. Examples include the Thai Union Frozen Company's purchase of the Chicken of the Sea brand; the South African Brewery's purchase of Miller Brewing (a major U.S. beer maker); and Malaysian Berjaya's purchase of Taiga, the largest Canadian distributor of building materials. Developing country firms may also purchase foreign firms to acquire R&D capacity. For example, the Chinese company Shanghai Automotive Industry Corporation bought Sangyong of the Republic of Korea to enhance its R&D capabilities in sport utility vehicles. Accessing foreign technology also takes the form of establishing R&D centers in developed countries. For example, Huawei Technologies and ZTE Corporation, both Chinese companies, have established R&D centers in Sweden.

Developing countries can also license foreign technologies

Developing countries can also gain access to technology through licensing, which typically

Table 3.4 Selected purchases of high-tech firms by companies in developing countries, early 2000s

Acquiring company	Country of acquirer	Year	Acquired firm	Country of acquired	Industry
Netcare	South Africa	2006	General Health Care	United Kingdom	Health
Tata Tea	India	2006	Tetley	United Kingdom	Tea
Videocon Industries Ltd.	India	2006	Daewoo Electronics	Korea, Rep. of	Electronics
Chalkis	China	2005	Le Cabanon	France	Food processing
Essel Propack	India	2005	Telcon Packing	United Kingdom	Tube packing
Wipro	India	2005	New Logic	Austria	Semiconductors
Orascom	Egypt, Arab Rep. of	2005	Wind	Italy	Telecommunications
Lenovo	China	2004	IBM	United States	PC manufacturing
TCL	China	2004	Alcatel	France	Telecommunications
Ranbaxy	India	2004	RPG	France	Pharmaceuticals
BOW Technology Group	China	2003	Hynix	Korea, Rep. of	PC manufacturing
PKN Orlen	Poland	2002	BP (500 petrol stations)	United Kingdom	Downstream oil

Source: World Bank 2007a.

involves the purchase of production or distribution rights for a product and the underlying technical information and know-how for producing it. As measured by the payment of international royalties and fees in countries' balance of payments, licensing fees paid by developing countries increased from $7 billion in 1999 to $22 billion in 2006, about a fivefold increase when expressed as a percentage of developing country GDP.[16] The increase was sharpest for oil- and mineral-exporting countries, reflecting higher prices for oil and contracts that often expressed these fees as a percentage of revenues or profits. Nevertheless, licensing fees paid by other developing countries also tripled, and for both low- and middle-income countries these fees represented a larger share of overall GDP than they did for oil- and mineral-exporting countries (figure 3.5).

Licensing can be used as a substitute for FDI. Uncertainty about the policy environment may lead multinationals to sell technology rather than to exploit the technology through foreign investment (domestic firms may have more information or may be better placed than foreigners to deal with a poor policy environment). Evidence suggests that both FDI and licensing respond to an adequate business environment, and factors such as patent protection may shift incentives for investors from FDI toward licensing (Maskus 2002). Where protection of intellectual property rights is weak, multinationals may be less willing to license technology for fear of it being copied by domestic firms. Alternatively, they may only be willing to license out-of-date technologies (Maskus 2000). Data on U.S. multinationals show that the likelihood of entering into licensing agreements increases as developing countries increase their protection of intellectual property rights (Antras, Desai, and Foley 2007).

Some countries have pursued a licensing-based strategy of technology acquisition in the

Figure 3.5 Licensing payments have risen sharply

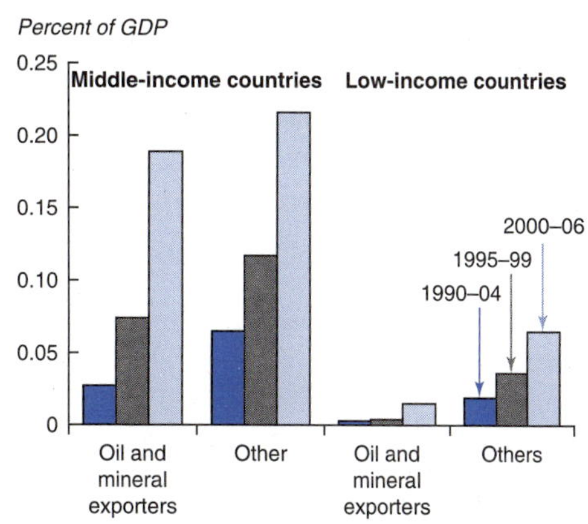

Sources: Balance of Payments Database (IMF) and World Development Indicators.

belief that domestic firms will be able to upgrade their own technological capacities by working with licensed technology. For example, in the 1950s and 1960s, Japan kept its economy relatively closed to FDI to encourage multinationals that wished to gain from the growing Japanese market to license technology to domestic firms (Pack and Saggi 1997). China has also encouraged joint ventures, as opposed to FDI, to maximize technology transfers to local firms. This strategy is likely to work only if the country has sufficient market power. Moreover, such discriminatory policies run the risk of resulting in the transfer of substandard technologies (Hoekman and Javorcik 2006). In contrast, several Latin American countries discouraged the licensing of technology from abroad because of concerns about unfair pricing and competition with local technologies, a strategy that retarded or skewed technological development in that region (Pack and Saggi 1997).

The bulk of international royalties and fees stems from intrafirm transfers. In part, this may reflect a preference by multinational firms to transfer more advanced technologies only to wholly owned subsidiaries rather than to partially owned affiliates and to enter markets through wholly owned subsidiaries rather than through joint ventures (Javorcik 2006; Mansfield and Romeo 1980). However, it may also mean that these fees are being used as a mechanism for repatriating profits, perhaps for tax reasons. As a result, the level of royalties and fees may not be a market-based reflection of the value of technology purchased by the local subsidiary (Robbins 2006).

Partly because of intrafirm payments and of the close relationship between licensing and FDI, economists have had difficulty in evaluating the impact of licensing on technology transfer. Nevertheless, a few case studies have documented its benefits. Brazil and Korea achieved considerable success in absorbing new technologies through licensing (Correa 2003), and licensing agreements were an important factor for the success of floriculture in Kenya, maize in India, and the electronics sector in Taiwan, China (Chandra and Kolavalli 2006). The latter study also highlights that even though licensing may enable rapid acquisition of product and process know-how, it also requires a significant level of local technological capability to put the licensed technology to work.

International migration

Along with trade and FDI, international migrants are another important channel for the transmission of technology and knowledge. From the perspective of developing countries, however, the direction of technology transfer can be both outward (as migrants take away scarce skills) or inward (through contacts with the diaspora).

The direction and scale of technology flows that result from international migration are less clear than for FDI and trade. On the one hand, the brain drain associated with better educated citizens of developing countries working in high-income countries is a serious problem for many developing countries. On the other hand, the contribution that these individuals would have made had they stayed home is uncertain given the lack of opportunities in some countries. Moreover, developing countries can benefit from the immigration, albeit often temporary, of managers and engineers that often accompanies FDI; the return of well-educated developing country emigrants; and the contacts with a technologically sophisticated diaspora.

High rates of skilled out-migration imply a net transfer of human capital and scarce resources (in the form of the cost of educating these workers) from low- to high-income countries (UNCTAD 2007; World Bank 2006a). For some countries, the brain drain represents a significant problem: emigration rates of highly educated individuals can exceed 60 percent in some small countries (figure 3.6), and since 1990, the highly educated diaspora of developing countries has doubled in size.[17] However, the share of developing country tertiary-educated individuals living abroad remained stable and relatively low,

Figure 3.6 The brain drain is a severe problem in a number of small countries

% of tertiary-educated individuals in OECD countries, 2000

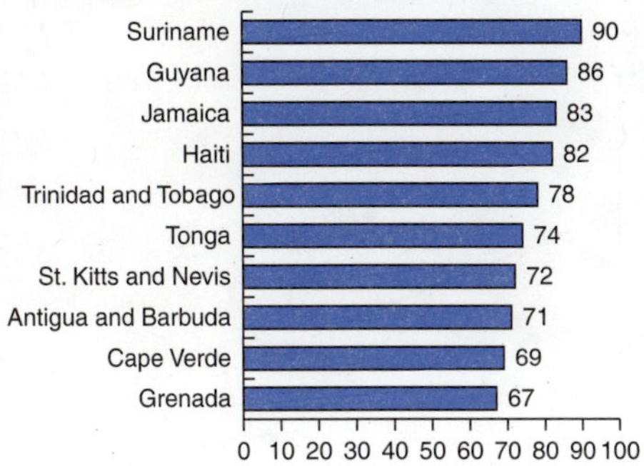

% of low-, medium-, and high-skilled individuals living in OECD countries, 2000

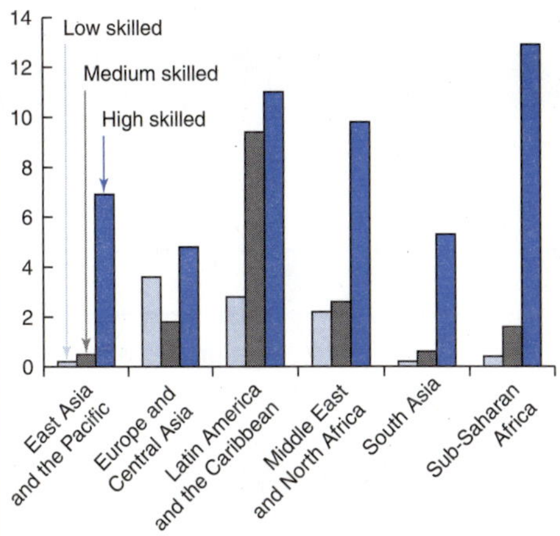

Source: World Bank staff calculations based on Docquier and Marfouk 2004.

Note: OECD = Organisation for Economic Co-operation and Development.

ranging from 5 to 13 percent depending on the region (figure 3.6), because the number of such individuals also doubled.

The emigration of professionals who make a direct contribution to production, such as engineers, may result in reduced rates of domestic innovation and technology adoption (Kapur and McHale 2005a). Emigration rates for scientists, engineers, and members of the medical profession tend to be higher than for the general university-educated population. For example, in India, the emigration rate for those with a tertiary education is 4 percent, but the rate for graduates of the elite Indian Institutes of Technology ranged from 20 to 30 percent in the 1980s and 1990s (Docquier and Marfouk 2004; Khadria 2004).

More moderate migration rates may be beneficial, especially when domestic opportunities are limited, because of technological transfers from the diaspora and because most migration is not a one-way flow. For example, a majority of foreign students from many developing countries who earn their doctorates in the United States return home (figure 3.7), bringing with them a great deal of technological and market knowledge that represents an important technological transfer in favor of the developing country.

The share of recent doctoral graduates from developing countries who remain in the host country varies significantly across countries of origin. In part, these cross-national differences reflect differences in opportunity costs. The likelihood that a student remains in the United States after graduation falls as average per capita incomes in the home country rise. However, even at a given income level, the length of stay varies significantly across countries, with fewer graduates returning home to countries such as Argentina, China, India, and the Islamic Republic of Iran than would be expected based on income alone. Other factors explaining high retention rates include the quality of living conditions and research facilities in high-income countries, as well as the density of research networks and the size of the preexisting diaspora. Factors favoring a return include proximity to family, cultural affinities, and emigrants' desire to contribute to technological progress in their native country.[18]

The diaspora is a major source of skills and capital

Repeated waves of emigration have led to the creation of vibrant diasporas that possess cutting-edge technology, capital, and professional contacts. For example, developing countries accounted for three-quarters (approximately 2.5 million) of the 3.3 million

Figure 3.7 Share of Ph.D. students still living in the United States five years after graduation

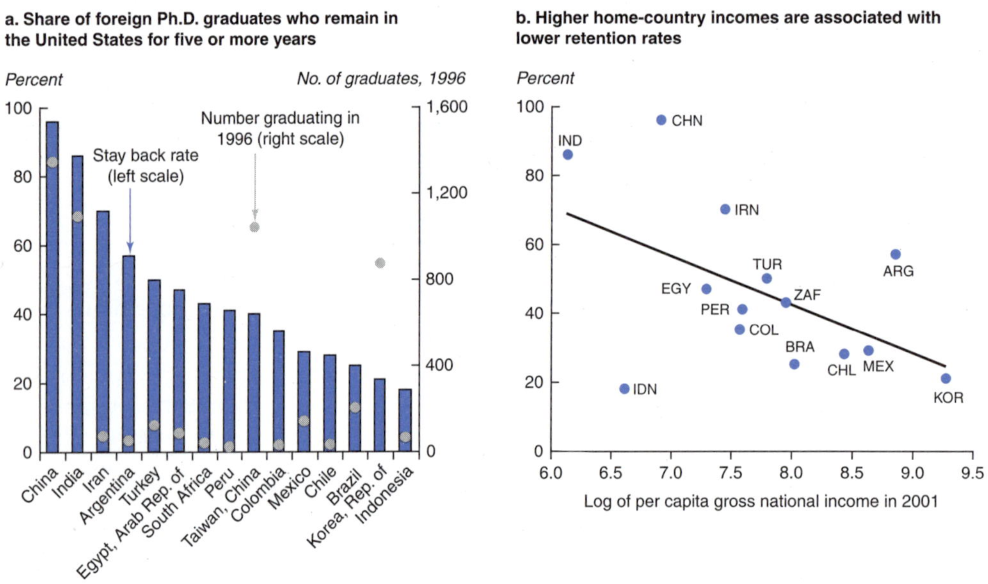

Source: World Bank calculations based on Finn 2003.
Note: Country mnemonics follow ISO standards.

immigrant scientists and engineers living in the United States in 2003.[19] Moreover, because out-migration rates are higher for high-skilled individuals than for low-skilled individuals, on average, the diaspora is much more skilled than the home-country population and represents an important concentration of expertise (figure 3.8). Notwithstanding the size of the diaspora, relatively little rigorous empirical research exists on whether and to what extent it influences technology adoption and creation in emigrants' home countries.[20] The primary evidence of diaspora contributions to knowledge transfers comes in the form of case studies. At a minimum, the technical, market, and marketing knowledge of national diasporas is a huge potential technological resource.[21]

Returning migrants can be a major source of entrepreneurship, technology, marketing knowledge, and investment capital (Brinkerhoff 2006a, 2006b; Kapur 2001).[22] Migrants returning to Egypt tend to have higher levels of human capital than nonmigrants and are likely to be more entrepreneurial the longer they work abroad (McCormick and Wahba 2003; Wahba 2007). Returning migrants and members of national diasporas who are still abroad

Figure 3.8 High-skilled emigrants are disproportionately represented in the diaspora

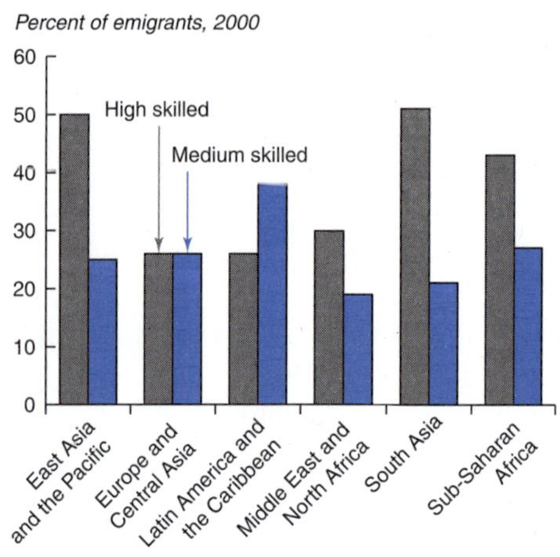

Source: Docquier and Marfouk 2004.

Box 3.5 Technological transfers through the diaspora and return migrants: Some examples

An émigré from Bangladesh working in the financial sector in the United States returned to help create the Grameen Phone network and make mobile phones available to poor people in remote villages (Sullivan 2007). Through its successful Village Phone Program, the network has provided business opportunities to some 260,000 Village Phone operators, mostly poor rural women. Grameen Phone now has 15 million customers, more than 10 times the maximum potential client base initially estimated by Bangladesh Telecom.

In India, Sam Pitroda, a global entrepreneur who divides his time between India and the United States, founded the Center for Development of Telematics, which developed rural automatic telephone exchanges and introduced shared public call offices all over the country, thus expanding access to cheap and reliable domestic and international calling. The relatively low-cost telephone exchanges are designed to operate without air conditioning and require significantly less maintenance than conventional exchanges. The technology has been exported to several other developing countries.

Bata Shoes of the Czech Republic is an early example of technology diffusion through migration and return. Faced with the threat of bankruptcy at his small shoemaking business in the early 1900s, the founder of the company, Tomas G. Bata Sr. went to the United States in 1904 to learn more efficient mass production methods. Bata returned to the Czech Republic to apply these production techniques. He eventually expanded production to several other countries, including India, Poland, and the former Yugoslavia, and became the world's leading footwear maker by the 1930s. Faced with nationalization in 1945, the founder's son moved his family and the company's headquarters to Canada, returning to the Czech Republic once again in 1989 with a further transfer of technology and business know-how acquired over the intervening years. Since then, the Bata company has continued to spread technology. It has opened stores in Croatia, Poland, Russia, and Slovenia, as well as a production facility in China, and is modernizing its Batanagar factory complex in India.

Source: http://www.bata.com; Factiva; Telenor press releases.

have made major contributions to technological progress in their home countries (box 3.5).

The diaspora also contributes to technology transfers and adoption by strengthening trade and investment linkages. The high-skilled diaspora of countries such as India has contributed to the growth of the information technology sector, outsourcing (Kapur and McHale 2005b; Pandey and others 2006), and FDI in their home countries. The flow of outward FDI from the United States is strongly correlated with the stock of migrants from the origin country.[23] Nearly half of the $41 billion in FDI that China received in 2000 may have originated from its diaspora abroad (Wei 2004). Similarly, 60 percent of the increase in bilateral trade in differentiated products within Southeast Asia may be attributable to ethnic Chinese networks (Rauch and Trindade 2002).[24] Moreover, technology appears to diffuse more efficiently through culturally and nationally linked groups, and shared ethnicity appears to counteract the kind of home bias effects that underpin the geographic network or the cluster effects that give high-density R&D zones an innovation advantage (Agrawal, Kapur, and McHale 2004).

Diaspora networks and returnees help promote technology adoption

The diaspora's political engagement in home countries can also improve local technological absorptive capacity, both through return and by exercising pressure on home country politicians from afar. Many leaders of developing countries were educated abroad and returned to strengthen political institutions in their countries of origin (Easterly and Nyarko 2005). In addition, migrants have often played a valuable role in the transfer of market-based institutions, such as venture capital, entrepreneurship, and corporate transparency, to their countries of origin.[25] Overseas Taiwanese engineers and returnees, for example, worked closely with policy makers to establish a successful venture capital industry. This has provided local entrepreneurs with an alternative source of finance, which has helped them overcome the constraint posed by the reluctance of state-owned financial institutions to lend to high-risk entrepreneurial activities in the technology sector (Kuznetsov 2007).

Expatriate knowledge networks have been created to foster regular contacts; transfers of skills; and opportunities for business with researchers, scientists, and entrepreneurs in the country of origin. Brown (2000) identified 41 such networks for 30 different countries. These networks tend to be rich depositories of talent with high concentrations of members with advanced degrees, many earned in the host countries.[26] Colombia's Red Caldas network, set up with government assistance in 1991, was one of the first diaspora networks that succeeded in promoting collaborative research between domestic scientists and Colombian researchers abroad through workshops and symposiums, joint research programs, visiting researchers, scientific events, publications, and research and training opportunities (Chaparro, Jaramillo, and Quintero 2006). Less formal networks played an important role in the transition of the Republic of Korea and Taiwan (China) from developing to high-income economies.[27] Some diaspora networks have failed, principally because they were too ambitious, particularly in cases where the policy and institutional environment in the home country were not supportive.[28] Research suggests that the most successful models start small to build up trust and credibility before attempting to sponsor a major research project or cooperative agenda (Kuznetsov 2006).

Remittances can promote technology diffusion by making investments more affordable

Remittances to developing countries have grown steadily in recent years, reaching $207 billion in 2006, and are now are larger than FDI and equity inflows in many countries, especially small, low-income countries. Remittances can support the diffusion of technology by reducing the credit constraints of receiving households and encouraging investment and entrepreneurship (Fajnzylber and López 2007; Puri and Ritzema 1999; Woodruff and Zenteno 2007; World Bank 2006a). A survey of self-employed workers and small firms in Mexico found that remittances were responsible for one-fifth of the capital invested in microenterprises in urban Mexico (Woodruff and Zenteno 2001). In the Philippines, households work more hours in self-employment and become more likely to start relatively capital-intensive household enterprises in response to an exogenous increase in remittances (Yang 2006).

Remittance flows have also contributed to the extension of banking services (often by using innovative technologies), including microfinance, to previously unserved, often rural, sectors. This has improved the access of households and firms to financial services (box 2.8; Gupta, Pattillo, and Waugh 2007), and their ability to purchase and invest in technology. For example, remittance revenues may have helped Ghana's ApexLink and Mongolia's Xac banks to expand their networks and services (Isern, Donges, and Smith 2006). Cell phone money transfers, such as G-cash and Smart Padala in the Philippines, and card-based remittances are becoming prevalent in a number of countries, including Mozambique, South Africa, and the United Arab Emirates, and are likely to expand to other countries in the coming years (Helms 2006; Jordan 2006). Remittances have also helped domestic banks foster links with banks in high-income countries. In turn, such links have fostered technology transfers as banks in high-income countries have helped local partners to upgrade their systems to comply with the anti-money-laundering, antiterrorism, and know-your-customer regulations in developed countries.

A summary index of trends in the exposure of developing countries to external technology

The preceding paragraphs have argued that developing countries gain access to foreign technology through trade, FDI, and the diaspora and that these links have been increasing over time. This section reports on the results of an effort to summarize these trends by applying principal components analysis to five data series covering trade and FDI following the same basic methodology as used in chapter 2 to create the index of technological achievement.[29]

The index shows that the relationship between income levels and exposure to external technology is relatively weak across countries. Even though the average exposure is higher as one moves from low-income to upper-middle-income developing countries, substantial variation is apparent across countries. This variation partly reflects issues of country size (smaller countries tend to be more open than larger countries), but it also stems from varying degrees of specialization among countries.

The index also shows that many countries have increased their exposure to technology during the 1990s (figure 3.9). Of the developing countries for which data are available, 17 experienced a reduction in exposure to foreign technologies over the 1990s and 70 saw their exposure rise. The average percentage increase was highest in low-income and in upper-middle-income countries, with the increase among lower-middle-income countries actually being below that observed among high-income countries. These average results reflect a mix of strong increases in excess of 100 percent in a number of countries and less spectacular increases in others.

Much of the variation is attributable to strong increases in the degree of openness among the transition economies. The average improvement in the index of exposure to foreign technology for the countries of Europe and Central Asia was 80 percent. Excluding these countries from the sample lowers the average increase in middle-income countries significantly, resulting in a clear negative relationship between the observed increase in exposure to foreign technologies and incomes (table 3.5). This is particularly encouraging for low-income countries, as the gains from such exposure tend to be nonlinear and enduring (Lumenga-Neso, Olarreaga, and Schiff 2005). For middle-income countries and South Asia, however, this result suggests that many countries (notably those in South Asia) may be missing out on the potential benefits to be achieved from increased openness.

Nurturing technological adaptive capacity

Openness to trade, FDI, and international communication through the diaspora, other networks, and various media all serve to expose a country to technologies and applications of technologies that may not have been exploited domestically. Exposure does not, however, guarantee that these new technologies will spread and grow within the domestic economy. Too often technologically sophisticated processes or products are limited to a few major centers or foreign-owned enclaves. How far these technologies diffuse within a country is determined by its technological adaptive capacity, that is, the quality of its labor force and the business environment (including access to finance) in which firms operate and are able (or unable) to start up, expand, and reap the financial rewards of their new-to-the-market innovations. In the following sections we explore recent trends in technological adaptive capacity among developing countries and the roles firms, governments, and individuals play in creating and supporting that capacity.

Governance and the business climate

A stable and predictable economic environment reduces the risk that returns to investments in technology and innovative business activities will be lost to conflict or widely variable inflation and exchange rates. A stable regulatory environment that facilitates the conduct of business by enforcing property

Figure 3.9 Most developing countries have increased their exposure to external technology

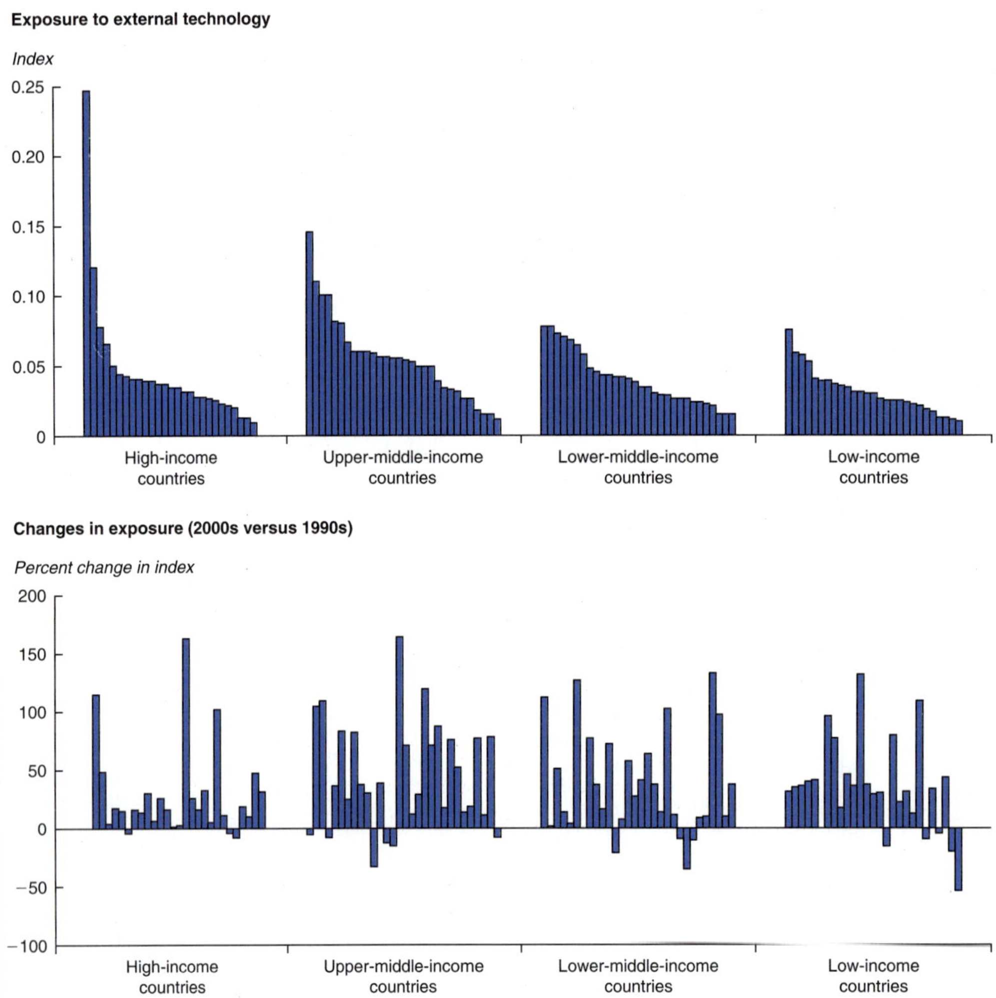

Source: World Bank.

rights, by limiting corruption, and by not imposing onerous requirements that make the creation or expansion of firms or their adoption of new technologies unnecessarily difficult also contributes to an economy's technological adaptive capacity.

Political and macroeconomic stability have improved countries' ability to exploit technology

Over the past 15 years, the number of countries involved in international or domestic conflict, as measured by the International Crisis Behavior Project, has declined significantly (figure 3.10). The decline has been most pronounced in Sub-Saharan Africa, where the total number of countries in conflict declined from a peak of 10 in 1998 to only 2 in 2004. Among its many benefits, the cessation of conflict can provide an environment that is more conducive to both private and public sector investments in technology. For example, 12 years after the end of hostilities, the government of Rwanda launched an ambitious

Table 3.5 Increases in exposure to external technologies index, 1990s to 2000s

	All countries	(excluding Europe and Central Asia)
Regions	*(percent change)*	
East Asia and the Pacific	13.4	
Europe and Central Asia	83.7	
Latin America and the Caribbean	33.4	
Middle-East and North Africa	37.8	
South Asia	13.7	
Sub-Saharan Africa	33.4	
Income groups		
High-income countries	27.7	27.7
Upper-middle-income countries	45.1	24.4
Lower-middle-income countries	36.2	31.7
Low-income countries	33.5	33.5

Source: World Bank.
Note: Values are unweighted averages of country-specific changes.

program of technological capacity building (Watkins and Verma 2007).

Improved macroeconomic stability and growth in developing countries has also contributed to an environment that is more friendly toward technological investment.[30] High and variable inflation and high exchange rate volatility increase the risk involved in investments in technology and increase the returns to financial manipulation relative to investment. High government deficits and debt also increase uncertainty, especially when combined with a rigid exchange rate regime, a combination that increases the likelihood of an abrupt revaluation that would further cloud expected future returns. The median inflation rate in developing countries fell from 19 percent in the early 1990s to 4 to 6 percent during the first half of this decade, exchange rate volatility is down, and government deficits have declined across the board and are now below 3 percent of GDP in every developing region except South Asia. Moreover, the acceleration of per capita income growth over the past 15 years, which has been most marked over the past 6 years, has improved the overall affordability of technology (table 3.6).

A weak business environment and poor governance can impair technological progress

Regulatory restrictions that impair the economy's flexibility may limit the absorption of technology. Restrictions on labor mobility and rules that constrain firms' ability to reallocate workers within the firm can be important barriers to the adoption of new technologies (Parente and Prescott 1994). For example,

Figure 3.10 Number of countries in conflict worldwide

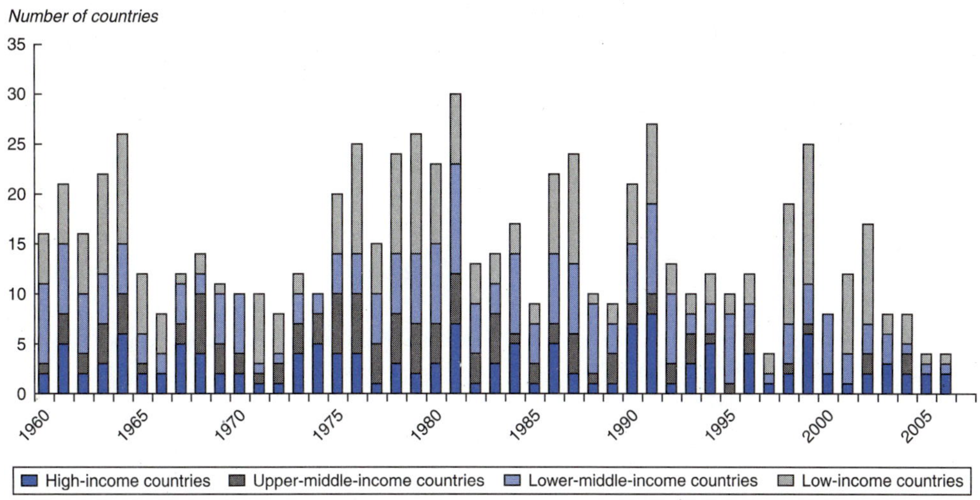

Source: International Crisis Behavior database. http://www.cidcn.umd.edu.icb.

Table 3.6 Macroeconomic stability has improved in developing countries

	Median inflation rate[a]			Real effective exchange rate volatility[b]		
	1990–94	2002–06	Difference	1990–94	2002–06	Difference
World	11.1	3.6	−7.5	3.7	1.4	2.3
High-income countries	3.4	2.1	−1.3	1.6	0.8	0.8
Upper-middle-income countries	19.2	4.5	−14.7	2.8	1.4	1.4
Lower-middle-income countries	16.3	4.7	−11.6	6.5	1.2	5.3
Low-income countries	9.2	4.0	−5.2	3.9	2.0	1.9
Developing countries	18.8	4.2	−14.5	4.5	1.5	3.0
East Asia and the Pacific	7.1	3.4	−3.7	1.3	1.2	0.1
Europe and Central Asia	326.8	4.3	−322.5	10.6	1.2	9.4
Latin America and the Caribbean	17.1	5.5	−11.6	2.9	1.3	1.6
Middle East and North Africa	8.9	3.7	−5.2	1.9	1.2	0.7
South Asia	9.8	5.4	−4.4	1.4	1.1	0.3
Sub-Saharan Africa	9.2	4.6	−4.6	3.9	2.1	1.8

	General government balance[c]			General government debt[d]		
	1990–94	2002–06	Difference	1990–94	2002–06	Difference
World	−5.0	−1.5	3.5	62.6	64.1	1.5
High-income countries	−4.3	0.8	5.1	58.7	55.6	−3.0
Upper-middle-income countries, excluding ECA	−2.3	−2.1	0.2	55.1	74.5	19.4
Lower-middle-income countries, excluding ECA	−3.8	−2.9	0.9	64.3	57.5	−6.8
Low-income countries, excluding ECA	−5.4	−1.9	3.5	97.9	106.5	8.7
Developing countries, excluding ECA	−4.1	−2.2	1.9	73.3	78.7	5.4
East Asia and the Pacific	−2.0	−2.1	−0.1	45.6	57.0	11.4
Europe and Central Asia	−9.4	−1.9	7.5	38.9	37.2	−1.7
Latin America and the Caribbean	−2.2	−2.8	−0.6	67.5	69.7	2.2
Middle East and North Africa	−6.6	−2.8	3.9	71.6	71.3	−0.3
South Asia	−7.7	−6.1	1.5	78.2	76.3	−1.9
Sub-Saharan Africa	−5.3	−1.4	3.9	88.6	97.6	8.9

	GDP per capita growth[e]		
	1985–94	1995–2006	Difference
World	1.8	2.5	0.7
High-income countries	2.1	2.5	0.4
Upper-middle-income countries, excluding ECA	2.9	2.1	−0.8
Lower-middle-income countries, excluding ECA	1.1	2.1	1.0
Low-income countries, excluding ECA	−0.5	1.6	2.1
Developing countries, excluding ECA	2.0	2.0	0.0
East Asia and the Pacific	3.7	2.5	−1.1
Europe and Central Asia	−2.4	4.9	7.3
Latin America and the Caribbean	2.1	1.7	−0.5
Middle East and North Africa	3.2	2.1	−1.1
South Asia	2.6	3.3	0.7
Sub-Saharan Africa	0.6	2.6	2.0

Source: DataStream, International Monetary Fund, JP Morgan, World Bank.
Note: ECA = Europe and Central Asia.

a. Calculated as the mean over each indicated period of the median monthly (year over year) Consumer price index inflation rates of the countries in each grouping.
b. Calculated as the period average of the absolute value of the month-over-month percent change of the real effective exchange rate of countries in each grouping.
c. Calculated as the period average of the simple mean across countries of the central government budget deficit as reported by the International Monetary Fund.
d. Calculated as the period average of the simple mean across countries of the government debt as reported to the World Bank (for low- and middle-income countries and as per the IMF for high-income countries).
e. Calculated as the period average of the simple mean across countries of the growth in GDP per capita.

stringent labor market regulations in Brazil undermine productivity and technical efficiency (World Bank 2005), and the removal of labor market regulations that result in involuntary overstaffing would increase labor productivity by 7 percent in India (World Bank 2004b). Similarly, restrictions on firm exit and entry can impede technological progress by propping up inefficient firms and limiting the expansion and creation of innovative firms.[31]

Rules and regulations governing firm start-up can be particularly important, because they have the potential to prevent a new technology or new-to-the-market product or process from seeing the light of day. The World Bank's indicators on doing business suggest substantial room for improvement in most developing regions. On average, an entrepreneur seeking to begin a new business must undertake more than 9 separate procedures, which can take almost 50 days to complete (table 3.7). Among high-income countries that belong to the Organisation for Economic Co-operation and Development (OECD), the equivalent figures are 6 procedures and 17 days. Moreover, in developing countries the associated fees are particularly onerous given income levels, consuming more than an amount equivalent to 1.5 years worth of per capita income for a person living in South Asia, compared with 5 days worth of the per capita income of someone in an OECD country. Minimum capital requirements are also high compared with income and likely limit the size of formal small and medium enterprise sectors, particularly in the Middle East and North Africa and in Sub-Saharan Africa, where they represent more than two years of average earnings.

Ensuring timely and efficient exit by failed businesses also promotes technological progress by freeing unemployed and underemployed capital and workers for more efficient uses. Developing countries, on average, require much more time to resolve insolvencies (ranging from 2.7 years for East Asia and the Pacific to 5.0 years for South Asia) than OECD countries (which require an average of 1.3 years). In addition, the amount recovered averages less than 30 cents on the dollar in all developing regions (and only 20 cents in South Asia and 17 cents in Sub-Saharan Africa), compared with 74 cents on the dollar in OECD countries.[32]

The quality of regulation, including its enforcement, and of the business legal environment are critical determinants of the capacity of new and innovative firms to grow and expand. For example, the ability of such firms to finance their initial operations or conduct arms-length operations, both of which are crucial for technologically advanced companies that require a large customer base to exploit economies of scale, depend on the

Table 3.7 The regulatory burden is heavier in developing countries than in the OECD

	Procedures	Duration	Cost	Minimum capital requirements
	(number)	*(days)*	*(% of GNI per capita)*	*(% of GNI per capita)*
East Asia and the Pacific	8.2	46	43	60
Europe and Central Asia	9.4	32	14	54
Latin America and the Caribbean	10.2	73	48	18
Middle East and North Africa	10.3	41	75	745
South Asia	7.9	62	163	1
Sub-Saharan Africa	11.1	33	47	210
Developing-country average	**9.5**	**47.8**	**65**	**181**
OECD countries	**6.2**	**16.6**	**5**	**36**
Memo:				
Ratio of developing-country average to OECD average	1.5	2.9	12.2	5.0

Source: World Bank; Doing Business. http://www.doingbusiness.org
Notes: Procedures required to register a firm, average time spent during each procedure, offical cost of each procedure, and minimum capital required as a percent of income per capita; GNI = gross national income.

Figure 3.11 Efficiency of contract enforcement

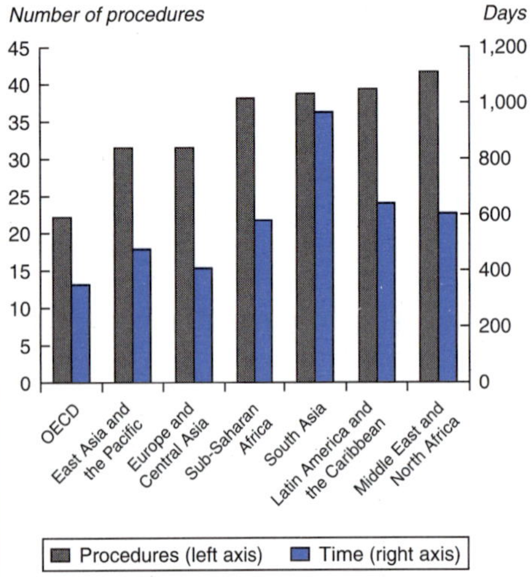

Sources: World Bank; Doing Business. http://www.doingbusiness.org.

Figure 3.12 Developing country governance scores relative to OECD average

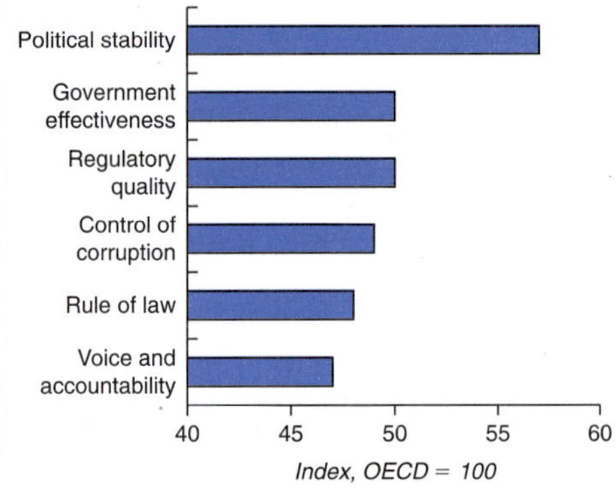

Source: Kaufmann, Kraay, and Mastruzzi 2007.

system's ability to enforce contracts, establish property rights, and enforce court decisions in a timely and cost-effective manner.

Although the number of procedures required to enforce a court decision in the case of a contract dispute in developing countries is significantly higher than in OECD countries, the time taken to reach a decision is not too much greater (with the notable exception of South Asia), generally less than 25 days, compared with 13 days in OECD countries (figure 3.11). However, the time required to enforce legal decisions approaches two years in four of six regions. This seriously affects firms' (and consumers') ability to effect arms-length transactions with confidence, and is therefore an important inhibitor to the growth of technologically sophisticated firms.

Corruption can also prevent entrepreneurs from making investments in technology and expanding their businesses in a manner that helps extend the penetration of technologies into the economy, while increasing the relative return to activities aimed at influencing policy makers. Moreover, better governance is also associated with improvements in process technology, particularly in the delivery of government and regulated services. For example, Kaufmann, Kraay, and Mastruzzi (2007) estimate that an improvement of one standard deviation in the summary governance indicator is associated, in the long term, with a two-thirds reduction in infant mortality and a tripling of incomes.

Surveys suggest that developing countries lag behind high-income countries on a wide range of governance indicators (figure 3.12). For example, government effectiveness and regulatory quality are typically considered to be at half of OECD levels, with indicators for corruption, rule of law, and voice and accountability being even lower.

These aggregate results hide a certain amount of variation across countries and regions (figure 3.13). Governance in the Caribbean and in Eastern Europe and the Baltic countries appears to be much stronger (more than 70 percent of the OECD level) than in the rest of the developing world, while countries in the former Soviet Union and Sub-Saharan Africa have the lowest ratings, only 34 and 28 percent of OECD levels, respectively.

In contrast to other indicators of performance, such as inflation and openness, there is little evidence that developing countries have

Figure 3.13 Regional averages of six governance indicators

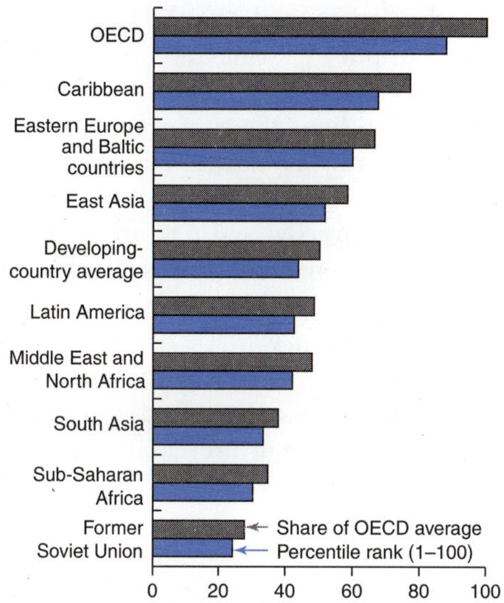

Sources: World Bank; Doing Business. http://www.doingbusiness.org.

markedly improved their governance over the past decade. Despite individual country improvements and marked gains in the regulatory environment in Europe and Central Asia, on average, the quality of governance around the world has not improved much over the past decade (see the World Bank's *Governance Matters* series). For each country that has done well, one has experienced deterioration in its governance indicators. Two countries that have experienced notable deterioration are Belarus and the República Bolivariana de Venezuela. Many countries have not experienced any significant change in either direction. On the positive side, the *Governance Matters* series shows that where countries are committed to reform, improvements can take place relatively quickly. For example, during the relatively brief period of 2002–06, Kenya, Liberia, and Ukraine made significant advances in voice and accountability, while Algeria and Angola made substantial progress in political stability. Thus the potential exists for a rapid, substantial improvement in the quality of governance in many developing countries, an improvement that would encourage technological progress.

Basic technological literacy

While the policy environment is critical to the absorption of technology, technological progress also requires a literate workforce. The process by which external technologies are absorbed, adapted, and integrated into an economy is not a mechanical one, but one that depends on the quality, quantity, and distribution of human capital, that is, on the technological competencies and the health of the people that use and implement the technology. For this reason, efforts to increase the technological competency, knowledge, and understanding of populations, firms, and governments lie at the heart of the World Bank's technology agenda. Especially among poor countries and in rural areas, existing deficits in terms of basic skills are a binding obstacle to technological progress and income growth.

Low incomes and poor health impair skill formation for technological progress

Low income and poor health are perhaps among the most basic constraints to technological progress. Even if profitable investments in technology are available, inadequate income limits the ability to generate resources for investment. At the level of the economy, low income is both a cause and an effect of low levels of human capital, limited funds allocated to research, thin financial markets, often poor governance, and sometimes violence and macroeconomic instability, all of which limit the ability to absorb technological innovations.

Recent developments in relation to income levels are heartening. Growth rates of GDP per capita have picked up throughout the developing world over the past 15 years (figure 3.14). The number of people living in absolute poverty has declined by more than 250 million, and their share in the population of the developing world is expected to fall from 18 percent in 2004 to around 11 percent by 2015 (chapter 1).

Figure 3.14 Per capita incomes have accelerated in recent years

Average growth in annual per capita incomes

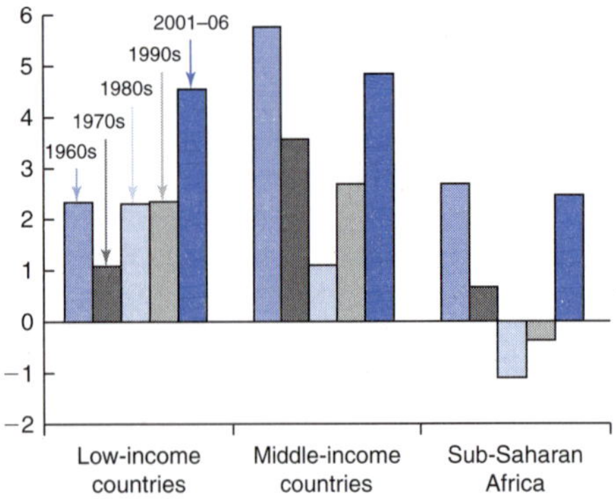

Source: World Bank.

Similarly, welcome developments have taken place in basic health. Life expectancy at birth has reached 70 years in middle-income countries and continues to converge to still-rising high-income country levels (figure 3.15). Among low-income countries, life expectancy is also converging with high-income countries. Excluding Sub-Saharan Africa, where life expectancy has been declining because of HIV/AIDS, life expectancy in low-income countries increased from 59 years in 1990 to 64 years in 2005, suggesting that in much of the world, poor health should be decreasing as a factor impeding technological progress.

Figure 3.15 Except in Sub-Saharan Africa, life expectancy is improving

Life expectancy at birth (years)

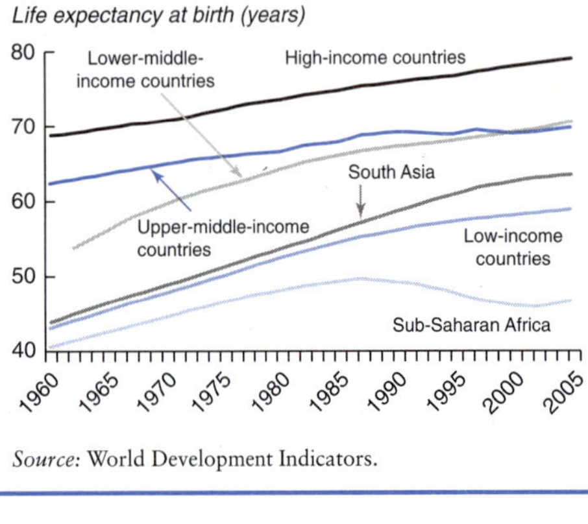

Source: World Development Indicators.

In Sub-Saharan Africa, the combination of incomes that are still extremely low and the ravages of HIV/AIDS are more problematic. The failure to control HIV/AIDS is itself an example of poor dissemination of technology and problems of affordability, as both the know-how to limit the spread of the disease and to control its health effects are well known, even though implementation strategies are controversial and tend to be country specific. Some countries, such as Uganda, have succeeded in reducing HIV infection rates. Other countries in western Africa have succeeded in limiting its spread. Still others, notably Botswana, are doing better at treating those infected than in preventing new infection. In too many countries, however, the epidemic continues to grow more or less uncontrolled, with widespread societal consequences (World Bank 2007b). Estimates suggest that in Burkina Faso, Rwanda, and Uganda, HIV/AIDS is likely to increase the percentage of people living in extreme poverty by as much as 6 percentage points between 2000 and 2015 (UNDP 2003). In Kenya, HIV/AIDS may reduce GDP per adult by 11 percent by 2040 compared with what it would have been in the absence of HIV/AIDS (Bell, Bruhns, and Gersbach 2006). In addition to the incalculable human costs implied, continued high death rates in the adult population will have further negative implications for the ability of these countries to acquire and to apply technology, both because the experience and technological competencies of the adults expected to die will be lost and because the educational attainment and literacy of their children and dependents will be impaired (Bell, Devarajan, and Gersbach 2004).

Illiteracy is declining, but still blocks countries' ability to absorb new technologies

The level of human capital is a major determinant of an economy's ability to adapt and absorb both sophisticated and even more basic technologies.[33] In both high-income (Eaton and Kortum 1996) and developing countries

(Caselli and Coleman 2001), the extent to which a given technology is used within a country depends importantly on the educational attainment of the population, both because such skills help individuals learn how to make effective use of a new-to-the-firm or farm technique, and because they increase the likelihood that firms will learn of new innovations beyond the scope of their local communities.

Although the gap between the educational attainment of individuals living in developing countries and those in high-income countries remains wide, it is closing, both in terms of the most basic indicators (literacy and primary school completion rates) and more sophisticated indicators, such as tertiary education enrollment rates (table 3.8). Over the past 15 years, literacy rates have increased throughout the developing world, with the biggest increases recorded among low-income countries, particularly in South Asia. Reported literacy rates in Europe and Central Asia rival those in high-income countries, while in East Asia and the Pacific and Latin America and the Caribbean, literacy rates are at or close to 90 percent. Elsewhere literacy lags considerably, with only 73 percent of the population in the Middle East and North Africa being able to

Table 3.8 Educational attainment indicators

	Adult literacy rate		Female literacy rate		Expected years of schooling	
	1990–2005	2005[a]	1990–2005	2005[a]	2001–05	2005
Regions	*(% point change)*	*(% of population aged 15 and older)*	*(% point change)*	*(% of female population aged 15 and older)*	*(% change)*	*(years of schooling)*
East Asia and the Pacific	10.7	91	14.9	87	1.9	11.2
Europe and Central Asia	1.3	97	1.8	96	0.8	12.7
Latin America and the Caribbean	2.3	90	2.6	89	0.5	13.1
Middle East and North Africa	14.7	73	16.5	63	2.1	11.7
South Asia	11.6	58	12.8	46	4.0	9.7
Sub-Saharan Africa	5.1	59	5.2	50	3.5	8.0
Income groups						
World	**6.0**	**82**	**7.3**	**77**	**2.0**	**10.9**
High income	0.3	99	0.3	98	0.4	15.8
Upper middle income	0.8	93	1.9	92	0.5	13.3
Lower middle income	9.2	89	12.0	85	2.0	11.5
Low income	9.3	61	10.1	50	3.5	9.0

	Primary completion rate		Secondary completion rate		Tertiary completion rate	
	1991–2005	2005	1990–2000	2000	1990–2000	2000
Regions	*(% point change)*	*(% of relevant age group)*	*(% point change)*	*(% of population aged 15 and older)*	*(% point change)*	*(% of population aged 15 and older)*
East Asia and the Pacific	−1.7	97.7	1.5	13.7	0.8	2.5
Europe and Central Asia	2.2	94.9	0.1	13.5	1.6	5.5
Latin America and the Caribbean	16.9	98.5	1.1	8.7	1.2	4.9
Middle East and North Africa	13.7	90.7	2.1	10.0	1.4	3.4
South Asia	18.1	83.5	0.5	7.0	0.5	2.0
Sub-Saharan Africa	11.5	60.8	0.5	2.3	0.4	1.0
Income groups						
World	**n.a.**	**87.6**	**0.4**	**11.9**	**1.0**	**4.9**
High income	n.a.	97.4	−0.7	18.6	2.9	13.3
Upper middle-income	10.3	98.5	0.7	12.4	1.4	4.9
Lower middle-income	2.7	96.6	1.4	12.4	0.9	2.9
Low income	17.0	75.9	0.5	6.1	0.4	1.8

Source: World Development Indicators.
a. Actual reference year varies by country.

read and write and about 60 percent in South Asia and in Sub-Saharan Africa. Moreover, there are concerns about the comparability of these data, as some low-income countries reportedly define literacy as the ability to read and write one's own name.

Divergence in the literacy rates for women explain much of the disparity. For example, in South Asia fewer than half of women age 15 and older are literate. Women in the Middle East and North Africa and Sub-Saharan Africa fare somewhat better, with literacy rates of 63 and 50 percent, respectively. Although the technological consequences of such widespread illiteracy are difficult to quantify, illiterate mothers are much less successful in assisting their children to learn (Behrman and others 1999), have much more difficulty in absorbing new techniques and instructions that are transmitted in written form, and are likely to be less effective workers than their better educated peers. Indeed, female illiteracy and the resulting relative ignorance of best practices in child rearing may be a major causal factor in poor child health care and poor female labor force outcomes (Rosenzweig and Wolpin 1994).

Rising primary school completion rates should drive further improvements in adult literacy

The rise in literacy rates is due in no small part to increased and longer participation in formal education. Primary school completion rates approach 100 percent in about half of the developing regions and have increased substantially among poorer regions, notably South Asia and Sub-Saharan Africa. Although reflective of the average literacy in the geographical region, these numbers hide important variations across countries. Thus the low score for South Asia reflects mainly low literacy in India, and it masks the fact that some 95 percent of Sri Lankan youth can read and write. Similarly, China's relatively high literacy rates and its large weight in East Asia aggregate mask the less than 90 percent literacy rates of less populous countries such as Cambodia and the Lao People's Democratic Republic. In particular, the gap between school completion rates for girls and boys has narrowed significantly. Partly as a consequence, youth literacy rates are much higher than adult literacy rates in South Asia and Sub-Saharan Africa, which over time should be reflected in better literacy scores for women and improved transmission of knowledge and technology to future generations (table 3.9).

Table 3.9 Relatively high youth literacy rates

	Youth literacy rate	
	1990–2005	2005[a]
Regions	*(% point change)*	*(% of population age 15–24)*
East Asia and the Pacific	3.43	98
Europe and Central Asia	1.67	99
Latin America and the Caribbean	2.29	96
Middle East and North Africa	12.23	88
South Asia	13.72	73
Sub-Saharan Africa	5.42	70
Income groups		
World	**4.16**	**88**
High-income countries	0.23	99
Upper-middle-income countries	1.82	98
Lower-middle-income countries	3.68	96
Low-income countries	10.41	73

Source: World Bank; World Development Indicators.
a. Actual reference year varies by country.

Of course, progress in providing effective basic education is a necessary precursor of more formal secondary and tertiary education. Nevertheless, the more advanced technical and problem-solving skills that are taught at the basic level can significantly increase students' capacity to learn to work with, adapt, and maintain more technologically advanced goods. Indeed, the main obstacle to deepening the use of a given technique or process in a country is frequently a lack of sufficient numbers of individuals trained to maintain and install systems. For example, in Rwanda a shortage of plumbers and sheet metal workers has been identified as a principal factor constraining the deployment of the simple kind of rain-harvesting technologies that have succeeded in increasing the supply of sanitary drinking water in neighboring countries

(Watkins and Verma 2007). While nearly 19 percent of the population completes secondary school in high-income countries, secondary school attainment rates range between 10 and 14 percent in East Asia and the Pacific, Europe and Central Asia, and the Middle East and North Africa, but are below 9 percent in Latin America and the Caribbean, South Asia, and Sub-Saharan Africa (table 3.8). Between 1990 and 2000, secondary completion rates more than doubled in the Middle East and North Africa, East Asia and the Pacific, and Latin America and the Caribbean, but remain low. In contrast, improvements have been much less marked in South Asia and Sub-Saharan Africa, and no appreciable gain was apparent in Europe and Central Asia. By income grouping, the strongest gain in the secondary completion rate is reported by the lower-middle-income countries with an increase of 1.4 percentage points during 1990–2000, compared with half as much or less of an improvement among other income groupings.

This same general pattern is observed for tertiary-level students. In East Asia and the Pacific, South Asia, and Sub-Saharan Africa, 2.5 percent or less of the population aged 15 years or older has completed tertiary education. Europe and Central Asia and Latin America and the Caribbean have almost double the number of tertiary-level graduates, while the Middle East and North Africa falls in between these two groups of regions (table 3.8). The share of secondary graduates who go on to tertiary studies is relatively high in Latin America and the Caribbean, 60 percent, compared with 70 percent in high-income countries. However, the share of university students following a scientific as opposed to a social science curriculum is relatively low (Maloney 2006). Elsewhere, the ratio is 42 percent or lower, with only 18 percent of secondary graduates going on to the tertiary level in East Asia and the Pacific.

This performance in educational attainment across levels of schooling is largely consistent with patterns of public expenditures dedicated to education. For example, public expenditures

Figure 3.16 Educational expenditures have risen in some regions

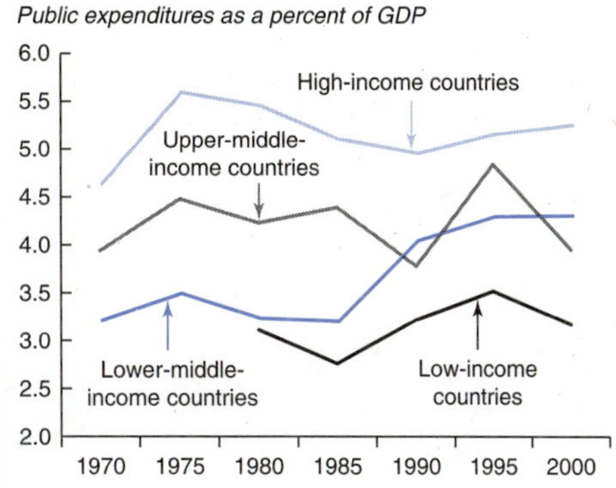

Sources: UNESCO Institute of Statistics; World Bank.

on education among lower-middle-income countries averaged about 3.3 percent of GDP during the 1970s and 1980s and rose to a fairly steady 4.3 percent during 1990 through 2000 (figure 3.16). Among low-income countries, the share of public outlays rose by about half a percentage point to an average of 3.3 percent of GDP during 1990–2000, up from an average of 2.9 percent during 1980 through 1985. These shares compare with government expenditures on education of close to 5.3 percent of GDP in high-income countries, down from a peak of just over 5.6 percent during the mid-1970s.[34]

While educational attainment rates and expenditure data are available for a fairly wide number of countries, the data are silent on the quality of the education (or knowledge) received, and it is the quality of education that determines the effectiveness with which individuals can absorb and exploit technology. Here significant concerns have been raised, particularly for poorer countries where the quality of educators and limited resources sap the value of time spent in school. This suggests that the education deficits in developing regions could be larger than indicated by national indicators, which, in turn, implies that the expansion of knowledge attained (and the capacity to adopt and adapt technological

Figure 3.17 Many developing country students fail to meet literacy standards

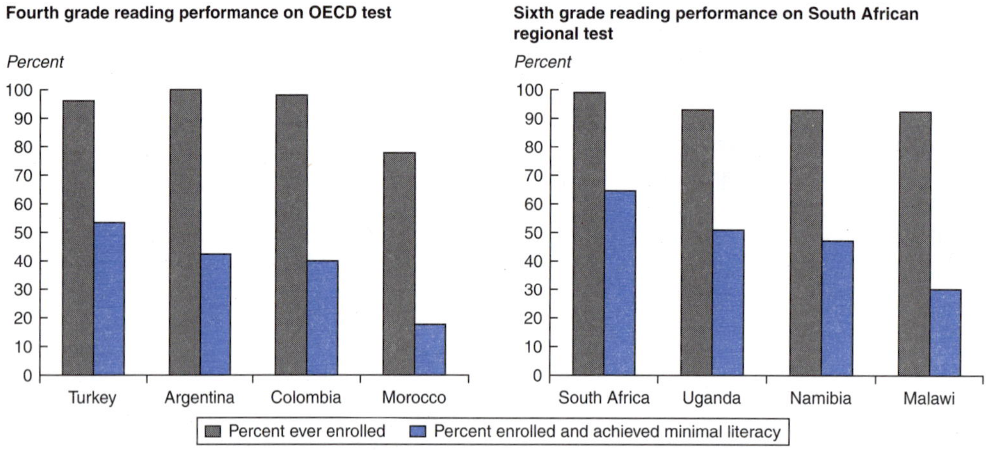

Source: World Bank 2007d.

knowledge) is not necessarily rising in accordance with higher educational attainment. The availability of international test scores across countries is very limited outside of high-incomes countries, but some data underscore these concerns. For example, in a number of middle-income countries, the majority of primary school students fail to meet OECD literacy standards. In Sub-Saharan Africa, despite enrollment rates of close to 100 percent, in some countries fewer than half of grade six students are deemed literate (figure 3.17). Although based primarily on data from high-income countries, research suggests that teacher quality is a key determinant of differences in student outcomes (Hanushek and Woessmann 2007).

Financing innovative firms

So far, the discussion has described how the policy environment and human capital can promote technology diffusion. At the same time, and as indicated in chapter 2, affordability, both at the level of the firm and of the consumer, can be a major impediment to the diffusion of technology within a country. In this regard, the success with which an economy's financial system succeeds in channeling resources (savings) toward their most productive use (investments) is an important determinant of its technological adaptive capacity.

Limited financial intermediation restricts technology diffusion

Neither the banking system, nor equity markets, nor private sector bond markets in developing countries have channeled savings into the private sector to the same extent as they have in high-income countries (table 3.10). As a result, the arm's-length channels through which private savings can be directed toward innovative firms are limited. While banks in high-income countries play a significant role in relaying private savings to investors (private-sector debt is equivalent to some 50 percent of GDP in high-income countries), this kind of intermediation occurs at about half that level in middle-income countries and almost not at all in low-income countries. On a more encouraging note, the run-up in international investors' appetite for risk has increased market capitalization in developing countries by significant margins since 2000 (with the exception of East Asia, where valuations declined). Valuation ratios are now much closer to those observed in high-income countries.

Table 3.10 Weak financial intermediation hinders technology in developing countries

	1990	2000	2005	% change 2005/1990	1990	2000	2005	% change 2005/1990
	Financial system deposits				Stock market capitalization			
	(% GDP)				(% GDP)			
Regions								
East Asia and the Pacific	40.9	41.7	45.6	11.5	38.7	44.1	51.3	32.5
Europe and Central Asia	23.8	22.8	31.2	31.0	8.5	13.8	19.7	130.8
Latin America and the Caribbean	31.1	39.9	39.8	28.1	11.7	28.2	46.4	298.3
Middle East and North Africa	46.5	47.4	59.8	28.7	16.0	26.1	63.8	298.3
South Asia	22.5	33.3	43.7	94.0	6.7	13.4	26.1	290.0
Sub-Saharan Africa	18.5	19.9	24.4	31.4	31.0	27.0	34.9	12.4
Income groups								
High-income countries	76.0	87.0	91.4	20.4	45.1	105.0	112.2	148.7
Upper-middle-income countries	34.3	43.6	45.2	31.8	37.7	36.5	50.2	33.4
Lower-middle-income countries	36.0	34.3	39.4	9.7	13.4	20.4	34.3	156.7
Low-income countries	16.7	17.4	21.8	30.7	7.6	10.8	22.3	194.7
	Private-sector credit				Private-sector debt			
	(% GDP)				(% GDP)			
Regions								
East Asia and the Pacific	30.3	36.7	44.9	48.2	—	37.5	31.0	..
Europe and Central Asia	22.3	18.2	27.9	25.3	—	12.7	12.2	.
Latin America and the Caribbean	28.6	40.6	32.1	12.3	—	27.2	23.3	..
Middle East and North Africa	35.3	40.5	46.1	30.7	—	—	—	..
South Asia	16.2	21.6	34.1	110.4	—	1.9	4.0	..
Sub-Saharan Africa	17.4	16.3	18.2	4.4	—	20.1	30.2	..
Income groups								
High-income countries	81.1	94.2	108.2	33.3	—	47.9	50.0	..
Upper-middle-income countries	32.8	42.5	40.5	23.6	—	27.5	26.1	..
Lower-middle-income countries	27.3	29.3	31.9	16.7	—	27.7	23.4	..
Low-income countries	14.9	13.4	16.4	9.7	—	1.9	4.0	..

Source: Beck, Demirgüç-Kunt, and Levine 2000. Financial Structure Dataset updated March 20, 2007. For Private Sector Debt the source is World Bank, Financial Sector Development Indicators. http://www.financial-indicators.org (February 2007).
Note: — = not available; .. = undefined.

Barriers to the finance of high-risk activities severely impede the spread of technology

Although weak intermediation is a general problem in developing countries, the problem for innovative firms or companies seeking to employ an untested new-to-the-market technique or product is more severe. Innovation can involve high risk, and traditional sources of capital—banks, stock exchanges, and bond markets—often lack the technical expertise to evaluate innovative investments. Thus in the absence of demonstrated cash flows or enforceable collateral, innovative firms or entrepreneurs are less likely to obtain financing than experienced entrepreneurs operating with proven techniques. Coupled with thin markets, this translates into higher capital costs for innovative firms in developing countries than for those in high-income countries, a fact that is reflected in lower R&D intensities (Lederman and Maloney 2006) and a reduced likelihood that their financing needs are met.[35]

Innovative firms in developing countries are also less likely to have access to equity financing than do their counterparts in high-income countries because of strict listing requirements imposed by the regulators of emerging-market exchanges[36] (Pfeil 2000). Less stringently regulated, so-called new markets, modeled after the NASDAQ in the United States, have been developed to fill the void. Many of these markets help investors by providing some, albeit less rigorous, due diligence of listed firms and by offering risk-pooling services (offerings of bundled shares that reduce investors' exposure to any one firm). Such capital pool companies allow listing firms to access equity finance in amounts that are too large for angel investors to provide, but are too small for institutional investors. However, the full promise of such markets has yet to be felt, in part because many of them have been obliged to maintain relatively strict listing requirements to attract foreign investors (Yoo 2007).

Increasingly, venture capitalists and "business angels" are playing a role in financing new technologically sophisticated firms in developing economies.[37] These investors tend to have more technological know-how than do traditional lenders and to be better able to judge the potential profitability of new ventures. Often the transfer of business and marketing expertise is as important as the infusion of capital in determining the difference between success and failure for young firms (Avnimelech and Teubal 2004; Mayer 2003). Even though empirical evidence is still scarce, this activity appears to be translating into increased innovation (Pfeil 2000). Western-based venture capitalists are increasingly becoming involved in markets in Asia (China and India), Eastern Europe (notably the Czech Republic, Hungary, and Russia), and South Africa. Notwithstanding this increased activity, Nastas (2007) reports that only 1 in 200 small and medium enterprises in emerging markets is likely to secure venture capital financing, and the ratio is undoubtedly lower for firms in less-developed countries.

Supporting innovative firms with R&D and outreach

While the process of technological advance occurs fundamentally at the firm level, the government, along with international and national organizations, including nongovernmental ones, can play a role in promoting the dissemination of knowledge within the domestic economy. In addition to the formal education system, less formal continuing education—notably, outreach programs and R&D programs that focus on adapting technologies to local conditions—have a central role to play.

R&D efforts to adapt existing technology to local conditions are expanding

Domestic R&D capacity is critical in determining an economy's capacity both to generate new technologies and to absorb technologies from abroad. Foreign technologies frequently need to be modified so that they are suitable for domestic circumstances. For example, equipment and processes may need to be adapted to differences in the quality of inputs and in the relative abundance of labor and capital, and a stock of researchers is often necessary to understand and evaluate advanced technology (Cohen and Levinthal 1989). Building up R&D capacity facilitates the imitation and adaption of foreign technologies and improves the extent to which positive spillovers from FDI and trade accrue to the rest of the economy (Fagerberg 1988; Kinoshita 2000). Moreover, countries tend to acquire technology more readily when domestic firms have R&D programs and when public research laboratories and universities have relatively close ties to industry (Maskus 2000).

Available data indicate that most developing regions have been increasing their R&D expenditures relative to GDP (table 3.11).[38] East Asia and the Pacific has experienced a particularly rapid rate of increase in R&D expenditures and also has the highest level of such expenditures among those regions for which data are available. In contrast with other regions, in Latin America and the Caribbean, both the number of researchers and expenditures on R&D have been falling or stagnant, reflecting both a reorientation of policy away from university-led R&D (Maloney 2006) and tighter fiscal policies.

Table 3.11 R&D intensities have increased

	R&D expenditure		Researchers in R&D	
	1997–2002	2002	1997–2002	2002
Regions	*(% point change)*	*(% of GDP)*	*(% change)*	*(per million people)*
East Asia and the Pacific	0.45	1.06	4.4	545.3
Europe and Central Asia	0.06	0.88	-1.4	2008.7
Latin America and the Caribbean	0.01	0.57	—	—
Middle East and North Africa	—	—	—	—
South Asia	0.13	0.77	—	—
Sub-Saharan Africa	—	—	—	—
Income groups				
World	**0.12**	**2.18**	—	—
High-income countries	0.12	2.43	2.6	3750.0
Upper-middle-income countries	0.09	0.71	—	—
Lower-middle-income countries	0.46	1.01	3.9	499.9
Low-income countries	0.18	0.80	—	—

Source: World Development Indicators.
*Note:** Interpolation applied where appropriate; — = not available.

While developing countries spend less on R&D than high-income countries, the gap is not extreme. Relative to GDP, low-income countries spend about one-third as much on R&D than high-income countries. One issue with the data is that the coverage of commercial R&D expenditures is poor in many developing countries, so the figures largely reflect R&D expenditures by the public sector and universities. As firms in many developing countries probably focus on adapting foreign technology to local conditions, a significant portion of this important activity may therefore not be captured.

Firm-level R&D is most effective in promoting technological progress

All R&D can contribute to an economy's capacity to create, adapt, and adopt technology. Nevertheless, because of the fundamental role that firms play in diffusing technology through the economy, the most productive R&D tends to be that conducted by firms or by public or university laboratories working actively with the private sector. Across developing countries, the share of R&D conducted by firms (as opposed to government or university laboratories) is highest in East Asia and the Pacific, where it rivals the share in

Table 3.12 Private-public sector R&D

		Sector of performance			Sector of funding		
	R&D spending	Business	Government	Higher education	Business	Government	Higher education
	(% GDP)	*(share of total)*			*(share of total)*		
World	2.28						
High-income countries	2.45	63	13	27	49	34	2.1
Developing countries	0.83	—	—				
East Asia and the Pacific	1.44	62	22	14	54	35	2.3
Europe and Central Asia	0.94	43	29	20	38	54	0.5
Latin America and the Caribbean	0.56	29	27	33	33	37	27
Middle East and North Africa	—	—	—	—	—	—	—
South Asia	0.73	—	—	—	—	—	—
Sub-Saharan Africa	—	—	—	—	—	—	—

Source: Gill and Karas 2007.
Note: — = not available.

high-income countries (table 3.12). Note, however, that in China, despite rapid technological progress, the efficiency of R&D spending is relatively low and the impact of R&D is impaired because of poor linkages among government R&D institutes, businesses, and universities (Zeng and Wang 2007). In Europe and Central Asia and in Latin America and the Caribbean, academia and the government are responsible for a much higher share of R&D. Moreover, in the latter region coordination between R&D carried out by government institutions and private firms has been poor, reducing the impact of R&D on productivity growth (de Ferranti and others 2003).

Research on OECD countries suggests that the more R&D is conducted at the firm level, the higher the rate of return to public and academic R&D, presumably because having R&D expertise close to the firm increases the likelihood of successful adaptation of a technology created in government, academic, or even foreign laboratories (Guellec and Pottelsberge de la Potterie 2004). Maloney (2006) concludes that state-funded R&D that is too academic and/or too disconnected from the private sector is less effective at promoting technological progress than firm-conducted R&D or state-supported R&D that has a strong connection to business needs. Indeed, the relatively high share of private sector R&D in East Asia and South Asia may have contributed to the more rapid technological progress in those regions than in Latin America and the Caribbean and Europe and Central Asia.

Outreach plays a critical role in bringing technology to the broader population

Too often the overall effectiveness of R&D undertaken by government and specialized research institutes is reduced because such organizations are divorced from their eventual clients and their incentives are poorly aligned with the ultimate dissemination of their inventions and adaptations.[39] Especially in poor countries plagued by illiteracy and weak communication networks, technology outreach programs can play a critical role in increasing the diffusion of often simple but important technologies. Agricultural outreach programs were instrumental to the green revolution, even though it took much longer than initially expected for those programs to bear fruit (World Bank 1998). Difficulties encountered in other efforts to disseminate technology include a lack of skilled personnel to staff the outreach program and the need to earn the trust of the local population. Here challenges include minimizing the risks people run in trying a new technology, listening to their experiences, and adapting techniques as a consequence (World Bank 2007d). Enhancing the role of farmers in agricultural outreach programs and relying more on cooperation between government and the private sector—in those areas where private benefits from technology transfer can be substantial—may improve both the impact and financial sustainability of outreach efforts.

Direct government policies to promote technology

Innovation requires entrepreneurs: people who are willing to take risks to invest in uncertain projects and who have the organizational skills required to bring new products to the market. Given the high risks involved, the returns to successful entrepreneurship must be high, but the returns to investment in new technology in developing countries can be limited, because potential profits may be reduced by imitation, because of a lack of coordination between firms that produce complementary inputs, or because economies of scale and agglomeration generate threshold effects that prevent firms from breaking into mature markets (box 3.6).

Government policy can play a central role in helping firms overcome market failures

The difficulties that these externalities pose for firms in certain sectors and those seeking to adopt a new-to-market (or even new-to-the-firm) technology imply that specific government interventions may be necessary to encourage investment in technology.

Box 3.6 Principal market failures impeding technological progress in developing countries

The nonpatentability of new-to-the-market products and processes. The vast majority of innovation that occurs in developing countries involves the adaptation of already discovered techniques and products to the domestic market, and such innovation is not patentable. Lack of patent protection facilitates imitation, which may speed diffusion, but reduces the returns to the individual or firm introducing the technique or product to the domestic market. As a result, private entrepreneurs underinvest in easily reproduced techniques, even though they could have large social benefits.

Coordination failures limit investment in technology. Some technologies rely on the availability of complementary inputs. Coordination failures can arise when new industries exhibit scale economies and some of the inputs require geographical proximity. For example, producing cut flowers for export requires an adequate electrical grid, irrigation, logistics and transport networks, quarantine and other public health measures, and resources devoted to marketing the country as a dependable supplier (Rodrik 2004). However, these services have high fixed costs and will not be supplied unless demand is sufficient, creating a vicious circle where demand is not forthcoming because of the lack of supply. The market for training is another example of potential coordination failure, as workers will demand training only if a demand for trained workers exists, but in the absence of training there is no demand (Rodriguez-Clare 2005). Perhaps reflecting such factors, in almost all the successful case studies of innovation reported in Chandra (2006), government played an important role by providing infrastructure, marketing, or training support.

Threshold effects caused by economies of scale in many manufacturing sectors prevent entry by firms into global markets or the introduction of a new process in a small market dominated by a preexisting, large-scale competitor. Economies generated from learning by doing and the productivity boosts generated by the accumulation of small innovations are related impediments that imply that start-ups must endure an initial period of relatively high costs, which in the absence of adequate intermediation, may prevent them from accumulating sufficient experience or scale to attain adequate levels of profitability. For example, Arrow (1962) cites evidence that productivity in the production of airframes is a decreasing function of the total number of airframes of the same type produced previously.

Knowledge spillovers tend to be geographically bounded within a region where the new economic knowledge is created (Audretsch and Feldman 2004). Audretsch and Feldman (1996) find that the propensity of innovative activity to cluster geographically tends to be greater in industries where new economic knowledge plays a more important role as has occurred in, for example, Silicon Valley and Bangalore. Studies also find that access to venture capital in the United States is heavily skewed by region (Sorenson and Stuart 2001).

Agglomeration effects, whereby firms benefit from the knowledge and human resource spillovers arising from the geographical proximity of firms in the same area of business, may also prevent developing economy firms from breaking into established markets (Glaeser and others 1992). The absence of such effects represents an important barrier to development in Sub-Saharan Africa and in more remote areas of China and India, where lack of physical proximity both raises trading costs and minimizes the potential for benefits from interactions with more rapidly growing areas.

Source: World Bank.

Governments in developing countries have undertaken a host of direct interventions in productive activities to provide demonstration effects, encourage innovation that otherwise would not occur because imitators reap the lion's share of benefits, resolve coordination failures, and move an industry toward efficient technologies that it would not otherwise adopt because of capital market imperfections. These steps have included the following:

- *Providing support for industry-specific research.* For example, Malaysia funded industry-specific R&D, provided

Box 3.7 Government sponsored innovation: Brazilian biofuels

Brazil launched its National Alcohol Program in 1975 to reduce its dependence on crude oil imports and to guarantee the profitability of the sugar industry by allowing excess sugar production to be converted into alcohol (ethanol) in special distilleries located near sugar mills.

Government support for the initiative has been extensive. Initially it was supported by legislation that mandated that 24 percent of fuel sold for automobiles must be in the form of ethanol. This requirement was complemented by sponsored research into the production of, and eventually the subsidization of sales of, cars that ran entirely on ethanol. Moreover, government credit guarantees and low-interest loans to construct the refineries amounted to some 29 percent of the overall investment cost of these ventures. At the same time, the state oil company, Petrobras, was required to make infrastructure investments in ethanol distribution and to keep the cost of ethanol to consumers significantly cheaper than the cost of gasoline. Overall, the government spent $12.3 billion on the National Alcohol Program during 1975–98.

During periods of high oil prices the program has been relatively successful, with ethanol-powered cars representing 90 percent of sales between 1983 and 1988. However, as oil prices fell, the technology became less attractive and the costs of supporting the industry rose. At the same time, world sugar prices rose and sugar growers shifted their cane to the production of sugar for export instead of ethanol for the domestic market. Ethanol shortages developed and ethanol-powered car sales dropped. As a result, the government gradually rescinded the program's incentives and subsidies, although it still mandated that all gasoline contain roughly 20 percent ethanol, citing environmental benefits to justify the mandate.

The flex-fuel car engine, which was able to run on any combination of ethanol and gasoline, was introduced in 2002 and, along with the surge in crude oil prices, led to a revival of ethanol in Brazil. With the recent rise in oil prices, ethanol-based cars are once again competitive, and ethanol produced from Brazilian sugar can be produced for less than the equivalent quantity of gasoline. Other developing countries are increasingly interested in adopting the Brazilian technology to reduce their energy dependence and also to support their sugar sectors.

Source: Coelho and Goldemberg 2004; World Bank 1994; Xavier Marcos 2007.

financing, built infrastructure, and offered tax incentives to encourage the processing of palm oil (Chandra and Kolavalli 2006).[40] Governments have also encouraged innovation by improving networking among enterprises, universities, and government research institutes (Goldman and Ergas 1997). For example, government-funded technology parks in Taiwan, China, encouraged research by providing high-quality facilities and by facilitating interactions among scientists. Many governments finance agricultural research and support farmers' efforts to exploit new technologies.

- *Providing direct subsidies for specific products.* The government started the first commercial-scale salmon farming operation in Chile to demonstrate its feasibility (Rodrik 2004). Korea and Japan provided fiscal subsidies to create "national champions" in key sectors (Hoekman, Maskus, and Saggi 2005). Similarly, the Brazilian aircraft and biofuel sectors (box 3.7), the Indian pharmaceuticals sector, and the South African automobile industry were developed using tax incentives, regulatory policies that encouraged domestic competition, science and technology support, and collaboration with foreign firms (UNCTAD 2003).
- *Imposing more dirigiste policies.* Some countries, particularly in East Asia, have guided production decisions through initially high import tariffs, export

Box 3.8 A successful government program of technological development and innovation financing in the Republic of Korea

GDP per capita in Korea increased from $150 in 1960 to $16,000 in 2005, with GDP growing particularly rapidly during the 1980s and early 1990s as technological progress accelerated. Although an outcome of many factors, Korea's technologically intensive growth spurt had a strong public policy element. Government-funded research institutes, including the Korea Science and Engineering Foundation in the 1970s, recognized the need to enhance cooperative research between universities and industry (80 percent of the nation's research capability was university based in the 1970s). The government created research centers located within corporations to supply industry with high-tech research capability and industry dictated the focus and area of research.

With time, industry realized that domestically-developed technology could be internationally competitive and began investing heavily. As a result, Korean industry transformed itself from a low-tech, labor-intensive exporter to one of the world's leading high-tech producers. Private sector expenditures on R&D have increased rapidly since 1990—almost doubling over the past decade—and are now the main source of R&D financing. Nanotechnology, information technology, and biotechnology are the main axes of the government's focus on R&D at the generation stage.

Source: World Bank.

subsidies, government influence over the allocation of production, and directed credit programs. The extent to which such policies were necessary to these countries' success has generated some controversy (Hernandez 2004), and the forms of intervention in high-growth East Asian economies were by no means identical. For example, Korea (box 3.8) favored tariff protection and constraints on FDI to maximize technology transfer; Singapore encouraged FDI; and Hong Kong, China, practiced laissez-faire policies. Nevertheless, some observers doubt that such interventions were pervasive in many of the most successful East Asian economies.

But government efforts at promoting technological champions have often failed

Notwithstanding the wide range of support policies that governments have tried and the existence of many apparent success stories, such policies have often been spectacular failures. Even among the examples cited, it is not clear that all should be considered successes. For example, the Brazilian aircraft maker Embraer did not become commercially successful until it was privatized. More generally, the import-substitution policies followed by many countries in Latin America and Africa and India's inward-focused policies severely hampered economic and technological development. To take two of the countless examples, first, rather than promoting the development of a technologically sophisticated export industry, the tariffs, price harmonization, and import licensing programs imposed in Côte d'Ivoire diminished incentives for efficiency in its textile industry, making it internationally uncompetitive. Second, Brazil's attempts to promote its domestic personal computer sector by banning imports and FDI, awarding licenses for production, providing fiscal incentives, and establishing a public research center resulted in an inefficient industry, high domestic prices, and lagging technology (World Bank 1998).

Two important issues distinguish industrial policies in the successful East Asian countries with those in many other countries. First, in contrast to Latin America, where subsidies were often provided free of performance criteria, East Asian countries conditioned subsidies on performance (often export performance), essentially relying on external competition to discipline the market.[41] Second, East Asian countries maintained high-quality bureaucracies that for the most part avoided capture by industrial interests, thereby maintaining a balance between knowledge and involvement in productive activities and state autonomy. In Latin America, industrialists often captured bureaucracies, while in many Sub-Saharan African countries, the interests of industrialists or corrupt officials dominated government interventions.

Imitation opportunities may boost technological diffusion, but have costs

The possibility of adopting technologies already elaborated in more technologically advanced economies represents a fundamental advantage of less-advanced developing economies and is the basis for much of their R&D and outreach activity. Indeed, many developing countries with relatively advanced levels of technological achievement (Brazil, China, India, the Republic of Korea, Mexico, and Malaysia), as well as Japan, initially used an explicit policy of copying foreign technologies. While this strategy proved successful to a point, eventually the successes that these economies had in the markets of their higher-technology competitors meant that these competitor countries became increasingly unwilling to share technology with them.

A substantial literature attempts to grapple with the trade-off between the impact of weaker intellectual property regimes and the potential for increased technological diffusion in a host country and with the impacts that such regimes might have on foreign partners' willingness to undertake FDI and licensing agreements. Although the theoretical literature emphasizes the importance of intellectual property regimes (Lai 1998; Taylor 1994), the empirical evidence is ambiguous overall.

Some studies find no relationship between the level of intellectual property rights and FDI or licensing (Primo Braga and Fink 2000; Branstetter, Fisman, and Foley 2005; Maskus and Konan 1994). Other studies show a positive effect of strong intellectual property regimes on FDI both in influencing location decisions by multinational corporations and in inducing foreign firms to invest in production rather than in distribution activities (Javorcik 2004; Lee and Mansfield 1996; Mansfield 1994; Maskus 1998).[42] Some evidence suggests that while a stronger intellectual property rights regime is associated with a rise in flows of knowledge to affiliates and in inward FDI toward middle-income and large developing countries, this is not the case for poor countries (Fink 2005; Hoekman, Maskus, and Saggi 2005; Smith 2001).

Overall, the impact of intellectual property rights on FDI depends on the nature of the sector. Intellectual property rights appear to have little impact on investment in lower-technology goods, such as textiles and apparel; services sectors, such as distribution and hotels; or in sectors where the sophistication of the technology itself or the cost of production already serves as an effective barrier to entry. Indeed, the increased ease with which some products such as pharmaceuticals, chemicals, food additives, and software are reproduced

Figure 3.18 Levels of intellectual property protection

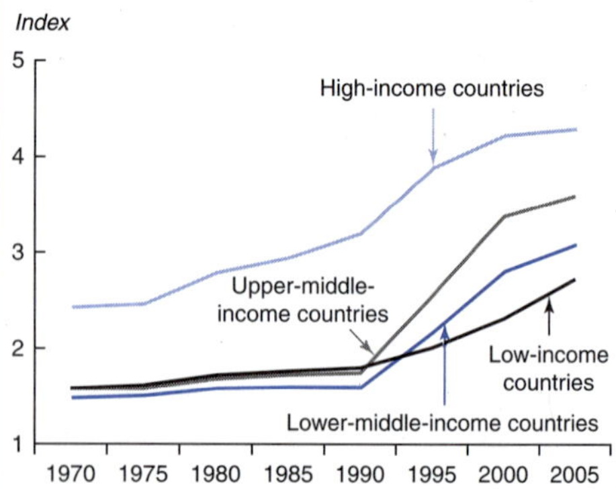

Source: World Bank calculations based on individual country data provided by Walter Park, American University.

Note: A higher score on the index indicates stronger intellectual property rights.

may explain the rising interest in establishing intellectual property rights (Maskus 2000).

Perhaps reflecting such considerations, a general trend toward strengthening the legal protection afforded by intellectual property rights has been apparent since the latter half of the 1980s (figure 3.18). Among developing countries, the legal basis for such rights has progressed most in upper-middle-income countries, where levels of protection now exceed the levels in high-income countries in the mid-1990s. Progress in lower-middle-income and low-income countries has been less marked, reaching about the same level as in high-income countries in the 1990s and 1970s respectively (note, however, that the index in figure 3.18 refers to the protection offered in statutes, not in practice).

Governments can also promote technological progress in their own operations . . .

In many developing countries the government accounts for a significant share of productive activities. Using technology to increase the productivity of government operations can help raise the efficiency of the economy as a whole by improving health and education services (see chapter 2 and the foregoing discussion of human capital); enhancing the effectiveness and reducing the costs of publicly-provided power, telecommunications, and water and sanitation; providing approaches to regulation and tax administration that are less burdensome to firms; and demonstrating the feasibility of new technology that firms can copy. One area where dramatic efficiency gains are possible is greater use of technology in government procurement. Countries that have implemented Internet-based procurement systems include Brazil (including in some local governments), Chile, Mexico, and the Philippines.[43] Implementing e-procurement systems may require changes in laws and policies governing government operations (for example, ensuring that government agencies can contract with foreign firms that can provide such systems. Although procurement is often a focus of corruption and is frequently biased in favor of local products (most developing countries provide preferential treatment to local suppliers in government procurement [Kohr 2007]), the use of advanced communications and information technologies can raise the transparency and efficiency of government procurement and can ensure greater competition, thereby contributing to an overall improvement in the quality of government services.

More broadly, the integration of information and communications technology tools has tremendous potential for improving access to government information, increasing public participation in government decision making, and making government services more readily available to the public (World Bank Information for Development Program and Center for Democracy and Technology 2002). In addition to enhancing government efficiency, such improvements can help reduce costs and improve services to private sector firms, thereby increasing the potential for technological progress. While many industrial countries have used the Internet to improve local access to information and services, its potential remains largely unexploited in many developing countries. Nevertheless, some developing countries are implementing e-government systems that are as or more sophisticated than those used in some high-income countries (United Nations 2003). Also, the use of electronic systems has helped improve the efficiency of customs services in many countries.

A survey of case studies in developing countries outlines some initial steps in use of the Internet to improve tax administration and general services and to enhance the transparency and efficiency of government operations (Ndou 2004). The survey underlines the importance for the success of e-government initiatives of appropriate stocktaking of the current state of telecommunications networks; of raising awareness of the potential for, information and communications technology beginning with relatively small projects to test feasibility; of stimulating collaboration among government departments; and of making substantial investments in equipment and software, human capital, and appropriate organizational changes. Other important issues pertinent to implementing e-government systems include its coverage (comprehensive, national efforts may be appropriate for small countries, but may be too complex and difficult in large countries); the ability of the enabling environment to support e-government initiatives, for instance, adequate infrastructure, an appropriate legal framework, political commitment, and public involvement; and the availability of strong project management skills (Bhatnagar and Deane 2002).

. . . and encourage improved technology through product standards

Governments can play a key role in boosting technological progress by defining and promoting standards for products made by private firms and by facilitating quality control to help firms comply with standards. Good standards support technological progress by increasing consistency and ensuring minimum product performance; facilitating the connection of components in complex systems by standardizing the interfaces between different parts of the system; offering buyers a greater choice of suppliers at lower risk and lower cost and the prospect of faster and more reliable system development; and offering manufacturers and vendors easier entry to markets, economies of scale, and lower product liability risks (Yokota and Weiland 2004). The transmission of information about standards can be an extremely useful channel for technology transfer. Implementing well-defined standards, including testing and sanctions for noncompliance, can be critical in maintaining a country's reputation for quality, which is important for establishing and maintaining access to global markets.

The value of a country's reputation, the benefits of coordination, and the protection of health and safety underline the government's role in promoting and enforcing standards, even in competitive product markets, but the government's specific role will depend on the product and the market structure involved. Standards may be defined by private firms with dominant market shares or agreed on through a collaborative process negotiated within the context of professional organizations. They may also be imposed by government regulation, or they may derive from some combination of collaboration and imposition. Participation in international organizations can help developing countries understand and influence international standards. The International Organization for Standardization, with 132 developing country members, is a forum for agreement on technical specifications for a variety of products.[44]

Coherent policies and committed government leadership are critical for technological progress

No single blueprint for technological progress exists, but most success stories have involved strong central leadership to ensure a consistent and effective policy framework that supports the development and commercialization of innovations. Technological progress is largely implemented by private firms. However, progress at the firm level requires government support, elements of which include the following: an appropriate incentives framework, including overall political and economic stability and government transparency, along with specific technology policies such as protection of intellectual property rights; investments in human capital, including general education and technical training where firms underinvest in training because of the potential mobility of trained staff; support for R&D of new-to-the-market technologies because of difficulties in appropriating the full benefits from such efforts; and, where appropriate, government interventions to overcome market failures involving coordination, threshold effects, and agglomeration effects (box 3.6). Most technological success stories, including Germany in the 19th century, Japan before and after World War II, the East Asian miracle countries, Chile, Ireland, and Israel have involved strong national leadership

Figure 3.19 Level of and recent changes in technological absorptive capacity

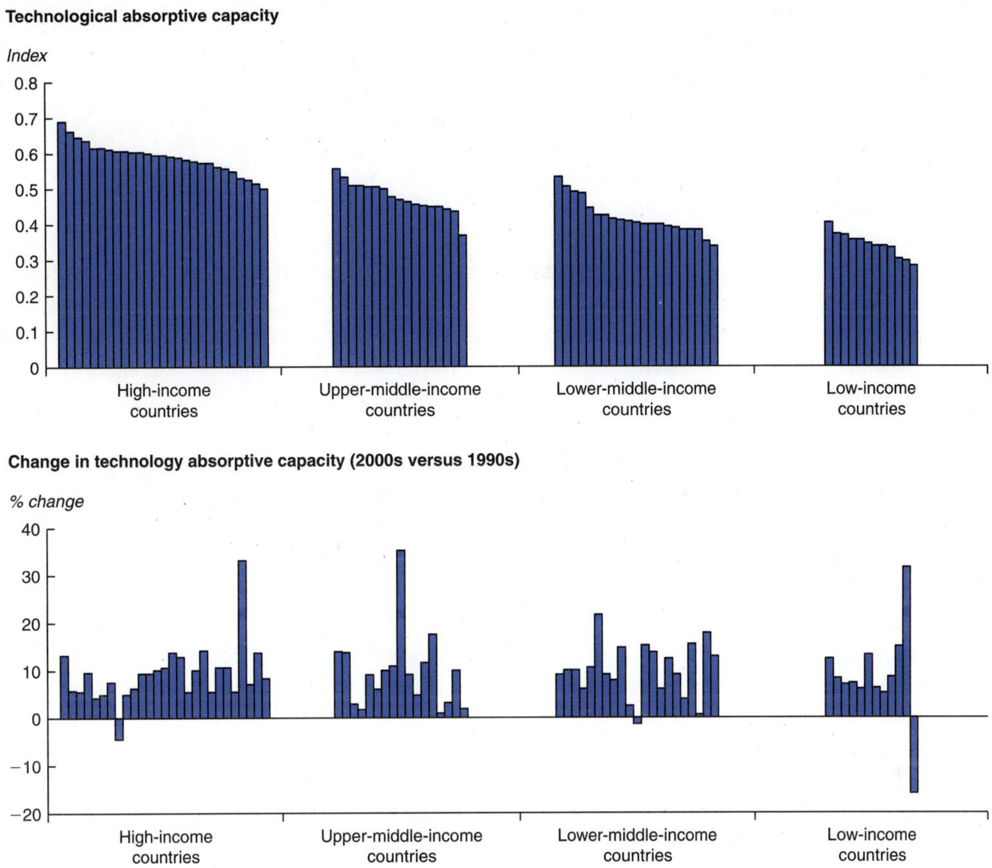

Source: World Bank.

and a coherent strategy for promoting technology.

An overall index of technological absorptive capacity

Figure 3.19 summarizes countries' level of technological absorptive capacity and changes over the past 10 years. The overall index was generated following the same methodology used to construct the index of technological achievement discussed in chapter 2 and the index of exposure to external technologies discussed earlier in this chapter. As was the case for technological achievement, a two-step procedure was followed. The first step was to estimate a separate summary index of the quality of the macroeconomic environment, financial market intermediation, human capital, and governance. The technical annex to chapter 2 describes the estimation process used and the results of the principal components analysis in more detail than provided here and table A2.2 summarizes the individual indicators that went into the index.

The most important determinants of the overall index are the governance variables (with a 37 percent weight), followed by human capital variables (with a 25 percent weight), and financial intermediation (with a 27 percent weight), followed by the macroeconomic environment (with an 11 percent weight).

Compared with the technological achievement index, technological absorptive capacity is more clearly correlated with income, with less of an overlap across countries in different income groups. This probably results from the complex causal relationship that may exist between technological absorptive capacity, technology, and income, in which technology is a function of technological absorptive capacity and affordability, income is a function of technology, and affordability is a function of income, with income being both an indirect cause and an effect of technological absorptive capacity.

Reflecting the complexity of the institutions that generate technological absorptive capacity and the difficulties of reforming some of the measures included in the index (see technical annex to chapter 2), progress has been more limited than was the case for technological achievement (where the index increased by 160 percent for low-income countries). Relatively few countries improved their overall score for absorptive capacity by more than 10 percent between 1990 and 2000 (the strongest negative score in low-income countries was recorded by Zimbabwe and reflects mainly the deterioration in macroeconomic and governance conditions there in recent years). Moreover, in contrast to technological achievement, there is little sign of catch-up. Developing countries are improving their technological absorptive capacity at about the same rate as high-income countries.[45]

The relatively weak improvements in absorptive capacity notwithstanding, the relative strength of the technological improvement observed to date might be comforting. At the same time, the relatively weak increases in technological achievement in Latin America and the Caribbean and in the Middle East and North Africa may reflect that technological progress (and TFP growth) in those countries has reached the limits that can be achieved from relatively easy adoption and imitation of existing technologies given current levels of absorptive capacity and that further improvement may require substantial enhancement of absorptive capacity.

Conclusion

Technology diffusion in developing countries depends both on access to foreign technology (through trade, FDI, international migration, and other networks) and on the ability to absorb technology (as determined by the quality of government policy and institutions, the stock of human capital, the efforts at R&D, and the financial system). One implication of the analysis and data presented in the preceding two chapters is that prospects for further technological progress in low- and middle-income countries are good. Over the past 15 years, the main international channels through which technology is transferred have increased. Developing countries' imports of high-tech goods and of capital goods have risen relative to GDP, and their share in global high-tech export markets has increased. Inflows of FDI have increased sixfold relative to developing countries' output, and opportunities to purchase technology have risen along with FDI outflows.

Simultaneously, the absorptive capacity of developing countries has been increasing, albeit more slowly. Youth literacy rates are as much as 15 percentage points higher than for the adult population. As a result, the basic technical literacy of the population has been increasing, and it should continue to do so for many decades. The macroeconomic instability that plagued developing countries during the 1970s and 1980s has declined, and the business climate has improved, although not by as much or as uniformly as one might have hoped. Technological achievement should continue to rise over the medium term as long as these trends continue and assuming there are no major disruptions to global trade and financial systems.

Of particular note is the speed with which communications technologies are evolving and diffusing in the developing world. Only 27 years after the introduction of cell phone technology, mobile phones are being used in virtually every country, and penetration rates are rising rapidly. Moreover, the range of economic activities that were once heavily dependent on infrastructure and that are now being conducted using mobile phone technology is impressive and growing daily. Already mobile phones are bringing banking, remittances, and arm's-length financial transactions to regions of the world that until recently were unserved. Given the pace at which things are changing, most developing countries should continue to see a rise in their ability to communicate and process information over the next few decades, which should help speed the diffusion of other technologies as well.

For middle-income countries, the relatively rapid technological progress of the past few years and the improvements in both openness and technological adaptive capability suggest that their level of technological sophistication should continue to converge with that of higher-income countries. However, even the most advanced of the middle-income countries will be unable to benefit fully from the new technologies that are expected to become both technically and economically viable over the next several years because of inadequacies in their infrastructure (unreliable power or communications systems), insufficient technical literacy, or the absence of a critical mass of scientists and engineers necessary to exploit the technology (box 3.9). For some countries, the relative slowness with which technological absorptive capacity has been advancing could slow the pace of convergence as missing competencies become an increasingly binding constraint on the absorption of additional technologies.

For low-income countries, the prospects are more complex. On average, among the low-income countries for which sufficient data are available to calculate recent increases in technological achievement, convergence is occurring and is doing so more quickly than in middle-income countries. However, this finding reflects rapid progress in a few countries and more modest performance in many others that are only maintaining their ground relative to high-income countries.

Notwithstanding strong technological progress in some cities and greater openness to technological flows, the gap between existing competencies and those needed to converge with technological progress in high-income countries is immense, especially in rural areas. Moreover, the pace at which absorptive capacity is rising is disappointing. While some countries have recorded significant increases, on average, developing countries are not catching up to high-income countries, suggesting that the gap in their technology potential is not closing. As a result, unless substantial steps are taken to raise basic competencies and invest in local networks that successfully disseminate technologies and technological competencies, many of these countries are not expected to be able to master anything more than the simplest of forthcoming technologies (box 3.9).

One bright spot is the relatively rapid diffusion of some new technologies in low-income countries. Declining computing costs and prospects for rapid declines in the cost of wireless Internet connections may enhance the efficiency of ongoing economic activities in low-income countries and may enable them to leapfrog into more advanced technologies (Primo Braga, Daly, and Sareen 2003).[46] However, successful exploitation of these new technologies will require stepped-up investments in human capital and reforms in policy and regulation to provide an appropriate incentives structure for investments in information and communications technology.

A rigorous road map for achieving rapid technological progress does not exist. Nevertheless, the evidence presented in this report points to a number of conclusions, principles, and policy directions that appear likely to promote technological progress and that may be able to guide policy makers. Exactly how

Box 3.9 Technology in 2020

A recent report by the Rand Corporation (Silberglitt and others 2006) examines some 56 emerging technologies expected to be commercially available by 2020 and evaluates in detail the 16 judged to be most important on the basis of technical feasibility, marketability, and societal impact. These applications include improvements in health services (targeted drug delivery, improved diagnostic and surgical methods), in access to information (rural wireless communications, quantum cryptography), and in the environmental sustainability of products and services (improved water purification, green manufacturing, hybrid vehicles). It then examines the technical base a country requires to make effective use of each technology and the likelihood that each of 80 representative economies, including both high-income and developing countries from every region in the world, will be able to exploit these technologies by 2020.

While many countries are expected to be able to take advantage of some of the simpler-to-use technologies, a wide range of countries are not expected to be able to do so because they lack the required technological infrastructure, because their population is not sufficiently technically literate, or because a critical mass of scientists and engineers is not present to exploit the technology (see the table). The report finds that most high-income countries will be able to adopt and exploit all the technologies effectively. A second group of countries, including China, India, Russia, and the countries of Eastern Europe, are found to have a considerable level of scientific and technological proficiency in specific applications. However, barriers to technology adaptation are likely to limit their ability to take advantage of the most sophisticated network applications. A third group of middle-income countries, which consists of several Latin American countries, Indonesia, South Africa, and Turkey, lacks more prerequisites and is therefore expected to exploit fewer of these technologies. A final group that comprises most of the world's poorest countries, including most of the countries of Africa, the Middle East, and Oceania, is projected to make use of only the simplest of the new technologies.

This analysis provides a useful snapshot of the prospects for technological progress based on current data. However, it does not incorporate the potential for dynamic improvements in technological progress, for example, through the rapid dissemination of existing new technologies, which could rapidly improve developing countries' ability to absorb new technologies.

Technological adaptive capacity may restrict the diffusion of future technologies

Requires increased technological sophistication ↓

Technology application	Most of Africa, Middle East, Oceania	Latin America, South Africa, Turkey, Indonesia	China, India, Russia, Eastern Europe	Industrial countries
	Technologies likely to be mastered by 2020 (✓)			
Cheap solar energy	✓	✓	✓	✓
Rural wireless communication	✓	✓	✓	✓
Genetically modified crops	✓	✓	✓	✓
Filters and catalysts	✓	✓	✓	✓
Cheap autonomous housing	✓	✓	✓	✓
Rapid bioassays		✓	✓	✓
Green manufacturing		✓	✓	✓
Ubiquitous RFID tagging		✓	✓	✓
Hybrid vehicles		✓	✓	✓
Targeted drug delivery			✓	✓
Improved diagnostic and surgical techniques			✓	✓
Quantum cryptography			✓	✓
Ubiquitous information access				✓
Tissue engineering				✓
Pervasive sensors				✓
Wearable computers				✓

Source: Silberglitt and others 2006.
Note: RFID = radio-frequency identification.

much weight to give to each of these conclusions and how they interact depends on specific country circumstances and should be the subject of future research. These policy directions include the following:

- Openness to external technologies through foreign trade, FDI, diasporas, and other international networks is critical for technological progress for both low- and middle-income countries, where most progress occurs through the adoption, adaptation, and assimilation of preexisting but new-to-the-market or new-to-the-firm technologies.
- The capacity of firms or individuals to use a technology depends critically on the basic technological literacy of workers and consumers. The level of technological literacy, in turn, depends on the government's capacity to deliver a quality education to the largest number of people possible.
- The preeminent vehicles for the dissemination and diffusion of technology in a market economy are firms and entrepreneurs. Their success in doing so depends on their ability to undertake and expand new activities. This requires a stable macroeconomic environment, together with a regulatory environment that effectively enforces property rights and the rule of law, does not excessively restrict firms' ability to hire and fire, and does not impose excessive regulatory or financial burdens.
- The capacity of firms or individuals to take advantage of a technology can be constrained by affordability and by liquidity, thereby placing a premium on the efficiency with which the financial system intermediates between savers and borrowers both domestically and abroad.
- Given the existence of market failures, the government has a role to play in assisting firms to learn how to adapt, adopt, and market new technologies. In addition to focusing on R&D in new-to-the-market technologies, applied R&D agencies need to emphasize outreach, testing, marketing, and dissemination activities. The huge rural–urban divide in both technology and absorptive capacity in many developing countries underlines the importance of such activities to inclusive development.
- The government can also have an important impact on economic progress by integrating new technology into its own operations, including in the provision of education, health, and publicly-provided infrastructure; in the procurement of goods and services; in the provision of information and in fostering public dialogue; and in the definition of standards for commercial products.
- The principal challenge facing many low-income countries is not their access to technology, but their absorptive capacity, including physical, human, and institutional capacity; their limited financial resources; and the extent to which their social and political environments are supportive of entrepreneurship, investment, and technological progress.

These conclusions highlight the critical role of the government in establishing the general conditions that support rapid technological progress, in helping to overcome market failures that constrain innovations by firms, and in providing (and purchasing) high-quality goods and services. Countries that have achieved sustained and rapid technological progress have generally benefited from committed national leadership that follows coherent development policies, although the nature of these policies—in particular, the degree of public sector intervention in private markets—has varied enormously.

Notes

1. The econometric evidence is mixed. Harrison (1994) for Côte d'Ivoire and Haddad, de Melo, and Horton (1996) for Morocco find no statistically significant impact of import penetration on productivity following trade liberalization. Nishimizu and Page (1982) for the former Yugoslavia; Tybout, de Melo, and Corbo (1991) for Chile; and Tybout and Westbrook

(1995) for Mexico find a positive relationship between import penetration and firm efficiency. Grether (1999) and van Wijnbergen and Venables (1993) for Mexico, Earle and Estrin (2001) for Russia, Falk and Dierking (1995) for Poland, Levinsohn (1993) for Turkey, and Roberts (1996) for Colombia find a positive impact of import penetration on either industry markups or measured labor productivity.

2. Keller (1998) casts doubt on these results by showing that the relationship also holds for randomly generated import shares, but Lumenga-Neso, Olarreaga, and Schiff (2005) find that imports from countries that import from other R&D centers are positively related to productivity and that these indirect spillovers are at least as important as direct spillovers.

3. Lall (2000, 2001) identifies four categories of products: resource-based products; low-tech products, which include textiles and fashion; medium-tech products; and high-tech products. According to this classification, which is defined using SITC 3-digit rev. 2, technological products do not include agricultural products, moderately processed food products, tobacco products, minerals, construction materials, and energy products.

4. Available data provide only a rough indication of the sophistication of economic activity, because ascertaining the level of sophistication of the capital goods imported is not possible. Also some countries may import relatively sophisticated capital goods for use in enclave production (for example, oil and minerals) with little spillover into the rest of the economy.

5. Chandra and Kolavalli (2006) cite important spillover effects from exporting electronics and software.

6. The contradictory evidence from case studies and econometric studies may be due to the different impacts of exports across industries and countries, as well as difficulties inherent in classifying firms (some studies classify exporters on the basis of surveys with yes-no answers rather than measuring the volume of exports) (Keller 2004). Also the argument for technology transfers through exports refers only to some exports—namely, new products or products that have evolved over time, and export statistics may not capture such subtleties. Firms that export the same product that is not subject to significant upgrading may not benefit from spillovers. If some firms improve their productivity through exports and some do not, and available data do not permit distinguishing between these firms, measuring the extent of productivity improvements over time may be difficult. For specific examples, see Tybout and Westbrook (1996), who find that trade liberalization in Mexico benefited exporters because of declines in prices of imported inputs, but had no effect on productivity. Soderbom and Teal (2000) find that Ghanaian firms with higher technical efficiency become exporters. Isgut (2001) finds that exporting firms in Colombia had higher labor productivity than nonexporters three years before entering the export market, but that afterward there is no difference in the growth of labor productivity of exporters as compared with nonexporters. Fafchamps, Zeufack, and El Hamine (2002) find that in Morocco, more productive firms move into exports. However, after initiating exports they do not achieve more rapid reductions in production costs than nonexporters, although they do learn to improve product design to suit foreign markets.

7. Following Lall (2001), the nomenclature used is SITC 3-digit, Rev. 2.

8. Costa Rica has emerged as a high-tech platform for foreign investors and increased its world market share of high-tech products from 0.01 to 0.20 percent between the mid-1990s and 2002–04.

9. Between 1992 and 2003, developing countries made some 2,563 favorable changes to national laws and regulations relating to FDI. The most frequent changes concerned FDI promotion and incentives (855), sectoral restrictions (497), operational conditions (406), guarantees (304), and corporate regulations (153). During the same period, 113 developing countries became members of the World Trade Organization, which required the elimination of many restrictions and impediments to FDI, particularly in the services sector (World Bank 2004a).

10. The world's largest R&D investors conducted an average of 28 percent of their R&D outside their home territory in 2003 (UNCTAD 2005).

11. This section builds on many studies of FDI spillovers that have identified possible channels for technology transfers and knowledge spillovers through FDI (Görg and Greenaway 2004; Görg and Strobl 2001; Javorcik 2007; Lipsey 2002; Moran 2007; Saggi 2002).

12. Javorcik (2004) finds that the TFP of Lithuanian firms is positively correlated with the extent of potential contacts with multinational customers in downstream sectors. Blalock and Gertler (forthcoming) and Kugler (2006) find strong evidence that vertical supply chains were a channel for technology transfers in Colombian and Indonesian manufacturing sectors. Swinnen and others (2006) show that investments by foreign companies in processing and retailing in Eastern Europe have introduced higher standards, which in turn led to significant efficiency gains by suppliers.

13. Javorcik (2007) documents the increased competitive pressures from foreign entry in Czech and Latvian firms, and the McKinsey Global Institute (2003) cites case studies where competition is a key factor in diffusing FDI-introduced innovations.

14. Ayyagari and Kosova (2006), using Czech FDI data for 1994 to 2000, show that spillovers vary substantially across industries. Although service industries benefited from huge FDI spillover effects through both horizontal and vertical channels, manufacturing industries did not show any significant positive spillover effects from FDI.

15. Belderbos, Capannelli, and Fukao (2000) find that the proportion of inputs sourced locally by Japanese multinationals increases with the number of years of operation in a given host country.

16. These data are incomplete, as only 90 of 150 developing countries (on average across 1999–2006) reported royalty and license fee payments. The data may also overstate payments for technology transfer, as developing countries with mineral or oil investments abroad may report the payment of substantial royalties that represent fees for extraction rights rather than for the purchase of technology.

17. Between 1990 and 2000, the number of tertiary-educated emigrants from developing countries that resided in OECD countries rose from 19.1 million to 37.8 million (Docquier and Marfouk 2004).

18. Even though a majority of Argentine doctoral graduates in the United States prefer to remain in the host country, most respondents in a survey of high-skilled Argentine diaspora members in Europe, the United States, and elsewhere expressed their willingness and interest in helping develop science, technology, and education in their home country (Kuznetsov, Nemirovsky, and Yoguel 2006).

19. Of these technologically sophisticated émigrés, 56 percent were born in Asia, with Latin America and the Caribbean accounting for another 15 percent (Kannankutty and Burrelli 2007).

20. Agrawal, Kapur, and McHale (2007), using patent data, find evidence of the influence of the diaspora in technology transfers to home countries.

21. The Mexican Ministry of Science and Technology views the presence of 1 million tertiary-educated Mexican migrants in the United States, with an estimated 400,000 in managerial positions, as a unique, unexplored opportunity for knowledge transfers (Kuznetsov 2006). Emigrants from China and India were running almost 30 percent of Silicon Valley's (California) technology businesses by the end of the 1990s (Saxenian 2000, 2002). In addition, 25 percent of all engineering and technology companies started in the United States during 1995–2005 had a foreign-born person as a key founder (Wadhwa and others 2007).

22. Page and Plaza (2006) argue that technology transfer by migrants takes place through several channels: (a) licensing agreements between diaspora-owned or managed firms in host countries and firms in sending countries, (b) knowledge spillovers when returning migrants assume managerial positions in their home country, (c) networks of diaspora researchers and scientists performing research directed at the needs of their country of origin, (d) "virtual" return through extended visits and electronic communication in fields such as medicine and engineering, and (e) return to permanent employment in the country of origin after gaining work experience in the host country.

23. Estimates suggest that a 10 percent increase in skilled migrant stock in the United States is associated with a 4 percent increase in the flow of FDI (in current dollars) to the home country (Mattoo, Özden, and Neagu 2005).

24. This result is supported by work on high-income countries that shows immigrant ties have been important determinants of U.S and Canadian bilateral trade (Gould 1994; Head and Ries 1998; Wagner, Head, and Ries 2002).

25. Kuznetsov (2007) argues that diasporas can act as global search networks by leveraging their contextual knowledge of their home countries' economy and institutions to identify untapped resources and opportunities, such as research capabilities, availability of technical manpower, and business-friendly local governments.

26. Among members of the Philippines Brain Gain Network, 35 percent have a master's degree and 23 percent hold a doctorate, while 49 percent of the members of the South African Network of Skills Abroad have a master's degree and another 30 percent have a doctorate (Brown 2000).

27. The Taiwanese diaspora and returning migrants were active conduits for technology transfers. For example, in 2000, 113 out of 289 companies at the Hinschu Science-Based Industrial Park in Taiwan, China, were started by U.S.-educated Taiwanese (O'Neil 2003).

28. Countries with strong institutions such as Chile, the Republic of Korea, and Scotland have been able take advantage of their high-skilled diasporas, while others such as Argentina, Armenia, and Colombia have not succeeded as well despite having many programs (Kuznetsov 2006).

29. Finding a relevant, available indicator of the size of the diaspora to include in the index proved difficult. The data series used included FDI net inflows, royalties and license fee payments, imports of high-tech goods, imports of capital goods, and imports of intermediate goods—all as a percent of GDP. Imports of intermediate goods and net FDI inflows have the largest weight in the calculation, accounting for more than half the total.

30. The productivity benefits from the adoption of new technology are best realized in the context of low

inflation, stable exchange rates, sustainable government finances, and positive income growth (Pack 2006).

31. Liu and Tybout (1996) and Roberts and Tybout (1997) present data from Chile, Colombia, and Morocco confirming that the entry and exit of firms makes an important contribution to productivity growth.

32. Data are taken from the World Bank's Doing Business Web site (http://www.doingbusiness.org).

33. See Keller (2004) for a survey of the economic literature on this topic. Education levels are typically important in empirical studies of cross-country differences in growth rates and in labor productivity (Chen and Dahlman 2004), but these studies do not determine the channel through which human capital contributes to growth.

34. In some countries, the limited rise in public expenditures on education may have been balanced by increases in private expenditures.

35. Ayyagari, Demirgüç-Kunt, and Maksimovic (2007) find a positive correlation between financial market depth (proxied by credit to the private sector as a percent of GDP) and R&D intensities.

36. These requirements are generally imposed to reduce volatility in these often thin markets and to bolster investor confidence in the safety of investing in listed firms. While they enable some well-established firms to access global capital markets by providing the exchanges with legitimacy, they exclude more speculative firms less well. Similarly, the use of American deposit receipts, which make investing in emerging-market firms easier for foreign investors, is largely restricted to large, well-established, and mainly export-oriented firms (Claessens and Schumkler 2007).

37. The OECD (2005) defines venture capital "as capital provided by firms who invest alongside management in young companies that are not quoted on the stock market. The objective is high return from the investment. Value is created by the young company in partnership with the venture capitalist's money and professional expertise." The flow of venture capital from the investor to a start-up company and back can be thought of as a cycle that runs through several phases. The International Finance Corporation monitors about 90 venture capital funds active in developing countries.

38. Internationally comparable data have been available only since 1997.

39. See the discussion from the World Bank Global Forum on Science, Technology, and Innovation, February 13–15, 2007, in Washington, DC. http://go.worldbank.org/DWODQ7E3E0.

40. Note that an OECD (2003) study found that fiscal incentives to support R&D in rich countries were not very effective on average, with success being heavily dependent on the design of the tax measures.

41. Such programs are more difficult to implement today in light of World Trade Organization restrictions on export subsidies (Rodrik 2004).

42. The intellectual property regime is only one consideration among many, including various local market and sector characteristics, that enter into multinational corporations' decisions on how to deploy technology internationally (Mansfield 1994, 1995).

43. See World Resources Institute Digital Dividend (http://www.digitaldividend.org) and the Working Group on E-Government in the Developing World (http://www.pacificcouncil.org/pdfs/e-gov.paper.f.pdf).

44. See http://www.iso.org.

45. There is a slightly inverted U shape to the distribution of improvements in technological absorptive capacity, with high-income countries recording a 9.1 percent improvement, compared with 9.4 percent for upper-middle-income countries, 9.8 percent for lower-middle-income countries, and 8.6 percent among those low-income countries for which data are available.

46. The development of simple, low-cost computers and the spread of open-source technology has already enhanced the affordability of new technologies for low-income countries.

References

Acemoglu, Daron, and Fabrizio Zilibotti. 2001. "Productivity Differences." *Quarterly Journal of Economics* 116 (2): 563–606.

Agrawal, Ajay K., Devesh Kapur, and John McHale. 2004. "Defying Distance: Examining the Influence of the Diaspora on Scientific Knowledge Flows." Unpublished paper. Queen's School of Business, Queen's University, Ontario. Presented at the Fourth Annual Roundtable for Engineering Entrepreneurship Research, Georgia Institute of Technology, College of Management, December 4.

______. 2007. "Brain Drain or Brain Bank? The Impact of Skilled Emigration on Poor-Country Innovation." Unpublished paper. *University of Toronto, Rotman School of Management, Ontario.*

Aitken, Brian J., and Ann E. Harrison. 1999. "Do Domestic Firms Benefit from Foreign Direct Investment? Evidence from Venezuela." *American Economic Review* 89 (3): 605–18.

Antras, Pol, Mihir A. Desai, and C. Fritz Foley. 2007. "Multinational Firms, FDI Flows, and Imperfect Capital Markets." Working Paper 12855. National Bureau of Economic Research, Cambridge, MA.

Arrow, Kenneth. 1962. "The Economic Implications of Learning by Doing." *Review of Economic Studies* 29 (3): 155–73.

Audretsch, David B., and Maryann P. Feldman. 1996. "R&D Spillovers and the Geography of Innovation and Production. *American Economic Review* 86 (4): 253–73.

_____. 2004. "Knowledge Spillovers and the Geography of Innovation." In *Handbook of Urban and Regional Economics*, vol. 4, ed. J. V. Henderson and J. F. Thisse, 2,713–39. New York: North Holland.

Avnimelech, G., and M. Teubal, 2004: "Venture Capital Policy in Israel: A Comparative Analysis and Lessons for Other Countries." In *Financial System, Corporate Investment in Innovation and Venture Capital*, ed. M. Sunil A. and Bartzokas. Cheltenham, U.K.: Edward Elgar.

Ayyagari, M., and R. Kosova. 2006. *Does FDI Facilitate Domestic Entrepreneurship? Evidence from the Czech Republic*. Washington, DC: George Washington University, School of Business.

Ayyagari, Meghana, Asli Demirgüç-Kunt, and Vojislav Maksimovic. 2007. "Firm Innovation in Emerging Markets: The Roles of Governance and Finance." Policy Research Working Paper Series 4157. World Bank, Washington, DC.

Barro, Robert J., and Jong Wha Lee. 2000. "International Data on Educational Attainment: Updates and Implications." Center for International Development Working Paper No. 42, April.

Beamish, P. W. 1988. *Multinational Joint Ventures in Developing Countries*. London: Routledge.

Beck, Thorsten, Asli Demirgüç, and Ross Levine. 2000. "A New Database on Financial Development and Structure." *World Bank Economic Review* 14, 597–605.

Behrman, Jere R., Andrew D. Foster, Mark R. Rosenzweig, and Prem Vashishtha. 1999. "Women's Schooling, Home Teaching, and Economic Growth." *Journal of Political Economy* 107 (4): 632–714.

Belderbos, Rene, Giovanni Capannelli, and Kyoji Fukao. 2000. "The Local Content of Japanese Electronics Manufacturing Operations in Asia." In *The Role of Foreign Direct Investment in East Asian Economic Development*, ed. Takatoshi Ito and Anne O. Krueger, 9–41. Chicago: University of Chicago Press.

Bell, C., R. Bruhns, and H. Gersbach. 2006. "Economic Growth, Education, and AIDS in Kenya: A Long-Run Analysis." Policy Research Working Paper 4025. World Bank, Washington, DC.

Bell, C., S. Devarajan, and H. Gersbach. 2004. "Thinking about the Long-Run Economic Costs of AIDS." In *The Macroeconomics of HIV/AIDS*, ed. M. Haacker, 96–133. Washington, DC: International Monetary Fund.

Bhatnagar, Subhash, and Arsala Deane. 2002. "Building Blocks of E-Government: Lessons from Developing Countries." Poverty Reduction and Economic Management Note 91. World Bank, Washington, DC.

Blalock, Garrick, and Paul J. Gertler. Forthcoming. "Welfare Gains from Foreign Direct Investment through Technology Transfer to Local Suppliers." *Journal of International Economics*.

Blomstrom, M., A. Kokko, and M. Zejan. 2000. *Foreign Direct Investment. Firm and Host Country Strategies*. London: Macmillan.

Borensztein, E., J. de Gregorio, and J.-W. Lee. 1998. "How Does Foreign Direct Investment Affect Economic Growth?" *Journal of International Economics* 45 (1): 115–35.

Branstetter, Lee G., Raymond Fisman, and C. Fritz Foley. 2005. "Do Stronger Intellectual Property Rights Increase International Technology Transfer? Empirical Evidence from U.S. Firm-Level Panel Data." Working Paper 11516. National Bureau of Economic Research, Cambridge, MA.

Brinkerhoff, Jennifer M. 2006a. "Diasporas, Mobilization Factors, and Policy Options." In *Converting Migration Drains into Gains: Harnessing the Resources of Overseas Professionals*, ed. Clay Wescott and Jennifer Brinkerhoff, 127–53. Manila: Asian Development Bank.

_____. 2006b. "Diasporas, Skills Transfer, and Remittances: Evolving Perceptions and Potential." In *Converting Migration Drains into Gains: Harnessing the Resources of Overseas Professionals*, ed. Clay Wescott and Jennifer Brinkerhoff, 1–32. Manila: Asian Development Bank.

Broadman, Harry G., and Francesca Recanatini. 2005. "Is Russia Restructuring? New Evidence on Job Creation and Destruction." Policy Research Working Paper 2641. World Bank, Washington, DC.

Brown, Mercy. 2000. "Using the Intellectual Diaspora to Reverse the Brain Drain: Some Useful Examples." In *Brain Drain and Capacity Building in Africa*, ed. S. J. M. Tapsoba, S. Kassoum, P. V. Houenou, B. One, M. Sethi, and J. Ngu. Economic Commission for Africa, International Development Research Centre, and International Organization for Migration.

Bureau of Economic Analysis. 2007. "Operations of Multinational Companies." U.S. Department of Commerce. http://www.bea.gov. Accessed September 1, 2007.

Caselli, Francesco, and Wilbur John Coleman II. 2001. "Cross-Country Technology Diffusion: The Case of Computers." *American Economic Review Papers and Proceedings* 91 (2): 328–35.

Chandra, Vandana, ed. 2006. *Technology, Adaptation and Exports: How Some Developing Countries Got It Right*. Washington, DC: World Bank.

Chandra, Vandana, and Shashi Kolavalli. 2006. "Technology, Adaptation and Exports: How Some Developing Countries Got It Right." In *Technology, Adaptation and Exports: How Some Developing Countries Got It Right*, ed. Vandana Chandra, 1–41. Washington, DC: World Bank.

Chaparro, Fernando, Hernan Jaramillo, and Vladimir Quintero. 2006. "Promise and Frustration of Diaspora Networks: Lessons from the Network of Colombian Researchers Abroad." In *Diaspora Networks and the International Migration of Skills*, ed. Yevgeny Kuznetsov, 187–98. Washington, DC: World Bank Institute.

Chen, Derek H. C., and Carl J. Dahlman. 2004. "Knowledge and Development: A Cross-Section Approach." Policy Research Working Paper 3366. World Bank, Washington, DC.

Claessens, Stijn, and Sergio L. Schumkler. 2007. "International Financial Integration through Equity Markets: Which Firms from Which Countries Go Global?" Policy Research Working Paper 4146. World Bank, Washington, DC.

Coe, David T., Elhanan Helpman, and Alexander W. Hoffmaister. 1997. "North-South R&D Spillovers." *Economic Journal* 107 (January): 134–49.

Coelho, S.T., and J. Goldemberg. 2004. "Alternative Transportation Fuels: Contemporary Case Studies." In *Encyclopedia of Energy*, Vol. 1. Elsevier.

Cohen, Wesley M., and Daniel A. Levinthal. 1989. "Innovation and Learning: The Two Faces of R&D." *Economic Journal* 99 (September): 569–96.

Correa, Carlos M. 2003. "Can the TRIPS Agreement Foster Technology Transfer to Developing Countries?" Unpublished manuscript. Duke University, Durham, NC.

Dahlman, Carl J., Bruce Ross-Larson, and Larry E. Westphal. 1987. "Managing Technological Development: Lessons from the Newly Industrialising Countries." *World Development* 15 (6): 759–75.

de Ferranti, David, Guillermo Perry, Indermit Gill, J. Luis Guasch, William F. Maloney, Carolina Sanchez-Paramo, and Norbert Schady. 2003. *Closing the Gap in Education and Technology*. Latin American and Caribbean Studies. Washington, DC: World Bank.

Docquier, Frederic, and Abdeslam Marfouk. 2004. "Measuring the International Mobility of Skilled Workers (1990–2000)." Policy Research Working Paper Series 3381. World Bank, Washington, DC.

Earle, John S., and Estrin, Saul. 2001. "Privatization and the Structure of Enterprise Ownership." In *Russia's Post-Communist Economy*, ed. Brigitte Granville and Peter Oppenheimer, 149–68. Oxford, U.K.: Oxford University Press.

Easterly, William, and Yaw Nyarko. 2005. "Is the Brain Drain Good for Africa?" Unpublished paper. New York University, New York.

Eaton, Jonathan, and Samuel Kortum. 1996. "Trade in Ideas: Patenting and Productivity in the OECD." *Journal of International Economics* 40: 251–78.

______. 2001. "Trade in Capital Goods." *European Economic Review* 45 (7): 1195–235.

Enos, John, and W. H. Park. 1987. *The Adoption and Diffusion of Imported Technology*. London: Croom Helm.

Fafchamps, Marcel, Albert Zeufack, and Said El Hamine. 2002. "Learning to Export: Evidence from Moroccan Manufacturing." Policy Research Working Paper 2827. World Bank, Washington, DC.

Fagerberg, Jan. 1988. "Why Growth Rates Differ." In *Technical Change and Economic Theory*, ed. Giovanni Dosi, Christopher Freeman, Richard Nelson, Gerald Silverber, and L. Soete. London: Pinter Publishers.

Fajnzylber, Pablo, and J. Humberto López. 2007. *Close to Home: The Development Impact of Remittances in Latin America*. Washington, DC: World Bank.

Falk, J., and L. Dierking, eds. 1995. *Public Institutions for Personal Learning: Establishing a Research Agenda*. Washington, DC: American Association of Museums.

Fink, Carsten. 2005. "Intellectual Property Rights and U.S. and German International Transactions in Manufacturing Industries." In *Intellectual Property Rights and Development: Lessons from Recent Economic Research,* ed. Carsten Fink and Keith Maskus, 75–110. Washington, DC: World Bank.

Finn, Michael G. 2003. "Stay Rates of Foreign Doctorate Recipients from U.S. Universities, 2001." Unpublished paper. Oak Ridge Institute for Science and Education, Science and Engineering Education Program, Oak Ridge, TN.

Fosfuri, A., M. Motta, and T. Ronde. 2001. "Foreign Direct Investment and Spillovers through Workers' Mobility." *Journal of International Economics* 53: 205–22.

Gereffi, Gary. 1999. "International Trade and Industrial Upgrading in the Apparel Commodity Chain." *Journal of International Economics* 48: 37–70.

Gill, Indermit, and Homi Kharas. 2007. *An East Asian Renaissance*. Washington, DC: World Bank.

Girma, Sourafel, and Katherine Wakelin. 2001. "Are There Regional Spillovers from FDI in the UK?" Research Paper 2000/16. University of Nottingham, School of Economics, Centre for Research on Globalization and Labour Markets, Nottingham, U.K.

Glaeser, Edward L., Hedi D. Kallal, Jose A. Scheinkman, and Andrei Shleifer. 1992. "Growth of Cities." *Journal of Political Economy* 100 (6): 1126–52.

Glass A. J., and K. Saggi. 2002. "Multinational Firms and Technology Transfer." *Scandinavian Journal of Economics* 104 (4): 495–513.

Goldman, Melvin, and Henry Ergas. 1997. "Technology Institutions and Policies: Their Role in Developing Technological Capability in Industry." Technical Paper 383. World Bank, Washington, DC.

Görg, Holger, and David Greenaway. 2004. "Much Ado about Nothing? Do Domestic Firms Really Benefit from Foreign Direct Investment?" *World Bank Research Observer* 19 (2): 171–97.

Görg, Holger, and Eric Strobl. 2001. "Multinational Companies and Productivity Spillovers: A Meta-Analysis." *Economic Journal* 111: 723–39.

Gould, David. 1994. "Immigrant Links to the Home Country: Empirical Implications for US Bilateral Trade Flows." *Review of Economics and Statistics* 76 (2): 302–16.

Grether, J. M. 1999. "Determinants of Technological Diffusion in Mexican Manufacturing: A Plant-Level Analysis." *World Development* 27 (7): 1287–98.

Guellec, Domininque, and Bruno van Pottelsberge de la Potterie. 2004. "From R&D to Productivity Growth: Do the Institutional Settings and the Source of Funds of R&D Matter?" *Oxford Bulletin of Economics and Statistics* (July): 353–78.

Guerrieri, P., and C. Milana. 1998. "High-Technology Industries and International Competition." In *Trade Growth and Technical Change*, ed. D. Archibugi and J. Michie, 188–207. Cambridge, U.K.: Cambridge University Press.

Gupta, Sanjeev, Catherine Pattillo, and Smita Waugh. 2007. "Impact of Remittances on Poverty and Financial Development in Sub-Saharan Africa." Working Paper 07/38. International Monetary Fund, Washington, DC.

Haddad, Mona, Jaime de Melo, and Brendan Horton. 1996. "Morocco 1984–1989: Trade Liberalization, Exports and Industrial Performance. In *Industrial Evolution in Developing Countries*, ed. Mark J. Roberts and James R. Tybout. New York: Oxford University Press.

Handoussa, Heba, Mieko Nishimizu, and John Page. 1986. "Productive Change in Egyptian Public Sector Industries after the 'Opening,' 1973–79." *Journal of Development Economics* 20 (1): 53–73.

Hanushek, Eric A., and Ludger Woessmann. 2007. "The Role of Education Quality in Economic Growth." Working Paper 4122. World Bank, Washington, DC.

Harrison, Anne E. 1994. "Productivity, Imperfect Competition, and Trade Reform: Theory and Evidence." *Journal of International Economics* 36 (1–2): 53–73.

Head, Keith, and John Ries. 1998. "Immigration and Trade Creation: Econometric Evidence from Canada." *Canadian Journal of Economics* 31 (1): 47–62.

Helms, Brigit. 2006. *Access for All: Building Inclusive Financial Systems*. Washington, DC: Consultative Group to Assist the Poor.

Hernandez, Zenaida. 2004. "Industrial Policy in East Asia: In Search of Lessons." Background Paper for the *World Development Report 2005*. World Bank, Washington, DC.

Hobday, Michael. 1995. *Innovation in East Asia: The Challenge to Japan*. Aldershot, U.K.: Edward Elgar.

Hoekman, Bernard, and Beata Smarzynska Javorcik. 2006. "Lessons from Empirical Research on International Technology Diffusion through Trade and Foreign Direct Investment." In *Global Integration and Technology Transfer*, ed. Bernard Hoekman and Beata Smarzynska Javorcik, 1–28. New York: Palgrave MacMillan.

Hoekman, Bernard, Keith E. Maskus, and Kamal Saggi. 2005. "Transfer of Technology to Developing Countries: Unilateral and Multilateral Policy Options." *World Development* 33 (10): 1587–1602.

Hou, Chi-Ming, and San Gee. 1993. "National Systems Supporting Technical Advance in Industry: The Case of Taiwan." In *National Innovation Systems: A Comparative Analysis*, ed. Richard R. Nelson, 384–413. New York: Oxford University Press.

Isern, Jennifer, William Donges, and Jeremy Smith. 2006. "Making Money Transfers Work for Microfinance Institutions: A Technical Guide to Developing and Delivering Money Transfers." Draft for public review. Consultative Group to Assist the Poor, Washington, DC.

Isgut, Albert E. 2001. "What's Different About Exporters? Evidence from Colombian Manufacturing." *Journal of Development Studies* 37 (5): 57–82.

Jaffe, A. B. 1989. "Real Effects of Academic Research." *American Economic Review* 79 (5): 957–70.

Javorcik, Beata Smarzynska. 2004. "Does Foreign Direct Investment Increase the Productivity of Domestic Firms? In Search of Spillovers through Backward Linkages." *American Economic Review* 94 (3): 605–27.

______. 2006. "Technological Leadership and the Choice of Entry Mode by Foreign Investors." In *Global Integration and Technology Transfer*, ed. B. Hoekman and B. Javorcik, 179–206. New York: Palgrave Macmillan.

______. 2007. "Foreign Direct Investment and International Technology Transfer: What Do We Know? What Would We Like to Know?" Unpublished paper. World Bank, Washington, DC.

Javorcik, Beata Smarzynska, Wolfgang Keller, and James Tybout. 2006. "Openness and Industrial Responses in a Wal-Mart World: A Case Study of Mexican Soaps, Detergents, and Surfactant Producers." Working Paper 12457. National Bureau of Economic Research, Cambridge, MA.

Javorcik, Beata Smarzynska, and Mariana Spatareanu. 2005. "Disentangling FDI Spillover Effects: What Do Firm Perceptions Tell Us?" In *Does Foreign Direct Investment Promote Development?*, ed. Theodore Moran, Edward Graham, and Magnus Blomstrom, 45–72. Washington, DC: Institute for International Economics.

Jordan, Mary. 2006. "New Conductors Speed Global Flows of Money: Cellphones Make Transfers Faster, Cheaper." *Washington Post*, October 3, p. A01.

Kannankutty, Nirmala, and Joan Burrelli. 2007. "Why Did They Come to the United States? A Profile of Immigrant Scientists and Engineers." *InfoBrief* NSF07-324, Science Resources Statistics, Directorate for Social, Behavioral, and Economic Sciences, United States National Science Foundation, Arlington, VA. June.

Kapur, Devesh. 2001. "Diasporas and Technology Transfer." *Journal of Human Development* 2 (2): 265–86.

Kapur, Devesh, and John McHale. 2005a. *Give Us Your Best and Brightest: The Global Hunt for Talent and Its Impact on the Developing World.* Washington, DC: Center for Global Development.

______. 2005b. "Sojourns and Software: Internationally Mobile Human Capital and High-Tech Industry Development in India, Ireland and Israel." In *Underdogs to Tigers: The Rise and Growth of the Software Industry in Some Emerging Economies*, ed. Ashish Arora and Alfonso Gambardella. Oxford University Press.

Kaufmann D., A. Kraay, and M. Mastruzzi. 2007. *Governance Matters VI: Governance Indicators-for 1996–2006*. Washington, DC: World Bank.

Keller, Wolfgang. 1998. "Are International R&D Spillovers Trade Related? Analyzing Spillovers among Randomly Matched Trade Partners." *European Economic Review* 42: 1469–81.

______. 2004. "International Technology Diffusion." *Journal of Economic Literature* 42 (September): 752–82.

Khadria, Binod. 2004. "Human Resources in Science and Technology in India and the International Mobility of Highly Skilled Indians." Science, Technology and Industry Working Paper 2004/7. Organisation for Economic Co-operation and Development, Paris. http://www.olis.oecd.org/olis/2004doc.nsf/43bb6130e5e86e5fc12569fa005d004c/c1912c8b0517eba3c1256ea1003a038d/$FILE/JT00164994.PDF.

Kinoshita, Yuko. 2000. "R&D and Technology Spillovers via FDI: Innovation and Absorptive Capacity." William Davidson Institute Working Paper No. 349. Available at SSRN: http://ssrn.com/abstract=258194.

Kohr, Martin. 2007. "Government Procurement in FTAs: An Outline of the Issues." Third World Network. http://www.twnside.org.sg. Accessed November 15, 2007.

Kugler, Maurice. 2006. "Spillovers from Foreign Direct Investment: Within or between Industries?" *Journal of Development Economics* 80 (2): 444–77.

Kui-Yin, Cheung, and Ping Lin. 2007. "Spillover Effects of FDI on Innovation in China: Evidence from the Provincial Data." http://ssrn.com/abstract=419020. Accessed November 15, 2007.

Kuznetsov, Yevgeny. 2006. "Leveraging Diasporas of Talent: Towards a New Policy Agenda." In *Diaspora Networks and the International Migration of Skills*, ed. Yevgeny Kuznetsov, 221–37. Washington, DC: World Bank Institute.

______. 2007. "The New Argonauts: Global Search and Local Institution-Building." Unpublished paper. World Bank Institute, Washington, DC.

Kuznetsov, Yevgeny, Adolfo Nemirovsky, and Gabriel Yoguel. 2006. "Argentina: Burgeoning Networks of Talent Abroad, Weak Institutions at Home." In *Diaspora Networks and the International Migration of Skills*, ed. Yevgeny Kuznetsov, 153–70. Washington, DC: World Bank Institute.

Lai, Edwin L. C. 1998. "International Property Rights Protection and Rate of Product Innovation." *Journal of Development Economics* (February): 133–53.

Lall, Sanjaya. 2000. "The Technological Structure and Performance of Developing Country Manufacturing Exports, 1985–98." *Oxford Development Studies* 28 (Part 3): 337–69.

______. 2001. "Competitiveness Indices and Developing Countries: An Economic Evaluation of the Global Competitiveness Report." *World Development* 29 (9): 1501–25.

______. 2003. "Indicators of the Relative Importance of IPRs in Developing Countries." Issue Paper 3. UNCTAD-ICTSD Project on IPRs and Sustainable Development.

Lederman, Daniel, and William F. Maloney. 2006. "Innovation in Mexico: NAFTA Is Not Enough." In *Global Integration and Technology Transfer*, ed. Bernard Hoekman and Beata Smarzynska Javorcik, 305–339. New York: Palgrave MacMillan.

Lee, Jeong-Yeon, and Edwin Mansfield. 1996. "Intellectual Property Protection and U.S. Foreign Investment." *Review of Economics and Statistics*. 78 (2): 181–86.

Lemoine, Françoise, and Deniz Ünal-Kesenci. 2003. "Trade and Technology Transfers: A Comparative Study of Turkey, India, and China." Working Paper 2003-16. Centre d'Etudes Prospectives et d'Informations Internationales.

Levinsohn, James. 1993. "Testing the Imports-as-Market-Discipline Hypothesis." *Journal of International Economics* 35 (1): 1–22.

Lipsey, Robert. 2002. "Home and Host Country Effects of FDI." Working Paper 9293. National Bureau of Economic Research, Cambridge, MA.

Lipsey, Robert E., and Fredrik Sjoholm. 2005. "The Impact of Inward FDI on Host Countries: Why Such Different Answers?" In *Does Foreign Investment Promote Development?*, ed. Theodore H. Moran, Edward M. Graham, and Magnus Blomstrom. Washington, DC: Institute for International Economics.

Liu, Lili, and James Tybout. 1996. "Productivity Growth in Colombia and Chile: Panel-Based Evidence on the Role of Entry, Exit and Learning." In *Industrial Evolution in Developing Countries*, ed. Mark J. Roberts and James R. Tybout. New York: Oxford University Press.

Lumenga-Neso, A., M. Olarreaga, and M. Schiff. 2005. "On 'Indirect' Trade-Related R&D Spillovers and Growth." *European Economic Review* 49 (7): 1785–98.

Maloney, William. 2006. "Missed Opportunities: Innovation and Resource-Based Growth in Latin America." World Bank, Washington, DC.

Mansfield, Edwin. 1994. "Intellectual Property Protection, Foreign Direct Investment, and Technology Transfer." International Finance Discussion Paper 19. Washington, DC, World Bank.

______. 1995. "Intellectual Property Protection, Direct Investment, and Technology Transfer: Germany, Japan, and the United States." Discussion Paper. World Bank and International Finance Corporation, Washington, DC.

Mansfield, E., and A. Romeo. 1980. "Technology Transfer to Overseas Subsidiaries by U.S.-Based Firms." *Quarterly Journal of Economics* 95 (4): 737–50.

Maskus, Keith. 1998. "The International Regulation of Intellectual Property." *Weltwirtschaftliches Archiv* 134 (2): 186–208.

______. 2000. "Intellectual Property Rights and Foreign Direct Investment.: Policy Discussion Paper 22. University of Adelaide, Centre for International Economic Studies, Adelaide, Australia.

______. 2002. "Intellectual Property Issues for the United States and Japan: Disputes and Common Interests." In *Issues and Options for U.S.–Japan Trade Policies*, ed. R.M. Stern, 165–90. Ann Arbor, MI: University of Michigan Press.

Maskus, Keith, and D. Konan. 1994. "Trade-Related Intellectual Property Rights: Issues and Exploratory Results. In *Analytical and Negotiating Issues in the Global Trading System*, ed. A. Deardorff and R. Stern, 401–46. Ann Arbor, MI: University of Michigan Press.

Mattoo, Aaditya, Caglar Özden, and Cristina Neagu. 2005. "Brain Waste? Educated Immigrants in the U.S. Labor Market." Policy Research Working Paper 3581, World Bank, Washington, DC.

Mattoo, Aaditya, and Lucy Payton, eds. 2007. *Services Trade and Development: The Experience of Zambia*. Washington, DC: World Bank.

Mayer, School Yafeh. 2003. *Sources of Funds and Investments Activities of Venture Capital Funds*. Oxford University Press.

McCormick, Barry, and Jackline Wahba. 2003. "Return Migration and Geographical Inequality: The Case of Egypt." *Journal of African Economies* 12 (4): 500–32.

McKinsey Global Institute. 2003. *New Horizons: Multinational Investment in Emerging Economies*. San Francisco: McKinsey & Company, Inc. http://www.mckinsey.com/mgi/publications/newhorizons/.

Moran, Theodore. 2007. "How to Investigate the Impact of Foreign Direct Investment on Development and Use the Results to Guide Policy." Unpublished report. Georgetown University, Washington, DC.

Nastas, Tomas. 2007. "*Scaling up Innovation: The Go-Forward Plan to Prosperity.*" Development Outreach, World Bank Institute. Washington, DC.

Ndou, Valentina. 2004. *E-Government for Developing Countries: Opportunities and Challenges.* Albania: University of Shkoder, Department of Business Administration.

Nishimizu, Mieko, and John M. Page Jr. 1982. "Total Factor Productivity Growth, Technological Progress and Technical Efficiency Change: Dimensions of Productivity Change in Yugoslavia, 1965–78." *Economic Journal* 92 (368): 920–36.

OECD (Organisation for Economic Co-operation and Development). 2003. *Tax Incentives for Research and Development: Trends and Issues.* Paris: OECD.

———. 2005. "Financing ICTs for Development Efforts of DAC Members." Development Assistance Committee, OECD.

______. 2007. *Reviews of Innovation Policy.* China, Synthesis Report. Paris: OECD.

O'Neil, Kevin. 2003. *Brain Drain and Gain: The Case of Taiwan.* Migration Information Source. Washington, DC: Migration Policy Institute. http://www.migrationinformation.org/Feature/display.cfm?ID=155).

Pack, Howard. 2006. "Econometric Versus Case Study Approaches to Technology Transfer." In *Global Integration and Technology Transfer*, ed. Bernard Hoekman and Beata Smarzynska Javorcik, 29–50. New York: Palgrave MacMillan.

Pack, Howard, and Kamal Saggi. 1997. "Inflows of Foreign Technology and Indigenous Technological Development." *Review of Development Economics* 1 (1): 81–98.

Page, John, and Sonia Plaza. 2006. "Migration, Remittances and Development: A Review of Global Evidence." *Journal of African Economics* 15 (Supplement 2): 245–336.

Pandey, Abhishek, Alok Aggarwal, Richard Devane, and Yevgeny Kuznetsov. 2006. "The Indian Diaspora: A Unique Case?" In *Diaspora Networks and the International Migration of Skills*, ed. Yevgeny Kuznetsov, 71–97. Washington, DC: World Bank Institute.

Parente, Stephen L., and Edward C. Prescott. 1994. "Barriers to Technology Adoption and Development." *Journal of Political Economy* 102 (2): 298–321.

Pfeil, Andreas. 2000. *Venture Capital: New Ways of Financing Technology Innovation.* Human Development Report Office.

Primo Braga, Carlos A., John Daly, and Bimal Sareen. 2003. "The Future of Information and Communication Technologies for Development." Paper presented at the Information and Communications Technology Development Forum, Petersburg, Germany, May 21.

Primo Braga, Carlos A., and Carsten Fink. 2000. "International Transactions in Intellectual Property and Developing Countries." *International Journal of Technology Management* 19: 35–56.

Puri, Shivani, and Tineke Ritzema. 1999. "Migrant Worker Remittances, Micro-Finance, and the Informal Economy: Prospects and Issues." Working Paper 21. International Labour Organisation, Social Finance Unit, Geneva.

Rauch, James, and Vitor Trindade. 2002. "Ethnic Chinese Networks in International Trade." *Review of Economics and Statistics* 84 (1): 116–130.

Reserve Bank of India. 2007. "Balance of Payment Data." Reserve Bank of India. http://www.rbi.org.in/scripts/Statistics.aspx. Accessed September 1, 2007.

Rhee, Yung Whee, Katharina Katterback, and Jannette White. 1990. *Free Trade Zones in Export Strategies.* Washington, DC: World Bank.

Rhee, Yung Whee, Bruce Ross-Larson, and Gary Pursell. 1984. *Korea's Competitive Edge: Managing the Entry into World Markets.* Washington, DC: World Bank.

Robbins, C. 2006. "Measuring Payments for the Supply and Use of Intellectual Property." U.S. Department of Commerce, Bureau of Economic Analysis, Washington, DC.

Roberts, Mark. 1996. "Colombia 1977–1985: Producer Turnover, Margins, and Trade Exposure." In *Industrial Evolution in Developing Countries: Micro Patterns of Turnover, Productivity, and Market Structure.* New York: Oxford University Press.

Roberts, Mark J., and James R. Tybout. 1997. "Producer Turnover and Productivity Growth in Developing Countries." *World Bank Research Observer* 12 (1): 1–18.

Rodriguez-Clare, Andres. 2005. *Coordination Failures, Clusters and Microeconomic Interventions.* Washington, DC: Inter-American Development Bank.

Rodrik, Dani. 2004. *Industrial Policy for the Twenty-First Century.* Cambridge, MA: Harvard University.

Rosenberg, Nathan. 1976. *Perspectives on Technology.* Cambridge, U.K.: Cambridge University Press.

Rosenzweig, Mark R., and Kenneth I. Wolpin. 1994. "Are There Increasing Returns to the Intergenerational Production of Human Capital? Maternal Schooling and Child Intellectual Achievement." *Journal of Human Resources* 29 (2): 670–93.

Saggi, Kamal. 2002. "Trade, Foreign Direct Investment and International Technology Transfer: A Survey." *World Bank Research Observer* 17 (2): 191–235.

Saxenian, AnnaLee. 2000. "Silicon Valley's New Immigrant Entrepreneurs." Working Paper 15. University of California, Center for Comparative Immigration Studies, San Diego.

______. 2002. "Brain Circulation: How High-Skilled Immigration Makes Everyone Better Off." *Brookings Review* 20 (1): 28–31.

Schiff, Maurice, and Yanling Wang. 2006a. "North–South and South–South Trade-Related Technology Diffusion: An Industry-Level Analysis of Direct and Indirect Effects." *Canadian Journal of Economics* 39 (3): 831–44.

______. 2006b. "On the Quantity and Quality of Knowledge Diffusion: The Impact of Openness and Foreign R&D on North–North and North–South R&D Spillovers." In *Global Integration and Technology Transfer*, ed. Bernard Hoekman and Beata S. Javorcik. New York: Palgrave McMillan.

Silberglitt, Richard, Philip S. Anton, David R. Howell, and Anny Wong. 2006. *The Global Technology Revolution 2020*. Santa Monica, CA: RAND Corporation, National Security Research Division.

Sjoholm, F. 1998. "Joint Ventures, Technology Transfer, and Spillovers: Evidence from Indonesian Establishment Data." In *Foreign Direct Investment in Asia*, ed. Economic Planning Agency, 587–616. Tokyo: Economic Planning Agency.

Smith, Pamela J. 2001. "How Do Foreign Patent Rights Affect U.S. Exports, Affiliate Sales, and Licenses?" *Journal of International Economics* 55 (2): 411–40.

Soderbom, Mans, and Francis Teal. 2000. "Skills, Investment and Exports from Manufacturing Firms in Africa." *Journal of Development Studies* 37 (2): 13–43.

Sorenson, Olav, and Toby E. Stuart. 2001. "Syndicated Networks and the Spatial Distribution of Venture Capital Investments." *American Journal of Sociology* 106 (6): 1546–88.

Soubbotina, Tatyana P. 2006. "Generic Models of Technological Learning by Developing Countries." Draft. World Bank, Science and Technology Program, Washington, DC.

Sullivan, Nicholas P. 2007. *You Can Hear Me Now: How Microloans and Cell Phones are Connecting the World's Poor to the Global Economy*. Jossey-Bass.

Swinnen, J. F. M., L. Dries, N. Noev, and E. Germenji. 2006. "Foreign Investment, Supermarkets, and the Restructuring of Supply Chains: Evidence from Eastern European Diary Sectors." Working Paper Series WP 165/2006, 2006. LICOS Centre for Transition Economics.

Taylor, M. S. 1994. "TRIPS, Trade and Growth." *International Economic Review* 35: 361–81.

Tybout, James R., Jaime de Melo, and Vittorio Corbo. 1991. "The Effects of Trade Technical Efficiency: New Evidence from Chile." *Journal of International Economics* 31 (3–4): 231–50.

Tybout, James R., and M. Daniel Westbrook. 1995. "Trade Liberalization and the Dimensions of Efficiency Change in Mexican Manufacturing Industries." *Journal of International Economics* 39 (1–2): 53–78.

———. 1996. "Trade Liberalization and the Dimensions of Efficiency Change in Mexican Manufacturing Industries." *Journal of International Economics* 39 (1–2): 53–78.

UNCTAD (United Nations Conference on Trade and Development). 2001. *World Investment Report 2001: Promoting Linkages*. New York and Geneva: United Nations.

______. 2003. *Transfer of Technology for Successful Integration into the Global Economy*. UNCTAD/ITE/IPC/2003/6. Geneva: UNCTAD.

______. 2005. *World Investment Report 2005: Transnational Corporation and Internationalization of R&D*. New York and Geneva: United Nations.

______. 2007. *The Least Developed Countries 2007: Knowledge, Technological Learning and Innovation for Development*. Geneva: UNCTAD.

UNDP (United Nations Development Programme). 2003. *Millennium Development Goals: A Compact among Nations to End Human Poverty*. New York: Oxford University Press.

United Nations. 2003. *United Nations World Public Sector Report 2003: E-Government at the Crossroads*. New York: United Nations.

van Wijnbergen, Sweder, and Anthony Venables. 1993. "Trade Liberalization, Productivity, and Competition: The Mexican Experience." Discussion Paper 345. London School of Economics.

Wadhwa, Vivek, AnnaLee Saxenian, Ben Rissing, and Gary Gerefi. 2007. *America's New Immigrant Entrepreneurs*. Report prepared for the University of California–Berkeley, Master of Engineering Management Program.

Wagner, Don, Keith Head, and John Ries. 2002. "Immigration and the Trade of Provinces." *Scottish Journal of Political Economy* 49 (5): 507–25.

Wahba, Jackline. 2007. "Returns to Overseas Work Experience: The Case of Egypt." In *International Migration, Economic Development, and Policy*, ed. Çaglar Özden and Maurice Schiff. Washington, DC: World Bank.

Watkins, Alfred, and Anubha Verma. 2007. "Government of Rwanda-World Bank, Science, Technology and Innovation Capacity Building Assistance Program: Developing Practical Solutions to Practical Problems." Internal report. World Bank, Washington, DC.

Wei, Yingqi. 2004. "Foreign Direct Investment in China." In *Foreign Direct Investment: Six Country Case Studies*, ed. Yingqi Wei and V. N. Balasubramanyam, 9–37. Cheltenham, U.K.: Edward-Elgar.

Woodruff, Christopher, and Rene Zenteno. 2001. "Remittances and Microenterprises in Mexico." Working Paper. University of California, San Diego, Graduate School of International Relations and Pacific Studies.

______. 2007. "Migration Networks and Microenterprises in Mexico." *Journal of Development Economics* 82 (2): 509–28. March.

World Bank. 1994. "Sugar Ethanol Policy." In *Brazil: The Management of Agriculture, Rural Development, and Natural Resources.* Vol. 2. Report No. 11783–BR. July 31.

———. 1998. *World Development Report: Knowledge for Development.* New York: Oxford University Press.

______. 2004a. *Global Development Finance 2004.* Washington, DC: World Bank.

______. 2004b. *India: Investment Climate and Manufacturing Industry.* Washington, DC: World Bank.

______. 2005. *Brazil Investment Climate Assessment.* Washington, DC: World Bank.

______. 2006a. *Global Economic Prospects 2006: Economic Implications of Remittances and Migration.* Washington, DC: World Bank.

———. 2006b. *World Development Report.* Washington, DC: World Bank.

______. 2007a. *Global Development Finance: The Globalization of Corporate Finance in Developing Countries.* Washington, DC: World Bank.

______. 2007b. *Our Commitment: The World Bank's Africa Region HIV/AIDS Agenda for Action 2007–2011.* Report No. 40513-AFR. Washington, DC: World Bank.

______. 2007c. *World Development Indicators.* Washington, DC: World Bank.

———. 2007d. *Global Monitoring Report.* 2007. Washington, DC: World Bank.

______. 2008. *World Development Report.* Washington, DC: World Bank.

______. Forthcoming. "Export Diversification in Egypt, Jordan, Morocco, and Tunisia." World Bank, Washington, DC.

World Bank Information for Development Program and Center for Democracy and Technology. 2002. *The E-Government Handbook for Developing Countries.* Washington, DC: World Bank Information for Development Program and Center for Democracy and Technology.

Xavier, Marcos Renato. 2007. "The Brazilian Sugarcane Ethanol Experience." Competitive Enterprise Institute, February 15.

Xu, Bin. 2000. "Multinational Enterprises, Technology Diffusion, and Host Country Productivity Growth." *Journal of Development Economics* 62: 477–93.

Yang, Dean. 2006. "International Migration, Remittances, and Household Investment: Evidence from Philippine Migrants' Exchange Rate Shocks." Working Paper 12325. National Bureau of Economic Research, Cambridge, MA.

Yokota, Toshiyuki, and Richard J. Weiland. 2004. "ITS Standards for Developing Countries." ITS Technical Note 4. Washington, DC: World Bank.

Yoo, JaeHoon. 2007. "Financing Innovation: How to Build an Efficient Exchange for Small Firms." *Public Policy Journal. No. 315.* World Bank Washington, DC.

Zeng, Douglas Zhihua, and Shilin Wang. 2007. "China and the Knowledge Economy: Challenges and Opportunities." Staff Working Paper 4223. World Bank, Washington, DC.

Appendix
Regional Economic Prospects

East Asia and the Pacific

Recent developments

Growth in the developing countries of East Asia and the Pacific strengthened in 2007, with gross domestic product (GDP) advancing a full 10 percent in the year, up from 9.7 percent in 2006. The expansion was powered by China's 11.3 percent gain, with other countries in the region growing at a 5.9 percent pace (figure A1). Domestic demand was a key driving force for many economies, as a downturn in the global high-tech cycle for most of 2006–07 served to blunt the momentum of exports for technology-producing countries in the region. The pickup in regional growth was all the more notable because it occurred despite a slowdown in the U.S. economy: total U.S. imports fell from 5.8 percent growth in 2006 to 2 percent in 2007. Regional exports nonetheless advanced 17.8 percent, a modest pickup from 2006 outturns.

East Asia appears to have absorbed the effects of the financial turmoil in the high-income markets well. Stock markets in the main East Asian economies dropped a median 14 percent during July and early August, with equity prices increasing a median 22 percent to mid-October. Similar developments were witnessed in foreign exchange markets and in sovereign bonds. Since the beginning of the year, several East Asian currencies have appreciated sharply against the dollar, with the Philippine peso up 12 percent and the Thai baht up 11.3 percent. The Chinese yuan continued its gradual rise against the dollar, a 4.7 percent gain since the beginning of the year, but at the same time, the yuan depreciated against many other currencies.

On the policy front, East Asian central banks generally tightened monetary conditions from mid-2004 to the early part of 2006 to curb rising inflation. As a result, inflation stabilized in 2007 (although headline inflation rates, which include fuels and food, have turned up recently in some countries because of higher food price inflation), allowing central banks to keep policy rates stable, and even to begin easing in Indonesia and Thailand

Figure A1 East Asian growth moves up in 2007

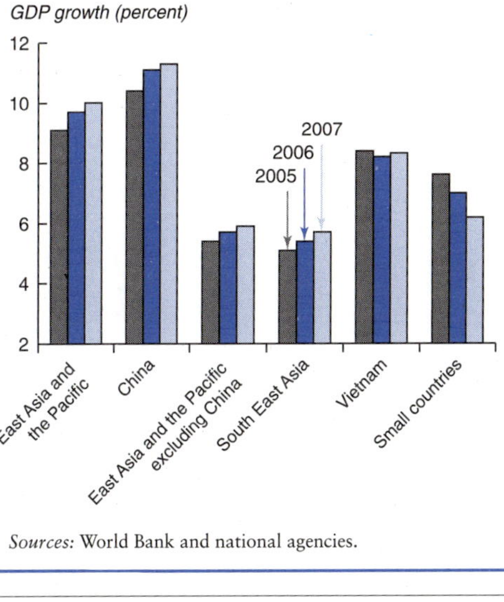

Sources: World Bank and national agencies.

Figure A2 Except for China, inflation is now stabilizing across East Asia

Consumer price inflation (percent change year over year)

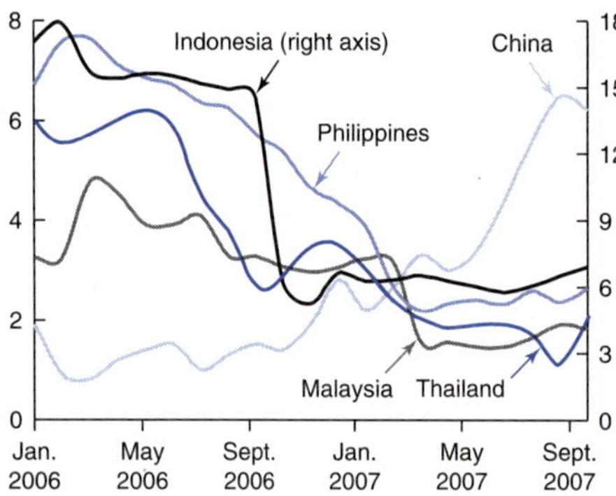

Source: World Bank.

(figure A2). Fiscal balances have improved and government debt has declined over the course of the decade in most of the larger East Asian economies thanks to fiscal consolidation efforts, relatively low interest rates, and sustained economic growth since 2001.

External conditions during 2007 remained sufficiently positive for surplus positions to widen across countries. Central banks in China, Indonesia, Malaysia, the Philippines, and Thailand continued to build up reserves as their current accounts remained in surplus. East Asia's aggregate current account surplus as a share of GDP increased to 10.1 percent in 2007, up from 8.4 percent in 2006. Gross capital flows, including bond and equity issuance and net bank borrowing, amounted to a remarkable $170 billion over the year through October. This contrasts favorably with inflows of $153 billion for all of 2006 and $107 billion for 2005, indicating that market access has remained largely unencumbered. At the same time, the contribution of net exports to GDP growth increased 3 percentage points, as exports expanded by 17.8 percent, significantly outpacing the 15.3 percent growth in imports (table A1).

Table A1 East Asia and Pacific forecast summary

(annual percent change unless indicated otherwise)

					Forecast		
	1991–2000[a]	2004	2005	2006	2007	2008	2009
GDP at market prices[b]	8.4	9.0	9.1	9.7	10.0	9.7	9.6
GDP per capita[c]	7.1	8.1	8.2	8.8	9.1	8.8	8.7
Purchasing Power Parity GDP[d]	—	9.2	9.3	9.9	10.2	9.9	9.7
Private consumption	7.3	6.8	7.5	7.4	7.6	7.6	7.6
Public consumption	9.0	6.7	10.9	8.5	9.0	8.5	8.6
Fixed investment	10.3	11.5	12.7	10.9	11.3	9.9	9.6
Exports, GNFS[e]	11.7	22.6	17.8	17.7	17.8	15.2	18.5
Imports, GNFS[e]	11.3	20.6	10.5	14.8	15.3	14.2	19.4
Net exports, contribution to growth	0.3	1.8	3.9	2.8	3.0	2.3	2.1
Current account balance/GDP (%)	0.1	3.4	5.7	8.4	10.1	8.6	7.6
GDP deflator (median, LCU)	6.5	6.1	3.8	4.3	4.6	2.9	3.8
Fiscal balance/GDP (%)	−0.7	−1.5	−1.4	−0.5	−0.9	−1.1	−1.2
Memo items: GDP							
East Asia, excluding China	4.8	6.1	5.4	5.7	5.9	5.9	6.2
China	10.4	10.1	10.4	11.1	11.3	10.8	10.5
Indonesia	4.2	5.1	5.7	5.5	6.3	6.3	6.5
Thailand	4.5	6.2	4.5	5.0	4.3	4.6	5.2

Source: World Bank.
Note: — = not available.
a. Growth rates over intervals are compound averages; growth contributions, ratios, and the GDP deflator are averages.
b. GDP measured in constant 2000 U.S. dollars.
c. Measured in U.S. dollars.
d. GDP measured at purchasing power parity exchange rates.
e. Exports and imports of goods and nonfactor services.

In China, growth continued at a robust pace in 2007, underpinned by strong contributions to GDP from net exports and by buoyant domestic demand, led by investment. Growth achieved a 11.5 percent run-up in the first half of the year, including an exceptional 11.9 percent advance during the second quarter. The soaring current account surplus of about $380 billion in 2007, some 12 percent of GDP, is adding to domestic liquidity and contributing to asset price increases, while supporting, along with other factors such as sharp gains in food prices, an upward drift in consumer price inflation.

Elsewhere investment growth picked up in most economies, as capacity utilization reached high levels, corporate profits rose, and the health of balance sheets improved. In Indonesia, fixed investment surged 11.3 percent (seasonally adjusted annual rate) in the second quarter, and GDP growth increased to 6.3 percent, up from 5.5 percent in 2006. Against this background, inflation is now a growing concern, reaching 6.9 percent in September (year-on-year), at the upper end of the central bank's target range. GDP growth should register a solid 6.3 percent for the year.

Malaysia suffered subpar export performance during the first half of 2007, tied in part to sluggish demand for semiconductors and other high-tech inputs, slow hydrocarbon shipments, and difficulties in several exportable food and raw material commodities. Export growth declined to 2.5 percent in the first half of 2007, down from 6 percent in the second half of 2006, contributing to a slowdown in GDP growth to 5.6 percent in the first half of the year. Equity markets were depressed for a short time during the period of global financial stress, but have bounced back sharply since mid-August. Domestic demand is expected to sustain growth, offsetting weakness in trade and allowing Malaysia to register 5.7 percent GDP growth for 2007.

In the Philippines, GDP growth ramped up to 7.3 percent during the first half of 2007 based on strong investment outlays and a pickup in services; growth for the year is expected to register 6.7 percent. The country is beginning to enjoy the benefits stemming from the substantial fiscal adjustment, public debt reductions, and balance-of-payments surpluses of recent years. The current account surplus rose sharply as a result of large remittance inflows and a diminishing trade deficit. Foreign direct investment (FDI) inflows increased 70 percent from 2006 to $1.6 billion in the first half of the year, while international reserves have increased to some $30.7 billion, enough to cover 5.5 months of imports.

In Thailand, where continuing political and policy uncertainties have significantly dampened business and consumer confidence, GDP is anticipated to grow by 4.3 percent in 2007, down from 5 percent in 2006. Growth has relied on conditions in the external environment, where the news is somewhat discouraging, given an 11 percent appreciation of the baht against the dollar over 2007 to date and sluggish conditions in the U.S. market.

Growth has also continued to run at strong 7 to 10 percent rates in several low-income economies of the region, including Cambodia, the Lao People's Democratic Republic, Mongolia, and Vietnam, powered by across-the-board strength in exports and domestic demand. Growth is also above historical rates in some of the small island states of the region, pushed up by high commodity prices, and in some cases by improved economic management. At the same time, political instability and social tensions continue to undermine performance in some of the Pacific islands, including Fiji, where GDP is expected to contract this year.

Medium-term outlook

Growth in East Asia and the Pacific is projected to remain strong, with GDP easing by just 0.3 percentage points to 9.7 percent in 2008 and retaining strength in 2009 with an advance of 9.6 percent. Growth in China is expected to slow modestly, dropping less than a percentage point over the period to 10.5 percent by 2009, as authorities' long-standing attempts to rein in certain investment projects

Table A2 East Asia and Pacific country forecasts
(annual percent change unless indicated otherwise)

	1991–2000[a]	2004	2005	2006	Forecast 2007	2008	2009
Cambodia							
GDP at market prices[b]	—	10.0	13.5	10.8	9.5	8.0	9.0
Current account balance/GDP (%)	—	−3.7	−7.1	−5.8	−7.8	−11.2	−9.0
China							
GDP at market prices[b]	10.4	10.1	10.4	11.1	11.3	10.8	10.5
Current account balance/GDP (%)	1.5	3.6	6.9	9.4	11.9	10.3	9.1
Fiji							
GDP at market prices[b]	2.1	5.3	0.7	3.6	−3.1	1.9	2.8
Current account balance/GDP (%)	−3.1	−16.8	−22.7	−22.2	−20.1	−24.0	−26.2
Indonesia							
GDP at market prices[b]	4.2	5.1	5.7	5.5	6.3	6.3	6.5
Current account balance/GDP (%)	−0.4	0.6	0.4	3.1	2.7	1.5	0.9
Lao People's Democratic Republic							
GDP at market prices[b]	—	6.4	7.1	7.6	7.1	7.9	7.5
Current account balance/GDP (%)	—	−6.3	−26.4	−18.7	−16.8	−19.0	−19.0
Malaysia							
GDP at market prices[b]	7.1	7.2	5.0	5.9	5.7	5.9	6.0
Current account balance/GDP (%)	−0.4	12.6	15.3	17.1	13.8	12.2	10.2
Papua New Guinea							
GDP at market prices[b]	4.8	2.7	3.4	2.6	5.2	4.0	4.2
Current account balance/GDP (%)	2.2	−1.5	2.6	4.4	2.7	3.6	2.8
Philippines							
GDP at market prices[b]	3.0	6.2	4.9	5.4	6.7	6.2	6.5
Current account balance/GDP (%)	−3.1	1.9	2.0	5.3	4.3	2.4	1.8
Thailand							
GDP at market prices[b]	4.5	6.2	4.5	5.0	4.3	4.6	5.2
Current account balance/GDP (%)	−1.2	1.7	−4.6	1.6	2.4	1.4	1.5
Vanuatu							
GDP at market prices[b]	4.1	4.0	6.5	7.2	5.0	5.0	5.0
Current account balance/GDP (%)	−8.2	−19.7	−20.2	−22.1	−19.9	−20.8	−20.4
Vietnam							
GDP at market prices[b]	7.6	7.7	8.4	8.2	8.3	8.2	8.3
Current account balance/GDP (%)	−5.1	−1.0	−0.3	1.1	−1.1	−0.6	−1.8

Source: World Bank.
Note: Growth and current account figures presented here are World Bank projections and may differ from targets contained in other World Bank documents. American Samoa, Dem. Rep., the Federated States of Micronesia, Kiribati, Korea, Northern Mariana Islands, Marshall Islands, Mongolia, Myanmar, Palau, Solomon Islands, Timor-Leste, and Tonga are not forecast because of data limitations.
— = not available
a. Growth rates over intervals are compound averages; growth contributions, ratios, and the GDP deflator are averages.
b. GDP measured in constant 2000 U.S. dollars.

and to avoid overheating in several sectors come to fruition (table A2 and figure A3). Substantial reform efforts in several countries of the Association of Southeast Asian Nations should yield acceleration in activity through the forecast period. Growth among East Asian economies other than China is expected to register 6.2 percent by 2009.

A projected slowdown in export growth from 17.8 percent in 2007 to 15.2 percent in 2008 echoes a softening in demand by countries of the Organisation for Economic Co-operation and Development (OECD)—with U.S. imports increasing by a meager 1.3 percent—as well as second-round effects on intraregional trade. However, the decline

Figure A3 Performance improves for East Asian countries other than China

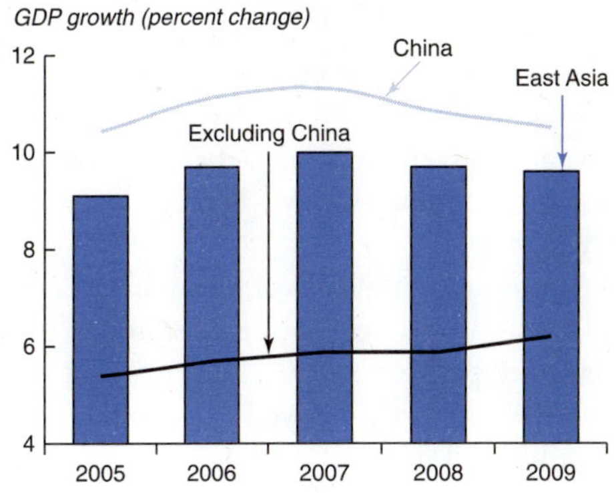

Source: World Bank.

should not make a serious dent in regional GDP, and the contribution of net trade to growth is projected to fall only moderately, from 3 percentage points in 2007 to 2.3 in 2008. Largely reflecting developments in China, the momentum underlying fixed investment begins to dissipate during 2008, easing from 11.3 percent in 2007 to 9.9 percent. By 2009, the external environment is expected to feature a revival in U.S. GDP growth complemented by recovery in Europe and Japan. OECD import demand is forecast to increase from 5 percent in 2008 to 7.8 percent in 2009, and conditions in financial markets are expected to stabilize.

Risks

The year 2008 will likely be challenging for policy makers, with a large number of interrelated downside risks. These include the possibility of a full-fledged recession in the United States, higher oil prices, and further escalation of turbulence in financial markets linked to the U.S. subprime debacle.

Among principal concerns is the extent to which both financial and real side effects of the U.S. subprime crisis might increase in the coming year. China should be well positioned to weather the continuing turmoil in financial markets. The impact on Chinese financial institutions holding overseas collateralized debt obligations and other U.S. mortgage-backed securities appears likely to be small in relation to the size of China's economy and its huge international reserves ($1.4 trillion), but other countries may be more vulnerable to effects flowing through both direct and indirect channels.

Should losses by large international institutions mount to substantial levels, other investments, including those in East Asia, could be called in an effort to rebalance portfolios and mitigate the effects on trading profits. Several countries in East Asia are exposed to this risk, particularly those that have been recipients of large capital inflows intermediated through the yen carry trade. Policy makers will need to keep a close eye on the volume, direction, and volatility of short-term flows, including those into local equity markets. Nevertheless the large holdings of foreign exchange reserves and the current account surplus positions of most East Asian economies should provide a significant buffer and reduce macroeconomic vulnerability to a reversal in capital flows.

The obverse of this risk is that interest rate reductions in high-income economies may boost liquidity to the point of touching off another upward cycle in equities, including in emerging markets, setting the stage for an even more pronounced adjustment later. Even in the absence of such a scenario, many economies in the region have been struggling to curb liquidity growth caused by burgeoning current account surpluses and large-scale buildup of reserves. If not managed properly, excess liquidity could jeopardize price stability, form asset price bubbles, and expose a country to serious financial and macroeconomic vulnerabilities. Finally, a slowdown in the high-income countries that is more severe than projected would subject many East Asian economies to a substantial downdraft in export growth.

Europe and Central Asia

Recent developments

GDP growth in the Europe and Central Asia region eased slightly, from 6.9 percent in 2006 to 6.7 percent in 2007, reflecting a modest softening of both external and domestic demand (table A3). With a stable population in the region, this means that per capita production continued to increase at remarkable rates of more than 6 percent. High productivity gains have been made possible by technology diffusion, double-digit growth in investment supported by rapid credit expansion through lending by domestic and foreign banks, high energy prices for hydrocarbon exporters, and large remittance inflows from workers overseas. These same factors have boosted private consumption and consistently raised import growth 3 or more percentage points above the already robust expansion of exports. These developments, which have helped to rapidly increase standards of living, are not without shadow costs. Capital inflows have created challenges for macroeconomic management; inflation remains high relative to that in the Euro Area, making it more difficult for several countries to maintain effective exchange rate pegs; and current account deficits in many oil-importing countries have become unsustainably high.

At the subregional level, growth in Central and Eastern Europe (CEE) moderated to a still robust 6.0 percent in 2007 from 6.5 percent in 2006 (figure A4), buoyed by rapid growth in credit and in real wages, strong capital inflows, and high remittance inflows. The falloff in growth in CEE is attributable in large measure to a slowdown in Hungary, where a program of fiscal consolidation pushed growth down 3.2 percentage points to 2.2 percent in 2007. The decline in growth in CEE also stems from continued moderation in

Table A3 Europe and Central Asia forecast summary

(annual percent change unless indicated otherwise)

					Forecast		
	1991–2000[a]	2004	2005	2006	2007	2008	2009
GDP at market prices[b]	−1.0	7.4	6.1	6.9	6.7	6.1	5.7
GDP per capita[c]	−1.2	7.4	6.2	6.9	6.7	6.0	5.7
Purchasing Power Parity GDP[d]	−0.9	7.6	6.1	7.1	7.0	6.2	5.8
Private consumption	0.5	8.6	7.8	7.4	7.3	6.9	6.8
Public consumption	0.1	2.3	3.4	5.0	4.5	5.4	3.4
Fixed investment	−6.6	14.1	11.5	16.5	14.9	13.0	10.3
Exports, GNFS[e]	0.9	12.4	7.0	10.3	9.2	8.5	8.7
Imports, GNFS[e]	−1.6	17.4	10.2	14.0	12.8	12.2	11.2
Net exports, contribution to growth	0.9	−1.7	−1.4	−1.8	−2.0	−2.3	−1.9
Current account balance/GDP (%)	—	0.8	1.5	0.6	−1.3	−1.9	−2.6
GDP deflator (median, LCU)	118.5	6.6	5.8	7.3	6.9	6.4	5.5
Fiscal balance/GDP (%)	−6.1	−0.7	2.0	2.9	1.6	1.6	1.5
Memo items: GDP							
Transition countries	2.0	6.9	5.7	6.3	5.7	5.5	5.3
Central and Eastern Europe	1.2	5.7	4.7	6.5	6.0	5.5	5.2
Commonwealth of Independent States	−4.2	8.0	6.8	7.8	8.2	6.8	6.2
Russian Federation	−3.9	7.1	6.4	6.7	7.5	6.5	6.0
Turkey	3.6	8.9	7.4	6.1	5.1	5.4	5.7
Poland	3.8	5.3	3.6	6.1	6.5	5.7	5.1

Source: World Bank.
Note: — = not available.
a. Growth rates over intervals are compound averages; growth contributions, ratios, and the GDP deflator are averages.
b. GDP measured in constant 2000 U.S. dollars.
c. Measured in U.S. dollars.
d. GDP measured at purchasing power parity exchange rates.
e. Exports and imports of goods and nonfactor services.

Figure A4 Mixed growth outturns across Europe and Central Asia

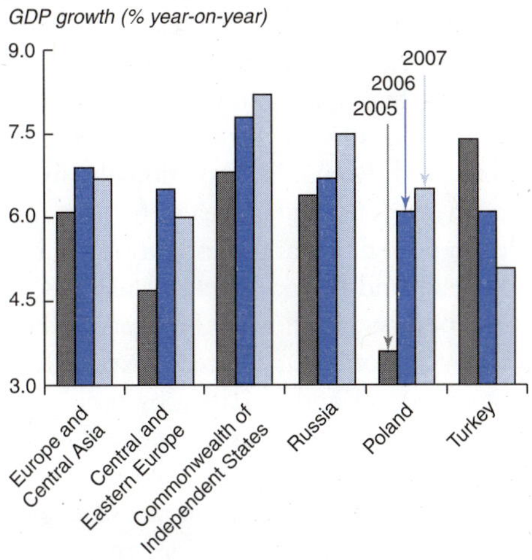

Sources: World Bank and national agencies.

Figure A5 External positions vary widely across Europe and Central Asia

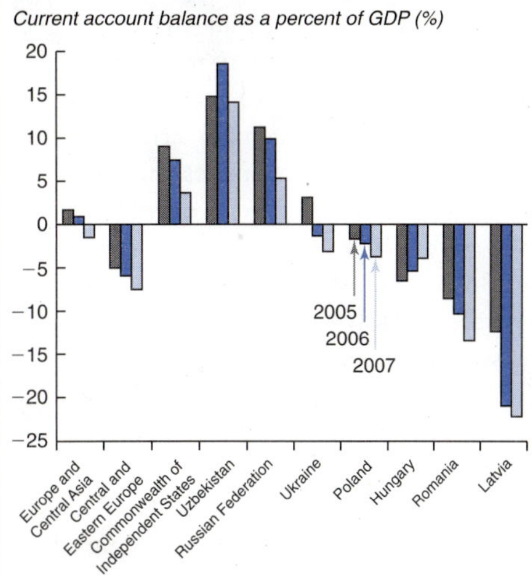

Sources: World Bank and national agencies.

Turkish GDP, which slowed by 1 percentage point to 5.1 percent in 2007 from an unsustainable 8.9 percent pace posted in 2004.

In contrast with CEE, growth in the Commonwealth of Independent States (CIS) accelerated sharply from 7.8 percent in 2006 to 8.2 percent in 2007 (figure A4). A strong increase in public consumption and investment, combined with a slightly improved contribution from net exports, formed the foundation for this pickup in growth. Revenue gains for the oil-exporting economies, notably Azerbaijan, Kazakhstan, and the Russian Federation, continue at robust rates, given increasing oil prices, and are providing ongoing support to demand growth through fiscal linkage. A construction boom in residential, commercial, and civil engineering (infrastructure) projects is contributing to a rise in the non-oil sectors. Among the smaller CIS economies, high worker remittance inflows, FDI, and vibrant demand from regional oil exporters (notably Russia) and from Asia (especially China) are underpinning growth. Gross worker remittances represented a substantial share of GDP for several of the region's countries in 2006, ranging from the equivalent of 4 percent of GDP to as much as 38 percent: Albania (15 percent), Armenia (19 percent), Azerbaijan (4 percent), Georgia (7 percent), the Kyrgyz Republic (12 percent), Moldova (38 percent), and Tajikistan (20 percent). Remittances are anticipated to maintain this strong level in 2007.

Europe and Central Asia's regional current account position shifted to a modest deficit equivalent to 1.3 percent of GDP in 2007 after posting a surplus of 0.6 percent in 2006 (figure A5) and an average surplus of nearly 1 percent of GDP over 2000–05. Strong domestic demand is driving import volume growth of 12.8 percent, well in excess of exports at 9.2 percent. Sizable current account deficits among countries in CEE have been financed to a large extent by FDI, although for the Baltic states, foreign borrowing by banks has come to represent a substantial share of external finance, leading to higher external debt-to-GDP ratios. In the case of Latvia, that ratio reached 112 percent in 2006 and is projected to remain above 100 percent during 2007–09. Moreover, short-term debt as a share of total external debt is high in a number of countries, reaching more than 40 percent in Latvia, Lithuania, and the Slovak Republic. These indicators point to potential future problems with currency and maturity mismatches.

In the CIS, worker remittances have helped finance significant external deficits in a number of smaller countries. In Kazakhstan and the Kyrgyz Republic, external debt as a share of gross national income stood at 83 and 86 percent, respectively, in 2005, and in the case of Kazakhstan, this share has increased by 12 percentage points since 2001. Indeed, the rise in the international indebtedness of Kazakh banks has recently focused attention on the country, given the turbulence in international financial markets. In the Kyrgyz Republic, debt burdens remain at high levels, but they have been reduced sharply since 2000—by more than 50 percentage points as a share of gross national income—largely because of debt rescheduling by the Paris Club in 2002 and an improvement in debt management strategy.

Fiscal positions in the region generally deteriorated in 2007, with the largest shifts posted in the CIS. The most notable decline has been in Tajikistan, where the fiscal balance shifted from a surplus of 1.6 percent of GDP in 2006 to a deficit of 10.3 percent. This reflects, in part, an effort to offset weakening exports to sustain domestic consumption and investment. Marked deteriorations in fiscal positions of 2 percentage points or more during 2007 have been recorded in Belarus (2.0 points), Bosnia and Herzegovina (3.4 points), Kazakhstan (3.0 points), Russia (2.2 points), and Turkey (3.4 points). In contrast, notable consolidation has been achieved in Hungary, where the austerity program reduced the deficit from 9.2 percent of GDP in 2006 to 6.4 percent. Firming government revenues underpinned by stronger than expected GDP growth helped manage a reduction of Poland's deficit from 3.9 percent of GDP in 2006 to 3.0 percent in 2007. In Azerbaijan, increasing oil revenues and new productive capacity have led to a considerable rise in the fiscal surplus, which is equivalent to 5.0 percent of GDP, up from 0.1 percent in 2006.

Monetary policy across the region has become more restrictive to counter rising inflationary pressures. Price increases are stemming from sustained high domestic demand growth and rising fuel and grain prices, the latter aggravated locally by drought conditions in Bulgaria and Romania and globally by the surge in the use of cereals for biofuels. Moldova posted the largest escalation in prices. In Hungary and Latvia, prices were up 3 percentage points; inflation in Hungary is being driven by increases in indirect taxes and administered prices and in Latvia by rapid credit expansion tied to vibrant capital inflows. In Azerbaijan, inflation is expected to rise to 16 percent in 2007, double the rate of 2006; in Ukraine and Uzbekistan inflation is expected to average 17.5 and 17.0 percent, respectively.

In several countries, however, inflationary pressure has eased. In Romania, consumer prices fell from 6.6 percent during 2006 to 4.6 percent in 2007, thanks to currency appreciation and a delay in regulated price adjustments. The Slovak Republic is also projected to see an easing of inflation of some 2 percentage points. Tighter domestic conditions and exchange rate appreciation helped moderate inflationary pressures in Croatia, Kazakhstan, and Turkey during the year. Nonetheless, inflation pressures are expected to rekindle, in part reflecting higher food prices and energy costs, which are affecting a wide spectrum of countries.

The impact of market turbulence tied to the U.S. subprime mortgage market has been fairly limited in the region, and initial downside adjustments in currency and asset prices have largely been recouped. Bond spreads increased, but not as much as in other markets. Nevertheless, concerns about potential spillovers remain for a number of countries in the region, particularly those that have experienced rapid credit growth and private sector borrowing from abroad, the proportions of which may be underestimated. Signs of overheating are clearly evident in Bulgaria and the Baltic states, where already worrisome external positions have deteriorated even further during 2007. Given that foreign inflows are financing much of the credit expansion in these economies, increased market volatility points to heightened concerns in relation to currency mismatches, sudden stops, and contagion. A potential exchange rate risk is present in a number of countries where loans denominated in foreign currencies make up a large share of total loans by domestic banks. In the Baltic states, Hungary, Kazakhstan, Romania, and Ukraine, this ratio was 40 percent or more in 2006, and in the case of Latvia, the share increased by more than 15 percentage points since 2001 to nearly 80 percent in 2006.

Medium-term outlook

From GDP gains of 6.7 percent in 2007, growth is projected to continue easing, falling off to 6.1 percent in 2008 and to 5.7 percent in 2009 (tables A3 and A4, figure A6). The slowdown in 2008 is expected to be widespread across countries in the region, given heightened risk aversion and volatility on international financial markets, which could spill over to the region both directly and also indirectly through a faltering of external demand. Slower growth in the OECD countries, especially in Germany and the Euro Area, may dampen export growth for CEE during the year. Difficulties among European financial institutions would also have repercussions throughout Europe and Central Asia. Domestic demand growth is anticipated to moderate from recent highs, with the contribution to growth from both private consumption and investment projected to fall by 0.2 percentage points during 2008. The contribution of trade to growth—reflecting weakened external demand, and despite a degree of softening import growth—is expected to become still more negative in 2008.

Figure A6 Growth in Europe and Central Asia eases into 2009

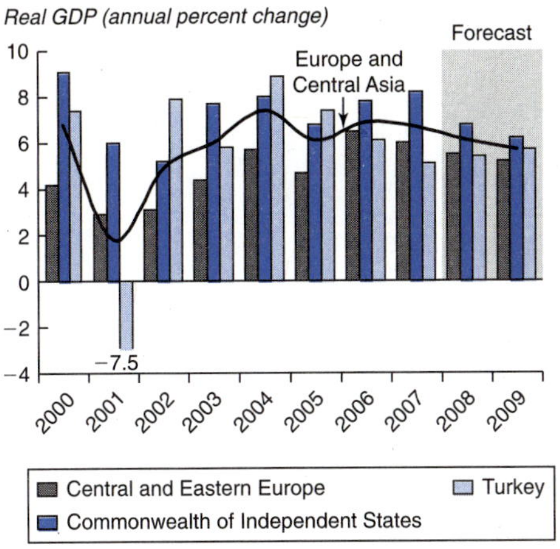

Source: World Bank.

Three notable exceptions to the projected growth slowdown in 2008 are Albania, Hungary, and Turkey. In Albania, continued strong domestic demand is expected to help firm up growth. A key component of that demand is increased public investment to mitigate the power shortages that have created a bottleneck to growth. In Hungary and Turkey, improvements in domestic conditions should permit additional easing of monetary policy, bolstering demand sufficiently to bring about a pickup in GDP growth.

By 2009, external demand is projected to strengthen in concert with GDP growth in the OECD, leading to an improvement in contributions to growth from net exports, equivalent to 1.9 percentage points in 2009 (following a drop by 2.3 percentage points in 2008). A further falloff in domestic demand growth; particularly the investment in the CIS countries, is projected to offset this improvement somewhat, resulting in modest deceleration in regional growth to 5.7 percent in 2009. In large measure, the projected slowdown in the CIS is driven by the near completion of major hydrocarbon investment projects that led to the expansion of production and export capacity in recent years.

Despite a rise in external demand and continued moderation in domestic demand, the regional current account is anticipated to

Table A4 Europe and Central Asia country forecasts

(annual percent change unless indicated otherwise)

	1991–2000[a]	2004	2005	2006	Forecast 2007	2008	2009
Albania							
GDP at market prices[b]	1.4	5.9	5.5	5.0	5.5	6.0	6.2
Current account balance/GDP (%)	−5.6	−4.8	−7.8	−7.2	−8.4	−8.4	−8.0
Armenia							
GDP at market prices[b]	−3.8	10.5	13.9	13.3	11.0	8.5	7.5
Current account balance/GDP (%)	−12.0	−4.5	−4.4	−4.7	−5.7	−5.6	−4.8
Azerbaijan							
GDP at market prices[b]	−5.2	10.2	26.4	34.5	33.5	19.4	14.9
Current account balance/GDP (%)	−15.8	−29.8	1.3	18.2	24.2	31.6	33.3
Belarus							
GDP at market prices[b]	−1.2	11.4	9.4	9.9	7.8	6.4	5.7
Current account balance/GDP (%)	—	−5.2	1.8	−4.1	−8.0	−8.4	−8.3
Bulgaria							
GDP at market prices[b]	−1.7	5.7	5.5	6.3	6.1	6.0	5.2
Current account balance/GDP (%)	−2.3	−6.9	−12.2	−15.8	−19.2	−18.1	−17.3
Croatia							
GDP at market prices[b]	−1.5	3.8	4.3	4.8	5.8	4.9	4.5
Current account balance/GDP (%)	1.1	−5.2	−6.7	−7.7	−8.4	−8.0	−7.9
Georgia							
GDP at market prices[b]	−9.3	5.9	9.6	9.8	10.0	9.0	8.0
Current account balance/GDP (%)	—	−8.3	−9.8	−13.8	−15.0	−14.1	−12.0
Hungary							
GDP at market prices[b]	0.8	5.2	6.0	5.4	2.2	3.1	3.8
Current account balance/GDP (%)	−5.4	−8.5	−6.8	−5.7	−4.2	−5.0	−5.9
Kazakhstan							
GDP at market prices[b]	−3.6	9.6	9.7	10.7	8.5	7.1	6.4
Current account balance/GDP (%)	−1.8	0.8	−1.9	−2.2	−2.0	−4.6	−7.7
Kyrgyz Republic							
GDP at market prices[b]	−4.0	7.0	−0.6	2.7	7.5	7.0	6.7
Current account balance/GDP (%)	−10.6	−4.6	−9.3	−6.6	−17.9	−15.1	−12.2
Lithuania							
GDP at market prices[b]	−3.3	7.0	7.5	7.4	7.8	6.8	6.0
Current account balance/GDP (%)	−5.9	−7.7	−7.1	−10.8	−13.3	−13.6	−12.3
Latvia							
GDP at market prices[b]	−2.8	8.6	10.2	11.9	9.7	7.4	6.4
Current account balance/GDP (%)	−1.6	−12.9	−12.7	−21.4	−22.7	−19.5	−15.3
Moldova							
GDP at market prices[b]	−9.8	7.4	7.5	4.0	6.0	6.8	7.0
Current account balance/GDP (%)	—	−2.2	−9.0	−9.3	−8.0	−14.9	−12.7
Macedonia, FYR							
GDP at market prices[b]	−0.9	4.1	4.1	3.0	5.0	5.0	5.5
Current account balance/GDP (%)	—	−8.0	−1.5	−0.4	−2.9	−5.0	−6.1
Poland							
GDP at market prices[b]	3.8	5.3	3.6	6.1	6.5	5.7	5.1
Current account balance/GDP (%)	−3.5	−4.2	−1.9	−2.4	−4.3	−5.3	−5.7
Romania							
GDP at market prices[b]	−1.7	8.4	4.1	7.7	6.1	5.9	5.5
Current account balance/GDP (%)	−4.8	−8.5	−8.7	−10.5	−13.9	−15.3	−14.9
Russian Federation							
GDP at market prices[b]	−3.9	7.1	6.4	6.7	7.5	6.5	6.0
Current account balance/GDP (%)	—	10.0	11.1	9.7	5.7	4.3	2.2

Table A4 (*continued*)

(annual percent change unless indicated otherwise)

	1991–2000[a]	2004	2005	2006	Forecast 2007	2008	2009
Slovak Republic							
GDP at market prices[b]	0.3	5.2	6.6	8.8	8.7	7.1	6.8
Current account balance/GDP (%)	—	−3.1	−8.4	−8.0	−4.3	−3.5	−3.1
Turkey							
GDP at market prices[b]	3.6	8.9	7.4	6.1	5.1	5.4	5.7
Current account balance/GDP (%)	−1.1	−5.2	−6.2	−8.1	−7.5	−7.7	−7.6
Ukraine							
GDP at market prices[b]	−8.0	12.1	2.7	7.1	6.3	5.5	5.0
Current account balance/GDP (%)	—	10.7	2.9	−1.5	−3.6	−6.5	−7.4
Uzbekistan							
GDP at market prices[b]	−0.2	7.7	7.0	7.3	7.7	5.0	5.0
Current account balance/GDP (%)	—	10.1	14.9	18.7	14.3	11.9	8.7

Source: World Bank.
Note: Growth and current account figures presented here are World Bank projections and may differ from targets contained in other World Bank documents. Bosnia and Herzegovina, Serbia and Montenegro, Tajikistan, and Turkmenistan are not forecast because of data limitations.
— = not available.
a. Growth rates over intervals are compound averages; growth contributions, ratios, and the GDP deflator are averages.
b. GDP measured in constant 2000 U.S. dollars.

continue to deteriorate through 2009, largely because of declines in the terms of trade for hydrocarbon-exporting countries as oil prices begin to soften. Inflationary pressures are likely to ease over the medium term, with median GDP inflation coming down from 6.9 percent in 2007 to 6.4 percent in 2008 and 5.5 percent in 2009. This decline is tied to generally tighter credit conditions in both international and domestic markets. However, this somewhat sanguine picture masks an expected rise in inflation pressures in Belarus and Georgia and slower progress toward stabilization of consumer price inflation among oil exporters (as well as in Moldova and Ukraine) because of strong demand pressures. Among the new EU member countries, only the Slovak Republic is anticipated to join the Euro Area in the coming years following Slovenia's entry in 2007.

Risks

Downside risks to regional growth are tied to potential overheating and a sudden unwinding of large external imbalances. The presence of large foreign banks in several countries in the region, and the fact that many of these countries share common creditors and investors, appears to expose them to higher contagion risk in the event of a nondiscriminatory pullout, similar to what occurred in East Asia in 1997. In particular, large current account deficits (equivalent to about 12 percent or more as a share of GDP) in Bulgaria, Georgia, Latvia, Lithuania, and Romania remain a concern.

Risks to growth are also associated with the slowing of reform momentum in the new EU member states and other countries in CEE. In the CIS, slow progress with economic reforms and only gradual diversification from commodity market dependence remain a concern, pointing to slower medium-term growth prospects. And a more protracted workout of the housing situation in the United States and associated financial distortions there and in other OECD markets present a substantial downside risk.

Higher than anticipated oil prices also present risk for energy-importing countries in the form of higher import bills and increased inflationary pressures. With respect to the latter, while countries with free-floating currency regimes in CEE have direct policy levers to manage inflationary pressures, those with currencies pegged to the euro, such as the Baltic states and Bulgaria, have more limited options. Higher than projected grain prices could also lead to increased inflationary pressures, particularly among the low-income countries, where food expenditures represent a large share of consumption.

Despite gains in a number of Millennium Development Goal indicators, some countries in the region, particularly in Central Asia and the Caucasus, have shown regressing trends and slower progress toward achieving the goals. The Caucasus have met the goals related to carbon emissions and primary education, but concerns remain about the nonincome poverty indicators, such as malnutrition, access to tertiary education, HIV/AIDS, the environment, and soil and water management.

Figure A7 Growth outturns were mixed across Latin America in 2007

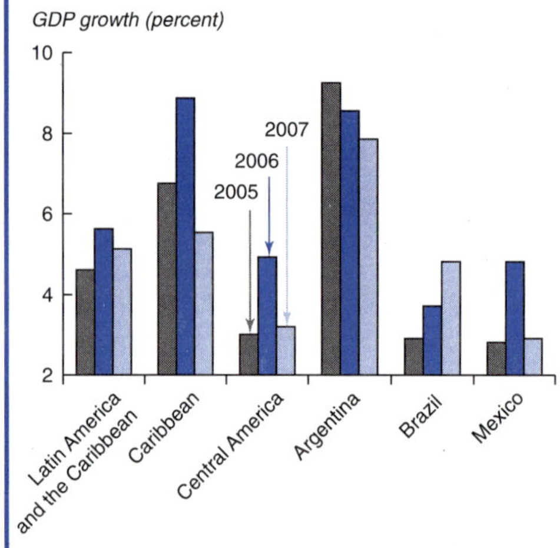

Sources: World Bank and national agencies.

Latin America and the Caribbean

Recent developments

Marking the fourth consecutive year of sustained advances, GDP growth in Latin America and the Caribbean registered 5.1 percent in 2007, following a 5.6 percent gain in 2006. The average yearly rate of output growth since 2004 has been 5.3 percent, twice the 2.7 percent registered during the previous 15 years. Recent growth has been more broadly based, with positive results shared by all subregions: the Caribbean, Central America, and South America. A favorable external environment together with improved domestic macroeconomic conditions helped strengthen fundamentals and enhanced growth and stability (figure A7).

During 2006, the region recorded large current account surpluses, which have diminished to a degree in 2007. Growing foreign exchange revenues made up of export earnings linked to high commodity prices for food, metals, and energy and continued large FDI; portfolio investment; and remittance flows have all contributed to the maintenance of high levels of foreign reserves and helped support equity markets. This positive external situation has underpinned government finances by boosting revenues that, despite a significant increase in public spending, limited the region's primary deficit to 0.3 percent of GDP in 2007, from 0.5 percent the previous year.

Monetary authorities, helped by stronger fiscal positions and supportive exchange rates, have been able to achieve inflation targets in most countries (figure A8). Excluding Argentina and the República Bolivariana de Venezuela, average consumer price inflation was stable in 2007 at 5.7 percent after declining by almost 1.0 percentage point in 2006. Only one country in the region has experienced inflation above 10 percent in each of the last five years.

The recent turmoil in financial markets that originated in the U.S. subprime mortgage market appears to have had limited effects on the region to date. Spreads have increased, though capital flows have continued (figure A9). Indeed, growth in 2007 continued to be strong, and although any sharp slowdown in the United States would eventually affect Latin American and the Caribbean prospects, the region seems better prepared for exogenous shocks than it was during earlier periods of crisis or financial dislocation.

Figure A8 Latin American inflation eases over the last 15 years

Median consumer price inflation in the seven largest Latin American countries (percent change)

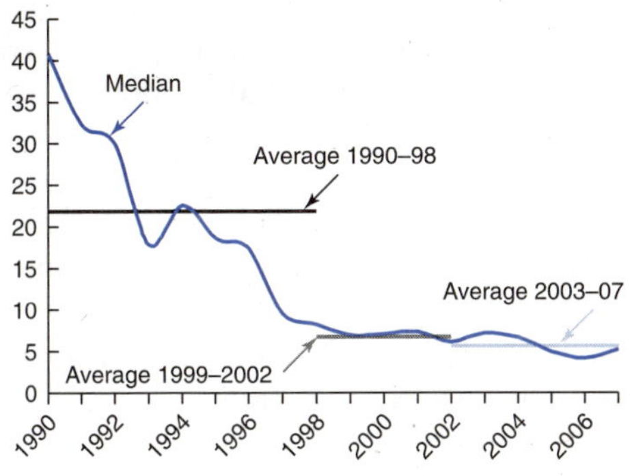

Source: World Bank.

Figure A9 Latin America and the Caribbean sovereign bond spreads decline, then increase again

Basis points

Source: JPMorgan-Chase.

This broadly positive picture for the region is qualified by substantial variations from country to country. Between 2005 and 2007, Brazil, which accounts for about one-third of the region's GDP, stepped up growth by almost 1 percentage point a year. Significant monetary policy easing has been a key factor behind increasing private demand, which together with higher public spending, has boosted GDP growth. The policy interest rate was reduced further in the first half of 2007 in line with expectations of additional easing in inflation. Following the credit crisis in the United States, the exchange rate of the Brazilian *real* had depreciated from R/\$1.86 in mid-July to R/\$2.06 in mid-August. The currency had fully recovered and appreciated further against the U.S. dollar to R/\$1.78 by the end of November, a move of 9.5 percent. Ample international reserves, a continuing current account surplus, and other strong macroeconomic fundamentals suggest increased resilience. In 2007, Chile resumed rapid 5.7 percent growth at the same level as in 2005 despite a dip to 4 percent in 2006 caused by the delayed effects of monetary tightening, countercyclical fiscal policy, mining stoppages, and energy constraints.

In Mexico, despite uncertainties surrounding the presidential election during the first half of 2007, investment demand rose 10.3 percent. High oil prices supported export revenues, which offset increased spending on imports and helped contain the trade deficit to \$13 billion, up from \$6 billion in 2006. Despite the positive performance of investment, private consumption, and manufacturing output in the first half of 2007, concerns regarding a weakening U.S. economy and its repercussions for Mexico have mounted because of the trade and financial links, including migrants' remittance flows, between Mexico and its northern neighbor. Mexico's GDP is anticipated to grow by 2.9 percent for the year.

Growth in Colombia and Peru has been above the regional average thanks to sustained strength in investment, which was up 18 percent in Colombia and 19 percent in Peru during 2006. Investment has been led by the private sector, with foreign companies playing an important role. The improved security situation in Colombia and several massive projects in the mining and energy sectors in Peru have attracted investors, and FDI has risen considerably. These factors will continue to support the pace of economic activity in 2007 at rates of 6.5 for Colombia and 7.5 percent for Peru.

Central American countries have also performed exceptionally well in recent years.

Average growth for the aggregate of Costa Rica, El Salvador, Guatemala, Honduras, Nicaragua, and Panama has amounted to 5.5 percent over 2004–07, the strongest since the early 1990s. Strong remittance inflows and the recent implementation of the Dominican Republic–Central American Free-Trade Agreement (a bilateral free trade agreement between the United States, Central America, and the Dominican Republic) have underpinned increasing consumer and business confidence and domestic spending. By increasing exports of manufactured goods to the United States, this agreement is helping Central America reduce export market losses in the garment sector resulting from the expiration of the Multi-Fiber Agreement and increased competition from China.

Growth in Argentina has been easing gradually from extremely high rates. GDP increased 7.8 percent in 2007, down from 8.5 percent in 2006. The prolonged expansion in Argentina can be explained in part by an undervalued real exchange rate, an expansionary fiscal policy, and an accommodative monetary stance. Contrasted with the experience of Brazil, where the currency appreciated and fiscal deficits contracted, in Argentina, intervention in the foreign exchange market has prevented nominal appreciation, while sterilization operations have contained expansion of the monetary base. Argentina has also put a series of supplementary measures in place to suppress inflation (actual levels of inflation remain unclear given the lack of transparency in official consumer price inflation calculations): the government raised export taxes on food and fuel and imposed direct controls on basic consumer prices, formal wages, and the tariffs on most energy products and public services. Despite massive revenue growth, the government's fiscal policy has been procyclical (increasingly so in the first half of 2007). Were external conditions to deteriorate, Argentina would have little margin to devalue the real exchange rate further or to contract its fiscal surplus in a meaningful way.

In the República Bolivariana de Venezuela, massive oil earnings have continued to finance large and procyclical government spending. These outlays supported growth of 8.3 percent in 2007, down 2 percentage points from the previous year. Apart from a clear acceleration in inflation, substantial export revenues have masked the adverse effects of increased state intervention on the economy. Significant declines in oil prices or oil production could lead to large liquidity problems in the future, especially in light of the increased spending, including spending on nationalized enterprises and numerous social programs.

The outcomes of seven presidential elections held in the region during 2006 did not result in major shifts in macroeconomic policy for the region as a whole. However, policy in Argentina, Bolivia, the República Bolivariana de Venezuela, and more recently Ecuador and Nicaragua is now more oriented toward an increasing role for the state in the economy.

Medium-term outlook

Regional GDP is expected to slow further in the years ahead, coming in at 4.5 percent in 2008 and at 4.3 percent in 2009 (figure A10). This measured slowdown is supported by continued strong growth in Brazil and a rebound from a weak 2007 for Mexico. Growth in other countries—notably Argentina and the República Bolivariana de Venezuela—is likely to slow. Excluding those two countries, regional GDP growth is expected to moderate only marginally from 4.4 percent in 2007 to 4.2 percent in 2008—because of weakness in the United States—before picking up to 4.3 percent in 2009.

Should these outturns be realized, they would represent the longest positive growth spell for Latin America since the 1960s. Despite a gradual worsening of current account balances due to stabilizing commodity prices and slower growth in global demand, this stronger growth is likely to persist, supported by continued expansion in consumption and investment and buoyed by an environment of low inflation (excluding Argentina

Figure A10 Growth in Latin America and the Caribbean eases into 2009

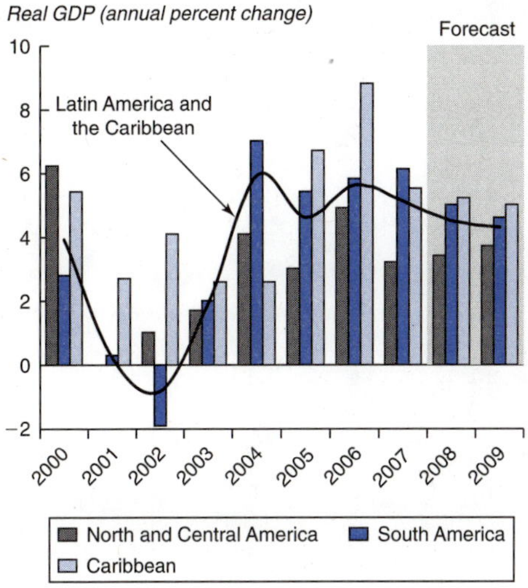

Source: World Bank.

and the República Bolivariana de Venezuela); improved fiscal policy (particularly in Mexico); and continued strong capital inflows (especially to Brazil).

Among various groupings of Latin American economies, a number of themes emerges. Growth among agricultural exporters is expected to slow from 7.1 percent in 2007 to 4.6 by 2009. However, if Argentina—where growth is expected to slow to more sustainable rates—is excluded from the group, the deceleration is less marked, from 5.0 percent in 2007 to 4.5 in 2009. Growth among metals exporters is projected to remain buoyant, easing from 5.1 percent in 2007 to 4.7 percent by 2009, in large part because of expansionary policies in Brazil and Chile. Growth among energy exporters is expected to slow gradually, from 5.2 percent in 2007 to 4.4 percent in 2008, easing further to 4.2 percent in 2009 as oil prices begin to soften. A reduced pace

Table A5 Latin America and the Caribbean forecast summary
(annual percent change unless indicated otherwise)

					Forecast		
	1991–2000[a]	2004	2005	2006	2007	2008	2009
GDP at market prices[b]	3.4	5.9	4.6	5.6	5.1	4.5	4.3
GDP per capita[c]	1.7	4.6	3.3	4.3	3.8	3.2	3.0
Purchasing Power Parity GDP[d]	4.3	5.6	4.5	5.4	5.1	4.6	4.4
Private consumption	3.4	4.9	5.2	6.2	5.7	4.9	4.6
Public consumption	1.5	1.7	3.2	3.3	4.2	3.0	2.8
Fixed investment	4.7	9.7	9.7	12.2	10.2	9.5	8.2
Exports, GNFS[e]	8.1	12.5	8.6	7.8	4.7	5.5	5.8
Imports, GNFS[e]	10.7	15.2	12.2	13.6	9.4	9.5	8.4
Net exports, contribution to growth	−0.3	−0.4	−0.7	−1.4	−1.3	−1.2	−0.9
Current account balance/GDP (%)	−2.8	1.0	1.4	1.6	0.5	0.1	−0.2
GDP deflator (median, LCU)	10.9	7.2	6.6	10.0	8.7	5.1	4.2
Fiscal balance/GDP (%)	—	0.0	−0.7	−0.5	−0.3	−0.9	−1.1
Memo items: GDP							
LAC excluding Argentina	3.2	5.5	3.9	5.1	4.7	4.3	4.3
Central America	3.6	4.1	3.0	4.9	3.2	3.4	3.8
Caribbean	3.6	2.6	6.7	8.8	5.5	5.2	5.0
Brazil	2.7	4.9	2.9	3.7	4.8	4.5	4.5
Mexico	3.5	4.1	2.8	4.8	2.9	3.2	3.6
Argentina	4.5	9.0	9.2	8.5	7.8	5.7	4.7

Source: World Bank.
Note: — = not available.
a. Growth rates over intervals are compound averages; growth contributions, ratios, and the GDP deflator are averages.
b. GDP measured in constant 2000 U.S. dollars.
c. Measured in U.S. dollars.
d. GDP measured at purchasing power parity exchange rates.
e. Exports and imports of goods and nonfactor services.

Table A6 Latin America and the Caribbean country forecasts

(annual percent change unless indicated otherwise)

	1991–2000[a]	2004	2005	2006	Forecast 2007	2008	2009
Argentina							
GDP at market prices[b]	4.5	9.0	9.2	8.5	7.8	5.7	4.7
Current account balance/GDP (%)	−2.9	1.9	2.8	3.4	2.2	2.0	1.3
Antigua and Barbuda							
GDP at market prices[b]	3.3	4.3	5.3	11.5	5.0	4.4	4.2
Current account balance/GDP (%)	−6.0	−11.9	−8.7	−16.0	−16.6	−17.6	−16.3
Belize							
GDP at market prices[b]	5.9	4.6	3.1	5.6	3.5	3.3	3.4
Current account balance/GDP (%)	−7.3	−14.4	−14.6	−1.9	−4.4	−6.5	−5.7
Bolivia							
GDP at market prices[b]	3.8	3.9	4.1	4.6	4.1	4.4	4.2
Current account balance/GDP (%)	−6.1	3.9	5.4	11.8	9.2	8.4	7.9
Brazil							
GDP at market prices[b]	2.7	4.9	2.9	3.7	4.8	4.5	4.5
Current account balance/GDP (%)	−2.1	1.9	1.7	1.4	0.7	−0.1	−0.2
Chile							
GDP at market prices[b]	6.4	6.2	5.7	4.0	5.7	5.1	5.0
Current account balance/GDP (%)	−2.7	2.2	1.1	4.0	4.0	1.6	0.8
Colombia							
GDP at market prices[b]	2.5	4.8	4.7	6.8	6.5	5.3	4.8
Current account balance/GDP (%)	−1.9	−0.9	−1.6	−1.5	−1.6	−1.1	−1.0
Costa Rica							
GDP at market prices[b]	5.2	4.1	5.9	8.2	6.1	5.0	4.9
Current account balance/GDP (%)	−3.6	−4.3	−4.9	−4.9	−4.8	−5.4	−5.0
Dominica							
GDP at market prices[b]	1.8	3.2	3.4	4.1	3.2	3.1	3.0
Current account balance/GDP (%)	−16.6	−19.5	−28.8	−18.4	−19.2	−20.6	−20.7
Dominican Republic							
GDP at market prices[b]	6.0	2.0	9.3	10.7	7.2	5.4	4.8
Current account balance/GDP (%)	−3.2	5.7	−2.0	−2.6	−2.9	−3.8	−4.2
Ecuador							
GDP at market prices[b]	1.8	7.9	4.7	4.1	2.4	2.5	2.7
Current account balance/GDP (%)	−2.3	−1.7	0.8	3.5	1.6	2.9	2.3
El Salvador							
GDP at market prices[b]	4.6	1.8	3.1	4.2	4.2	3.8	4.0
Current account balance/GDP (%)	−2.0	−4.0	−5.4	−4.7	−5.2	−6.1	−5.7
Guatemala							
GDP at market prices[b]	4.1	2.7	3.2	4.6	5.0	4.6	5.0
Current account balance/GDP (%)	−4.6	−4.4	−4.4	−4.3	−4.1	−5.3	−5.0
Guyana							
GDP at market prices[b]	4.9	3.3	−1.9	4.7	4.5	3.7	3.5
Current account balance/GDP (%)	−15.1	−2.5	−12.0	−26.6	−21.2	−22.8	−16.4
Honduras							
GDP at market prices[b]	3.3	5.0	4.1	6.0	6.0	5.5	4.7
Current account balance/GDP (%)	−7.7	−5.7	−1.4	−1.9	−4.9	−5.0	−5.2
Haiti							
GDP at market prices[b]	−1.3	−2.2	2.0	2.3	3.5	3.8	4.0
Current account balance/GDP (%)	−1.8	−1.7	1.4	−0.3	−2.0	−3.8	−3.8
Jamaica							
GDP at market prices[b]	1.9	1.1	1.8	2.5	1.1	3.0	3.1
Current account balance/GDP (%)	−2.7	−5.7	−11.1	−10.7	−11.5	−13.7	−13.6
Mexico							
GDP at market prices[b]	3.5	4.1	2.8	4.8	2.9	3.2	3.6
Current account balance/GDP (%)	−3.7	−1.0	−0.6	−0.2	−1.0	−0.9	−1.0

Table A6 (*continued*)

(annual percent change unless indicated otherwise)

	1991–2000[a]	2004	2005	2006	Forecast 2007	2008	2009
Nicaragua							
GDP at market prices[b]	3.4	5.1	4.4	3.7	4.2	4.7	4.5
Current account balance/GDP (%)	−28.7	−14.6	−13.0	−13.9	−11.4	−12.1	−10.2
Panama							
GDP at market prices[b]	5.1	7.6	6.4	7.5	8.3	7.2	7.1
Current account balance/GDP (%)	−4.8	−7.5	−5.1	−0.2	−5.6	−6.8	−7.5
Peru							
GDP at market prices[b]	4.0	5.2	6.7	7.6	7.5	6.4	6.1
Current account balance/GDP (%)	−5.5	0.0	1.5	2.9	1.8	0.8	0.4
Paraguay							
GDP at market prices[b]	1.8	4.1	2.7	4.0	4.0	3.9	3.8
Current account balance/GDP (%)	−2.2	2.0	0.0	−2.6	−2.6	−3.8	−3.8
St. Lucia							
GDP at market prices[b]	3.1	3.9	5.8	5.4	5.2	5.1	5.0
Current account balance/GDP (%)	−11.4	−16.6	−22.5	−18.9	−16.8	−16.9	−15.0
St. Vincent and the Grenadines							
GDP at market prices[b]	2.1	5.4	2.2	4.5	5.5	6.3	5.9
Current account balance/GDP (%)	−19.8	−29.0	−29.1	−24.2	−19.8	−17.7	−13.9
Uruguay							
GDP at market prices[b]	3.0	11.8	6.8	7.0	5.5	4.2	3.8
Current account balance/GDP (%)	−1.5	0.0	0.0	−2.7	−2.7	−3.3	−2.9
Venezuela, R.B. de							
GDP at market prices[b]	2.1	17.9	10.3	10.3	8.3	5.8	4.2
Current account balance/GDP (%)	2.6	14.1	18.5	14.4	7.4	6.9	4.7

Source: World Bank.

Note: Growth and current account figures presented here are World Bank projections and may differ from targets contained in other World Bank documents. Barbados, Cuba, Grenada, and Suriname are not forecast because of data limitations.

a. Growth rates over intervals are compound averages; growth contributions, ratios, and the GDP deflator are averages.

b. GDP measured in constant 2000 U.S. dollars.

of economic activity in Argentina and the República Bolivariana de Venezuela could speed up the regional slowdown for energy exporters, but a pickup in growth in Mexico would offset that to some extent.

Despite the gradual reduction in oil prices, growth among small energy importers is likely to moderate from 6 percent in 2007 to 5.1 percent by 2009. This outturn reflects the combined effects of weaker import demand in the United States, reduced remittance inflows (linked to a slowdown of construction activity in the United States), and increasing competition from China following the phaseout of textile and apparel quotas under the Multi-Fiber Agreement. At the same time, GDP should find support through continued strong FDI inflows following implementation of the Dominican Republic–Central American Free-Trade Agreement.

Growth in Brazil is expected to moderate from 4.8 percent in 2007 to 4.5 percent in both 2008 and 2009. The positive fundamentals observed in 2006 and 2007—low interest rates, a strong currency, and falling unemployment—should continue to underpin a robust pace of domestic activity. At the same time, a further near-term acceleration in growth is unlikely. The Central Bank has taken a pause in interest rate reductions, while quarter-on-quarter GDP figures show a slight moderation from the first quarter to the second quarter of 2007.

Argentina's growth is expected to decelerate sharply from 7.8 percent in 2007 to 5.7 percent in 2008 and to 4.7 percent in

2009. Despite rising fiscal revenues, persistent and accelerating inflation and increased public intervention in private sector activity appear likely to discourage growth prospects. Recent production and goods trade numbers underscore a weakening in the pace of activity, caused in large part by the imposition of energy rationing. Industrial output gained 2.3 percent in July (year-on-year), the weakest showing in more than five years, while steel production contracted by 26 percent.

Growth in Mexico is likely to rebound from 2.9 percent in 2007 to 3.2 percent in 2008 and to 3.6 percent in 2009. Although remittances will contribute less to domestic activity as growth in the United States slows, increased domestic credit to consumers and businesses should support spending. Recent fiscal reforms also point toward better growth prospects, as improved revenue collection should allow the government to boost needed infrastructure outlays. With a rebound of U.S. activity in the second half of 2008 and 2009, Mexican exports will make a stronger contribution to growth.

Finally, activity in the República Bolivariana de Venezuela is anticipated to slow fairly rapidly, with GDP growth declining from 8.3 percent in 2007 to 5.8 percent in 2008 and 4.2 percent in 2009. Activity in late 2006 and early 2007 was supported by large-scale run-ups in fiscal outlays associated with the presidential elections, but falling oil revenues over the forecast period make continued expansion in government spending unlikely. Private activity is also expected to slow substantially. Higher inflation will likely result in declines in real wages, a sharp falloff in FDI will reduce the contribution of investment to growth, and an uncertain regulatory environment (notably with regard to property and contract rights) is anticipated to hamper private sector startups and job creation.

Risks

A stabilization of growth in Latin America and the Caribbean at high rates in a historical context and broad improvements in the region's fundamentals have been supported by an exceptionally favorable external environment. Should that environment deteriorate substantially, growth is likely to slow. Moreover, despite improved fundamentals, some countries may be vulnerable to a sharp reversal in conditions.

Overall, the region's resilience to shocks has improved, and better economic policies have supported this improvement. In particular, the structure of external debt—in terms of maturity and foreign currency exposure—has improved; the accumulation of reserves has, in most cases, surpassed external borrowing requirements; the region's fiscal and current accounts have been in surplus during the current growth cycle; and independent central banks are imposing countercyclical monetary policies, especially in those countries where inflation targeting is the adopted policy regime. Notwithstanding these advances, some risks linked to a worsening of the external environment may remain a concern for the region.

In a potentially difficult phase of rising risk aversion in global financial markets, the region has, up to now, demonstrated that it has developed a stronger "immune system." As shown in figure A11, the responsiveness of the spreads on sovereign bonds (noninvestment grade) for Latin American and the Caribbean countries with respect to changes in risk aversion, though still elevated, is much lower when contrasting the July 2006 to end-2007 period with the August 1997 to August 1999 period (the period of the financial crises in East Asia and Russia). Contagion effects to Latin America and the Caribbean through the financial channel seem less likely than during past challenging phases. However, there are still some country-specific issues: Argentina (because of the INDEC incident—the national statistics agency producing questionable infection data) and Ecuador (because of the outright discussion of default) have undermined the perception of their willingness to pay, regardless of their reserves cushion, and therefore were hit harder and earlier than the other countries. The República Bolivariana de Venezuela was also affected because of political concerns.

Figure A11 Financial test: Credit

Lower elasticity of LAC EMBI with respect to risk aversion (HY bonds)...

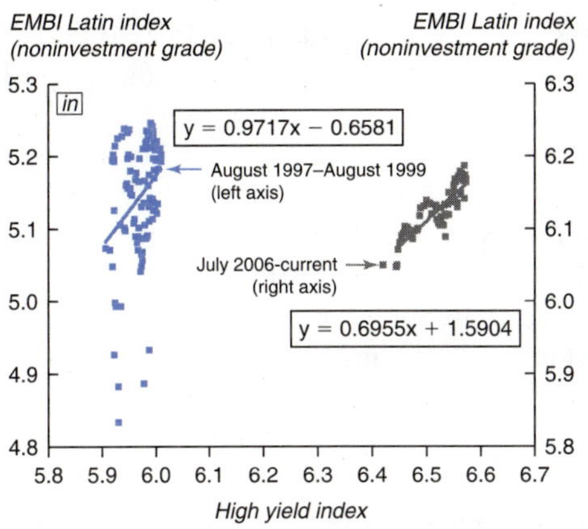

Source: Bloomberg weekly data; Credit Suisse high-yield index; JP Morgan EMBI.

Note: EMBI = Emerging markets bond index.

Figure A12 Exchange rate policy dilemmas?

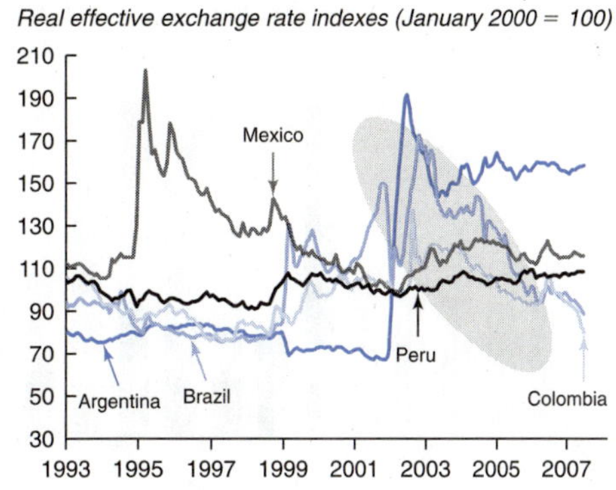

Source: International Monetary Fund.

Figure A13 Export product (value) concentration is increasing

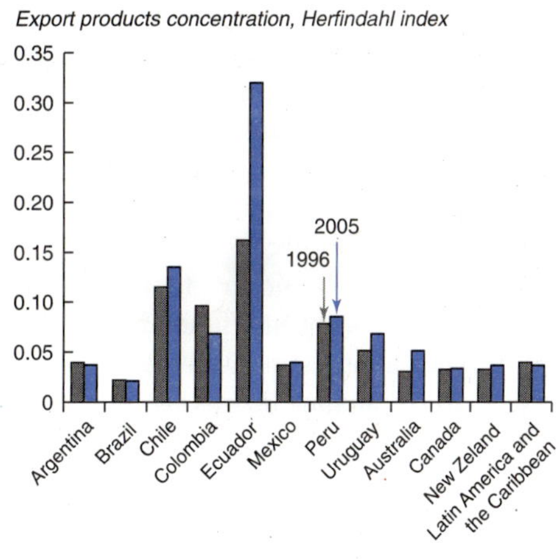

Sources: World Integrated Trade System.

The region could still suffer adverse consequences from a worsening and spreading of the U.S. subprime crisis through real channels. Lower remittances may hurt some of the poorest among Latin America and the Caribbean's recipient countries, while lower external demand may be exacerbated by weaker competitiveness resulting from appreciating currencies, as shown in figure A12.

Finally, terms-of-trade deterioration may also exert negative pressure on aggregate output. Figures A13 and A14 summarize the region's vulnerability to commodity price shocks. In recent years, export concentration for the region, as captured by the Herfindahl index of exported goods, did not decline. Indeed, it increased in many countries, possibly because of an increase in specific commodity prices (as the index is measured in nominal terms). Increases in this index signal a potential worsening of the risk associated with volatility of global commodity prices. Counterbalancing this tendency is the geographic diversification of Latin American and the Caribbean's export markets. The concentration of Latin exports to the U.S. market is quite strong, especially for countries such as Mexico, but the overall trend is toward diversification.

The emergence of China and India played a role in explaining the trade patterns displayed in figures A13 and A14, and on a positive note, may have permanently and favorably changed the terms of trade faced by the region. In this rosier situation, the region may be drawn into intensive activities in areas

Figure A14 Export market (value) concentration is falling

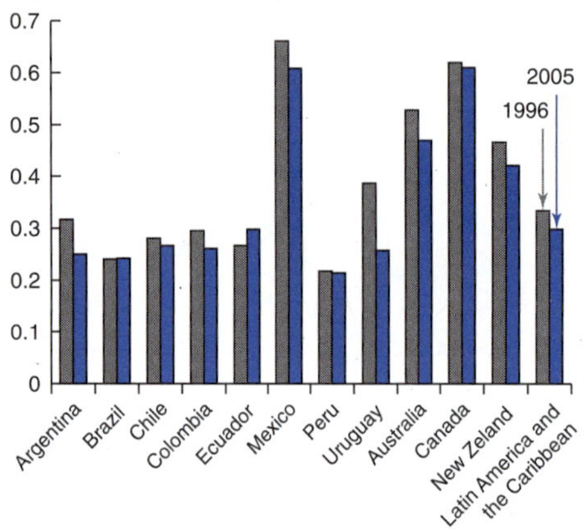

Sources: World Integrated Trade System.

of comparative advantage, such as natural resources and skills and technology, but additional progress on some structural factors is needed to take full advantage of these opportunities. In particular, the region has to improve its investment climate and the skill composition of its labor force.

Compared with other regions, Latin American and Caribbean fundamentals may appear to be unimpressive, and the region does not seem to be catching up in a significant way. Even for the most recent period, aggregate GDP growth, gross fixed capital formation (as a share of GDP), and TFP growth remain well below averages for other developing regions. The Latin America and the Caribbean region does not appear, at least not yet, to have been capitalizing on the favorable external environment to raise its growth path.

Middle East and North Africa

Recent developments

GDP for the developing countries of the Middle East and North Africa region grew nearly 5 percent in 2007, matching the decade-high pace achieved the preceding year (table A7 and figure A15).[1] Continued growth in hydrocarbon receipts among the region's developing (and high-income) oil exporters was a key factor supporting growth, as world oil prices breached records at close to $100 a barrel toward the end of the year. Notwithstanding the severe drought that afflicted countries in the Maghreb, notably Morocco, a revival in European demand helped underpin exports for the resource-poor, labor-abundant countries in the region, especially the Arab Republic of Egypt, where a depreciation of the pound against the euro also assisted, and Jordan.[2] Moreover, record inflows of FDI, ample liquidity, and strong domestic demand all bolstered growth across the diverse countries of the region.

Oil exporters registered growth of 4.5 percent for the year, up from 4.0 percent in 2006, as GDP in Algeria and the Islamic Republic of Iran moved higher. The group of diversified exporters witnessed an easing of growth from 6.2 percent in 2006 to 5.4 percent, largely as output gains in Morocco plummeted from 8 percent to 2 percent. However, GDP in all other countries picked up or repeated its strong performance of 2006.

Oil-related revenues for the year increased 9 percent for developing exporters in the

Figure A15 Growth in Middle East and North Africa picks up

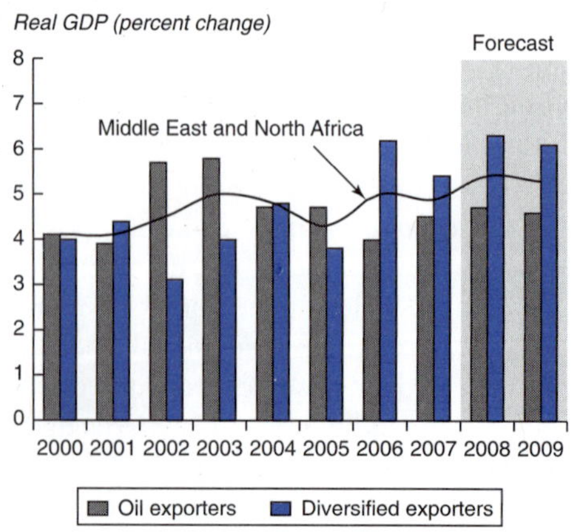

Source: World Bank.

Table A7 Middle East and North Africa forecast summary

(annual percent change unless indicated otherwise)

	1991–2000[a]	2004	2005	2006	Forecast 2007	2008	2009
GDP at market prices[b]	3.8	4.8	4.3	5.0	4.9	5.4	5.3
GDP per capita[c]	1.6	3.0	2.5	3.1	3.1	3.6	3.5
Purchasing power parity GDP[d]	4.7	4.8	4.3	5.0	4.9	5.4	5.1
Private consumption	3.8	6.3	5.0	5.2	4.9	4.9	5.2
Public consumption	4.3	2.7	5.9	5.6	7.0	7.4	4.7
Fixed investment	3.3	8.1	8.2	11.6	13.9	11.7	11.1
Exports, GNFS[e]	4.4	8.6	9.1	9.5	4.3	3.8	5.2
Imports, GNFS[e]	1.6	15.2	12.5	13.5	10.2	7.2	8.0
Net exports, contribution to growth	0.7	−1.9	−1.2	−1.6	−2.3	−1.5	−1.5
Current account balance/GDP (%)	−0.5	7.4	9.6	9.6	8.2	9.5	6.2
GDP deflator (median, LCU)	7.4	9.1	11.7	8.7	4.4	6.1	4.3
Fiscal balance/GDP (%)	−2.8	−2.7	3.4	2.2	−0.9	−1.8	−1.8
Memo items: GDP							
MENA Geographic region[f]	3.4	5.0	5.2	4.8	4.6	5.1	4.9
Resource poor-labor abundant[g]	4.2	4.8	3.8	6.2	5.4	6.3	6.1
Resource rich-labor abundant[h]	3.3	4.9	4.6	3.8	4.4	4.6	4.4
Resource rich-labor importing[i]	3.0	5.2	6.8	4.7	4.2	4.6	4.5
Egypt, Arab Rep. of	4.6	4.1	4.5	6.8	7.1	7.0	6.8
Iran, Islamic Rep. of	3.7	5.1	4.3	4.6	5.0	5.0	4.7
Algeria	1.7	5.2	5.1	1.8	3.4	4.0	3.8

Source: World Bank.
a. Growth rates over intervals are compound averages; growth contributions, ratios, and the GDP deflator are averages.
b. GDP measured in constant 2000 U.S. dollars.
c. Measured in U.S. dollars.
d. GDP measured at purchasing power parity exchange rates.
e. Exports and imports of goods and nonfactor services.
f. Geographic region includes high-income countries: Bahrain, Kuwait and Saudi Arabia.
g Egypt, Jordan, Lebanon, Morocco and Tunisia.
h. Algeria, Iran, Syria and Yemen.
i. Bahrain, Kuwait, Oman and Saudi Arabia.

region, rising to $160 billion. Among high-income oil exporters, oil-related revenues rose 13 percent to $382 billion, sufficient to fund ongoing infrastructure and social programs while also adding to massive reserve levels.[3] Among developing country oil exporters, which are dominated in size by Algeria and the Islamic Republic of Iran, but also include Oman, Syria, and the Republic of Yemen, the upturn in oil prices had varying effects (figure A16). For example, in Algeria, hydrocarbon receipts increased moderately to $54 billion, widening Algeria's current account surplus slightly to $29 billion, or 23 percent of GDP. In the Islamic Republic of Iran, hydrocarbon revenues grew 12 percent to $65 billion, but rapid growth in consumer and government spending (as well as imports), together with volume constraints on oil production and shipment, caused the current account surplus to narrow from $34.5 billion in 2006 to $31 billion in 2007, or from 13.3 to 11.1 percent of GDP.

The dollar's swift decline—tied in part to reductions in U.S. interest rates to shore up the country's interbank market—has had differing effects in the region. Oil exporters find their dollar-based receipts falling sharply in relation to the euro, the currency in which a major proportion of imports are denominated, and are consequently suffering a form of terms-of-trade loss. In contrast, diversified exporters may find their competitiveness enhanced in the EU market, with local currencies depreciating moderately against the euro.

Figure A16 Hydrocarbon exports continue to rise on higher prices, modest volume gains

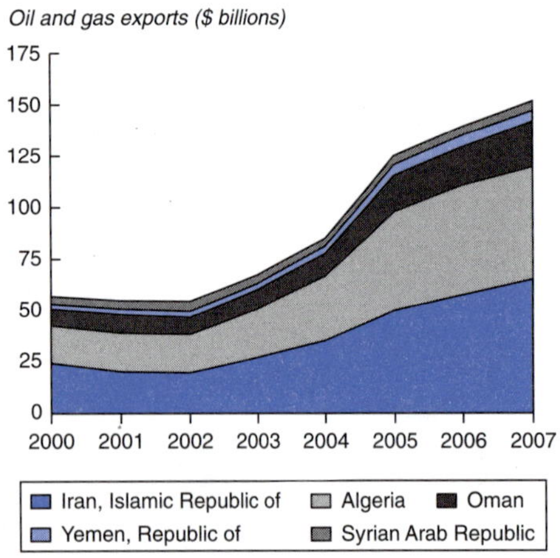

Source: United Nations Comtrade Database; World Bank.

A fall in hydrocarbon output has constrained growth in Algeria, with GDP advancing just 1.8 percent in 2006 and 3.4 percent in 2007. Oil and gas output growth declined 2.6 percent in 2006, but activity unrelated to hydrocarbons expanded by a robust 6 percent in 2007. A major government investment initiative got under way and is slated to expend more than $22 billion over the coming years on housing, transport, and agriculture. This is boosting job growth in construction and related sectors and underpinning strong household spending.

In the Islamic Republic of Iran, despite major fiscal expansion in 2007—seen in the widening of the budget deficit from 0.2 percent of GDP in 2006 to 2.4 percent—growth is likely to step up just 0.4 percentage points, to 5 percent given the extent of leakage into imports that occurred over the year. Exports advanced a modest 1.3 percent against a 13.5 percent gain in imports.

For the diversified exporters, or resource-poor, labor-abundant economies, 2007 marked a watershed for several countries in the area of finance. The Fitch Agency raised Egypt's Issuer Default Rating to a positive outlook, with growth supported by double-digit gains in investment. Morocco was awarded investment grade status for its sovereign bonds and quickly raised $675 million at a low 55 basis-point spread. GDP growth for the group—excluding Morocco, where the effects of drought bias figures for 2007—increased from 5.8 percent in 2006 to 6.2 percent in 2007 on the strength of 7.1 percent growth in Egypt, 6.0 percent in Jordan and Tunisia, and recovery for Lebanon from the downturn of 2006.

Growth in Egypt is broadly based, with non-oil manufacturing and retail trade accounting for half of overall output gains. The fastest-growing sectors include construction, Suez Canal traffic, communications, and tourism. Exports have boomed by 23 percent over 2007 to date, especially non-oil goods, but at 29 percent growth, import demand is even stronger and has kept the contribution of trade to growth negative while widening the country's deficit on trade. But for Egypt and many of the diversified exporters, services receipts and burgeoning remittances outweigh shortfalls on trade, allowing countries to maintain current account surplus positions (figure A17).

In Egypt, Morocco, and Tunisia, reforms are improving the business climate and increasing the competitiveness of the export sector. Egypt, Jordan, Morocco, and Tunisia signed a free trade agreement (the Agadir Agreement) to help promote intraregional trade while addressing rules-of-origin questions that often are part of broader frameworks, such as the European Union–Mediterranean agreements. FDI is becoming an important driver for private investment and growth in this group of countries, and as reforms proceed, the potential for attracting additional FDI grows in step.

Indeed, large-scale FDI has been flowing into the region for the last three years on the back of emerging and increasingly sustained economic growth, diversification, and ongoing reforms. Flows to the geographic region

Figure A17 Tourism and remittances offset widening trade deficits for Maghreb and Mashreq countries

Balance of nonfactor services and net transfers ($ billions)

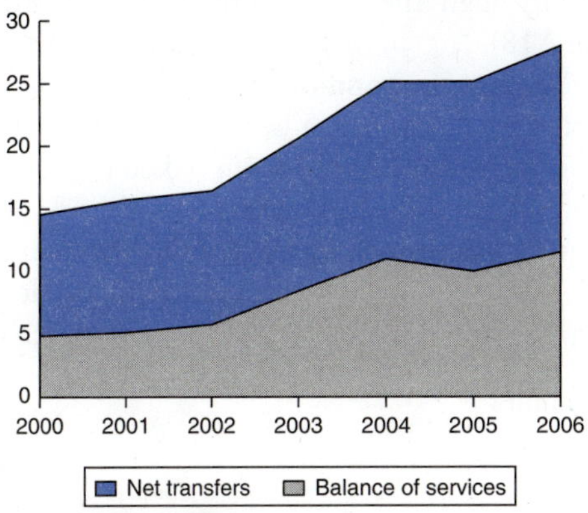

Source: International Monetary Fund balance of payments statistics.

(including the high-income oil exporters) increased 38 percent, to $64 billion in 2006, after doubling to $46 billion in 2005. Among the diversified exporters, the share of FDI in GDP doubled from 3.0 percent, on average, over 2000–04 to 5.6 percent in 2006. FDI flows are tending to focus on the services sector, including finance, telecommunications, and real estate, as well as hydrocarbons and related industries. Direct investment flows to Egypt, in particular, are booming, reaching $11 billion during the country's fiscal 2007, up from $6 billion the previous year. High-income countries in the region have emerged as major investors in the Middle East and North Africa. The United Arab Emirates, for example, invested $8 billion in Egypt in transport and tourism infrastructure during 2006. Evidence suggests that FDI continues to flow into the region's developing and high-income countries, setting a strong foundation for future growth and eventual alleviation of the region's unemployment problem.

Median inflation in the region currently stands at 5.0 percent, up from 3.2 percent in 2006. Inflation has become an important issue for several countries, including the Islamic Republic of Iran (18 percent year-on-year at latest readings) and Egypt (10.9 percent), where consumer price inflation has trended higher because of domestic supply shocks, for example, the partial elimination of subsidies in September 2006. More recent acceleration in Algeria and other oil exporters has accompanied rapid growth in domestic demand. Moreover, the ratcheting up of food and energy costs—the former notably in grains, with a 40 percent jump over 2007 related, in, part to increased global production dedicated to biofuels—presents difficulties for a number of economies, causing price pressures through imports as well as strains on fiscal positions from widespread subsidies covering fuels and cereals.

Medium-term outlook

Prospects for developing countries in the region appear relatively bright, with aggregate GDP gains projected to top 5 percent in 2008 and 2009. Despite uncertainties looming in the external environment for 2008 related to the financial and real implications of the U.S. subprime mortgage crisis, growth among developing oil exporters is anticipated to pick up, in large part tied to domestic developments, although oil prices will likely remain at high levels ($84 per barrel), thereby helping to sustain revenues supporting large, project-related expenditures. GDP gains for the oil exporters are projected to reach 4.7 percent in 2008 before receding to 4.6 percent in 2009 as global oil prices begin to recede.

For the diversified exporters, growth should pick up sharply in 2008, to 6.3 percent from 5.4 percent in 2007. A rebound in Morocco to 5.5 percent growth from the depths of drought is a factor in this outlook. Investment-led growth appears to be increasingly well established in Egypt, where activity is expected to remain within a higher 7 percent range over the forecast period. Sustained growth of around 6 percent in Jordan and Tunisia is likely, grounded in services exports and increasingly in investment and construction funded by FDI. In Lebanon, stronger growth on a sustained basis is unlikely until the political environment has improved (table A8).

Risks

The region appears to have suffered little in the way of direct effects from the financial turbulence of mid-2007. Yet the increasing sophistication of reserves management among high-income oil exporters and the movement toward establishing large-scale sovereign wealth funds may increase the exposure of such portfolios to innovative, yet complex and hard to price, securities. Regional equity markets slumped only briefly during the bout of global volatility, and indeed, stock exchanges in the Gulf states have outperformed the Morgan-Stanley emerging market average through the final months of 2007 (figure A18).

Markets for non-oil commodities, manufactures, and tourism services may suffer a more pronounced slowdown linked to the ripple effects of financial difficulties already present in the United States and the Euro Area. Should a significant credit crunch occur, slowing growth across the OECD as well as across

Table A8 Middle East and North Africa country forecasts

(annual percent change unless indicated otherwise)

				Estimate	Forecast		
	1991–2000[a]	2004	2005	2006	2007	2008	2009
Algeria							
GDP at market prices[b]	1.7	5.2	5.1	1.8	3.4	4.0	3.8
Current account balance/GDP (%)	3.2	13.1	20.7	24.2	23.0	24.4	21.2
Egypt, Arab Rep. of							
GDP at market prices[b]	4.6	4.1	4.5	6.8	7.1	7.0	6.8
Current account balance/GDP (%)	0.0	4.3	3.3	1.6	2.1	2.4	1.9
Iran, Islamic Rep. of							
GDP at market prices[b]	3.7	5.1	4.3	4.6	5.0	5.0	4.7
Current account balance/GDP (%)	1.2	15.9	16.2	13.3	11.1	12.7	6.8
Jordan							
GDP at market prices[b]	5.1	8.4	7.3	6.3	6.0	5.8	6.0
Current account balance/GDP (%)	−4.3	−0.2	−18.7	−15.0	−13.5	−14.6	−12.6
Lebanon							
GDP at market prices[b]	7.2	6.3	1.0	0.0	1.0	3.5	4.5
Current account balance/GDP (%)	—	−22.5	−23.2	−16.7	−19.6	−19.0	−15.9
Morocco							
GDP at market prices[b]	2.2	5.2	2.4	8.0	2.0	5.5	4.5
Current account balance/GDP (%)	−1.4	1.7	1.9	2.8	2.3	0.6	0.5
Oman							
GDP at market prices[b]	4.6	3.1	5.8	6.0	6.0	6.3	5.8
Current account balance/GDP (%)	−3.7	2.3	13.7	12.4	12.2	17.2	11.3
Syrian Arab Republic							
GDP at market prices[b]	5.1	3.9	4.5	5.1	3.9	3.7	4.8
Current account balance/GDP (%)	1.0	2.4	1.1	2.8	2.5	3.2	0.8
Tunisia							
GDP at market prices[b]	4.7	6.0	4.0	5.4	6.0	6.2	6.0
Current account balance/GDP (%)	−4.3	−2.0	−1.1	−2.1	−2.5	−2.6	−2.1
Yemen, Rep. of							
GDP at market prices[b]	5.5	2.5	4.6	4.0	3.8	4.3	4.0
Current account balance/GDP (%)	−4.3	1.7	2.3	0.4	−2.2	−2.3	−5.1

Source: World Bank.

Notes: Growth and current account figures presented here are World Bank projections and may differ from targets contained in other World Bank documents. Djibouti, Gaza, Iraq, Libya, and West Bank are not forecast because of data limitations.

— = not available.

a. Growth rates over intervals are compound averages; growth contributions, ratios, and the GDP deflator are averages.

b. GDP measured in constant 2000 U.S. dollars.

Figure A18 Middle East and North Africa equities rebound from the mid-2007 slump

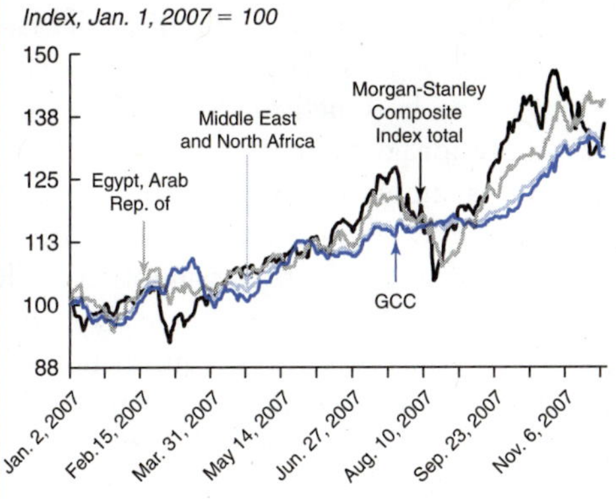

Source: Morgan-Stanley.

developing countries, demand for crude oil and refined petroleum products could decline and lead to a sharp fall in prices with the attendant effects ensuing for revenues and growth.

Notes

1. For the purposes of this report, coverage of the region is restricted (for the sake of consistency across all regions) to include only low- and-middle-income countries. These countries include Algeria, the Arab Republic of Egypt, the Islamic Republic of Iran, Jordan, Lebanon, Morocco, Oman, the Syrian Arab Republic, Tunisia, and the Republic of Yemen. Because of data limitations, the middle-income economies of Djibouti, Iraq, Libya, and the West Bank and Gaza are not included in the aggregates. High-income countries in the region are Bahrain, Kuwait, Qatar, Saudi Arabia and the United Arab Emirates, to which references are made. Qatar and the United Arab Emirates are not included in the high-income aggregate because of data limitations.

2. For the developing countries in the region, the resource-poor, labor-abundant countries are Egypt, Jordan, Lebanon, Morocco, and Tunisia. The resource-rich, labor-abundant countries are Algeria, the Islamic Republic of Iran, Syria, and the Republic of Yemen. Oman is the developing, resource-rich, labor-importing country. However, memo items in table A7 cover the full geographic region, including Bahrain, Kuwait, and Saudi Arabia. For reference, the GDP of the developing countries of the Middle East and North Africa region accounts for just 62 percent of the geographic region.

3. Changes in the volume of oil and gas production have been modest in recent years, ranging from 0.5 to 1.0 percent annual gains in Algeria to a decline in the Islamic Republic of Iran and the Republic of Yemen. Hence the buildup in export revenues is largely due to the large-scale increase in global oil prices over 2005 through 2007.

South Asia

Recent developments

South Asia's regional GDP was vibrant at 8.4 percent growth in 2007, easing only moderately from the 8.8 percent outturn of 2006. The region continues to build on the momentum of recent fiscal and business-oriented reforms. Private consumption and investment accelerated in 2007 despite more restrictive monetary policies. Large capital inflows, rising incomes, and strong worker remittances have supported private spending. Improvement in business sentiment—both foreign (toward India) and domestic—and rising corporate profits have provided a strong foundation for investment. Growth in government spending has come down from 12.5 percent in 2006 and is now in line with overall economic activity. The decline in government spending is primarily attributable to a sharp falloff in Pakistan's outlays following a spike in 2006 linked to recovery and reconstruction efforts after the December 2005 earthquake.

Among the larger economies, a modest easing of GDP growth in India, from 9.4 percent in 2006 to 9.0 percent in 2007 reflects a firming in Indian import demand that yielded a negative net export position, further underpinned by strong appreciation of the rupee (figure A19). The falloff in growth in Pakistan from 6.9 percent in 2006 to 6.4 percent in 2007 stems from a decline in private sector credit growth, a slowdown in FDI inflows beginning in July 2007, and weaker exports. In Bangladesh, tighter domestic credit conditions induced a softening in investment growth, while net exports turned negative, explaining

Figure A19 South Asian economies ease into 2007

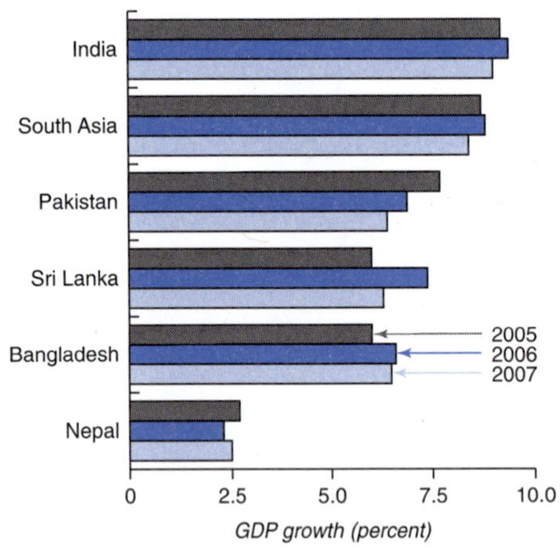

Sources: World Bank and national agencies.

the slight moderation in growth from 6.6 in 2006 to 6.5 percent in 2007. In Sri Lanka, an escalation of the conflict between government-led forces and separatists dampened prospects in the tourism industry and contributed to a 1.1 percentage point falloff in growth to 6.3 percent in 2007. In contrast, growth in Nepal is on course to pick up modestly from 2.3 percent in 2006 to 2.5 percent in 2007 as the peace process moves forward, bringing increases in foreign assistance and a gradual recovery in the tourism sector.

At the regional level, robust investment demand drove rapid import growth—which averaged 11 percent a year and exceeded export growth by 2.5 percentage points—while currency appreciation also increased demand for imports. Exports remained healthy at 8.5 percent, but were slowed by softening demand in high-income countries and real appreciations that have made export markets more competitive.

The regional current account deficit increased as a share of GDP, moving from 1.3 percent in 2006 to 2.4 percent. Current account positions worsened in a number of countries over the course of 2007, with deficits reaching close to 5 percent of GDP in Pakistan and about 2 percent in India. Pakistan's current account is of some concern, having deteriorated by the equivalent of more than 5 percentage points of GDP in the last four years. Strong flows of worker remittances into the region have helped contain the extent of deterioration in current account positions. Remittances amount to substantial proportions of GDP in many South Asian countries, helping to smooth private consumption while offering a buffer for external trade shortfalls. Remittance receipts are the equivalent of a large 16 percent of GDP in Nepal, 9 percent in Sri Lanka, 7 percent in Bangladesh, and 4 percent in Pakistan. Strong foreign capital flows to India and Pakistan, in particular, have complemented remittances to provide generally comfortable levels of external finance.

Inflation pressures in India and Pakistan eased over the first three quarters of 2007 (figure A20). In India, the appreciating rupee contributed to an easing of wholesale price inflation to 3 percent as of early November (year-on-year), breaching a five-year low. However, risks of a regional revival in inflation remain, stoked by an incomplete

Figure A20 Monetary policy is tightened in response to a buildup in inflation

Consumer price inflation (percent change year-on-year) and policy interest rates (percent)

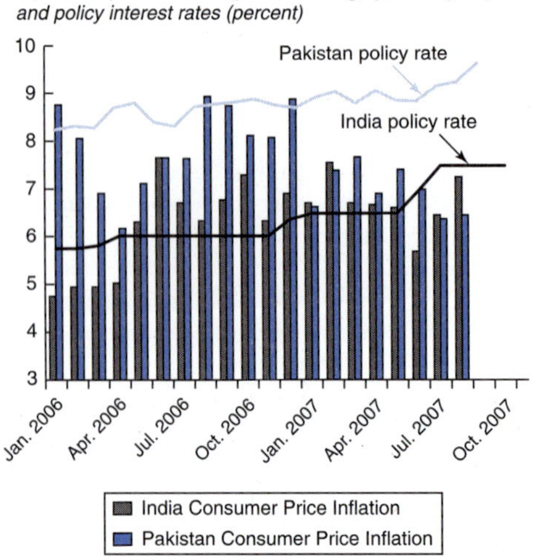

Source: World Bank.

pass-through of higher energy costs to the final consumer in several countries, increasing and widespread upward pressure on food prices, strong credit growth, and sharp gains in equity markets that have fueled liquidity. In Sri Lanka, inflation reignited in 2007, with 12-month moving average inflation increasing to 18 percent in September, up from 6.8 a year earlier. Inflation has also picked up in Maldives, from 3.7 percent in 2006 to 7.0 percent in 2007, reflecting expansionary government spending and a budget deficit anticipated to reach 24 percent of GDP in 2007, caused in part by continuing post-tsunami reconstruction and large tourism construction projects. Inflation also appears to be stepping up in Bangladesh in the wake of the recent cyclone.

In India, monetary tightening and large capital inflows led to significant currency appreciation during 2007, with the rupee reaching a near decadal high of Rs 39.2 against the dollar by the end of November. This development has contributed to an easing of inflationary pressures through prices of imports, while at the same time it has reduced the price competitiveness of India's exporters. The strong currency gains prompted the Reserve Bank of India to sell rupees to help contain the rate of appreciation and to introduce selected capital control measures. Pakistan's currency had been appreciating slightly against the dollar over much of the year, but it began to depreciate in response to heightened uncertainty on international capital markets and the president's imposition of a state of emergency in early November.

The increased volatility of international credit markets during mid-2007 tied to the housing market downturn in the United States initially led to a falloff in equity prices in India and Pakistan, but markets in both countries have since recouped their losses. In October, India's Sensex index rose above 19,000 for the first time, driven by overseas fund purchases. According to the Securities and Exchange Board of India, foreign investors bought an average of nearly $500 million more than they sold in Indian equities during the first half of October, compared with daily net purchases of $232 million in September. In relation to local currencies, equity markets were up 36 percent in India (50 percent in dollar terms) and 20 percent in Pakistan (19 percent in dollar terms) from January 1 to October 31, 2007.

Medium-term outlook

Tighter credit conditions, volatility in international financial markets, a risk of recession in the United States, and slowing growth in the European Union should yield a fairly pronounced slowing of external demand for South Asia's exports during 2008. This is likely to worsen the region's overall current account deficit, as will increases in global oil prices into 2008. Nonetheless, contributions to growth from domestic demand—both private consumption and investment—are expected to remain relatively high, despite facing headwinds from tighter monetary conditions and further consolidation in fiscal positions.

These factors are expected to lead to an easing of regional GDP growth from 8.4 percent in 2007 to 7.9 percent in 2008, with most countries experiencing a modest deceleration (tables A9 and A10). In Bangladesh, however, heightened political tensions and severe flooding were curbing demand in the second half of 2007 and will contribute to a full percentage point reduction in growth to 5.5 percent for 2008. Regional growth is expected to pick up to 8.1 percent by 2009, as recovering growth in the OECD firms up external demand and as receding oil prices ease pressures on the import bill. Domestic absorption is projected to regain momentum in 2009, assuming that price conditions permit an easing of monetary policy during the second half of 2008.

Tighter credit conditions in international markets and a decreased appetite for risk among investors could result in a falloff in regional capital inflows, which have contributed to recent strong growth outturns, particularly in India and Pakistan. Although trade openness has generally increased (except in Afghanistan, Nepal, and Sri Lanka, which are

Table A9 South Asia forecast summary

(annual percent change unless indicated otherwise)

					Forecast		
	1991–2000[a]	2004	2005	2006	2007	2008	2009
GDP at market prices[b]	5.2	7.8	8.7	8.8	8.4	7.9	8.1
GDP per capita[c]	3.2	6.1	7.0	7.2	6.9	6.4	6.6
Purchasing power parity GDP[d]	6.4	7.9	8.7	8.9	8.5	8.0	8.2
Private consumption	4.0	5.7	7.1	5.6	6.4	6.3	6.6
Public consumption	3.9	5.3	8.8	12.5	8.4	8.3	8.7
Fixed investment	5.5	10.2	14.2	14.2	15.2	13.6	12.6
Exports, GNFS[e]	9.0	14.5	7.0	9.0	8.5	8.4	10.5
Imports, GNFS[e]	7.9	32.9	12.5	11.9	11.0	11.1	12.1
Net exports, contribution to growth	−0.1	−3.1	−1.3	−0.9	−0.9	−1.0	−0.9
Current account balance/GDP (%)	−1.5	−0.1	−1.2	−1.3	−2.4	−3.0	−2.7
GDP deflator (median, LCU)	8.0	4.9	5.7	7.5	7.0	7.0	6.4
Fiscal balance/GDP (%)	−7.8	−6.4	−6.4	−6.3	−6.1	−5.5	−5.1
Memo items: GDP							
South Asia, excluding India	4.4	6.1	6.7	6.7	6.3	6.0	6.5
India	5.5	8.3	9.2	9.4	9.0	8.4	8.5
Pakistan	3.9	6.4	7.7	6.9	6.4	6.5	6.7
Bangladesh	4.8	6.3	6.0	6.6	6.5	5.5	6.5

Source: World Bank.
a. Growth rates over intervals are compound averages; growth contributions, ratios, and the GDP deflator are averages.
b. GDP measured in constant 2000 U.S. dollars.
c. Measured in U.S. dollars.
d. GDP measured at purchasing power parity exchange rates.
e. Exports and imports of goods and nonfactor services.

Table A10 South Asia country forecasts

(annual percent change unless indicated otherwise)

					Forecast		
	1991–2000[a]	2004	2005	2006	2007	2008	2009
Bangladesh							
GDP at market prices[b]	4.8	6.3	6.0	6.6	6.5	5.5	6.5
Current account balance/GDP (%)	−0.4	−0.5	−0.3	1.8	1.3	0.9	0.2
India							
GDP at market prices[b]	5.5	8.3	9.2	9.4	9.0	8.4	8.5
Current account balance/GDP (%)	−1.1	0.1	−1.0	−1.1	−2.2	−2.8	−2.5
Nepal							
GDP at market prices[b]	5.0	3.7	2.7	2.3	2.5	4.0	4.5
Current account balance/GDP (%)	−6.4	−0.7	0.0	−0.1	−1.7	−2.4	−2.9
Pakistan							
GDP at market prices[b]	3.9	6.4	7.7	6.9	6.4	6.5	6.7
Current account balance/GDP (%)	−3.7	−0.8	−3.3	−4.3	−4.9	−5.8	−5.3
Sri Lanka							
GDP at market prices[b]	5.2	5.4	6.0	7.4	6.3	6.2	6.5
Current account balance/GDP (%)	−4.6	−3.4	−3.1	−4.9	−4.8	−5.1	−4.5

Source: World Bank.
Note: Growth and current account figures presented here are World Bank projections and may differ from targets contained in other World Bank documents. Afghanistan, Bhutan, and Maldives are not forecast because of data limitations.
a. Growth rates over intervals are compound averages; growth contributions, ratios, and the GDP deflator are averages.
b. GDP measured in constant 2000 U.S. dollars.

all suffering from civil strife), openness remains relatively low in most countries. As a consequence, the region is likely to be buffered to a degree from a falloff in external demand tied to the downturn in the credit cycle.

Risks

Relatively large current account deficits in Maldives, Pakistan, and Sri Lanka remain of concern, particularly in an environment of increased volatility in international financial markets. In Maldives and Sri Lanka, fiscal deficits exceed 7.3 percent of GDP, and foreign reserve positions were fairly tight as of mid-2007, equivalent to 2.5 months of import cover. Although import cover in Pakistan is still a relatively comfortable four months, it is on a declining trend, suggesting that further adjustments are required. Accordingly, a sudden and marked slowdown in capital inflows or a discrete adjustment in global financial markets could have noticeable adverse economic effects on these countries.

European and U.S. restrictions on some categories of Chinese textile and clothing exports will be lifted at the end of 2008, and increased competition in 2009 could hurt regional exporters. Potential effects may be discerned by examining developments in Canada, which has not imposed safeguard restrictions on China: Bangladesh's share of Canada's textile and clothing market declined from 7.4 percent in 2005–06 to 6.9 percent over 2007 to date. Among regional exporters, Sri Lanka appears to be most at risk: nearly one-third of its total merchandise exports to the EU and nearly one-fifth of its shipments to the United States are in categories in which Chinese trade will be liberalized (see box 1.1 in chapter 1).

High, and in some cases increasing, commodity prices also present a risk for the region's economies. Sharp gains in international food prices are a growing threat in a region where food imports represent 11–20 percent of total merchandise imports: Bangladesh (19 percent), Maldives (16 percent), Nepal (17 percent), Pakistan (11 percent), and Sri Lanka (12 percent). India's food imports account for just 3 percent of its total merchandise imports. Aside from putting increased pressure on external positions, higher international food prices carry potentially serious implications for the poorest members of these societies and could strain government coffers and generate increased inflationary pressures given widespread food subsidies. Similarly, further increases in energy prices remain a risk for the region, which is highly dependent on oil imports. In India and Pakistan, for example, fuel imports represent more than 30 percent and 20 percent of merchandise imports, respectively.

Internal political and military tensions continue to represent downside risks to the projections, as demonstrated, for example, by increased fighting in the civil war in Sri Lanka from mid-2006 through 2007. Correspondingly, improving relations represent potential upside opportunities, such as the ongoing progress in reestablishing ties between India and Pakistan with the opening on October 1, 2007, of the first overland truck route across the border after several decades of closed borders.

Sub-Saharan Africa

Recent developments

Economic growth in Sub-Saharan Africa accelerated from 5.7 percent in 2006 to 6.1 percent in 2007, the region's fastest pace of growth in more than three decades (figure A21). Robust 8.1 percent GDP growth among the region's oil exporters and 5.3 percent gains for oil-importing countries, not including South Africa, powered the growth. High oil prices and new oil production, notably in Angola and Sudan, helped propel growth in the oil-exporting countries to the highest rate in almost 35 years. At the same time, the boom in non-oil commodity prices, in conjunction with increased openness and improved macroeconomic stability, boosted growth in oil-importing economies to a 10-year high (table A11).

Figure A21 Growth in Sub-Saharan Africa has accelerated markedly...

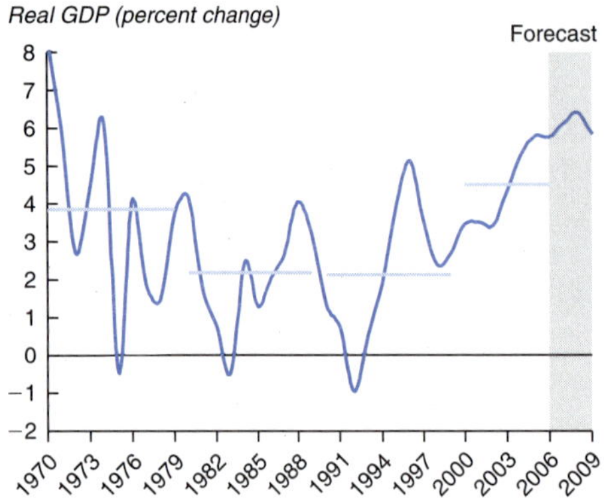

Source: World Bank.

Output expansion in South Africa, the region's largest economy, appears slated to ease to 5.0 percent in 2007 from 5.4 percent in 2006. Quarterly output readings point to robust expansion, with third-quarter growth accelerating to 4.7 percent (seasonally adjusted annual rate) from 4.4 percent in the second quarter. There are indications, however, that higher borrowing costs have dampened the pace of consumption growth, while higher interest rates and a stronger rand are undermining growth in the manufacturing sector. Meanwhile gross fixed capital formation continues to expand at a robust pace, and will likely do so in coming quarters as infrastructure spending is under way for the 2010 World Soccer Cup. Softer private consumption growth and a modest improvement in the terms of trade reduced South Africa's current account deficit to 6.5 percent of GDP in the second quarter of 2007, from a 6.9 percent gap in the previous quarter. Despite softer private consumption, increased capital and construction materials imports and deterioration in the terms of trade will cause the current account balance to widen (table A12).

Table A11 Sub-Saharan Africa forecast summary

(annual percent change unless indicated otherwise)

					Forecast		
	1991–2000[a]	2004	2005	2006	2007	2008	2009
GDP at market prices[b]	2.3	5.3	5.8	5.7	6.1	6.4	5.8
GDP per capita[c]	−0.4	2.9	3.4	3.7	4.0	4.4	3.8
Purchasing Power Parity GDP[d]	3.4	5.5	6.1	6.1	6.5	6.7	6.1
Private consumption	1.2	5.5	5.4	6.0	5.1	5.1	5.1
Public consumption	2.6	5.0	4.7	6.6	6.7	6.5	6.1
Fixed investment	3.7	9.1	13.7	15.7	13.2	12.5	11.8
Exports, GNFS[e]	4.7	6.7	11.6	4.4	5.7	7.3	6.6
Imports, GNFS[e]	4.4	9.3	14.6	12.3	8.2	8.6	8.9
Net exports, contribution to growth	0.2	−0.9	−1.1	−3.0	−1.2	−0.9	−1.4
Current account balance/GDP (%)	−2.1	1.0	−0.3	−0.2	−1.0	−0.9	−2.1
GDP deflator (median, LCU)	10.1	7.5	6.0	6.5	5.8	4.8	4.5
Fiscal balance/GDP (%)	−4.2	−0.7	0.6	1.6	−0.2	0.6	0.1
Memo items: GDP							
SSA excluding South Africa	2.6	5.5	6.2	5.9	6.7	7.2	6.2
Oil exporters	2.2	6.0	7.3	6.7	8.1	9.0	6.9
CFA countries	2.6	4.2	4.0	2.8	3.7	4.5	4.1
South Africa	1.8	4.8	5.0	5.4	5.0	5.1	5.3
Nigeria	2.8	6.0	6.6	5.6	5.9	7.4	6.1
Kenya	1.9	4.9	5.8	6.1	6.3	5.3	5.1

Source: World Bank.

a. Growth rates over intervals are compound averages; growth contributions, ratios, and the GDP deflator are averages.
b. GDP measured in constant 2000 U.S. dollars.
c. Measured in U.S. dollars.
d. GDP measured at purchasing power parity exchange rates.
e. Exports and imports of goods and nonfactor services.

Table A12 Sub-Saharan Africa country forecasts

(annual percent change unless indicated otherwise)

					Forecast		
	1991–2000[a]	2004	2005	2006	2007	2008	2009
Angola							
GDP at market prices[b]	0.8	11.2	20.6	16.9	24.3	21.7	13.4
Current account balance/GDP (%)	−6.1	5.9	15.1	13.6	12.4	9.6	3.7
Benin							
GDP at market prices[b]	4.8	3.1	2.9	3.6	4.4	5.1	5.3
Current account balance/GDP (%)	−6.8	−7.8	−6.3	−5.4	−5.7	−7.0	−7.4
Botswana							
GDP at market prices[b]	6.2	5.9	3.8	2.6	4.8	4.4	3.9
Current account balance/GDP (%)	8.1	2.9	16.6	18.0	17.6	14.7	12.8
Burkina Faso							
GDP at market prices[b]	4.0	3.9	7.1	6.1	5.3	5.5	5.9
Current account balance/GDP (%)	−5.6	−11.0	−10.5	−10.1	−10.2	−11.0	−11.3
Burundi							
GDP at market prices[b]	−1.7	4.8	0.9	5.4	4.2	5.3	5.1
Current account balance/GDP (%)	−3.4	−25.0	−17.9	−17.0	−15.5	−14.9	−13.7
Cape Verde							
GDP at market prices[b]	5.8	4.5	5.9	6.2	6.3	6.6	6.4
Current account balance/GDP (%)	−8.3	−16.3	−5.5	−12.0	−14.6	−15.8	−13.7
Cameroon							
GDP at market prices[b]	1.4	3.7	2.0	3.5	3.8	4.4	4.2
Current account balance/GDP (%)	−3.0	−2.6	−4.2	−0.7	−0.6	−0.9	−2.4
Central African Republic							
GDP at market prices[b]	1.6	1.3	2.2	3.3	3.5	3.8	4.1
Current account balance/GDP (%)	−4.3	−4.6	−4.9	−2.9	−2.9	−3.9	−4.6
Chad							
GDP at market prices[b]	2.3	29.5	7.9	1.4	−1.4	4.2	2.1
Current account balance/GDP (%)	−5.5	−18.7	−6.6	−7.3	−4.8	−2.6	−1.8
Comoros							
GDP at market prices[b]	1.1	−0.2	4.2	1.3	1.8	2.5	2.7
Current account balance/GDP (%)	−6.8	−3.4	−4.9	−5.9	−5.1	−5.2	−5.5
Congo, Dem. Rep. of							
GDP at market prices[b]	−5.6	6.6	6.5	5.1	6.1	7.3	6.8
Current account balance/GDP (%)	2.0	−8.8	−10.0	−8.9	−9.3	−9.5	−9.9
Congo, Rep. of							
GDP at market prices[b]	1.5	3.6	7.8	6.6	3.2	6.3	5.9
Current account balance/GDP (%)	−16.5	15.5	16.2	11.0	6.1	11.0	8.0
Côte d'Ivoire							
GDP at market prices[b]	2.3	1.8	1.8	0.9	1.7	2.8	3.1
Current account balance/GDP (%)	−4.0	1.6	0.4	3.3	2.5	1.0	−0.5
Equatorial Guinea							
GDP at market prices[b]	18.4	10.0	6.5	−5.2	8.8	9.0	−1.4
Current account balance/GDP (%)	−40.6	7.3	6.8	6.3	4.3	7.7	2.8
Eritrea							
GDP at market prices[b]	—	1.9	4.8	1.7	1.9	2.0	2.2
Current account balance/GDP (%)	—	−13.6	−28.0	−31.6	−30.9	−30.1	−28.5
Ethiopia							
GDP at market prices[b]	2.3	12.3	10.5	9.6	9.3	7.7	7.4
Current account balance/GDP (%)	−0.8	−6.9	−7.7	−9.6	−7.3	−7.4	−5.6
Gabon							
GDP at market prices[b]	2.4	1.4	3.0	1.2	4.8	3.9	3.7
Current account balance/GDP (%)	5.7	12.8	13.7	21.4	17.3	21.4	18.6

(continued)

Table A12 (*continued*)

(annual percent change unless indicated otherwise)

	1991–2000[a]	2004	2005	2006	Forecast 2007	2008	2009
Gambia, The							
GDP at market prices[b]	3.3	5.1	6.9	6.4	6.1	5.3	5.8
Current account balance/GDP (%)	−1.6	−11.1	−21.6	−21.5	−20.4	−21.2	−18.3
Ghana							
GDP at market prices[b]	4.3	5.6	5.9	6.2	4.9	5.4	6.1
Current account balance/GDP (%)	−6.4	−3.6	−6.5	−8.7	−10.3	−10.2	−8.4
Guinea							
GDP at market prices[b]	3.9	2.7	3.3	2.4	2.1	3.7	3.2
Current account balance/GDP (%)	−5.7	−4.3	−5.2	−6.1	−7.3	−10.7	−11.5
Guinea-Bissau							
GDP at market prices[b]	1.5	2.2	3.2	2.7	2.7	2.6	3.3
Current account balance/GDP (%)	−24.0	−4.9	−7.5	−11.3	−10.1	−4.3	−3.3
Kenya							
GDP at market prices[b]	1.9	4.9	5.8	6.1	6.3	5.3	5.1
Current account balance/GDP (%)	−1.6	−2.2	−0.8	−2.1	−3.2	−4.1	−3.6
Lesotho							
GDP at market prices[b]	3.4	3.1	2.9	6.9	4.1	4.8	4.4
Current account balance/GDP (%)	−13.3	−5.6	−7.4	3.0	0.1	−0.9	2.4
Madagascar							
GDP at market prices[b]	1.7	5.3	4.6	4.9	5.8	6.3	6.9
Current account balance/GDP (%)	−7.8	−12.4	−11.9	−8.9	−14.7	−21.7	−21.4
Malawi							
GDP at market prices[b]	3.4	7.1	2.7	7.4	6.3	6.1	5.6
Current account balance/GDP (%)	−8.5	−4.7	−9.5	−6.2	−4.0	−5.1	−4.1
Mali							
GDP at market prices[b]	4.0	2.2	6.1	4.9	5.1	5.2	5.3
Current account balance/GDP (%)	−8.9	−8.4	−8.3	−4.9	−4.6	−4.9	−5.2
Mauritania							
GDP at market prices[b]	2.9	5.2	5.4	11.7	2.1	5.7	6.7
Current account balance/GDP (%)	−0.3	−20.1	−46.3	−2.1	−4.0	−11.6	−19.3
Mauritius							
GDP at market prices[b]	5.3	4.7	3.1	3.5	4.1	4.4	3.9
Current account balance/GDP (%)	−1.6	−1.8	−3.7	−5.6	−8.4	−8.9	−7.6
Mozambique							
GDP at market prices[b]	5.2	7.5	6.2	8.5	9.1	7.4	6.7
Current account balance/GDP (%)	−18.2	−11.1	−12.6	−7.3	−9.0	−10.2	−9.2
Namibia							
GDP at market prices[b]	4.2	6.0	4.2	4.6	4.6	4.3	3.8
Current account balance/GDP (%)	4.1	10.0	7.2	13.0	15.0	11.3	10.6
Niger							
GDP at market prices[b]	1.8	0.0	7.0	4.2	4.8	4.5	4.6
Current account balance/GDP (%)	−6.9	−7.6	−9.4	−9.5	−10.3	−11.0	−10.8
Nigeria							
GDP at market prices[b]	2.8	6.0	6.6	5.6	5.9	7.4	6.1
Current account balance/GDP (%)	−0.8	23.4	10.9	13.7	9.2	12.6	9.5
Rwanda							
GDP at market prices[b]	0.2	4.0	6.1	6.4	6.7	5.1	4.7
Current account balance/GDP (%)	−3.5	−10.8	−3.9	−7.1	−8.3	−8.2	−7.4
Senegal							
GDP at market prices[b]	2.9	6.2	5.5	3.1	4.5	5.1	5.3
Current account balance/GDP (%)	−6.0	−6.7	−7.0	−9.6	−9.7	−8.4	−7.6

Table A12 *(continued)*
(annual percent change unless indicated otherwise)

	1991–2000[a]	2004	2005	2006	2007	2008	2009
					Forecast		
Seychelles							
GDP at market prices[b]	4.6	−2.0	1.2	5.3	5.5	5.1	5.7
Current account balance/GDP (%)	−7.4	−9.1	−23.8	−28.9	−30.4	−28.8	−20.4
Sierra Leone							
GDP at market prices[b]	−4.7	7.4	7.5	7.5	7.3	6.9	7.4
Current account balance/GDP (%)	−9.0	−13.1	−9.3	−6.0	−6.5	−8.3	−9.0
South Africa							
GDP at market prices[b]	1.8	4.8	5.0	5.4	5.0	5.1	5.3
Current account balance/GDP (%)	−0.2	−3.2	−3.8	−6.3	−6.8	−7.8	−7.7
Sudan							
GDP at market prices[b]	5.7	5.2	8.6	11.8	10.8	9.7	8.1
Current account balance/GDP (%)	−6.7	−4.1	−10.9	−14.2	−9.6	−6.5	−6.6
Swaziland							
GDP at market prices[b]	3.1	2.1	2.3	1.7	1.4	1.1	1.2
Current account balance/GDP (%)	−2.6	4.6	1.5	1.0	0.1	−3.2	−2.4
Tanzania							
GDP at market prices[b]	2.9	6.7	6.8	6.2	7.1	6.8	6.7
Current account balance/GDP (%)	−12.5	−2.2	−4.8	−8.0	−9.4	−11.0	−10.2
Togo							
GDP at market prices[b]	2.2	3.0	2.8	1.5	2.3	2.1	2.4
Current account balance/GDP (%)	−8.5	−10.0	−5.1	−5.7	−6.1	−9.3	−7.8
Uganda							
GDP at market prices[b]	6.8	5.5	6.6	5.4	5.5	5.3	5.9
Current account balance/GDP (%)	−7.0	−3.2	−2.2	−4.8	−3.0	−5.4	−4.9
Zambia							
GDP at market prices[b]	0.7	5.4	5.1	5.9	5.3	5.7	5.9
Current account balance/GDP (%)	−10.5	−10.0	−8.6	1.6	−0.7	−4.6	−6.2
Zimbabwe							
GDP at market prices[b]	0.9	−3.8	−5.3	−4.2	−6.3	−4.9	−2.1
Current account balance/GDP (%)	−7.5	20.7	25.7	45.0	71.9	81.7	82.7

Source: World Bank.
Notes: Growth and current account figures presented here are World Bank projections and may differ from targets contained in other World Bank documents. Liberia, Mayotte, São Tomé and Principe, and Somalia are not forecast because of data limitations.
a. Growth rates over intervals are compound averages; growth contributions, ratios, and the GDP deflator are averages.
b. GDP measured in constant 2000 U.S. dollars.

Recent turbulence in international financial markets resulted in a moderate depreciation of the rand against the dollar, but that followed a period of strong appreciation caused by, among other factors, anticipated capital inflows related to merger and acquisition activity. The rand has since returned to levels prevailing before the period of intense financial market disruptions of July. Volatility and declines in high-income financial markets affected capital markets in South Africa to some degree, but the change was limited. The country avoided sharp asset sell-offs, and the all-share Johannesburg Stock Exchange index reached new highs. Looking forward, limited spillovers to consumption and investment are anticipated.

Exceptional outturns in countries like Angola and Sudan underpinned growth among Sub-Saharan Africa's oil-exporting economies (figure A22). In Angola, the region's fastest-growing economy and its second largest oil producer, growth continues to be exceptionally robust, with both oil and non-oil sectors

Figure A22 ...reaching a 35-year high in oil-exporting countries...

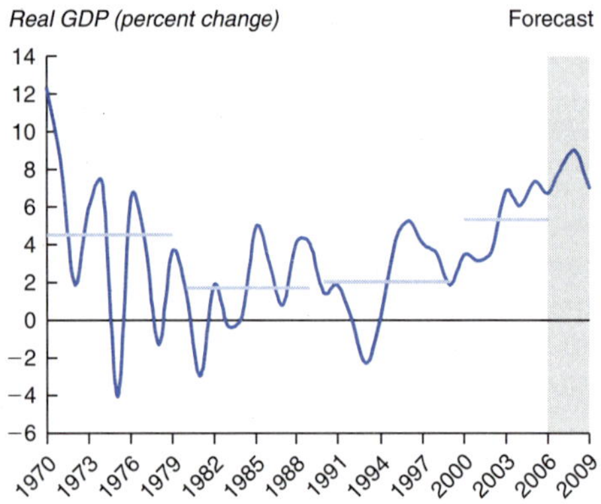

Source: World Bank.

advancing at double-digit rates. Diamond production has also been climbing, supplementing oil revenues and contributing to an increase in the current account surplus. Nevertheless, the increase in oil production was an impressive 18.7 percent in the first nine months of 2007 (year-on-year) after expanding 26 percent in 2005 and 13 percent in 2006. The new oil fields scheduled to come on line over 2007 to 2009 will ensure strong growth in the oil sector, while robust growth in agriculture, manufacturing, construction, and the power sector will boost activity in the non-oil sectors to near 20 percent.

Also notable among the oil-exporting economies is an improvement in macroeconomic stability, with inflation easing, notwithstanding large revenue inflows and stronger growth in government spending. Furthermore, recent monetary tightening should help bring inflationary pressures in Angola down further. Both fiscal and current account balances have improved tremendously as a result of the oil windfall. The non-oil fiscal balance also has improved, but largely as a result of capacity constraints that limit government spending increases.

Meanwhile, performance in Nigeria, the region's second largest economy, has improved marginally over the course of 2007. GDP growth rose modestly from 5.6 percent in 2006 to 5.9 percent, as strong gains in the non-oil sector offset substantial underperformance in oil. A 9.5 percent expansion in the non-oil sector during the third quarter of 2007 (year-on-year), driven by strong performance in agriculture and financial services, pushed overall growth up to 6.1 percent from 5.7 percent in the previous quarter. Crude oil production, including condensates and natural gas liquids, declined 7.1 percent during the third quarter (year-on-year), bringing output down 4.2 percent for the first nine months of 2007. This unfavorable result followed a contraction in production of 5.3 percent in 2006. Economic growth in Mauritania, the region's newest oil producer, has also been disappointing. Growth there was subdued largely because of a halving in oil output tied to a changeover in equipment.

Members of the Central African Economic and Monetary Community experienced mixed economic performance. For example, strong growth in the non-oil sector in Gabon led to a considerable pickup in GDP despite a decline in oil production. Growth also accelerated in Cameroon, underpinned by strong domestic demand, and on the supply side, by strong performance in the transport and telecommunications sectors. Meanwhile in the Republic of Congo, growth performance fell off as expansion in the oil sector softened, and delays in public investment affected growth in the non-oil sector. In Chad, another sharp decline in oil production and continued deceleration in growth within the non-oil sector caused the economy to contract during the year.

Among the region's oil importers, GDP advances were robust, especially in those countries that are further along the reform path, have achieved greater trade openness, and have improved macroeconomic stability (figure A23). Increases in nontraditional manufactured exports have helped propel growth in several countries. In East Africa, Tanzania recorded stronger growth in the agriculture sector and improved its performance in manufacturing, mining, and construction, pushing

Figure A23 ...and a 10-year high in oil-importing countries

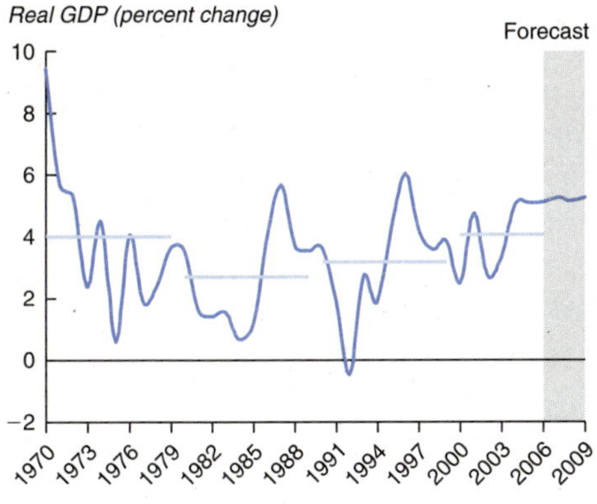

Source: World Bank.

overall GDP gains to 7.1 percent in 2007. In Kenya, at 6.3 percent, growth should surpass a 30-year record set in 2006 (6.1 percent) based on improved tourism arrivals and receipts, stronger gains in transport and communications, and better agriculture output. Growth accelerated to 7.1 percent in the second quarter of 2007 (year-on-year) as manufacturing expanded 8.6 percent, hotels and restaurants gained 11.1 percent, and communications expanded 11.8 percent. In Madagascar, large inflows of FDI to the mining sector are generating an important shift in the structure of the economy, while Uganda is benefiting from strong expansion in construction, transport, and communications, as well as from recovery in agriculture.

Growth among members of the West African Economic and Monetary Union also picked up in 2007, rising by almost a full percentage point to 3.7 percent, as GDP gains exceeded 4 percent in five of the eight economies. Yet inadequate energy supplies in many member countries and difficulties in several agriculture subsectors have kept growth from rising even further. Agricultural output and private consumption will take some time to recover in several countries in the union that sustained significant damage from flooding, slowing growth toward the end of 2007 into 2008.

In Mozambique, growth continues apace, with output up 8.8 percent in the first half of the year, but damage from cyclones and flooding slowed the rate of growth from 10 percent recorded a year earlier (year-on-year). The country boosted its GDP with investments of $1.4 billion in the Moatize Coal Project and $390 million in other projects during the first half of 2007.

Medium-term outlook

Growth in Sub-Saharan Africa is poised to remain buoyant by historic standards, nearing 6 percent over the near and medium terms, despite softening of demand in the Euro Area in 2008 and corrections to non-oil commodity prices, particularly metals, over the medium term (table A11). For many countries, the impetus for growth will come in part from robust domestic demand, in particular, strong growth in public and private fixed investment (figure A24).

Fixed investment is expected to remain strong, despite the credit crunch in international financial markets and the easing in

Figure A24 Contributions of investment and consumption have increased

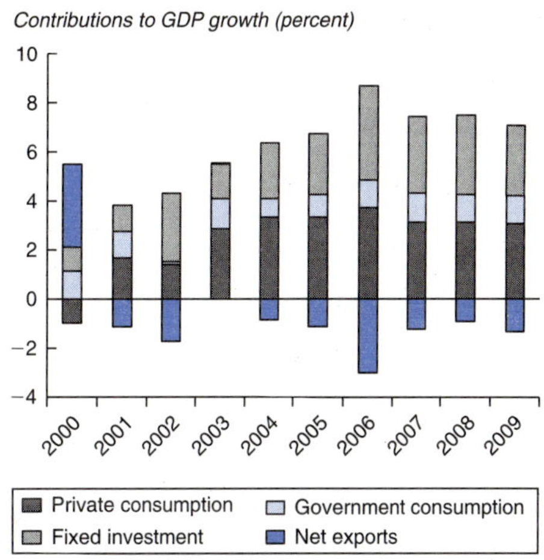

Source: World Bank.

non-oil commodity prices. Large, strategic, capital projects initiated by big, rapidly–growing, developing economies such as China and India are likely to underpin continued strong investment. Among recent notable deals is the $5 billion loan agreement reached between China and the Democratic Republic of Congo. According to the signed accord, about $3 billion will fund large infrastructure projects, including 2,000 miles of railway and 2,125 miles of highway. The project will also finance the construction of 31 hospitals, 145 health centers, and 2 universities. The remaining $2 billion will be used to set up a joint venture mining company between the two countries. Madagascar and Mozambique are also experiencing large-scale FDI flows into their economies.

Several years of strong non-oil commodity prices, together with rising private capital inflows and remittances, are supporting private consumption, although spending is anticipated to flatten over the medium term as income growth eases. In South Africa, higher interest rates and an erosion of real incomes is likely to curb real spending. Furthermore, the sharp decline in farmers' incomes in those countries affected by recent floods will constitute a drag on consumption, although private, government, and donor transfers may mitigate some of the effects. According to the latest estimates, the worst-affected countries are Burkina Faso, Ghana, and Uganda. Adverse spillovers to personal spending will be felt well into 2008. In other countries, recovery from drought is translating into improved performance in agriculture, adding impetus to growth, while the income effect resulting from several years of high prices for non-oil commodities continues to stimulate private consumption.

Growth among Africa's oil exporters is expected to slow to 6.9 percent by 2009, as oil prices are forecast to decline that year and as investment projects begin to unwind. However, this transition occurs from peak 9 percent GDP gains in 2008 led by continued advances in Angolan and Sudanese crude oil output and anticipated recovery in Nigerian production. Lower oil prices by 2009 could yield supply responses, at minimum slowing the pace of oil output growth for many smaller producers, where production costs remain high. For the region's major producers, however, output is projected to continue to increase.

Growth in Nigeria is projected to pick up markedly in 2008, buoyed by recovery in the oil sector and strong gains in the non-oil sector. Stabilization in the Niger Delta should allow oil production to recover gradually and to exceed 2005 levels, supporting gains near 10 percent in Nigeria's oil sector, following the contraction recorded in 2007. Investment growth should moderate, notwithstanding the government's plans to invest substantial amounts in roads, railways, and electricity infrastructure and in the dredging of the Niger River. This investment appears highly import-intensive, with import sourcing accounting for some 75–80 percent of expenditure, thereby limiting the direct positive effects on Nigeria's growth.

Difficulties in the cotton and groundnut subsectors in several West African countries are having negative spillover effects on growth, while electricity shortages and high energy costs are constraining faster expansion among oil-importing economies. Some countries are seeing surges in their oil import bills, in part because many companies use fuel-run power generators to supplement grid electricity. Growth among West African Economic and Monetary Union economies will be supported by improved performance in the primary sector and increased public investment spending, financed from savings made under the Highly Indebted Poor Countries and Multilateral Debt Relief initiatives. Furthermore, growth in oil-importing economies should benefit from strong investment growth, as well as continued demand for non-oil commodities from the rapidly expanding emerging market economies.

Risks

Among the most important downside risks to growth in Sub-Sahara African is a larger-than-expected falloff in high-income country growth and import demand. Such a falloff could be tied to continuing difficulties in financial markets, or it could be triggered by weaker growth outturns in major emerging market economies, such as in China and India, which might result in weaker export growth for Sub-Saharan Africa in general, and for the oil-importing countries in particular.

The risk of increasing inflationary pressure is also palpable. Should oil prices increase further or drought conditions affect the food supply, inflation could be the consequence. Increases in international prices of staple commodities such as cereals and vegetable oils, to a large degree already in the pipeline, could spill over to fuel domestic price pressures, particularly in countries that are heavily reliant on imports of wheat and vegetable oils.

In some countries, strong domestic demand and upward adjustments in public sector wages are already fueling inflationary pressures. Capacity constraints and overheating in some economies, especially the oil-producing economies, constitute further upside risks for inflation. Similarly, in South Africa, high confidence, strong domestic expenditures, rising employment, buoyant credit extension, and increasing asset prices all boost consumption through positive wealth effects and make the risk of a further buildup in inflationary pressures very apparent.

South Africa also faces a specific source of risk in the way it has financed its sizable current account deficit, anticipated to be in excess of 7 percent of GDP in 2008 and 2009: the country has relied largely on portfolio investments, which could potentially be reversed. Moreover, a marked depreciation of the rand in the event of a sell-off of South African assets by nonresidents would present the authorities with additional financial management issues to address as well as inflation pressures.

Finally, negative terms-of-trade shocks (lower non-oil commodity prices, further increases in oil prices, or both) may come to affect disposable incomes in oil-importing countries, undermining private consumption while also yielding worse external balances. Conversely, higher oil prices would benefit growth in oil-exporting countries. Sociopolitical tensions also remain a source of downside risk for countries such as Côte d'Ivoire, the Democratic Republic of Congo, Ethiopia, Guinea, Guinea-Bissau, Somalia, and Togo. In Nigeria, the risks associated with the activity of militant groups in the Niger Delta remain substantial, with oil production still about 25 percent below the 2.9 million barrels daily capacity.

Eco-Audit

Environmental Benefits Statement

The World Bank is committed to preserving endangered forests and natural resources. The Office of the Publisher has chosen to print ***Global Economic Prospects 2008*** on recycled paper with 30 percent post-consumer waste, in accordance with the recommended standards for paper usage set by the Green Press Initiative, a nonprofit program supporting publishers in using fiber that is not sourced from endangered forests. For more information, visit www.greenpressinitiative.org.

Saved:
- 21 trees
- 1247 lbs. of solid waste
- 7,539 gallons of wastewater
- 2,300 lbs. of net greenhouse gases
- 14 million BTUs of total energy

green press INITIATIVE